'Like previous editions, the fourth edition of Campbell and Kean's *American Cultural Studies* manages to address some of the most pertinent issues in the subject in a manner that is thought-provoking yet brief. The text blends history, theory, and analysis into a narrative that is intriguing, conceptually challenging, yet accessible for introductory humanities courses; the updated chapters on ethnicity and immigration, religion, and freedom are especially noteworthy in this regard.'

Veronica McComb, *Lenoir-Rhyne University, USA*

'*American Cultural Studies* is a key text for students that details a staggering wealth of US cultural history. Campbell and Kean not only look at a huge breadth of sources but they manage to weave this into a coherent and compelling interpretation of America's ideology that will be appreciated by all students of US history and politics. Indeed if you want to understand how the US affects us all through its cultural impact then you need to read this very enjoyable book.'

Lee Sartain, *University of Portsmouth, UK*

'Richly interdisciplinary and newly updated to include discussions of Barack Obama, long-form television, and "Hemispheric American Studies", the fourth edition of *American Cultural Studies* continues to provide the best and most up-to-date introduction to American Studies currently in print.'

Frederik Byrn Køhlert, *University of Calgary, Canada*

'The fourth edition of *American Cultural Studies* provides an introduction that is thoroughly informed by new directions in the discipline – especially, the turn to the transnational – and that reads more "traditional" topics alongside assessments of subjects that have generally received less attention on American Studies programmes, such as the presence of Islam in the United States, the growing significance of Hispanic culture, and the debates over same-sex relationships. The broad coverage is delivered with an expert knowledge of the field, encompassing an impressive combination of well-known and new readings of key moments and texts, and is supplemented with excellent lists of further reading.'

Chris Gair, *University of Glasgow, UK*

'This is an indispensable guide for students at all levels, covering the key themes, texts and debates of the "new" American Studies. Comprehensive, up-to-date, and thoroughly readable, it's probably the best introduction available; it is both practical and engaging and I highly recommend it.'

Tom Idema, *Utrecht University, The Netherlands*

'I've found *American Cultural Studies* to be a really strong and engaging text for American Studies students – both undergraduates and beginning Master's students. The authors get at key American themes and ideas, successfully elucidating their nuances and complexities and putting them into useful contexts. The international perspective (from writers not based in the USA) further enriches this look at American culture and the new edition includes timely updates so that the examples and case studies remain current.'

Stephanie A. Tingley, *Youngstown State University, USA*

American Cultural Studies

Exploring the central themes in modern American cultural studies and discussing how these themes can be interpreted, *American Cultural Studies* offers a wide-ranging overview of different aspects of American cultural life such as religion, gender and sexuality, regionalism, and ethnicity and immigration.

The fourth edition has been revised throughout to take into account the developments of the last four years. Updates and revisions include:

- discussion of Barack Obama's time in the White House
- consideration of 'Hemispheric American Studies' and the increasing debates about globalisation and the international role of the USA
- long-form television and American Studies
- up-to-date case studies, such as *Girls*, *The Wire* and *Orange is the New Black*
- more material on Detroit, the Mexican border, same-sex relationships and Islam in America
- updated further reading lists and new follow-up work.

Illustrated throughout, containing follow-up questions and further reading at the end of each chapter, and accompanied by a companion website (www.routledge.com/cw/campbell) providing further study resources, *American Cultural Studies* is a core text and an accessible guide to the interdisciplinary study of American culture.

Neil Campbell is Professor in American Studies at the University of Derby, UK. His recent publications include *Post-Westerns* (2013), *The Rhizomatic West: Representing the American West in a Transnational, Global, Media Age* (2008), *The Cultures of the American New West* (2000) and *The Radiant Hour: Versions of Youth in American Culture* (2000).

Alasdair Kean is a lecturer in American Studies at the University of Derby, UK.

American Cultural Studies

An introduction to American culture
Fourth Edition

Neil Campbell and
Alasdair Kean

Routledge
Taylor & Francis Group

LONDON AND NEW YORK

This edition published 2016
by Routledge
2 Park Square, Milton Park, Abingdon, Oxon OX14 4RN

and by Routledge
711 Third Avenue, New York, NY 10017

Routledge is an imprint of the Taylor & Francis Group, an informa business

First edition published 1997

Third edition published 2012
by Routledge

British Library Cataloguing-in-Publication Data
A catalogue record for this book is available from the British Library

Library of Congress Cataloging-in-Publication Data
Names: Caple, Chris, 1958– editor.
Title: Preservation of archaeological remains in-situ : a reader / edited by
Christopher Caple.
Description: New York, NY : Routledge, 2016.
Identifiers: LCCN 2015042830| ISBN 9780415832533 (hardback : alk. paper) |
ISBN 9780415832540 (pbk. : alk. paper)
Subjects: LCSH: Antiquities—Collection and preservation. | Archaeology |
Archaeological sites—Conservation and restoration. | Historic
sites—Conservation and restoration. | Cultural property—Protection. |
Historic preservation.
Classification: LCC CC135 .P716 2016 | DDC 930.1—dc23
LC record available at http://lccn.loc.gov/2015042830

ISBN: 978-1-138-83313-5 (hbk)
ISBN: 978-1-138-83314-2 (pbk)
ISBN: 978-1-315-64720-3 (ebk)

Typeset in Palatino and Helvetica
by Florence Production Ltd, Stoodleigh, Devon, UK

Contents

Plates

Acknowledgements

This is a newly revised fourth edition of the book previously published in 1997, 2006 and 2012. We would like to thank once again Professor Will Kaufman for all his productive comments on the first edition and subsequently all those anonymous readers who advised us on alterations for the second, third and fourth versions. We hope it meets some of their needs and will continue to stimulate students in their explorations of American culture. We would like to thank our colleagues, Dave Holloway, Simon Philo and Jo Bishton, and students at the University of Derby who have been involved in many classes in which these ideas have been worked out and whose voices may be heard echoing in these pages. Caroline Ball, Subject Librarian for American Studies, has been very helpful in guiding us to relevant material and helping with the updating of the website. We would also like to thank our respective families for their forbearance and encouragement. To Jane, as ever, 'Love knows no distance'. Love, too, to Trish, for continuing to give real meaning to the concept of 'new beginnings', and to Alex, Hannah, Oliver and Daniel for just being themselves.

All efforts have been made to contact copyright holders, but if any have been inadvertently overlooked, the publishers will be pleased to make the necessary arrangements at the first opportunity.

Introduction

The United States of America continues to be at the forefront of world events, with its foreign policy still engaged at home and abroad, with the varied consequences of the terrorist attacks of 11 September 2001 (9/11, or September 11th), now deeply entangled with events in Iraq, Afghanistan and Syria. The growing threat of Islamic State and the rise of Russian militarisation in Ukraine presents new, but related, challenges for the United States's role in global geopolitics. Closer to home, there is the threat of internal terrorism such as the Boston bombings (15 April 2013), urban unrest such as that following the murders of Trayvon Martin (2012) and Michael Brown (2014), as well as the continued effects of economic recession and environmental disasters such as Hurricane Katrina (2005), the *Deepwater Horizon* Gulf of Mexico oil spill (2010), and the prolonged drought in California and the desert southwest. What these different events 'mean', how they are dealt with and what they might tell us about the USA as a domestic and international power demonstrate why it is vitally important to continue to study and analyse the United States of America in all its formations. In recent years, ever-popular concepts in American history like 'nation', 'settler-colonial state', 'empire', 'homeland', 'freedom' and 'patriotism' have been given new meanings and inter- pretations, contested from the perspectives of those critical of the political project of President George W. Bush and celebrated by those who supported him. With the arrival of America's first African American president, Barack Obama, on 20 January 2009, many viewed the nation as entering a new phase, perhaps echoed in the optimistic words of the president's inaugural address: 'We gather because we have chosen hope over fear, unity of purpose over conflict and discord.' Yet as the speech progressed Obama restated what so many presidents had said before him: 'The time has come to reaffirm our enduring spirit; to choose our better history; to carry forward that precious gift, that noble idea, passed on from generation to generation: the God-given promise that all are equal, all are free and all deserve a chance to pursue their full measure of happiness.' Of course, spoken by an African American perhaps these

on an altered and more pointed meaning, reiterating old
re-emphasising them for a new age and a new audience.
ν-first century, how do Americans respond to notions of
rit', 'God-given promise' and concepts like freedom and
..though clearly echoing the Declaration of Independence,
does this mythic rhetoric still ring true for all Americans? As we write
this latest edition of *American Cultural Studies* there is even a possibility
of the first woman president in American history, something unthinkable
in the nation's recent past.

In a rapidly changing world where past and present are in continuous
negotiation, American Studies can be the focus for questions like these,
able to critique and analyse the discourses that have shaped and continue
to shape a nation and its complex relations with the world. Contrary to
some who have argued for the decline of the nation-state, it now remains
vital to any discussion of global events, with the United States of America
still a dominant world force, guarding its borders while engaging in the
policing of those of other nations, redefining new forms of power at the
very heart of our critical understanding of the twenty-first century.
However, the nature of what constitutes this 'nation' is still as problematic
as ever. As Dimock and Buell ask (2007: 2), 'Is "American" an adjective
that can stand on its own, uninflected, unentangled, and unconstrained?'
The American Cultural Studies employed in this book is, therefore,
interdisciplinary and international, exploring a range of ways to study
American culture, in order to encourage students, who may have little
experience either of America or interdisciplinary work, to develop their
engagement with both of these in tandem. Our focus is largely on the
twentieth- and twenty-first-century experience, but where appropriate, for
instance, in the chapters on regions, religion and African Americans,
we have included material from earlier periods in order to provide an
important context or sense of continuity. However, in the spirit of the
issues raised above, it does not seek to exceptionalise the 'American' in
American Studies but to suggest rather its fluid and interconnected
relations with other nations and fields of study.

AN EXCEPTIONAL PLACE OR WHAT IS AMERICA?

Since its inception in the 1930s, American Studies as an approach to the
study of the culture and history of the USA has been preoccupied with
certain key themes. One is what Michael Denning has described as the
founding question of the subject area, 'What is American?' (Denning 1986:
360). Although often phrased in different ways, the question is concerned
with the meaning of American national identity, and the ways in which
America might be distinguished from other nations. A particular answer
to this question has been to define the uniqueness or 'exceptional' quality

of the American experience in the form of a 'national narrative' – a story of agreed principles, values and myths that gives the country a coherent sense of identity, an 'image repertoire productive of the U.S. national community . . . through a recitation of the key terms in the national meta-narrative' (Pease 1994: 4). In other ways, however, examining the 'Americanness' of the USA has deep roots within American history itself. J.H. St John de Crevecoeur's famous question, 'What, then, is the American, this new man?', first posed in 1782, has echoed down subsequent generations of social and political commentary by both Americans and foreigners addressing the question of American identity. From Alexis de Tocqueville in the 1830s and 1840s through the founding fathers of American history like Frederick Jackson Turner, to post-Second World War cultural critics like David Riesman and Christopher Lasch, a considerable literature has built up dedicated to defining American character. American Studies, therefore, as the search for 'American exceptionalism', for some sense of the differences between American culture and other cultures, has come out of a deep-seated preoccupation with national self-definition. Even if American culture, on analysis, may turn out to be less distinctive from other modern societies than was once thought, one feature of it remains the durability of questions about a national identity. Indeed, as some commentators have argued, the centrality of the debate about American distinctiveness in the United States may in itself be a key component of American identity: 'The search for an American character is part of that character' (Wilkinson 1988: 2).

Simultaneously, there have been those set on contesting any coherent national narrative or essentialised sense of identity as ideological frameworks that exclude too much of the genuine experience of the USA. Criticisms of 'American exceptionalism' have tended to focus on two central weaknesses in many earlier attempts to define national difference. There is, first, the tendency to reduce questions of national identity to some essential singularity and in doing so to give undue weight to the experience of specific groups and traditions in explaining America, at the expense of other groups whose experience is, as a result, forgotten or marginalised. Second, there has been a tendency to study American society in isolation and from 'within', and in so doing to downplay those experiences the United States might have in common with other societies or that enable a comparative perspective to emerge. Increasingly in the twenty-first century some critics, as we shall see, prefer to rethink the USA as part of a 'hemisphere' or a 'world system' in order to understand its rather more interlinked histories (see Wilson and Connery 2007; Levander and Levine 2008; Dimock and Buell 2007; Edwards and Gaonkar 2010).

If we turn to the first major criticism, then the difficulties of generalising about national identity become evident. Americans, it has been overwhelmingly argued over the last seventy years, have been marked by division and opposition, rather than by agreement and consensus. Traditional conceptions of a unified American culture when examined turn out to be partial and selective views of what America has been or ought to be, grounded in the privileged status accorded to a white, male, middle-class, heterosexual perspective. America has presented itself as a classless society, marked by a powerful degree of consensus and a low level of conflict only because historians and cultural critics had tended not to emphasise those factors that indicated deep-seated divisions in American life, such as class, ethnicity, race and gender. Once these latter factors have been duly acknowledged, then, at the very least, it becomes much more difficult to accommodate them adequately within traditional notions of a seamless national identity. Americans, it is argued, are in the end divided as much as they are united. Where unity is apparent, this is only possible because difference has been hidden by the practice of power. The dominance of specific groups and perspectives in American life has obscured the fact that other groups were subordinate, and played little part in creating an 'official' American identity. As Elizabeth Fox-Genovese wrote in 1990: 'The last two decades have . . . witnessed a growing restiveness with any complacent assumptions that the culture of a privileged few could adequately represent the specific beliefs and practices of the many varieties of Americans' (Fox-Genovese 1990: 7). The construction of an American identity could thus no longer rely on a few privileged categories; Americans were 'female as well as male, black as well as white, poor as well as affluent, Catholic or Jewish as well as Protestant, and of diverse national and ethnic backgrounds' (ibid.).

A second major source of criticism has focused on a tendency in American Studies to examine American culture on its own without very much attention to cross-cultural comparison. In other words, 'exceptionalism' has often fed the very basis of American Studies as a discipline. The emphasis here tended to be on what set the United States apart from other cultures rather than what it might share with them. This approach, in turn, both fed off and encouraged that long-held belief in American history that the country had a special mission to fulfil, a mission which in the past had a strong religious, economic or racial gloss (as the 'errand into the wilderness' or 'Manifest Destiny'), but which was given renewed vigour by America's ideological role as the leader of the free world in the Cold War, and subsequently in its global 'War on Terror' (see Chapter 9). There are links between this argument and the tendency to underplay conflict in the American past for, as Giles Gunn has commented, 'wherever concern for American uniqueness was seen to wax, critical comprehension of its own inner divisions as well as its cultural complexity and contextual relations seemed to wane' (Gunn 1987: 151).

Again, this tendency drew on an understandable strain in American culture which sought to explain the country's identity from within, using American points of reference. Frederick Jackson Turner's elaboration of his Frontier thesis is only the most well-known attempt to provide an explanation of American development in terms of conditions within the country itself, arguing that the westward clash of civilisation and savagery created out of such conditions a composite American 'type' (see Chapter 5). What these various criticisms of 'American exceptionalism' suggest are the problems involved in generalising about the American experience. This is not to deny that the national dimension of historical and cultural analysis is significant, nor is it to dismiss the extensive literature on the American character, which, in any case, was rather more sensitive to matters of region and ethnicity than has sometimes been argued. It is, however, to emphasise that students, in seeking to understand American culture, need to take into account both internal variation and division as well as international and cross-cultural comparison. As we shall see later, one of the strongest themes in recent discussions of American Studies has focused on the need to 'internationalise' it, to relate it to the world and to global exchanges and transnational processes. One of the aims of this book, then, is to encourage students both to become aware of these internal divisions and at the same time to consider how they relate to conventional or accepted definitions of American identity.

WHAT IS AMERICAN STUDIES?

If the problematic nature of national identity is one major concern which recent enquiry in American Studies has addressed, a second is the process of interdisciplinary work. It may be helpful here to say something about what we mean by interdisciplinarity and in so doing to identify some of the benefits as well as potential problems involved in this kind of approach. American Studies, as practised both in the United States and abroad, has long advocated movement beyond traditional disciplinary boundaries and encouraged efforts to establish more open and cooperative projects between academic areas. As might be expected, however, such an enterprise has had a controversial and much disputed life, for a whole range of reasons, particularly in the last fifty years when the very nature of what we mean by an academic discipline has come under scrutiny from a number of different directions.[1] It is not our intention here to provide a review of this work; students who wish to follow its contours may be guided by the material in the notes and further reading, or follow the debates in the *American Quarterly* over the last thirty years. Rather, we want to open up areas of debate, and thus possible avenues of cultural exploration for students to develop in their own projects. In the individual chapters which follow, rather than providing interpretative overviews of the topics concerned, our aim is to suggest a range of potential approaches to American culture. What follows, then, by way of discussion of interdisciplinary issues, is a starting-point or a place of departure.

Central to any interdisciplinary enterprise is the relationship between texts to be studied and the contexts from which they come. There are two main issues to examine here. One is what we mean by 'texts'. Traditional approaches based on the study of literature, history and politics tended to favour certain kinds of texts at the expense of others, presenting an established canon of great works (often by 'dead white men', it is said) from which might be distilled the essence of American culture. Certain kinds of texts, such as *The Scarlet Letter* (1850) or *The Ambassadors* (1903), were appropriate for sustained examination while others, like popular films or detective novels, were not. The debate over what should be included in the canon has been hotly contested in recent years and is clearly related to the issues raised in the opening stages of this introduction. Whose America is reflected in any specific list of texts for close study? Can the works of key writers in themselves provide an adequate guide to the complexities of a culture as varied and as divided as that of the United States? Are certain kinds of texts worth more than others because they are more complex or contain particular revelatory or inspirational qualities? Can the USA only be represented from within? In attempting to come to terms with these questions, our approach has been to retain an emphasis on the importance of certain forms of literary and artistic production which seem to us to require sustained and careful reading, but at the same time not to limit ourselves to what has been traditionally included in such a category. For one thing, what might be defined as 'elite' or 'high' culture has clearly changed over time, as has the nature of the 'text' and how that text might be received and used. In the age of the Internet, social networking, Twitter and other electronic aids to communication, any assumptions about what a text constitutes are clearly changing.

If we define culture at its broadest as 'a way of life', then it also becomes clear that to restrict the study of cultural products to a small handful of approved texts runs the risk of omitting a great deal. One suggestion takes the opposite position stating texts are simply 'those stories that Americans tell one another in order to make sense of their lives' (Mechling 1989: 4). According to this definition, then, a whole range of cultural products and artefacts become available for analysis. It may still be that in such a scheme of study there remains room for qualitative judgement, that some stories carry greater conviction and resonance than others, but the possibilities for making connections between different aspects of the wider culture are greatly extended. The opening up of different kinds of texts for scrutiny, too, may yield surprising results. Listening closely to the stories they tell and how those stories fit or jar with other stories in the culture may reveal specific texts in the popular domain which repay close study, and which are as questioning and as complex as more ostensibly 'serious' works. In this collection, therefore, while retaining a strong emphasis on the works of a range of established writers from Edgar Allan Poe to Toni Morrison, we have also juxtaposed them with material from other sources including popular culture, photography, art, music, film, television and material artefacts. Moreover, in making connections between different texts, it might be argued that new kinds of texts are created which themselves can be read and interpreted. An example here might be the description of the city as a text, which can be read in a range of different ways, but which itself is made up of a range of different texts or stories.

More specifically, one might consider the television phenomenon *The Wire* (HBO 2002–8), which, over five series, explored Baltimore through different critical prisms: the illegal drug trade, the port system, the city government and bureaucracy, the school system and the print news media. Its large multicultural, multiclass cast provided a complex theatrical long form of television in which stories evolved over time allowing its audience to invest in its textured narrative threads. In this sense it offers a new and different form of 'text' for American Studies. Using established novelists like Dennis Lehane, Richard Price and George Pelecanos, the series referred to earlier traditions of crime writing and realist fiction while carving out a whole new form of television experience, at once demanding, thrilling and thoughtful. Yet its creator, David Simon, recognised its often powerful political themes as crucial to its purpose, such as when commenting on series two as 'a meditation on the death of work and the betrayal of the American working class . . . it is a deliberate argument that unencumbered capitalism is not a substitute for social policy; that on its own, without a social compact, raw capitalism is destined to serve the few at the expense of the many' (Simon in Richard Vine 2005; see also Busfield and Owen 2009; Simon 2009; Alvarez 2009).

An American Studies interdisciplinary approach to the study of *The Wire* is productive for it demands drawing on different theories and texts to comprehend how ideas are formed, sustained and adjusted over time. The goal of interdisciplinarity is to create a resulting understanding greater than the sum of its disciplinary parts by interlinking and comparing their lines of enquiry. The aim is not, however, a unified, smooth conclusion, but rather a means to explore the show's characteristic ambiguities, its battling voices and its moral complexity. With a rich and varied drama like *The Wire* ranging across different themes, this approach is vitally important. For these reasons, even Harvard University chose to use the series on its urban inequality course because it had the capacity to 'weave together the range of forces that shape the lives of the urban poor' and demonstrate how 'various institutions work together to limit opportunities for the urban poor' (Chaddha and Wilson 2010: n.p.). Indeed, David

Simon, *The Wire*'s creator, has written that it was 'an angry show' about how 'institutions themselves are paramount and every day human beings matter less' and he wanted to use the layered forms of the long-form television format (see discussion later) to enable a more nuanced recognition of social context and individual stories (in Alvarez 2009: 9, 30). The show's more novelistic form and its refusal to accept the 'simple paradigms' (ibid.: 1) of television formats that tailored the drama to fit neatly between advertisement breaks did not interest Simon. Instead, his aim was to find confrontational forms: slow, sprawling, poetic, accented and very intensely local (and yet universal), from which to break the habits of TV audiences and scripts that 'comfort the American comfortable and ignore the American afflicted, the better to sell Ford trucks and fast food' (ibid.).

If the concept of a text is open to redefinition, as David Simon suggests, then so too is the concept of context or 'history' that such new forms of 'telling' can produce. The implications of cultural theory for the discipline of history are considerable and remind us that written history is shaped and crafted in order to represent events to the reader, just as fiction is. Conventional notions of history as an empirically based quest for the truth about the past have been criticised as having an unquestioning and innocent approach to methodological and epistemological issues. Many of these criticisms are undoubtedly polemical in tone, and in their determination to make a theoretical case tend to ignore the sophistication, range and depth of much recent historical work. Ironically, they sometimes rely on particular versions of the past or models of historical interpretation which that work has undermined. Despite this tendency, however, it is nevertheless helpful to identify some of the central points in recent work on the philosophy of history, for they suggest ways of encouraging links between history and other disciplines in the humanities in a way which opens doors to interdisciplinary work. These points may be summarised as follows.

1   There is a critical distinction between 'the past' and 'history'.
2   History in the end is made by historians, defined here to include not just professional historians but all those who are interested in making some sense of the past. For example, an American historian like Frederick Jackson Turner established a narrative of Western history that sought to explain not just that region of the nation, but the entire make-up of a national character.
3   History as a discourse is a construct which cannot comprehend the whole of the past. The past, in its totality, is simply too big, too various, to encompass in any one account.
4   History, therefore, is made up of a range of different and contesting accounts of the past and we come to the past through its different

histories, and it is these histories which we must weigh against each other as we seek to make sense of the past. There is no accurate and unchanging historical record of the past out there against which we can check our stories for their truth. Thus new feminist or ethnic histories must be explored against the more 'traditional' male-centred constructions of historians like Frederick Jackson Turner.

5   Because history is a partial account of the past, it is subject to the same pressures as other stories; it is written according to certain conventions and rules, and employs a range of narrative devices, which may be explicit or implicit. The historian communicates by employing a range of strategies which are commonly thought of as the province of the novelist, such as metaphor, repetition, personification, closure and others. The same is true, of course, of the documentary materials which the historian consults.

6   These narratives are themselves contested, that is, they are in a dynamic relationship with each other. Particular kinds of narratives may have predominated at specific times, because they were the expression of dominant cultural forms or political systems. Other narratives remained unconstructed or silenced because they were not admitted into the dominant culture. Thus, until recently, Native Americans and African Americans have been silenced in history by a process that has denied them an authoritative historical voice.

7   Histories are written by historians who themselves are located in a specific social context, and whose observations, interpretations and judgements are partly shaped by the conceptual categories they bring to their task.

8   American history is part of a global system and cannot be viewed in isolation; it is *trans*-national.

It now may be possible to see how issues to do with the concept of an unproblematic national culture and identity mesh with methodological questions over what kinds of texts are worthy of scrutiny, and how these texts in turn link with the process of historical enquiry. An openness to a range of textual material – to include, for instance, popular and high culture, imaginative and documentary material, novels or films and histories – may in turn open up questions of national identity and its construction, move us beyond conventional disciplinary boundaries, and posit a range of alternative, competing discourses as the focus of analysis. Thus an event like the quincentennial of Columbus in 1992 was contested by different interpretations of the meanings of the 'discovery/conquest' of America (see Chapter 1), or one might examine Hurricane Katrina (2005) in a similarly diverse way as competing versions of events unfolded around race, economics and political mismanagement (see http://understandingkatrina.ssrc.org/ for work in this area), or, to return to

David Simon's *The Wire*, with its layered histories of Baltimore told through different voices from within its various communities, to understand how 'capital has triumphed completely, labor has been marginalized and monied interests have produced enough political infrastructure to prevent reform' (Simon in Alvarez 2009: 30).

As Shelley Fisher Fishkin put it in her call to redefine the field, 'The goal of American studies scholarship is not exporting and championing an arrogant, pro-American nationalism but understanding the multiple meanings of America and American culture in all their complexity' and to 'provide the nuance, complexity, and historical context to correct reductive visions of America' (Fishkin 2005: 20). One approach to this was suggested in 2008 when Levander and Levine called for 'Hemispheric American Studies' that 'focuses on the complex ruptures that remain within but nonetheless constitute the national frame, while at the same time moving beyond the national frame to consider regions, areas, and diasporan affiliations that exist apart from or in conflicted relation to the nation' (Levander and Levine 2008: 2). From apparently 'local' materials, such as those dramatised in *The Wire*, we need to look for connections and networks that produce these economic, cultural and political conditions. As one character in *The Wire* says when trying to steer the young Dukie away from the crime and drug trade in his neighbourhood, the 'world is bigger than that'. With a tinge of hope that his life might be different, Dukie asks: 'How do you get from here to the rest of the world?' The response: 'I wish I knew.' These critical tensions of inside and outside, local and global, national and transnational are very productive areas of debate within any current discussion of American Studies.

USING THE BOOK

In what follows we have not used the same mode of analysis in each chapter, since investigations of different themes or topics clearly demand different approaches. As we have stressed, this book is not a survey or an attempt to write a textbook with all the answers. As Michael Fischer has written, 'the text is not hermetically sealed, but points beyond itself' (Clifford and Marcus 1986: 201) and this book points to many other areas of study, avenues of exploration and research. Thus Chapter 6 on 'the American city' takes what might be described as a poststructuralist approach to the city as a text whose meanings are constantly shifting and unfixable, whereas Chapter 7 analyses the ways in which gender has defined power relations at work in America. We have, however, developed a self-conscious and explicit description of the practices we have adopted in the various chapters, as part of those chapters themselves. We have also included selected discussions of texts in a little more detail than a conventional survey would allow, again in an attempt to suggest possible approaches to a range of interdisciplinary textual material. The texts chosen for this purpose are not meant to be representative but, rather, to be helpful examples of what can be done through this kind of work.

At the end of each chapter and on the accompanying website for this book (see http://www.routledge.com/cw/campbell/), we have provided concrete suggestions for follow-up work that will allow students to develop their approaches to the topics concerned. Works cited in each chapter indicate a range of textual materials which might be used for further study. What we would encourage in these chapters, then, is open-mindedness and curiosity honouring and challenging a plurality of perspectives, relishing varieties of intellectual experience, while acknow-ledging the location and uncertainty of knowledge itself. At the same time, however, we also want to encourage students to explore some of the ways in which difference is connected to issues of power expressed through history, that 'the inherited notion of American culture is the product of historical struggles that have been won by some and lost by others' (Fox-Genovese 1990: 27) and that it is important to study the interaction between differing individuals and forces.

CRITICAL APPROACHES

For the remainder of this introduction, we will present, in more detail, some of the approaches and terms we see as informing the chapters that make up this book. It is our intention to begin with an overview of some of the concepts that structure and influence individual chapters, and provide a certain amount of explanation and context for these approaches. We have tried to explain them in the particular contexts in which they will be used in this book and we provide, through the notes and reading lists, ways of continuing the process started here through individual projects. It is important to emphasise, however, that individual chapters, with their specific applications of these critical approaches, will put the flesh and bones onto the skeleton assembled here.

Dream, myth and ideology

The American Dream was first defined by James Truslow Adams as 'that dream of a land in which life should be better and richer and fuller for everyone, with opportunity for each according to ability or achievement' (Adams 1932: 404). For all its faults as a concept, it does, however, express a dominant American national myth, a fundamental and long-held belief, like the promised land or Turner's Frontier thesis, which in different ways confirm certain qualities and attributes that function to define an 'American spirit'. These myths work to construct 'national character' and aspirations by suggesting that all people held these beliefs unanimously.

American Studies has often followed and explored, even helped to define, some of these mythic frameworks. Critical studies such as R.W.B. Lewis's *The American Adam* (1955) or Henry Nash Smith's *Virgin Land* (1950) are examples of texts that helped to enunciate American mythic sensibility by reinforcing specific notions of the nation as Edenic or as wilderness. In one sense, the purpose of myth is to make the world explicable, to magically resolve its problems and contradictions. 'Mythical thought always progresses from the awareness of oppositions toward their resolution' (Lévi-Strauss 1963: 224). Ronald Wright adds that, 'Myth is an arrangement of the past ... in patterns [that] create and reinforce archetypes so taken for granted, so seemingly axiomatic, that we live and die by them' (Wright 1992: 5).

Thus myths are the stories we tell each other as a culture in order to explain complexities and to banish contradictions, thus making the world seem simpler and more comfortable for us to inhabit. For example, if America was a 'virgin land', a wilderness, it was 'free' to be civilised and occupied by the pioneers, irrespective of the indigenous population. Roland Barthes warns against such complacency and reminds us to be vigilant and willing to interrogate the 'falsely obvious' (1973: 11) because 'By myth Barthes also means ideology understood as a body of ideas and practices which defend the status quo and actively promote the values and interests of the dominant groups in society' (Storey 1993: 78). For Barthes, myths alter the past by endowing the shifting, complex processes of history with the appearance of something 'natural', 'eternal' and taken for granted. Thus myth is 'depoliticised speech' because it is as if the complexities that we recognise in speech (and history) have been hollowed out until all that remains is 'what goes without saying' – a simple version denuded of political debate and difference.

Thus myths are ideological because they are concerned primarily with the ways in which particular images of the world are conveyed and reinforced through texts and practices. Ideology can be explained as those modes of feeling, valuing, perceiving and believing that exist within and inform our everyday lives and connect us to wider structures of power in society in ways that contribute to the maintenance and reproduction of social power (Eagleton 1983). Such ideological myths exist everywhere in American culture, helping to shape the way people think and write about the nation, its history and its life, and they need to be interrogated and critiqued. Every time we use the phrase 'American Dream' we must be critical of it, asking, for example, 'whose dream?' and 'at what cost?' For example, the idea of America as a new Eden, a place of new birth, mission and promise, has been perpetuated in various forms throughout its history. Through interrogating these myths and ideologies we see the lines of power that have structured and given preferred meanings to particular renditions of the past and privileged certain groups as a result. However, this is not a simple corrective, for that would imply that a 'myth' can be opposed by a 'truth' when, in fact, culture is more usefully viewed as a series of dynamic and contested ideological forces and interpretations. In this sense, these concepts need to be carefully related to that of 'discourse' (discussed later), as both myth and ideology contribute to the formations of discourse that construct 'America'.

Interdisciplinary Studies

The term 'Interdisciplinary Studies' suggests being at the boundary of the individual disciplines, where they begin to merge and intermingle, clash and jar, and relates to the condition of being at the margins of the normalised, accepted and official culture of America. These positions, both the abstract academic one and the real, ideological one, can be productive and invigorating. Being at these 'boundaries' or 'borders' can provide a new way of seeing a culture like the United States, because one is pushed beyond the centre where the world is defined, ordered and laid out, and permitted to see from a different perspective, through the decentred 'lens of alterity', as Paul Giles has termed it (2002: 255), including views from those excluded and marginalised by mainstream, dominant American culture. Here, a shift takes place giving a 'sense of disorientation, a disturbance of direction . . . an exploratory, restless movement' (Bhabha 1994: 1) because the established, safe sense of the 'real' has been questioned and replaced by an 'awareness of the subject positions – of race, gender, generation, institutional location, geopolitical locale, sexual orientation – that inhabit any claim to identity in the modern world' (ibid.). At the boundaries of American culture, there is a multicultural, multiperspectival, transnational way of seeing, from where one might gain both these new perspectives and grasp 'the possibility of a cultural hybridity that enter-tains difference without an assumed or imposed hierarchy' (ibid.: 4). This latter concern with cultural hybridity will be discussed later with regard to ethnicity and pluralism (see Chapter 2).

As a meeting place or 'crossroads' (as Fishkin writes) of many cultures, systems of ritual and belief, America can be seen as a vast borderland or 'contact zone' where, in the words of Mary-Louise Pratt, 'disparate cultures meet, clash and grapple with each other' and 'subjects are constituted in and by their relations to each other . . . in terms of co-presence, interaction, interlocking understandings and practices' (Pratt 1995: 6–7). Interdiscip-linary Studies, which interconnects *and* transgresses boundaries as a method of exploration, provides a suitable methodology through which to engage with and critique these dominant voices, and to appreciate and listen to other voices, recognising their mutual struggles to be heard.

Multicultural and multiperspectival

The development of critical Cultural Studies has been largely promoted by groups on the margins of power, excluded from the mainstream: women, ethnic minorities, gays, lesbians and others. Through their exploration of new critical approaches, old systems of representation and power have been interrogated and resisted, such as from within post-colonial studies (see Singh and Schmidt 2000; Madsen 2003). For example, multiculturalism – that is, the belief that a healthy culture is made up of many different people with diverse systems of belief and practice – has encouraged the analysis of relationships of control, oppression and social stereotyping, and focused on resistance to domination, the need for self-definition and the assertion of difference. Similarly, feminism has analysed the relations of power, finding many connections with the struggles of ethnic groups in America (see Adrienne Rich's work discussed in Chapter 7), but also contributed to the new critical voices that urge reconsideration, revision and the interdisciplinary search for new approaches beyond the simplistic 'either/or' mentality of thinking that suggests there are only opposites and no complex, negotiated terrains. Such terrains give voice to what Foucault calls 'subjugated knowledges' (1980: 81) – that is, to buried or marginalised cultural forms that have to be heard as part of the complex field of society. He emphasises the need to combine the 'erudite knowledge' with 'popular', 'local, regional . . . differential knowledge incapable of unanimity' (ibid.: 82), because in this mix there is a fuller picture of the multilayered cultural climate that we would associate with the United States. A multidimensional view of culture fostered by these new social movements has enabled approaches to texts that are challenging because they demand that we ask new questions about who speaks, who defines, who controls and who is included or excluded from this process. As Desmond and Dominguez put it, American Studies must 'move beyond a monocular [one-eyed] vision to one refracted by numerous simultaneous perspectives . . . as a body of scholarship on an "area" defined in dynamic relation to other "areas"' (Desmond and Dominguez 1996: 5).

A CULTURE OF MANY VOICES

For various reasons, certain powerful groups have sought to present America as a single nation and have played down its diverse components. This is exemplified by the significance of Noah Webster's dictionary and his call for a common American language in the 1790s. As Mikhail Bakhtin recognised, there are many voices running through language and litera-ture, as in culture itself, and these must be acknowledged in an ideally 'heteroglossic' (many-voiced) formulation of society:

at any given moment of its historical existence, language is heteroglot from top to bottom: it represents the co-existence of socio-ideological contradictions between the present and the past . . . these 'languages' of heteroglossia intersect each other in a variety of ways, forming new socially typifying 'languages'.

(Bakhtin 1990: 291)

For example, in watching a show like *The Wire* (discussed above and below), we are exposed to the 'heteroglossic' sense of Baltimore with its many competing voices, accents, communities engaged in complex struggles over power, place and meaning. As David Simon said of the show, in the end it was not about the characters, institutions, communities or crime, 'It was about the City' (Alvarez 2009: 3).

Poststructuralist thinking in particular (see Chapter 6 on the city) has recognised that texts are not closed, but plural with 'an endless play of signifiers which can never be finally nailed down to a single centre, essence or meaning' (Eagleton 1983: 138). To impose a single meaning or to attempt to find one is to misrepresent the complexity of the text itself (or nation in our case), for it is our contention that a variety of readings across the disciplines is one method of exploring the fullness of both the text and the nation, to hear the many voices that Bakhtin describes or Simon dramatises.

This reveals issues of power too: of whose voice is 'normally' heard in culture, what it enunciates and how it frames society in particular ways or as Simon put it earlier, 'capital . . . labor . . . monied interests' engaged in a struggle for authority (in Alvarez 2009: 30). These are the questions that emerge when we approach texts from outside their normal frame of reference. Diversity, difference, contest, dialogue are the watchwords of this approach, but crucially, too, a willingness to acknowledge the 'links and interrelationships' across what Bakhtin called 'the borderlines' (1984: 29) brings us back to our concern for the interdisciplinary method.

This book will pay attention to many voices and how they have recorded their lives, and recognise how history is always in a process of revision concerned with the analyses of power, ideology and representation. America as a nation of differences has to be examined with close consideration of the ways in which those differences relate to those who have the loudest voices, the most authority, status and wealth, and those who do not. Furthermore, such systems must be explored in order that such hierarchical structures are revealed and explained.

CULTURAL POLITICS/CULTURAL STUDIES

America, like all cultures, is multifaceted and ever-changing, and therefore it has to be constantly questioned and examined using the most appropriate tools available. In recent years, Cultural Studies has provided new analytical approaches through which many traditional attitudes towards 'culture' have shifted, allowing a wider interpretation of the word. Rather than just 'high' culture – the best-thought and -written, with eternal values and authority – there has been a perceived need to include other forms of cultural expression, drawn from popular culture, mass media (referred to in the past as 'low' culture) and to broaden what could be studied to include not just traditional forms of expression, but new forms (film, television, graphic novels) and a fuller definition of the concept of text. In this definition, culture is 'the ensemble of social processes by which meanings are produced, circulated and exchanged' (Thwaites *et al.* 1994: 1), and all these 'social processes' can be 'read', interpreted and contested as texts. A useful way of envisaging this is to see culture as 'an assemblage of texts, loosely and sometimes contradictorily united' (Clifford 1988: 41) which constitute meanings, ideologies and subjectivities as they weave together, collide and merge.

This leads us through a series of vital questions about cultural formation, power, ideology and representation:

> Whose culture shall be the official one and whose shall be subordinated? What cultures shall be regarded as worthy of display and which shall be hidden? Whose history shall be remembered and whose forgotten? What images of social life shall be projected and which shall be marginalized? What voices shall be heard and which be silenced? Who is representing whom and on what basis?
>
> (Jordan and Weedon 1995: 4)

In American terms, such questions reveal how certain non-white cultures have been 'hidden', or women's histories have been erased in favour of the dominant male stories of the nation. Through the close study of cultural expressions, texts and practices we can raise these questions and begin to see the ideological positions that are registered socially in cultural institutions such as the family, education, the media, the churches, the law and language. These are termed *discourses* that constitute – rather than simply describing or reflecting – reality, and form our concepts about our identity and about what the world means. Discourses organize statements, define texts, promote meanings, representations and stories, position subjects and are endlessly in competition for our attention as they *construct* our sense of what is right and wrong, normal and abnormal, important or not worthy of our attention. These competing discourses can at any one time achieve greater authority within the cultural system, and become *dominant discourses*, carrying more status, power and social significance. For example, a discourse of American patriotism in a time of war might be a gathering of texts such as the flag, emotional music, images of heroism and sacrifice and speeches of resolution and determination from the White House. Together these are discursive formations that construct patriotism as logical, acceptable and 'natural' – as if it is a timeless and eternal condition of all normal, good Americans. Anyone criticising these discursive elements would be seen as unpatriotic and threatening, as in some of the reactions post-11 September 2001.

The influence of such discursive formations within culture is immense, structuring power and influence, attitudes, beliefs and identity. After all, the effect of discourse is to *position us* in relation to a variety of social forces. It *subjects us*. So, using our example of patriotic discourse, Japanese Americans in the Second World War were imprisoned because they were perceived as a threat to the 'American' cause. They were 'subjected' and 'positioned' by this patriotic discourse and defined as dangerous outsiders as in John Sturges's film *Bad Day at Black Rock* (1955) where the Japanese American Komoko is killed by the racist locals. This is precisely the contested terrain into which Cultural Studies goes in order to debate issues of and assumptions about identity, gender, class, the family, education, ethnicity, the environment, religion and technology. In so doing, it reveals how power and ideology work to legitimate social inequalities, but it also explores how forms of resistance emerge as part of this complex cultural contest. For just as dominant discourses emerge in culture, so can resistant, counter-discourses, struggling to be heard in the cultural arena and attempting to alter the received and dominant modes of expression and definition. This is a central interest in this book, as in much Cultural Studies, for it is through these resisting and contesting voices that new and interesting critical challenges are made to the centralised and established order.

POWER, POSITION, HEGEMONY

America is a powerful nation, some would say an 'empire', with immense wealth, military strength and global influence, politically, economically, militarily and culturally and this is how it likes to represent itself to the world. But how is this power achieved, by whom, for whom and at what cost to others? It is vital that such assumptions and representations are questioned since power exists in different ways throughout culture and can be seen in all practices and signifying systems. In their creation of meaning and our relation to that meaning, we are positioned, that is, we are 'interpellated' or 'buttonholed' (Barthes 1973: 124–5) into a position which includes (or excludes) us in the relationship. The effect of this is ideological, for it serves to orient people in social contexts towards accepting certain values as natural, obvious and self-evident, and embodying these ideologies to such an extent that they appear to resolve contradictions and represent values which do not necessarily cohere with their lived experiences.

To modify an example from Barthes (1973) and Jordan and Weedon (1995), consider an image of an African American child, hand on heart, gazing on the Stars and Stripes at the beginning of the school day and reciting the Pledge of Allegiance. The child is 'hailed' as one of the people and a part of an ideological system from which 'history evaporates' (Barthes 1973: 117), for the 'long story' of slavery, segregation and lack of civil rights has been emptied out and replaced by a simple 'myth' – 'a rich, fully experienced, spontaneous, innocent, *indisputable* image' (ibid.: 118). This particular example stresses 'One nation under God' and there-fore promotes and makes 'natural' the ideology of a united and coherent America, ordained by God, 'with liberty and justice for all'. We may feel comfortable with these myths and values, and may go along with the positions they appear to offer us, or we may resist them and their attempts to place and define us. The power of discourse can contribute significantly to the formation of powerful notions of 'Americanness' or national identity. To reduce the image of the child to a single meaning is to denude it of possibility and to ignore the contradictory and competing meanings that have constructed it (its 'histories'). Of course, in a particular situation the image could be read simply as a signifier of patriotism, loyalty and equal opportunity – with an emphasis upon racial harmony, unity and the American Dream. This could be the dominant reading of the meanings on offer, fixed by social circumstance, cultural background, education and so on, and reinforced through powerful institutions (school, family, the media, etc.). Such subject positionings are difficult to resist for they anchor the image's meanings in very specific ways, but by adopting alternative perspectives one can provide different ways of seeing, redefine identities and present new forms of resistance.

Cultural Studies as an approach seeks to listen to marginal voices and to the perspectives they bring to debates about power, authority and meaning. These forces are connected to a term used throughout this book – *hegemony*. This is a term that helps explain the way that power works within culture that is in itself 'free and democratic', like America. Hegemony refers to the ways in which a dominant class 'doesn't merely rule but leads a society through the exertion of moral and intellec-tual leadership' (Storey 1993: 119) so that a consensus is established in which all classes appear to support and subscribe to its ideologies and cultural meanings, incorporating them into the existing power structure. Hegemony's embracing of consensus means that any opposition can be 'contained and channelled into ideologically safe harbours' (ibid.), not through imposition, but through negotiation. So subordinate groups are not necessarily ignored, but rather given a certain 'place', a position within the embrace of the dominant group, and their views articulated to a degree within the *master-narrative*. A master-narrative is the grand story told by the dominant groups to legitimate and justify their actions and policies. It attempts to encompass and totalise by a process of selection and exclusion of alternative, often critical, perspectives. For example, in the United States African Americans have been 'placed' within a dominant white cultural narrative, but through political struggle, cultural self-assertion and intervention they have developed an increasing role in the mainstream. Hegemony asserts cultural struggle and is best defined as 'a contested and shifting set of ideas by means of which dominant groups strive to secure the consent of subordinate groups to their leadership' (Strinati 1995: 170).

DIALOGISM

As we noted earlier, cultural anthropology and Cultural Studies have recognised the importance of the work of Mikhail Bakhtin and in particular his call for dialogism. Based on the study of linguistics and language use, Bakhtin's work can be very useful in the analysis of American culture. As Reising commented, it 'provides the basis for a new appreciation of the heterogeneity of American [culture], a heterogeneity often blurred or denied by the polarization of canonical/non-canonical, major/minor, aesthetic/social' (Reising 1986: 234; see also Lenz 1999; Giles 2002). Language is dialogical, interacting self and other in a constant process of 'intermingling of diverse points of view' (Reising 1986: 234), and culture can be seen as functioning in a similar manner, as 'an open-ended, creative dialogue of subcultures, of insiders and outsiders, of diverse factions' (Clifford 1988: 46). In adopting this approach to American Studies, 'the intention is to dialogize dominant monologues, indeed, to show that dialogue is not an abstract ideal . . . but that it is everywhere' (Krupat 1992: 237) and that in examining this dialogue we can move closer to 'a textured sense of being American' (Fischer 1986: 230). Dialogues are not, of course, necessarily equal but in recognising their existence we see culture as always in a process of negotiation, with positions and identities shifting, with official voices being parodied and satirised, with power being contested and realigned.

To summarise, we would agree that American 'culture is contested, temporal and emergent' (Clifford and Marcus 1986: 19) and through Cultural Studies we can examine these elements, both to identify patterns of power, inequality, domination and resistance, and also to see the possibilities for change and development in the future. America has always been a place of invention and of dreams, and this book will attempt in various ways to explore the possibilities that still exist within American culture. Some might argue that the emergence of Barack Obama is testament to this continuing power. To borrow from the anthropologist James Clifford, there is still a 'persistent hope for the reinvention of difference' within America (Clifford 1988: 15) which takes a variety of forms in its cultural life and energy. These 'histories of emergent differences require other ways of telling . . . there is no single model' (ibid.: 17), but as this book examines its various topics there are recurrent concerns about new forms revealed in interdisciplinary ways. The recognition and awareness of America as a still-emerging, creative and dynamic place in which new, hybrid identities are ever possible remains a prominent belief; but they are seen in the context of the histories and stories already told and often hidden, revealing a darker reality that has created the present from which anything new must emerge.

TRANSNATIONAL AND HEMISPHERIC AMERICAN STUDIES

Gunter Lenz has called for a 'dialogics of International American Culture Studies' (1999: 18) and Paul Giles writes of the need 'to rearticulate the . . . field dialogically and comparatively' (2002: 284). At the core of both arguments is the need to view American Studies as part of a complex, transnational dialogue that breaks down older, persistent notions of exceptionalism and essentialism by drawing on the disjunctions and similarities between cultures, challenging mythic unity with diversity and critique. Dialogues across and between cultures transform how America is viewed, decentring and rupturing the seamless 'cultural insiderdom' often associated with old school 'consensual' American Studies, whether from the 'borderlands' perspective of the US southwest as shown by Gloria Anzaldúa's or José David Saldivar's work, or from the 'transatlantic' perspectives of Paul Gilroy or Joseph Roach, or the Latin America perspectives of Walter Mignolo. This 'transnational turn' traces alternative spaces and modes of belonging that are not defined by the nation-state and reconceives immigration as diasporic, multidirectional movements (see Kaplan 2004; Fishkin 2005; Levander and Levine 2008; Fluck *et al.* 2011). In breaking out of the 'charmed circle' of representation from within the US, transnational perspectives work 'to reveal the circumference of national formations and thus to empty out their peremptory claims to legitimacy' (Giles 2002: 2, 17), raising important questions about established myths, values and hierarchies through redefining America as part of a global 'exchange'. In other words, it is not enough, as once thought, to simply incorporate more voices to the grid of American national identity and expand the canon, for this simply maintains the tradition of inclusiveness and 'unity'. Instead, one utilises external points of reference to relativise the whole field and to interrupt this circle of national representation. One consequence of such transnational (or postnational) thinking is to continually re-examine the idea of nation and its romantic attachment to 'roots' and essential, fixed identity, and supplement it with a sense of 'routes' – the multiple, fluid formation of identity through contact, motion, diaspora and hybridity. And perhaps in this, as Amy Kaplan has stated, American Studies can be engaged in the important work of 'translation', to 'contest the universalism of American exceptionalism and to participate in the "strain and stress of the world", which is interconnected in many more complex ways than through the military reach of empire' (Kaplan 2004: 15–16).

A further example of these ideas at work can be seen in the idea of 'Hemispheric American Studies', not as a distinct, defined methodology, but as a relational process by which 'nation-time' is interrupted in order to see 'the intricately intertwined geographies, movements, and cross-filiations among peoples, regions, diasporas, and nations of the American hemisphere' (Levander and Levine 2008: 3). Importantly for a revised American Studies, this would mean seeing nation as emergent, through 'constant collaboration, dialogue, and dissension' and its culture the product of 'subordinations, alliances, and cross-fertilisations that make the nation a richly suggestive but hardly an autonomous entity' (ibid.: 5, 6). Importantly, this re-places 'America' within its true hemispheric relation – that is, as not the only version of nation, but rather as one part in a complex web of relations called the Americas. We will examine some of these ideas in Chapter 2 when discussing the film *Frozen River*. Of course, in searching for new approaches and to continue this relativisation of American Studies, a further emphasis has been placed on the idea of 'worlding' or viewing American culture as intrinsically linked to wider flows of meaning and identity. 'Worlds' emerge in different places – on the streets of Baltimore in *The Wire*, on the border of El Paso and Juarez, in the rural backwoods of Montana – and 'remap relationships of power at different scales and localities ... by opening up new channels or reconfigure[ing] new social universes' (Ong 2011: 12). In this sense, as Dimock and Buell's 2007 collection argues, American literature might be seen as 'a constituted domain' within 'world literature' (2007: 1) contributing not to a single, unified vision, but rather to 'a living shifting network' (Ong 2011: 12).

LONG-FORM TELEVISION AND AMERICAN STUDIES

One emergent trend that has a huge influence on aspects of 'worlding' and the circulation of American Studies globally is the rise of new epic television shows that are now watched in different ways than the conventional weekly slots in a schedule. Streaming, 'catch-up' and 'box set' culture has altered the way television is produced and received, and therefore, has some significance in the transmission and discussion of all things American. Robert J. Thompson's *Television's Second Golden Age* (1996) argued for a significant change away from 'network fare' towards 'more sophisticated and more artistic' television epitomised by the rise of cable network Home Box Office (HBO) and its slogan, 'It's Not TV, It's HBO', signalling its belief in what some have called 'quality television'. He had in mind shows like *Hill Street Blues*, *St Elsewhere* and *thirty-something*, which helped to blaze a trail for later series such as *Oz* (1997–2003), *Sex and the City* (1998–2004), *The Sopranos* (1999–2007), *Six Feet Under* (2001–5) and, probably most significantly, as we discussed earlier, *The Wire* (2002–8). In recent years other companies like Netflix have entered the market to produce forms of television adapted to the new ways of both watching and accessing serial television (see *Orange is the New Black* in Chapter 7). There is no longer the need to wait for weekly showings when the show can be streamed or watched as 'catch-up' or as a box set, the viewer becoming immersed in the world constructed by types of television with high production values, crafted scripts and famous Hollywood stars. Serial, 'long-form' television gave writers and directors opportunities to work with extensive ensemble casts to explore broad narrative arcs across episodes and even seasons and allowing complex character development just not possible in the two hours of a typical feature film. Suddenly shows like *Breaking Bad* (AMC, 2009–13) told intricate, multiple-layered stories evolving across the luxury of twelve-episode series with a powerful sense of place (Albuquerque, New Mexico) and time, and surprising plot twists as well as quirky experimental styles of camera work.

What emerges from such serials is a new form of epic television telling more detailed social tales of the USA, whether historical, like *The Pacific* (2010), *Band of Brothers* (2001) or *Generation Kill* (2008) or cultural political, like *The Wire*, *Mad Men* (2007–15) or *Breaking Bad* in which long-form stories unravelled demanding narratives that engaged viewers in a television experience that tested their memories and their patience with alternative and unusual approaches. As Chris Bigsby has commented, such shows are novelistic and interested in 'social context more fully realised' (Bigsby 2013: 227), allowing, as in *The Wire*, alternative, often ambiguous perspectives to emerge to challenge 'the American comfortable' based on paradigms of 'good and evil, of heroes, villains, and simplified characterization' (in Alvarez 2009: 1). Mythic American narratives are cross-cut and interfered with by long-form television and demand more of the audience: 'to slow themselves down and pay attention, to immerse themselves in a way that the medium had long ago ceased to demand' (ibid.: 3).

These shows impact on American Studies, offering new challenges for myth-creation as well as critique, and above all immerse their audience in deep, layered experiences that provide time and space for more complex stories about a complex nation and its multiple identities to find their ways onto our screens wherever we are in the world. Hence, David Simon in *The Wire* used this format politically and provocatively to show not good and evil, like the mythic Western might have in the 1940s, but rather to dramatise a heteroglossic community, 'an America, at every level, at war with itself' (Simon in Bigsby 2013: 223).

THE CONTINUOUS 'PLAY' OF CULTURE, HISTORY AND POWER

This book will examine these heteroglossic identities, their constructions, their representations and their relationships to power and authority and show, through the attention to specific events, themes and texts, how and why the United States of America is 'historically evolving and contingent – rather than already formed' (Levander and Levine 2008: 6–7). If one of the central functions of historians is to 'lock up and unlock memory' (Appleby *et al*. 1994: 155), then this book is involved in the latter part of this process, engaged in the unlocking and 'dethroning' of long-held versions and myths of American culture and the 'simplified story that was told about the nation's past' (ibid.: 3, 294). Hence, the Wild West has given rise to immensely influential national myths and, through their interrogation, we can unlock relations of power that excluded women and ethnic minorities, attempted to erase the Indian and ravaged the land. We are concerned with ideologies, representations, power, discourse, hegemony and identity as constant factors in the construction of America as a broad, multifaceted and 'imagined community' whose cultural identity is:

> a matter of 'becoming' as well as of 'being' . . . [and] belongs to the future as much as to the past . . . not something that already exists, transcending place, time, history and culture . . . fixed in some essentialised past, [but] subject to the continuous 'play' of history, culture and power.
>
> (Hall 1990: 225)

It is within these contexts that this book will show 'a living mix of varied and opposing voices' (Bakhtin 1990: xxviii), constructed of many stories, told by many people from different positions and for different purposes. They change in value, worth and power, are argued for and against, are denied, hidden or celebrated, become official or remain unofficial, but taken together, in all their multiplicities, they construct and represent the United States of America, and it is this 'living mix' of stories that is the concern of this book. American Studies might, therefore, resist exceptionalist, imperialist perspectives and instead through such diverse narratives imagine a different relationship across cultures and between individuals based not on 'self-sufficiency and unbridled sovereignty' but on different forms of 'interdependency' and mutual acknowledgement of 'vulnerability' (Butler 2004: xii–xiii, 42). As Judith Butler explains, for America to alter its relations with the world it 'will need to emerge from the narrative perspective of US unilateralism and, as it were, its defensive structures, to consider the ways in which our lives are profoundly implicated in the lives of others' (ibid.: 7). What American Studies can do in the future through deep questioning, comparative work and constant revision is to contribute to this critical process and ultimately be 'open to narration that decenters [America] from [its] supremacy' and produces, in Butler's words, a '"we" traversed by a relationality that we cannot easily argue against' (ibid.: 18, 23).

NOTE

1 A very helpful and wide-ranging guide to recent work relevant to the interdisciplinary approach to American Studies may be found on Cultural Politics.net (2011) at http://culturalpolitics.net/.

REFERENCES AND FURTHER READING

Adams, J.T. (1932) *The Epic of America*, London: George Routledge and Sons.
Alvarez, R. (2009) *The Wire: Truth Be Told*, introduction by D. Simon, London: Canongate.
Anderson, B. (1991) *Imagined Communities*, London: Verso.
Anzaldúa, G. (1987) *Borderlands/La Frontera*, San Francisco: Aunt Lute Books.
Appleby, J., Hunt, L. and Jacob, M. (1994) *Telling the Truth About History*, London: W.W. Norton.
Bakhtin, M. (1984) *Rabelais and His World*, Bloomington: Indiana University Press.
—— (1990) *The Dialogic Imagination*, Austin: University of Texas Press.
Barthes, R. (1973) *Mythologies*, London: Paladin.
BBC (2011) 'Declinism', *Today Programme*, 16 February, at http://news.bbc.co.uk/today/hi/today/newsid_9399000/9399134.stm
Bhabha, H.K. (1994) *The Location of Culture*, London: Routledge.
Bigsby, C.W.E (2013) *Viewing America: Twentieth Century Television Drama*, Cambridge: Cambridge University Press.
Brantlinger, P. (1990) *Crusoe's Footprints: Cultural Studies in Britain and America*, London: Routledge.
Burgett, B. and Hendler, G. (eds) (2007) *Keywords for American Cultural Studies*, New York: New York University Press.
Busfield, S. and Owen, P. (2009) *The Wire Re-Up*, London: Guardian Books.
Butler, J. (2004) *Precarious Life: The Powers of Mourning and Violence*, London: Verso.
Chaddha, A. and Wilson, W.J. (2010) 'Why We're Teaching *The Wire* at Harvard', *The Washington Post*, 12 September, at http://www.washington post.com/wp-dyn/content/article/2010/09/10/AR2010091002676.html

Clayton, J. (1993) *The Pleasures of Babel: Contemporary American Literature and Theory*, Oxford: Oxford University Press.

Clifford, J. (1988) *The Predicament of Culture: Twentieth Century Ethnography, Literature and Art*, Cambridge, MA: Harvard University Press.

Clifford, J. and Marcus, G. (eds) (1986) *Writing Culture: The Poetics and Politics of Ethnography*, Berkeley: University of California Press.

Denning, M. (1986) 'Marxism and American Studies', *American Quarterly*, vol. 38, no. 3, p. 360.

Desmond, J.C. and Dominguez, V.R. (1996) 'Resituating American Studies in a Critical Internationalism', at http://xroads.virginia.edu/~DRBR2/desmond. html). Original in *American Quarterly*, vol. 48, no. 3 (1996), pp. 475–90.

Dimock, W.-C. and Buell, L. (eds) (2007) *Shades of the Planet: American Literature as World Literature*, Princeton: Princeton University Press.

Eagleton, T. (1983) *Literary Theory*, Oxford: Blackwell.

Edwards, B.T. and Gaonkar, D.P. (eds) (2010) *Globalizing American Studies*, Chicago: University of Chicago Press.

Fender, S. (1993) 'The American Difference' in M. Gidley (ed.) *Modern American Culture*, London: Longman.

Ferguson, R. *et al.* (eds) (1990) *Out There: Marginalization and Contemporary Cultures*, Cambridge, MA: MIT Press.

Fischer, M.M.J. (1986) 'Ethnicity and the Postmodern Arts of Memory' in J. Clifford and G. Marcus (eds) *Writing Culture*, Berkeley: University of California Press.

Fishkin, S.F. (2005) 'Crossroads of Cultures: The Transnational Turn in American Studies – Presidential Address to the American Studies Association, November 12, 2004', *American Quarterly*, vol. 57, no. 1, March, pp. 17–57.

Fluck, W., Pease, D.E. and Rowe, J.C. (eds) (2011) *Re-framing the Transnational Turn in American Studies*, Dartmouth: Dartmouth College Press.

Foucault, M. (1980) *Power/Knowledge: Selected Interviews and Other Writings 1972–77*, London: Harvester Wheatsheaf.

Fox-Genovese, E. (1990) 'Between Individualism and Fragmentation: American Culture and the New Literary Studies of Race and Gender', *American Quarterly*, vol. 42, no. 1, March, pp. 7–34.

Geertz, C. (1993) *The Interpretation of Cultures*, London: HarperCollins.

Giles, P. (2002) *Virtual Americas: Transnational Fictions and the Transatlantic Imaginary*, Durham, NC: Duke University Press.

Gilroy, P. (1993) *The Black Atlantic: Modernity and Double Consciousness*, London: Verso.

Giroux, H. and McLaren, P. (1994) *Between Borders: Pedagogy and the Politics of Cultural Studies*, London: Routledge.

Gunn, G. (1987) 'American Studies as Cultural Criticism' in *The Culture of Criticism and the Criticism of Culture*, Oxford: Oxford University Press.

Hall, S. (1990) 'Cultural Identity and Diaspora' in J. Rutherford (ed.) *Identity, Community, Culture, Difference*, London: Lawrence and Wishart.

Halliwell, M. and Morley, C. (2007) *American Thought and Culture in the Twenty-First Century*, Edinburgh: Edinburgh University Press.

Inglis, F. (1993) *Cultural Studies*, Oxford: Blackwell.

Jameson, F. (1984) 'Periodizing the Sixties' in S. Sayres *et al.* (eds) *The 60s Without Apology*, Minneapolis: University of Minnesota Press.

Jarvis, B., Jenner, P. and Dix, A. (2011) *The Contemporary American Novel in Context (Texts and Contexts)*, London: Continuum.

Jenkins, K. (1991) *Re-Thinking History*, London: Routledge.

Jordan, G. and Weedon, C. (1995) *Cultural Politics*, Oxford: Blackwell.

Kaplan, A. (2004) 'Violent Belongings and the Question of Empire Today – Presidential Address of the American Studies Association, October 17, 2003', *American Quarterly*, vol. 56, no. 1, March, pp. 1–17.

Kaplan, A. and Pease, D. (1993) *Cultures of United States Imperialism*, Durham: Duke University Press.

Kellner, D. (1995) *Media Culture: Cultural Studies, Identity and Politics Between the Modern and the Postmodern*, London: Routledge.

King, R. (1989) 'The Eighties' in M. Bradbury and H. Temperley (eds) *Introduction to American Studies*, London: Longman.

Krupat, A. (1992) *Ethnocriticism: Ethnography, History, Literature*, Berkeley: University of California Press.

Lenz, G.H. (1999) 'Towards a Dialogics of International American Culture Studies: Transnationality, Border Discourses, and Public Culture(s)', *Amerikastudien/American Studies*, vol. 44, no. 1, pp. 5–23.

Levander, C.F. and Levine, R.S. (eds) (2008) *Hemispheric American Studies*, New Brunswick: Rutgers University Press.

Levine, L. (1988) *Highbrow/Lowbrow: The Emergence of Cultural Hierarchy in America*, Cambridge, MA: Harvard University Press.

Lévi-Strauss, C. (1963) *Structural Anthropology*, New York: Basic Books.

Lipsitz, G. (1990) 'Listening to Learn and Learning to Listen: Popular Culture, Cultural Theory, and American Studies', *American Quarterly*, vol. 42, no. 4, December, p. 616.

—— (2001) *American Studies in a Moment of Danger*, Minneapolis: University of Minnesota Press.

Lowenthal, D. (1985) *The Past is a Foreign Country*, Cambridge: Cambridge University Press.

Madsen, D. (ed.) (2003) *Beyond the Borders: American Literature and Post-Colonial Theory*, London: Pluto Press.

Mechling, J. (1989) 'An American Culture Grid, with Texts', *American Studies International* vol. 27, April, pp. 2–12.

Metcalf, G. (2012) *The DVD Novel: How the Way We Watch Television Changed the Television We Watch*, New York: Praeger.

Mignolo, W. (2005) *The Idea of Latin America*, Oxford: Blackwell.

Obama, B. (2008) 'Address to the People of Berlin', 24 July, at http://www.americanrhetoric.com/speeches/barackobamaberlinspeech.htm

Ong, A. (2011) 'Introduction: Worlding Cities, or the Art of Being Global' in A. Roy and A. Ong (eds) *Worlding Cities: Asian Experiments and the Art of Being Global*, Oxford: Wiley-Blackwell.

Pease, D. (ed.) (1994) *National Identities and Post-Americanist Narratives*, Durham: Duke University Press.

Pease D. (2009) *The New Exceptionalism*, Minneapolis: University of Minnesota.

Pease, D. and Wiegman, R. (eds) (2002) *The Futures of American Studies*, Durham: Duke University Press.

Pratt, M.-L. (1995) (first 1992) *Imperial Eyes: Travel Writing and Transculturation*, London: Routledge.

Radway, J., Gaines, K., Shank, B., and Von Eschen, P. (eds) (2009) *American Studies: An Anthology*, London: Wiley-Blackwell.

Reising, R. (1986) *The Unusable Past: Theory and the Study of American Literature*, London: Methuen.

Roach, J. (1996) *Cities of the Dead: Circum-Atlantic Performance*, New York: Columbia University Press.

Rowe, J.C. (2002) *The New American Studies*, Minneapolis: University of Minnesota Press.

—— (ed.) (2010) *A Concise Companion to American Studies*, Oxford: John Wiley.

Rutherford, J. (ed.) (1990) *Identity, Community, Culture, Difference*, London: Lawrence and Wishart.

Saldivar, J.D. (1997) *Border Matters: Re-mapping American Cultural Studies*, Berkeley: University of California Press.

Sayres, S. *et al.* (eds) (1984) *The 60s Without Apology*, Minneapolis: University of Minnesota Press.

Shukla, S. and Tinsman, H. (eds) (2007) *Imagining Our Americas: Toward a Transnational Frame*, Durham: Duke University Press.

Siemerling, W. (2005) *The New North American Studies: Culture, writing and the politics of re/cognition*, London: Routledge.

Simon, D. (2009) *Homicide*, Edinburgh: Canongate.

Singh, A. and Schmidt, P. (eds) (2000) *Postcolonial Theory and the United States*, Jackson: University Press of Mississippi.

Smith, S. (1993) *Subjectivity, Identity and the Body*, Bloomington: Indiana University Press.

Storey, J. (1993) *An Introductory Guide to Cultural Theory and Popular Culture*, London: Longman.

Strinati, D. (1995) *An Introduction to the Theories of Popular Culture*, London: Routledge.

Tallack, D. (1991) *Twentieth Century America: The Intellectual and Cultural Context*, London: Longman.

Thompson, R.J. (1996) *Television's Second Golden Age*, New York: Syracuse University Press.

Thwaites, T., Davis, L. and Mules, W. (1994) *Tools for Cultural Studies: An Introduction*, Melbourne: Macmillan.

Trachtenberg, A. (1982) *The Incorporation of America: Culture and Society in the Gilded Age*, New York: Hill and Wang.

Vine, R. (2005) 'Totally Wired' (interview with David Simon), *The Guardian Unlimited* (London), at http://blogs.guardian.co.uk/theguide/archives/tv_and_radio/2005/01/totally_wired.html (accessed 4/9/2010).

Wilkinson, R. (1988) *The Pursuit of American Character*, New York: Harper & Row.

Wilson, R. and Connery, C.L. (eds) (2007) *The Worlding Project: Doing Cultural Studies in the Era of Globalization*, Santa Cruz: New Pacific Press.

Wright, R. (1992) *Stolen Continents: The 'New World' Through Indian Eyes*, Boston: Houghton Mifflin.

Chapter 1

New beginnings
American culture and identity

> Identity marks the conjuncture of our past with the social, cultural and economic relations we live within.
>
> (Rutherford 1990: 19)

Stuart Hall has written that cultural identity is not a 'fixed essence . . . lying unchanged outside history and culture', and is 'not [a] once-and-for-all . . . to which we can make some final and absolute Return', but is 'constructed through memory, fantasy, narrative and myth . . . made within the discourse of history and culture' and hence cannot be simply defined or 'recovered' like some lost, authentic being (in Rutherford 1990: 226). To grapple with the idea of cultural identity, therefore, is to examine the lines and discourses of its construction and to recognise the existence within it of many meanings. As the introduction suggested, the USA is a place where different identities mix and collide, an assemblage, a multiplicity, constantly producing and reproducing new selves and transforming old ones and, therefore, cannot claim to possess a single, closed identity with a specific set of values. Some Americans, however, prefer the notion of identity to be hegemonic, fixed and clearly surrounded by distinct boundaries and definitions. For example, some would care to think of white, male and heterosexual as the standard measure of 'Americanness', with a deep respect for the flag and a strong sense of regional identity, say, to the South or to Louisiana or Boston. However, these are ideological positions that are not shared by or representative of the nation as a whole; indeed, no set of beliefs or values can be, and this is precisely the point. Instead, America has to be interpreted or 'read' as a complex, multifaceted text with a rich array of different characters and events, within which exist many contesting voices telling various and different stories. And as with any such text, there are internal tensions, dramas and contradictions which contribute to, indeed constitute, what might be called its identity.

Postmodern and poststructuralist thought has recognised these kinds of knowledges and approaches, and began from the point of distrusting any 'meta-' or 'grand narratives' – that is, those totalising stories that claim to speak for all and explain all. For example, to argue that America is exceptional and that its history was divinely ordained and destined to follow a set course is to read America as a limited and 'closed' text through a controlling meta-narrative or 'master-story'. Rather than seek out the controlling, organising single meaning, it is more important to follow the different stories, however disjunctive they might be, that constitute the threads of the text – its texture, to persist with the metaphor. America is constructed from these threads which are diverse, divergent, coherent, contrary and competing, crossing and separating, clashing and merging, weaving in and out of one another, forming and de-forming, gathering and fraying all at the same time.

Of course, these metaphors are helpful only up to a point, for we must recognise the nature of the historical and political realm in which this American 'text' has formed. Certain stories are preferred and achieve greater status and power, while others are derided or erased. Traditionally in America, male, white heterosexual stories and versions of history have emerged as prominent and have therefore formed what we might term the dominant regime of representation or dominant ideological culture. These have tended to define American 'national identity'. Kristen Silva Gruesz asks a series of key questions that help us move closer to the issues in this chapter:

> Who gets to define what 'America' means? What institutions support or undermine a particular definition? Under what historical conditions does one's group's definition have more or less power than another's? How does the continued repetition of such ideological statements have real, material effects on the ways people are able to live their lives?
>
> (Gruesz in Burgett and Hendler 2007: 17)

Thus the rapid growth of industrialisation and urbanisation – the outward signs of modernity – encouraged the articulation of the nation as whole, unified, and progressive in order that production and economic growth could develop around common goals, shared beliefs and a sense of cohesion. These ideas formed examples of Gruesz's 'continued repetition of . . . ideological statements' that solidified a particular vision of nation with its emphasis upon the 'melting pot' as a way of bringing people together into the American nation. However, with the questioning of modernity and its values and the increasing rediscovery of ethnic, marginalised and minority histories in America, this semblance of unity has had to be revised. *E pluribus unum* – out of many, one – is a more controversial slogan for America today, for it suggests, on one level, the possibility of integration, of melting the parts into a universal whole, when in fact the parts may prefer to remain distinct and unmelted or multiply attached to different cultures, such as Mexican *and* American (see Chapter 2). There exists a tension between the conventional discourses of American identity – a complex set of statements, myths and ways of seeing that constitutes a core of values that equal 'America' to the people and the world – and a series of counter-discourses that question and resist the neatness and stability of such a view of national identity.

The following chapter will explore some of the key elements of the myth of national identity and suggest other, counter-discourses at work in American culture which propose a sense of the nation as always relationally defined. In particular, the following examples, deliberately drawn from diverse sources, offer differing perspectives on America's concern with beginnings and the 'dream' and how these have been used by both the right and left in creating persistent and competing notions of identity. Lauren Berlant has coined the phrase 'cruel optimism' to suggest the paradoxes of American aspiration and dreaming ('the fantasy of the good life', she calls it); defining it as 'when something you desire is actually an obstacle to your flourishing' (2011: 1). This chapter charts the movements of dreaming and disappointment in the USA and the complex relations between them.

READING COLUMBUS

One means by which America has unified itself is through an imagined communal mythology that all could share and that provided a cluster of beliefs through which the nation could be articulated, both to itself and to the world. The issue of how the 500th anniversary of Christopher Columbus's voyage of 1492 was commemorated is revealing here. Traditional mythology about Columbus's 'discovery' of the New World and the way in which it led to the republican and democratic values embedded in the history of the United States may be traced back to Joel Barlow's epic *Columbiad* (1807) and Washington Irving's *A History of the Life and Voyages of Christopher Columbus* (1828). In the nineteenth century Columbus became widely adopted as the basis of many American place names, and Columbus Day became part of the litany of national days of celebration. The Chicago World's Fair of 1893, marking the 400th anniversary of the first voyage, reinforced the narrative link between discovery and the power and progress of the United States at the end of the nineteenth century.

Columbus thus became integrated into Manifest Destiny, the belief that America's progress was divinely ordained. As part of this process the Columbian myth became anglicised, but it could also act as a symbol for immigrant groups like Italians as to the role they could play in contributing to America's historic mission. What became clear by the 1980s, however, as preparations were made for the 'Quincentenary Jubilee', was that many Americans found it hard, if not impossible, to see the anniversary as a 'jubilee'. There was nothing to celebrate in the legacy of Columbus. According to many of his critics, he had been the harbinger not of progress and civilisation, but genocide, slavery and the reckless exploitation of the environment. Leading the accusations were those minority groups who felt that the coming of the Spanish to America had brought an imperial project which had delivered not civilisation but catastrophe.

This reversal of the nineteenth-century myth of Columbus is revealing because it shows how the revival of concern for the interests of racial and ethnic minorities is closely linked to the reading and rewriting of American history. It is also significant in that it brings into focus some of the problems which emerge when one myth is discredited only to be replaced by another. At issue here, to some extent, is a debate about the functions of history. Some of the participants in the Columbus controversy assumed either that rewriting the Columbus myth would allow the 'truth' to emerge, as if there was a correct version of his life and its aftermath, once distortions had been cast aside. Others argued that older versions of the Columbus story were simply reflections of who held power at the time they were propagated. Historical truth from this perspective was determined by those who had the authority to make it seem convincing. Emotions ran so high over the issue in Berkeley, California, that 12 October 1992 was declared 'Indigenous Peoples' Day' instead of celebrating Columbus.

Many argued that historical enquiry must involve the constant re-examination and reassessment of evidence and argument using reason and intelligence, not skin colour and emotion, in coming to terms with controversial themes of the past. In an interview during the making of *When Worlds Collide: The Untold Story of the Americas After Columbus* for PBS, the writer Rubén Martinez (see Chapter 2), standing beside Columbus's tomb in Seville's massive cathedral, was torn between cursing or blessing the bones interred inside: 'It's kind of like that classic mestizo dilemma. . . . He's my dad. I'm a bastard kid. I hate him, I love him' (Martinez, 2010: n.p.). His language suggests how America is still struggling with its own identity in relation to Columbus and that an important part of its image is constructed through persistent myths that must be continually rethought and redefined from a variety of perspectives.

THE AMERICAN DREAM OF IDENTITY:
THE GREAT GATSBY (1925)

The Columbus myths enabled white Americans to find a beginning, to declare a courageous opening to their 'creation story'. It was part of the influential dream myth of origin so prevalent in America. 'America, said the founding documents, was the living incarnation of the search for

a common humanity . . . America declared itself as a dream . . . the micro-
cosm, or prefiguration of humanity' (Calhoun 1994: 159). F. Scott
Fitzgerald's *The Great Gatsby* (1925) is aware both of the power of American
dreams and the problems of seeking them out in lived experience. The
ideals of endless progress, self-creation, achievement and success – the
mythicised dream incorporated in the spirit of Columbus – are played out
in the figure of Jay Gatsby as seen through the eyes of Nick Carraway.
The novel concerns itself with issues of identity and in particular with the
temptation to believe in a 'dream' which is manifested in Gatsby's yearning
for Daisy Buchanan, a woman he almost married in the past, who encompasses 'the endless desire to return to "lost origins", to be one again with
the mother, to go back to the beginning' (Rutherford 1990: 236), and yet
proves to be beyond his reach and unattainable as all such dreams are.

> 'You can't repeat the past.'
>   'Can't repeat the past?' he cried incredulously. 'Why of course you
> can!'
>
> (Fitzgerald 1974: 117)

In Nick Carraway's story of Jay Gatsby one can uncover much about
the contradictions of identity and how these are central to any conception
of 'America'. In the same way that Nick constructs a history of Gatsby
through the telling of his narrative, so too has America been invented and
reinvented by each generation. On one level, Nick's story amplifies one
of the founding myths of American culture, the belief in the fresh start,
the new beginning. In the case of Gatsby, Nick tells us, he 'sprang from
his Platonic conception of himself' (ibid.: 105), that is, a self-making process
in which 'he invented just the sort of Jay Gatsby a seventeen-year-old boy
would be likely to invent', full of hope and 'romantic readiness' (ibid.: 8).
In 1980, Ronald Reagan spoke too of how 'we built a new breed of human
called an American' (quoted in Bercovitch and Jehlen 1986: 26), as if to
invoke the idea of self-creation as a core myth of American identity.
Gatsby comes to embody similar American ideological principles for Nick
and through him he records his own 'history' of America. It is a story,
however, marked by its contradictions, its ambiguities and its complexities.
As we read Nick's story, what emerges are some of the necessary doubts
and queries we bring to any consideration of America and American
identity.

At the close of the narrative, Nick returns to Gatsby's empty house
refusing to listen to the taxi driver's 'story' of his friend and erasing an
obscene word scratched on the steps by a boy, as if to remind us that it
is only Nick's story we will hear. The exclusion of other voices at the end
of the novel perpetuates the control that Nick has exercised throughout
the story. This history, this Gatsby, is one funnelled through Nick's eyes,

tempered by a total belief in what Nick wants to see in him – the Dream. In the moonlight, a characteristic time of romance and uncertain vision, Nick returns in his mind to another age when the houses of West Egg are replaced by a fresh vision of possibility, 'the old island that flowered once for Dutch sailors' eyes – a fresh, green breast of the new world' when 'the last and greatest of all human dreams' still seemed feasible (Fitzgerald 1974: 187). This dream, for Nick, links Gatsby with adventurers like Columbus and represents the 'last time in history' when mankind faced 'something commensurate to his capacity for wonder' – the moment in which mankind physically arrived at a place big enough to hold its dreams and allow it to invent new selves and new beginnings. For Nick – and this was also Gatsby's quest – there was a belief that all things were possible still and that the sense of the past was not lost but could be repeated and recovered. And yet, at the very moment that Nick reveals this equation to us, it is brought into question because the dream as a tangible achievement 'was already behind him' (ibid.: 188). What remains is the spirit of the quest, the indefatigable urge to go on looking and searching, 'boats against the current', for something in the future that is only held in the memory of the past.

'Past' is the last word of *The Great Gatsby*, and serves to remind us of the ambivalence of the novel's sense of time and history. Nick preserves a story of Gatsby by controlling what we are allowed to know about him, and yet there is still a sense of 'the foul dust' that surrounds his dream in the sub-texts of his business contacts and acquaintances. Nick admits at one point that Gatsby

> must have felt that he had lost the old warm world, paid a high price for living too long with a single dream. . . . A new world, material without being real, where poor ghosts, breathing dreams like air, drifted fortuitously about.
>
> (Ibid.: 168)

Here, the New World is a different vision, still of dreams, but trapped in a hopeless, lost cycle of despair symbolised throughout the novel by the wasteland of the 'valley of ashes'. Even Nick sees himself as 'within and without, simultaneously enchanted and repelled by the inexhaustible variety of life' (ibid.: 42). All people desire to invent and reinvent themselves, Fitzgerald suggests, and none more so than Americans, many of whom travelled to the land itself with that aim and belief. But there are complex reasons why they are denied those dreams in a culture not structured on simple myths, but on ideologies of power, class, race and gender.

The Great Gatsby's fascination with the multiple identities of America, embodied in the figure of Gatsby himself, are played out around the idea of the dream and the new beginning. Again and again in American culture, there has been a belief in the possibility of renewal set alongside doubts and questionings about the reality of such a concept. This has often been interpreted as a naïve, superficial dream associated with the mythic portrayals of America as the promised land and a new Eden. This 'new' continent seemed to offer the last great hope for mankind to begin again and put right all the wrongs of the Old World. The truth of such claims was quickly dispelled and yet it survived as a structural myth in American culture.

The very 'Americanness' of Fitzgerald's novel has much to do with its internal conflicts and contradictions, as if within itself a whole drama of American uncertainty and division is played out. Rather like Marshall Berman's definition of modernity, *The Great Gatsby* presents a world 'that promises . . . and at the same time . . . threatens to destroy everything we have, everything we know, everything we are'. It is a world of 'disintegration and renewal, of struggle and contradiction, of ambiguity and anguish' (Berman 1983: 15). Experiencing the narrative's dark moments and its radiant dreams is to fall into these contradictions embodied in Gatsby himself, 'the poet of openness, the future, the green light'. And 'On the other hand, his most profound profession of faith is that the past can "of course" be repeated; he is a prophet of stasis' (Holquist 1991: 180). This tension between stasis and the future is part of the web of contradictions and conflicts that fill the novel and suggest an American identity wrestling with diversity and unity, assimilation and separation, individualism and community, roots and routes, just as the self-made man 'Gatsby' himself is simultaneously of the West *and* the East, Old World *and* New.

MAYBE THIS IS HEAVEN: *FIELD OF DREAMS* (1989)

Fitzgerald's examination of America's dreamscape and its sense of identity born out of newness and beginning has become a major theme in American cultural expression. Individual courage, persistence and determination focused on idealism and 'dream' have become a strong, resilient strand in expressions of 'Americanness'. Phil Alden Robinson's film *Field of Dreams* (1989) dwells on possibility, rekindling a sense of wonder that the Reagan presidency had promised, but failed to deliver. In part, the film responds ambivalently to the so-called 'culture wars' debates of the 1980s and 1990s, in which issues of identity politics, multiculturalism and the representation of US history came to the fore, often embedded in the looser exchanges and controversies over so-called political correctness. Lynne Cheney, E.D. Hirsch, Allan Bloom and others began to attack new forms of history teaching for betraying particular established knowledges about America and its past. As Cheney wrote in 1988, history textbooks needed to be like those of the 'early decades of the century . . . filled with stories – the magic of myths, fables, and tales of heroes', providing 'symbols to share ... help[ing] us all, no matter how diverse our backgrounds, feel part of a common undertaking' (in Lipsitz 1990: 24–5). Cheney's belief that national identity was best served by the articulation of history as 'heroic' and unidirectional was at odds with the growing emphasis upon multi-cultural representations insisting upon 'the complex realities of American history itself' (ibid.: 27). Although broadly liberal, the film shares something of Cheney's conservatism in its celebration of fundamental ideological units, the individual and the family, following their 'heroic' dream. It belongs to a particular tradition in American thought, derived from strands of Puritan and republican traditions, 'a discourse of moral virtue and responsibility' stemming from 'a belief in chosenness and an original unity of communal virtue in a "city set upon a hill" or a "virtuous republic" of yeomen farmers' (King 1993: 364). Appropriately, it involves the land and an Iowa farmer Ray Kinsella (Kevin Costner) who hears voices from the fields telling him that 'if you build it, he will come'. Ploughing up his crops, and so rejecting economic security, he builds a baseball field in the belief that it will connect him with some lost sense of life that is unclear until the end of the film. The clue is the role of his own father:

> I never forgave him for getting old. ... He must've had dreams but he never did anything about them ... he could have heard voices but he sure didn't listen to them. ... He never did one spontaneous thing in all the years I knew him. I'm afraid of that happening to me.

Ray says, 'I'm scared to death of turning into my father' because the father is the Past, but not one to be restored or repeated as in the mythic return so prevalent in the American Dream. Rather, the father is a signifier of waste, of the failure of the dream rather than its fulfilment. Other characters gather around Ray and the film draws together the threads of their disparate dreams, as if all of them need to reconcile themselves with some aspect of their past. Just as Ray will ultimately be reconciled with his father, who returns as a ghost from the past, so the film reminds us of the values that the 1980s have destroyed: family, friendship, individualism, radicalism (the 1960s are a constant point of reference) and dreams.

> People will come ... as innocent as children, longing for the past ... it's money they have and it's peace they like ... they'll watch the game and it'll be like they dipped themselves in magic waters, the memories will be so thick they'll have to brush them away from their faces. This field, this game is part of our past ... it reminds us of all that was once good and could be good again.

of course, a link back to Gatsby here, for Shoeless Joe Jackson, to the baseball field, was cast out from the game by the 1919 fixing scandal. In Fitzgerald's novel, it is Gatsby's friend, ...sneim, who is said to have fixed the series and represents the individualism, the dream's inversion, corrupt and yet entrepreneurial, for as Gatsby says, 'he just saw the opportunity' (Fitzgerald 1974: 80). It is Wolfsheim's greed and power that *Field of Dreams* opposes with its renewal of past values, both of the 1960s counter-culture and the original 'capacity for wonder' that Nick Carraway longs for. The film criticises the book-burners of the Moral Majority, as well as the bankers foreclosing on Ray's farm, and thus connects to a wider liberal agenda that again underlines the ways stories can be appropriated by both right and left. But it is *the* American game, baseball, that has been corrupted, and the film uses it symbolically to represent all that has to be renewed, as Robinson said himself, 'it's symbolic of the better things about America that have been lost' (Robinson 1986: 6).

In all its powerful, emotive force, the film reiterates populist, mythic and traditional values – the pull of the land and the Puritan dream of the city on the hill (Ray's white house is prominent throughout) – as signifiers of goodness and vision. The community in which Ray lives mocks him, but in the end they will come to his vision, built from the individual power of his dream. Its values are those of the family, the home, the land, hard work and faith, but it also recasts the 1960s as a time of possibility, talks of reconciliation and moves towards some shared, multicultural vision of the future at odds with the conservative opinions voiced in the 'culture wars' debates. The final visual image of the film, as the camera moves heavenward, is of the baseball field at night with the lights of a thousand cars moving towards it across the mid-West. The field is the heart in the heart of America, a replenished 'homeland', and the people are its renewing blood surging to their dreams, unifying black and white, old and young, urban and rural in a new liberal consensus.

THE SURFACE OF AN IDENTITY: THE PAST AS PRESIDENTIAL DISCOURSE

The powerful emotional and mythic images employed in *Field of Dreams* speak of renewal and reconciliation of the homeland, popular themes in American political rhetoric. D.H. Lawrence celebrated a 'new voice' in American literature, 'a shifting over from the old psyche to something new', but this 'displacement . . . hurt' (Lawrence 1977: 7). It was about 'cutting away the old emotions and consciousness' (ibid.: 8) leading 'us back, through pang after pang of disintegrative sensation, back towards the end of all things, where the beginning is: just as the year begins where the year is utterly dead' (Lawrence 1962: 117). This poetic language suggests something of the impulse to reinvention and renewal that has characterised many of the myths of America, but whereas Lawrence's words are full of complexity and unspoken meanings, by the time the language has been selected and reused in the political sphere, it has become curtailed and simplified. It is no surprise perhaps to find the Inaugural Address of President Bill Clinton in 1993 employing similar seasonal imagery to describe his version of America's new hope. After the Republican presidencies of Bush Senior and Reagan, Clinton, a Democrat, called for 'the mystery of American renewal', 'a new season of renewal' to once again alter the country and replenish the nation/land through the fundamental core myths of American culture. First there is the belief in the capacity 'to reinvent America'; second, to 'define what it means to be an American'; and third, to 'begin anew with energy and hope, with faith and discipline' (Maidment and Dawson 1994: 197–200).

The implications of this speech reinforce key ideas and assumptions about American identity that connect it with a 'mystery', an invocation of the divine and Manifest Destiny of the nation as some final expression of the promised land where all Americans participate in its 'divine' mission, this dream. Individuals, wrapped in the nation, choose to define themselves, to invent their own identity and place within the idealised new 'spring reborn'. Nature itself is a part of the divine mystery of America's renewal, its capacity for change and for opportunity, and it is the heritage of this generation to 'rededicate' itself to the dream, 'the very idea of America' (ibid.: 200).

Clinton's speech implies American identity is free from ideology when he says, 'we march to the music of our time, [but] our mission is timeless' (ibid.: 197), as if history has been bypassed in the creation of the values and goals he talks of. He is, however, reinvoking the core myths, an essence, around which America has structured its dominant ideological meanings, myths whose 'meaning is *already* complete . . . a kind of knowledge, a past, a memory, a comparative order of facts, ideas, decisions' (Barthes 1976: 117). Clinton's speech, his story of America, 'thickens, becomes vitrified, freezes into an eternal reference meant to *establish* [American identity]' (ibid.: 125) by repeating the past, or the language of the past, and seeking to apply it to the present. 'Myth is speech *stolen* [from the past] and *restored* [to the present]' (ibid.) and the images it restores transform historical processes into apparently natural occurrences so that we fail to read them as a motive, only as a reason (see ibid.: 129).

These myths form a complex ideological system that appears simple and uncomplicated for it functions by assumption, and we *assume* its values for they seem to be natural, to belong, to fit the place they have been given in the order of things. Of course, we must suspect such a discourse and interrogate its operation, ideologies, assumptions and exclusions. For this mythic framework excludes by constructing a single narrative of America, fixing certain dominant meanings – of individuality, the nation, nature, rootedness, divinity, discipline and work – that cannot apply to all Americans, nor should they. The umbrella of myth tries to incorporate and *speak for* all while at the same time claiming that Americans can 'define what it means to be an American'. Here is the contradiction of myth/ideology, for it glosses over or elides difference, contingency and diversity in favour of clarity which 'goes without saying'; it functions to reassure (as presidential speeches must) and 'organizes a world without contradictions' (ibid.: 143). The Inaugural Address speaks to the American people as if they were 'one', seeking to reassure them of presidential new beginnings, of commitment to great visions and old traditions, and as such functions less at a level of policy-making than as a rallying cry for the continuity of the new presidential term of office. It serves to remind Americans of 'their' individual and collective dreams.

The presidential discourse of America is a tried and tested mythological system that attempts to speak of renewal and invoke new beginnings as an appeal that *'harmonizes* with the world, not as it is, but as it wants to create itself' (ibid.: 156). Thus, Clinton, a Democrat, employs similar rhetoric to Reagan, whose Inaugural Address of 1981 had also claimed the old territory of Dream, Frontier and renewal: 'let us review our determination, our courage, and our strength. And let us renew our faith and our hope. We have every right to dream heroic dreams. . . . Their values sustain our national life' (Maidment and Dawson 1994: 194). The broad, sweeping, general appeal is to 'eternal' values that nobody can disagree with, often cynically referred to as 'Mom and apple pie' – and its function is to evaporate history from the content of the discourse and remove 'all soiling trace of origin or choice' (Barthes 1976: 151).

For President George W. Bush, the rhetoric was similarly organic, emphasising America's role at home and in the world, but mixing it with a familiar mythic religiosity and dreamscape:

> The story of America is the story of expanding liberty: an ever-widening circle, constantly growing to reach further and include more. . . . In our world, and here at home, we will extend the frontiers of freedom. . . . Like generations before us, we have a calling from beyond the stars to stand for freedom. This is the everlasting dream of America and tonight, in this place, that dream is renewed.
>
> (Bush 2004)

Whereas the rhetoric remains in this mythic speech, any genuine call to the past as a truly destructive, or deconstructive, process has gone and been replaced by the actionless imagery of renewal. For Barack Obama in 2009 it was about 'Remaking America' following the risk-taking migrants of the past, creating an America 'bigger than the sum of our individual ambitions; greater than all the differences of birth or wealth or faction'. 'Starting today', he urged the people, 'we must pick ourselves up, dust ourselves off, and begin again the work of remaking America' (Obama 2009). Within the accepted rhetoric of the inaugural address, Obama bound his own history into the remaking possibility he urged on the nation, seeing himself as exemplary of America's greatness – 'a man whose father less than sixty years ago might not have been served at a local restaurant can now stand before you to take a most sacred oath'.

Barthes argues that criticism involves 'the essential destruction of the past' (Barthes 1976: 158) and not simply a 'restoring' and evocation of its images, for any harmonised narrative, any rendering of cultural wholeness is an improbable deception, a trick of mythology. Nick Carraway *wants* to believe in Gatsby's restorative dream, his wholeness of vision, but Fitzgerald's text encourages the reader to see beyond his 'single window' and 'partial view' to recognise that 'the rock of the world was founded securely on a fairy's wing' (Fitzgerald 1974: 10–11, 106). That novel's subtle contradictions, its doubts and tensions, remind us of America's diversity and the impossibility of any single, authoritative, totalising point of view. The mythic spin of presidential discourse, of the ideological past restored like Gatsby's mausoleum-like mansion, is finally empty and exists only 'at the surface of an identity' excluding the multifaceted details of cultural difference and the ambiguous nature of that 'past' (Barthes 1976: 101). America has to be 'read' as a polysemy, that is, a space of many signs, a rich text, 'a complex signifier, a contested textual construct that bears the name "America"' (Mathy 1993: 3).

Any 'partial view' that seeks to label America in a single manner misses the vast 'teeming nation of nations' that Walt Whitman recognised as its source of democratic hope. However, it is not enough to assert, as presidents do, that America is 'one nation', since it is clearly constructed from competing discourses, and presidential speeches simply tap into the deep tradition of myths of new beginnings and the dream, and ignore those counter- or border-discourses that are also 'America', but which exist on the edge of the frame fighting to be heard and yet vital to its future.

COUNTER-CULTURAL DREAMS

The radical criticism of the mainstream by the counter-cultures of the 1950s and 1960s is an interesting example of how the embodiment of possibility in America lived on as part of a counter-hegemonic alternative voice (see Gair 2007). Counter-cultural critics felt that the dream imagery had been hijacked by the corporate 'organisation man' and the values of the new beginning turned into the slogans of the consumer culture and presidential politics. In the works of many Beat writers, who emerged as rebellious figures willing to criticise and attack mainstream society, there is a determined effort to reclaim the identity of America as a statement of possibility rather than production. Allen Ginsberg wrote of

> an America gone mad with materialism . . . prepared to battle the world in defense of a false image of its Authority. Not the wild and beautiful America of the comrades of Whitman . . . where the spiritual independence of each individual was an America.
>
> (Allen 1960: 333)

This lost America has to be rediscovered, or reinvented, as a protest against the narrowing vision of 'Authority' – Ginsberg's expression for the dominant hegemonic power which dictates the terms of existence, spells out the dream through a 'fixed and universal monopoly on reality' (Allen and Tallman 1973: 243). 'America will be discovered' (Allen 1960: 321), and for Ginsberg and other artists, it was through a renewal of form, a challenge to the stasis that seemed only to serve the status quo of hegemony. As Michael McClure wrote, 'we wanted to make it new and we wanted to invent it . . . we wanted voice and we wanted vision' (1982: 12–13). The language recalls the mythic notion of new beginnings and celebrates the idealism of America, not as an imperial power, a conqueror of native lands or an oppressor of minorities, but as a place capable of change – make it new, he cries. For these critics there was something worth saving, something that was not mere rhetoric.

The counter-culture sought both the renewal of 'wonder' and the politics of opposition, both vision and action; and in this regard it was very much in an American tradition. The poet Lawrence Ferlinghetti called for 'a rebirth of wonder' and 'for someone to really discover America' (1968: 49), emphasising both the loss of spirit and the failure in American life to realise the true potential of the place. What had to be discovered was that which had been obscured by dominant, but limited definitions of American identity, which excluded or marginalised vital groups with much to contribute. It is significant that alongside and within the counter-culture emerged other alternative, previously marginalised voices (African Americans, Native Americans, women, gays, etc.) offering different expressions and definitions of identities.

In the Port Huron Statement (1962), 'the most authentically American expression of a new radicalism' (Sayres et al. 1984: 250), the counter-culture, voiced familiar calls for 'American values', which had been lost as a generation was 'maturing in complacency' (Maidment and Dawson 1994: 237), and demanded change. It repeated the plea to go 'beneath' 'the temporary equilibriums [or consensus] of our society', 'the stagnation of those who have closed their minds to the future' and to reject the feeling of 'the exhaustion not only of Utopias, but of any new departures as well' (ibid.: 238). The hegemonic, dominant culture promised stability and prosperity, but also perpetuated norms which excluded and limited the capacity for human potential. American identity has always involved tensions between the individual and the collective identity, for as the Port Huron Statement concludes, 'the object is not to have one's way so much as it is to have a way that is one's own' (ibid.: 241).

Thus in *Easy Rider* (1968), a key film often read as a counter-cultural text, one of the characters, Hanson (Jack Nicholson), says, 'This used to be a helluva country. I can't understand what's going on', and throughout the film we are presented with images of nostalgia for some half-remembered golden age, signified most often as an eternal, mythical West as opposed to the intolerance and corruptions of a modern world. The film's value system is contradictory throughout, but it does valorise certain traditional images such as the land and the family, very much in the way *Field of Dreams* did in the late 1980s. Sitting down to eat with a mixed American–Mexican family (another image of reconciliation and hope?), Wyatt (Peter Fonda) comments on the righteousness of 'living from the land' as if to celebrate a vision of timelessness and wholeness outside the mania of the city they have left behind.

The drug culture, as portrayed in the early parts of the film, supports the view that alternative perceptions were part of the process of re-visioning America and questioning its values, but this is also shown through the film's western landscapes and use of sacred Native American culture. Much of the journey is through Native American lands of Utah and New Mexico, with sequences in Monument Valley and Taos Pueblo, with references to the 'people' buried in the sacred land itself, as if to articulate the film's tentative portrayal of new identities and its challenges to the accepted culture of the times. Indeed, the film plays with alternatives to the dominant culture (such as the commune), but none is satisfactory and any sense of resistance is ultimately contained in the individual figures of Wyatt and Billy, who are destroyed and erased at the end of the movie. Change seems impossible, as the camera lifts above the final fiery destruction, in a shot reminiscent of the concluding shot of *Field of Dreams*, but unlike that film's sense of regeneration and possibility, *Easy Rider* ends in horror, death and the denial of alternatives.

The 1960s opened a dialogue with the stale imagery of the American Dream and sought to reinvent it with hope and to enlarge it through inclusiveness, by 'stressing the *utopian* aspects . . . as distinguished from its *economic* aspects' (Sayres *et al.* 1984: 249). As Fredric Jameson argues, the 1960s in America were part of a wider global reaction to colonialism involving 'those inner colonized of the first world – "minorities", marginals, and women – who became integral to a "coming to self-consciousness of subject peoples"' (ibid.: 181). Groups excluded from early visions of the 'dream', and silenced by the processes of history, sought to play some role in the rethinking of ideas of identity and nation. As the radical Chicana feminist Gloria Anzaldúa has written, 'We have come to realise that we are not alone in our struggles nor separate nor autonomous but that we – white black straight queer female male – are connected and interdependent' (Moraga and Anzaldúa 1983: foreword). This recognition of a diverse but connected struggle for renewal can still be expressed by appropriating the mythic language of nation-building: '*Women, let's not let the danger of the journey and the vastness of the territory scare us – let's look forward and open paths in these woods*' (ibid. – italics in the original). In 'unlearning to not speak', as the poet and novelist Marge Piercy puts it (1971), women and other excluded groups have explored and reinvented identities, not to reduce them down to a formulaic myth of consensus and unity, but to provide true scope for expansiveness and diversity (see Chapter 7).

MULTIPLICITY, DIFFERENCE AND RE-VISION

As we have seen in this chapter and in the introduction, identity is a constantly shifting territory in America, with renewal as a significant element in the recognition of difference and diversity, rather than fixity and stasis. American identity is characterised by re-vision as a process of renewal: 'Re-vision – the act of looking back, of seeing with fresh eyes, of entering an old text from a new critical direction' (Rich 1993: 167). The voices of people of colour, feminists and radicals coming from the margins of American culture and beyond the USA altogether have caused the 'assumptions' to which Adrienne Rich refers, to be examined and reviewed, but this is a process inherent in a radical interpretation of the myth of new beginnings. The French critic Gilles Deleuze argues, like D.H. Lawrence and others, that America is concerned with 'deterritorialisation' or the movement across lines and boundaries, unafraid to flee to new lands or leave old ones behind. He writes of the American passion for 'departure, becoming, passage' in its creation of 'a New Earth' (Deleuze and Parnet 1987: 36; see also Giles 2007).

The very act of movement is akin to the desire for renewal, for 'becoming' American. The constant 'passages' suggest that identity cannot in this scheme of things become fixed, nor arrive at some final point in which the authentic American is defined as an eternal essence. Deleuze touches upon the fact of American restlessness, its mobilities, or what we earlier termed the 'routes' of identity, as a sign of its 'multiplicity' – 'a set of lines or dimensions which are irreducible to one another' and in which 'what counts are not the terms or the elements, but what there is "between" ... *a set of relations which are not separable from each other*' (Deleuze and Parnet 1987: vi, vii – our italics).

This is crucial, for it suggests something of the nature of American identities as plural and irreducible to a single fixed idea of 'Americanness', but also, in contrast, dynamic, best recognised – to repeat – as 'a set of relations which are not separable from each other'. The implications of connection and dialogue come through here, and the idea of an American cultural identity derived through multiplicities rather than conformity and closure is in keeping with attitudes to cultural difference. 'The time for "assimilating" minorities to holistic and organic notions of cultural value has passed' (Rutherford 1990: 219) and what must be set alongside is a new definition of cultural identity, which is not based on any true Americanness, any 'oneness' of agreed values and history, but the recognition of difference. 'We cannot speak for very long, with any exactness, about "one experience, one identity", without acknowledging its other side – the ruptures and discontinuities which constitute ... [American] "uniqueness"' (ibid.: 225). These renegotiations are integral to discussions of identity in a contemporary culture where the fixities of big concepts like 'nation', 'identity' and 'culture' must be continually re-examined and challenged. Definitions are only provisional and 'subject to new analyses, new questions and new understandings if we are to unlock some of the narrow terms of the discourses in which we are inscribed' (Boyce-Davies 1994: 5).

The American sense of new beginnings, once demythicised, can still have a genuine and important meaning in the exploration of cultural practices and identity, for it is part of the endless efforts to trace the self, to follow the many lines that make up the 'teeming nation of nations' and to keep revisiting and redefining them from new perspectives for 'a new interrogation of meaning' (ibid.). In part, what is needed is Cornel West's 'new cultural politics of difference', which

> affirms the perennial quest for precious ideals of individuality and democracy by digging deep in the depths of human particularities and social specificities in order to construct new kinds of connections, affinities and communities across empire, nation, region, gender, age and sexual orientation.
>
> (West 1993: 29)

NEW INTERROGATIONS: GLORIA ANZALDÚA, BARRY LOPEZ AND TRINH T. MINH-HA

Barry Lopez and Gloria Anzaldúa combine a number of the perspectives that we have put forward in this chapter in an effort to both realise the complex nature of American identities and to suggest a constructive and realistic way ahead. They are both concerned with what James Clifford calls 'presents-becoming-futures' involving the recognition of both 'utopian, persistent hope for the reinvention of difference' and the realisation of the potential for the 'destructive, homogenizing effects of global economic and cultural centralization' (Clifford 1988: 15). They are interdisciplinary writers and activists, concerned with environmental issues, radical politics and cultural criticism, who have expressed their views in many voices: fiction, essays, travel writing and meditative poetic pieces. Their works attempt to redefine American identities to some extent by 'remapping' and decentring certain assumptions about the self and its relationships to place and others. Their work is hybrid (see Chapter 2) in that it merges with other cultural forms such as oral traditions, myths, trickster stories, and it unfixes itself from any obvious, stable tradition that one might too neatly term 'American'. They are border-writers, endlessly crossing boundaries between different cultural practices – becoming, challenging, redefining what it is to live in America and to think beyond simplistic national narratives towards the trans- or postnational perspectives discussed earlier. Between culture and nature, man and animal, life and death, space and place, wilderness and civilisation, new stories are told that remind us of William Carlos Williams's statement: 'History, history! We fools, what do we know or care? History begins for us with murder and enslavement, not with discovery' (Williams 1971: 55).

For Barry Lopez, whose work is broadly seen as environmental literature, America is a conquered land, colonised by Spaniards and other Europeans, and he writes of the horrors of conquest and imperial hegemony demanding that we 'rediscover the original wisdom' derived from pre-conquest cultures and their relationships 'with the nonhuman world'. To 'reclaim that metaphysics' is tied to the 'practical need' to see beyond the terrible history and seek an imaginative new beginning that refigures the relationship of humanity to place (Lopez 1988: 198). In *The Rediscovery of North America* (1990) Lopez brings together these ideas, tracing a 'tone' back to the conquest of America and agreeing with Tzvetan Todorov's claim that it 'heralds and establishes ... [America's] present identity' (Todorov 1987: 5). Since colonisation, argues Lopez, 'we have imposed, not proposed. ... We said what we thought, and bent to our will whatever resisted' (Lopez 1990: 18). In the New World 'we came to talk, not to listen' (ibid.: 19), thus establishing a monologue in which other voices were ignored, destroyed or marginalised. The first 'new beginning' ignored what the New World had to say and closed its mind to the wisdom of the place and its particular energies, preferring instead to view the land as 'empty' and awaiting the arrival of the European mind to 'write' itself onto the continent. Identity as such was formed around exclusions and denials, especially of Native cultures and existing traditions, rather than openness and possibility.

However, even in Lopez's dark remembrances there is still belief: 'It is still in some real sense the New World' (ibid.: 29), because the idea of American identity remains fluid. For him, this means a chance for new beginnings in which 'proposals' are made, a dialogue – 'opening an intelligent conversation' (ibid.: 36) – with the environment created, which would permit a new 'moral universe' where the land was included in 'the meaning of the word community' (ibid.: 34). He continues: 'In these ways we begin, I think, to find a home, to sense how to fit a place' (ibid.: 37), and it is this concept of home that is so important to Lopez, for it indicates 'a place where we take on the responsibilities of adults to the human community' (ibid.: 48). Unlike current appropriations of the term 'home-land' in terms of security and the policing of borders, Lopez sees home as expansive and open, a new beginning, and rejects any static 'dream' of some lost time.

Lopez recognises the New World not as a place to 'recover' but to 'rediscover'; that is, to see it differently, unlike before. There is no whole sense of America that can be recovered, so 'we need to sojourn in it again, to discover the lineaments of cooperation with it' – 'we have a monumental adjustment to make, and only our companions on the ship to look to. We must turn to each other, and sense that this is possible' (ibid.: 49, 58). This renewal of hope, based on the need to change and to look again at the way people live, carries with it the contemporary concern for ecology, the wisdom of ancient tribes, nature and the actual knowledge of modernity, working together and 'rethinking our relationships' (Lopez 1988: 198). As he wrote in *Arctic Dreams* (1986), there is a need for an

> altered perspective to imagine afresh the way to a lasting security of the soul and heart, and toward an accommodation in the flow of time we call history, ours and the world's. That dream . . . is the dream of great and common people alike.
>
> (Lopez 1987: 12)

And, in later work, he states 'other voices were as indispensable to our survival as variation in our DNA' (1999: 13).

Lopez's qualified optimism for a new 'dream' full of 'other voices' is echoed in the work of critic and film-maker Trinh T. Minh-ha, who has written that 'identity is a way of re-departing . . . to start again with re-departures, different pauses, different arrivals' (Trinh 1990: 328). Here the American sense of new beginning is empowering, learning from the past with the belief that one can begin again without repeating all the mistakes of the past. It becomes 'everything monologism has repressed. . . . Here again and anew, gender and sexuality and other struggles of borders. . . . The challenge is thus: how can one re-create without re-circulating domination?' (ibid.: 329). As in Barry Lopez's work, Trinh T. Minh-ha appropriates images of renewal and infuses them with new purposes to indicate the possibility of inclusion and expansion within America without stating the older definitions of totality. In her book *Woman Native Other*, Trinh states that what is desirable is a community 'built on differences . . . [that] . . . subverts every notion of completeness and its frame remains a non-totalizable one', articulated through a story that 'circulates like a gift' but which cannot be possessed by any one person or group, 'a gift built on multiplicity . . . inexhaustible within its own limits' (Trinh 1989: 2). In her vision, 'Life is a perpetual to and fro, a dis/continuous releasing and absorbing of the self' (ibid.: 128) where 'plurality adds up to no total' (ibid.: 330), but offers a source of renewal with its many voices, 'companions on the ship', to use Lopez's phrase, working towards different destinations and with different priorities. This suggests a sensitive and human response to the complexities of contemporary culture, which presents a possible way forward to make it over 'a-new a-gain', as she puts it (ibid.: 128).

Gloria Anzaldúa, writing as a Chicana lesbian feminist, sees herself as existing in the multiple 'borderlands' of American culture: 'that liminal landscape of changing meanings on which distinct human cultures encounter one another's "otherness" and appropriate, accommodate, or domesticate it through language' (Kolodny 1992: 9). Just as Lopez and Trinh are fascinated by the possibilities of the border, so too is Anzaldúa, recognising in it an 'inherently unstable locus . . . of environmental transitions and cultural interpenetrations' (ibid.: 10) which 'destabilizes easy assumptions about centers and margins' (ibid.: 12). The border, for Anzaldúa, is resistant to unitary explanations and neat stories; it is a place where 'different cultures, identities, sexualities, classes, geographies, races, genders and so on collide or interchange' (Boyce-Davies 1994: 16).

In many respects, as we discussed in the introduction, this is a description of American culture itself as a multiple and dynamic 'contact zone' giving rise to Anzaldúa's new, hybrid subjectivity – the mestiza – constituted by the acts of crossing and recrossing the border until 'a new life begins' (Anzaldúa 1987: 49). For her, the old ideas of being assimilated or 'rooted' as an 'American' are meaningless, for 'she learns to juggle cultures. She has a plural personality. . . . Not only does she sustain contradictions, she turns the ambivalence into something else' (ibid.: 79). It is a 'new birth' or beginning, what she terms a 'new consciousness' (ibid.: 80), but it is no easy, harmonious position – rather, one full of turmoil and pain, involving the 'uprooting of dualistic thinking' (ibid.) that constantly divides and sets one against the other. This 'third perspective' (ibid.: 46) offers a new subjectivity 'routed' beyond the norms and expectations of a narrowly defined 'American identity', seen as 'universal' (but in fact white, male, heterosexual, etc.). It is a visionary new beginning cast from the realities of a postmodern culture of difference and multiplicity with a sense of self that is open, plural, 'a space through which to negotiate ambivalence and heteroglossia' (Smith 1993: 175). Evoking once again Bakhtin's cultural ideal, Anzaldúa posits a new America where 'many languages intermingle with one another, in a state of nonhierarchical multiplicity, creating a hybrid language' (ibid.: 176). As Stuart Hall argues, this is a form of diasporic identity:

> people who belong to more than one world, speak more than one language (literally and metaphorically), inhabit more than one identity, have more than one home; who have learned to negotiate and translate *between cultures,* and who because they are irrevocably the product of several interlocking histories and cultures, have learned to live with, and indeed to speak from, *difference.*
>
> (Hall 1995: 206)

This position 'between' is 'always unsettling the assumptions of one culture from the perspective of another' providing an 'alternative framework' that 'cuts across the traditional boundaries of the nation-state, provides linkages across the borders of national communities', forcing us to rethink notions of identity, culture and place (ibid.)

The utopianism of these positions, despite their realistic acceptance of struggle and contest, asserts the persistence of the ideas of reinvention and new beginnings in American culture but refigured through the new positions of marginality, difference and diaspora. It is not necessarily an end to the 'broad-based democratic cultural discourse that implies more than a collection of marginalized groups' (King 1993: 378), but, rather, a reconstruction of American cultural identities in which new groups find a voice and new subjectivities emerge. As Trinh T. Minh-ha has said:

> the self . . . is not so much a core as a process, one finds oneself in the context of cultural hybridity, always pushing one's questioning of oneself to the limit of what one is and what one is not . . . Fragmentation is therefore a way of living at the borders.
>
> (Wheale 1995: 252)

Such a positive use of her multiple identities, as Vietnamese–African–French–American, is a recognition of how such unfixing of cultural identity can 'displace certainties in order to gain new ground' (ibid.). To borrow one of the titles from her films, one might term this new ground of identity as a 'reassemblage' acknowledging 'there is no real me to return to, no whole self . . . there are instead, diverse recognitions of self through difference, and unfinished, contingent, arbitrary closures that make possible both politics and identity' (ibid.: 255). Perhaps here in the postmodern shifting of identity, within the universal pressures of globalisation, diaspora and difference is the appropriate platform for a democratic America which recognises its own multiplicities and relates to wider, extra-national cultural connections to do with language, gender, race, ethnicity, religion and sexuality. In this re-vision there exists the timeless idea of the American Dream, recast, but still vibrant in its signification of creative regeneration and the quest for new beginnings, perhaps showing that 'the imagination is today a staging ground for action, and not only for escape' (Appadurai 2000: 7).

CONCLUSION: DIGGING DEEP – *LONE STAR* (1996)

John Sayles's film *Lone Star* begins literally in the American land, on the Mexican border, with the discovery of a skeleton, a Mason's ring, and a sheriff's badge buried in the desert. References to the 'Coronado Expedition' quickly locate the significance of colonial history to this film and suggest its continued relevance to the present-day lives of this border community, Frontera (border). 'This country's seen a good few disagreements over the years', we are told, but if 'You live in a place, you should learn something about it.' In this archaeological resurrection of the 'buried' and 'forgotten' pasts the film's interest in sites of memory and their relationships to official history is established, as well as its critique and expansion through 'learning' about place through uncovered memories and stories. *Lone Star*'s stories – Hispanic, African American, Anglo and women's – contribute to a multicultural layering of alternative, buried voices and versions of the past providing a framework for Sayles's reconsideration of relations of memory and history within his 'new cultural politics of difference'. Indeed, *Lone Star* was referred to as a 'prophetic allegory' by Mary Helen Washington in her Presidential Address to the American Studies Association in 1997, offering a new approach to studying America in which the 'differences of language, politics, historical vision' were not allowed 'to dissolve in a soothing movement toward consensus', but instead 'presents the multicultural moment as one of tension, struggle, discomfort and disagreement' (Washington 1998: 16). The following year Janice Radway reiterated the film's significance by using it too as a locus for her questioning of the meaning of 'American' within American Studies and the possibility of an interdisciplinary practice of 'intricate interdependencies' reflected in the 'cultural menudo' of Sayles's frontier community (Radway 1999: 6).

In this way, *Lone Star* examines multiple borders, from the ever-present geopolitical southwest border, to those drawn through the diverse lives that intersect within the community viewed not as unitary, but rather a complex contact zone. Through the film's central narrative Sam Deeds uncovers his own family history by demythicising his father's 'legend' and his secret relations with a Mexican woman – Mercedes Cruz. The final revelations of incest provide a metaphor for Sayles's interconnected community where blood and history are mixed and complex rather than separate and simple. The scene takes place in a disused drive-in movie theatre where Pilar, Sam's lover (and half-sister), calls for a clean break, a new beginning: 'We'll start from scratch. . . . All that other stuff, all that history, to Hell with it right? Forget the Alamo.' Looking up at the blank screen ravaged by time passing, Pilar and Sam are ready to 'project' their new vision upon it, ready to take over the role of the movie as the traditional 'escape' from the everyday borders and restrictions of their lives in the creative imagining of alternative identities. As the film *Lone Star* ends, Sayles suggests that the latent possibility inherent in the experience of movies can be carried forward into life itself – that is, into the imaginative reconstruction of identity, community and nation.

As Sayles has said, 'American culture is not monolingual or mono-racial. It's always been a mix' and in this moment of decision Sam and Pilar 'choose to cross that border of moral opinion' and assert this new 'family' (Carson 1999: 213, 216). Their incipient migratory movement and willingness to break the 'rule' and social taboo are signs of a wider recognition of the necessity for that very dialogical, hybrid mix that Sayles sees as fundamentally American. As if to directly respond to the kind of one-dimensional notions of identity and nation associated with conservative historians and theorists, Sayles allows Sam and Pilar a 'second life' as an anti-essentialist identity forged from movements and migrations rather than formed by a single and rooted attachment to one place.

In this Sayles echoes Gloria Anzaldúa's optimism for the future based on a similar belief that 'There will be a hybridity of equal parts instead of a graft and a major tree', and that identity

> is an arrangement or series of clusters, a kind of stacking or layering of selves, horizontal and vertical layers, the geography of selves made up of different communities you inhabit. . . . Where these spaces overlap is nepantla, the Borderlands. Identity is process-in-the-making . . . you shift, cross the border from one to the other.
>
> (Anzaldúa 2000: 278, 238–9)

Anzaldúa's 'nepantla' is an 'in-between' space that facilitates transformation since within it, as in *Lone Star*, traditionally assumed and fixed borders break down compelling us to find new ways of defining ourselves and our communities (see Mignolo 2000: x). The forbidden or taboo (like the incest motif and the hidden histories in the film) ruptures the smooth surfaces of the everyday, forming an 'interface' so that 'in the cracks between worlds and realities . . . changes in consciousness can occur. In this shifting space of transitions, we morph, adapt to new cultural realities' (ibid.: 280). The film is an example of a post-Western (see Chapter 5) in its refusal to accept a unanimous version of American identity or nation, as well as its questioning of the approved narratives of the 'West as America' (Campbell 2013). Through the retrieval of memory and the reconstruction of Frontera's multiple histories, *Lone Star* reaches points of knowledge and reconciliation from which choices can be made about living with the past rather than in its shadow and about identity as a process of 'routes' rather than a fixed and rooted essence

REFERENCES AND FURTHER READING

Allen, D. (1960) *The New American Poetry*, New York: Grove Press.
Allen, D. and Tallman, W. (eds) (1973) *The Poetics of the New American Poetry*, New York: Grove Press.
Anzaldiúa, G. (1987) *Borderlands/La Frontera*, New York: Aunt Lute Books.
—— (2000) *Interviews/Entrevistas*, London: Routledge.
Appadurai, A. (2000) *Modernity At Large*, Minneapolis: University of Minnesota Press.
Aton, J. (1986) 'An Interview with Barry Lopez', *Western American Literature*, vol. 21, no. 1, pp. 3–17.
Barthes, R. (1976) *Mythologies*, London: Paladin.
Bercovitch, S. and Jehlen, M. (eds) (1986) *Ideology and Classic American Literature*, Cambridge: Cambridge University Press.
Berlant, L. (2011) *Cruel Optimism*, Durham: Duke University Press.
Berman, M. (1983) *All That is Solid Melts into Air*, London: Verso.
Bigsby. C.W. (ed.) (2006) *The Cambridge Companion to Modern American Culture*, Cambridge: Cambridge University Press.
Boyce-Davies, C. (1994) *Black Women, Writing and Identity*, London: Routledge.
Brownell, K.C. (2014) *Showbiz Politics: Hollywood in American Political Life*, Chapel Hill: University of North Carolina Press.
Burgett, B. and Hendler, G. (eds) (2007) *Keywords for American Cultural Studies*, New York: New York University Press.
Bush, George W. (2001) 'In Announcement of Lesson of Liberty Initiative, Thomas Wootton High School, Rockville, Maryland, 30 October, 2001', at http:// www.whitehouse.gov/kids/connection/20011030–7.html
—— (2004) 'Republican National Convention Address', at www. americarhetoric. com/speeches/convention2004/georgewbushrnc.htm
Calhoun, C. (ed.) (1994) *Social Theory and the Politics of Identity*, London: Routledge.
Campbell, N. (2000) *The Cultures of the American New West*, Edinburgh: Edinburgh University Press.
—— (2013) *Post-Westerns: Cinema, Region, West*, Lincoln: University of Nebraska Press.
Carson, D. (ed.) (1999) *John Sayles Interviews*, Jackson: University of Mississippi Press.
Clifford, J. (1988) *The Predicament of Culture*, Cambridge, MA: Harvard University Press.
Deleuze, G. and Parnet, C. (1987) *Dialogues*, London: Athlone Press.
Ferlinghetti, L. (1968) *A Coney Island of the Mind*, San Francisco: City Lights.
Fitzgerald, F.S. (1974) (first 1925) *The Great Gatsby*, Harmondsworth: Penguin.
Foucault, M. (1980) *Power/Knowledge: Selected Interviews and Other Writings 1972–77*, London: Harvester Wheatsheaf.
Gair, C. (2007) *The American Counterculture, 1945–1975*, Edinburgh: Edinburgh University Press.
Gidley, M. (ed.) (1993) *Modern American Culture*, London: Longman.

Giles, P. (2007) 'The Deterritorialisation of American Literature' in W. Dimock and L. Buell (eds) *Shades of the Planet*, Princeton: Princeton University Press.

Gruesz, K. Silva, (2007) 'America' in B. Burgett and G. Hendler (eds) *Keywords for American Cultural Studies*, New York: New York University Press, pp. 16–22.

Hall, S. (1995) 'New Cultures for Old' in D. Massey and P. Jess (eds) *A Place in the World?*, Oxford: Oxford University Press.

Holquist, M. (1991) *Dialogism: Bakhtin and his World*, London: Routledge.

Humm, M. (1991) *Border Traffic: Strategies of Contemporary Women Writers*, Manchester: Manchester University Press.

King, R. (1993) 'American Cultural Criticism' in M. Gidley (ed.) *Modern American Culture*, London: Longman.

Kolodny, A. (1992) 'Letting Go Our Grand Obsessions: Notes Towards a New Literary History of the American Frontiers', *American Literature*, vol. 64, no. 1, March, pp. 1–18.

Lawrence, D.H. (1962) *The Symbolic Meaning*, London: Centaur Press.

—— (1977) *Studies in Classic American Literature*, Harmondsworth: Penguin.

Lipsitz, G. (1990) *Time Passages*, Minneapolis: University of Minnesota Press.

Lopez, B. (1987) (first 1986) *Arctic Dreams: Imagination and Desire in a Northern Landscape*, New York: Bantam.

—— (1988) *Crossing Open Ground*, London: Macmillan.

—— (1990) *The Rediscovery of North America*, New York: Vintage.

—— (1999) *About this Life*, London: Harvill.

Maidment, R. and Dawson, M. (eds) (1994) *The United States in the Twentieth Century: Key Documents*, London: Hodder and Stoughton.

Martinez, R. (2010) in 'The Birth of Latin American Identity', *LA Times* online, at http://articles.latimes.com/2010/sep/27/entertainment/la-et-martinez-2010 0927 (accessed 23/11/2010).

Mathy, J.-P. (1993) *Extreme-Occident: French Intellectuals and America*, Chicago: University of Chicago Press.

Matriko, J.W. (2005) *The American President in Popular Culture*, London: Greenwood Press.

McClure, M. (1982) *Scratching the Beat Surface*, San Francisco: North Point Press.

Mignolo, W.D. (2000) *Local Histories/Global Designs: Coloniality, Subaltern Knowledges, and Border Thinking*, Princeton: Princeton University Press.

Moraga, C. and Anzaldúa, G. (eds) (1983) *This Bridge Called My Back*, New York: Kitchen Table Press.

Morley, D. and Robins, K. (1995) *Spaces of Identity*, London: Routledge.

Obama, B. (2009) 'Inaugural Address, January 2009' at http://news.bbc.co.uk/1/hi/world/americas/obama_inauguration/7840646.stm (accessed 24/11/2010).

Piercy, M. (1971) *Unlearning to Not Speak*, Berkeley: Pacifica Foundation.

Radway, J. (1999) '"What's in a Name?" Presidential Address to the American Studies Association, 20 November 1998', *American Quarterly*, vol. 51, no. 1, pp. 1–32.

Rawlinson, M. (2009), *American Visual Culture*, Oxford: Berg.

Rich, A. (1993) *Adrienne Rich's Poetry and Prose*, New York: W.W. Norton.

Robinson, P.A. (1986) 'Ball Park Incident', *Films and Filming*, November, p. 6.

Rutherford, J. (ed.) (1990) *Identity: Community, Culture, Difference*, London: Lawrence and Wishart.

Sayres, S. *et al.* (eds) (1984) *The 60s Without Apology*, Minneapolis: University of Minnesota Press.

Smith, S. (1993) *Subjectivity, Identity and the Body*, Bloomington: Indiana University Press.

Soja, E.W. (1989) *Postmodern Geographies: The Reassertion of Space in Critical Social Theory*, London: Verso.

Todorov, T. (1987) *The Conquest of America*, New York: Harper Perennial.

Trinh T.M. (1989) *Woman Native Other*, Bloomington: University of Indiana Press.

—— (1990) 'Cotton and Iron' in R. Ferguson *et al.* (eds) *Out There: Marginalization and Contemporary Cultures*, Cambridge, MA: MIT Press.

Truettner, W. (ed.) (1991) *The West As American: Reinterpreting Images of the Frontier*, Washington, DC: Museum of American Art.

Washington, M.H. (1998) 'Disturbing the Peace: What Happens to American Studies If You Put African Americans at the Center?, Presidential Address to the American Studies Association, 29 October 1997', *American Quarterly*, vol. 50, no. 1, pp. 1–23.

West, C. (1993) *Keeping the Faith*, London: Routledge.

Wheale, N. (ed.) (1995) *Postmodern Arts*, London: Routledge.

Whitman, W. (1971) (first 1855) *Leaves of Grass*, London: Everyman.

Williams, W.C. (1971) *In the American Grain*, Harmondsworth: Peregrine.

FOLLOW-UP WORK

There are a number of additional resources, assignments and other materials to be found on the website that accompanies this new edition: http://www. routledge.com/cw/campbell/

1   Having read the introduction and Chapter 1, look at the article 'Dislocations: Transatlantic Perspectives on Postnational American Studies, Postnational Politics and American Studies' by Donald Pease at http://www.49thparallel.bham.ac.uk/back/issue8/pease.htm:

   • Summarise its key arguments on 'postnational American Studies'.
   • What do you see as the advantages and disadvantages of this approach?

2   Using a presidential speech, analyse its use of rhetoric and in particular the different ways it draws upon certain 'mythic' perceptions of America. What images does it use? What references to the dream, to the future, to the people?

3   Examine how landscape has been used as a powerful aspect of the American 'national narrative' using a range of appropriate sources. Refer to *Easy Rider*, *Field of Dreams*, *Frozen River* or *Slow West* or any other relevant film in your answer.

4   Read Gloria Anzaldúa's *Borderlands/La Frontera* and explain the different ways in which it explores the idea of living on the border. Then watch the Jennifer Lopez film *Bordertown* (2006, directed by Gregory Nava) and contrast how this explores similar themes on screen.

Chapter 2

Ethnicity and immigration
Between many worlds

ETHNIC AMERICA: 'A VAST INGATHERING' (FONER 1990: 251)

The ethnic mix of America is complex, consisting of indigenous peoples as well as voluntary and involuntary immigrants around whom revolve questions of religion, allegiance and national pride. Tension and ambivalence surround the whole idea of ethnicity in America, indeed some would argue that 'our grandparents were ethnic, not us', preferring to believe in the possibility of 'one homogeneous "American" community' (Singh *et al.* 1994: 5). However, the concept of assimilation asserted that all ethnic groups could be incorporated in a new American national identity, with specific shared beliefs and values, and that this would take preference over any previously held system of traditions. Assimilation stressed the denial of ethnic difference and the forgetting of cultural practices in favour of Americanisation which emphasised that one language should dominate as a guard against diverse groups falling outside the social concerns and ideological underpinnings of American society. Of course, within this particular vision, 'whiteness became the privileged grounding and metaphor for the empty abstraction of US citizenship' (Singh 2009: 10). Native Americans and African Americans, as well as immigrants from Europe and elsewhere, were seen as a threat to this vision until they were brought within the acceptable definitions of 'Americanness' or excluded from it entirely. These versions of assimilation argued for conformity and homogeneity as the means of guaranteeing democracy and equality for all in America. In the case of Native Americans, as we shall examine, the differences between tribal and white culture appeared too great for a satisfactory assimilation and the reservation system was employed instead (the case of African Americans is examined in Chapter 3).

Arguments about ethnicity in recent years, influenced by the post-1960s interest in multiculturalism, have moved away from the pressures to one central, uniform idea of America as the only definition of nationhood and towards cultural pluralism. This still allows for diverse ethnic groups to share common connections as Americans, without losing their links to older allegiances and identities. The Civil Rights movement helped to cement interests in ethnic pride and cultural diversity as strengths, asserting the possibility for self-definition and cultural autonomy rather than consensual conformity. The tensions between the call to ethnic assimilation through the abandonment of old values and the pull towards a new sense of plural, multicultural society have, however, remained persistent, and are very much the concerns of the ethnic cultural forms that this chapter will examine (Lowe 1996). In 1988 Peter Marin wrote of 'the generational legacy of every family, a certain residue, a kind of ash, what I would call "ghost-values" . . .'; the 'shreds and echoes' of the past (Singh *et al.* 1994: 8). It is, however, these 'ghost-values' that have become of greater and greater significance in the development of ethnic identities in America. No longer viewed as something to be denied, they are instead the sources of cultural strength and assertion. Through them many Americans have found a positive and empowering means to achieve a productive plural identity, as ethnic *and* American, allowing them to belong to different sets of values rather than be assimilated into only one. Not subjected to one version of identity, these Americans move between two (or more), with different languages, customs, traditions and values. This hybrid view of ethnicity runs through many of the texts we will examine in this chapter, from Native Americans to Jewish Americans, who have in different ways struggled with their own positions and identities within the nation.

For example, in Philip Roth's novel *The Counterlife* (1986), the central character, Nathan Zuckerman, on a visit to Israel finds himself defending his identity as an American Jew against the claims of an ageing Zionist who insists that there is no country for a Jew but Israel. 'I could not think of any historical society', Zuckerman narrates, 'that had achieved the level of tolerance institutionalised in America or that had placed pluralism smack at the center of its publicly advised dream of itself' (Roth 1987: 58). America was 'a country that did not have at its center the idea of exclusion' (ibid.). Zuckerman's American idealism, however much a performance it may be in the context of the novel, touches a central theme in the debates held about the relationship between ethnic identity and wider national values. From the beginnings of American society, as we discussed in the introduction, a central question has been whether or not there is a distinctive American identity. Is there such a thing as a national character and how does that character relate to the importance of ethnicity in American culture? And is any sense of identity forged only at the exclusion or denial of others?

The social historian Oscar Handlin, in one of the most well-known of all works on American immigration, *The Uprooted*, declared: 'Once I thought to write a history of immigrants in America. Then I discovered that the

immigrants *were* American history' (Handlin 1951: 3). What he clearly
excludes from this 'history' is the importance of Native Americans in this
process of identity formation since they were not immigrants in Handlin's
sense. They exist only, it would seem, as Others to be conquered, destroyed
and pitied by the immigrants that Handlin viewed as true Americans.

Earlier, Crevecoeur, in his survey of late eighteenth-century America –
Letters From an American Farmer (1782) – also concentrated on the influx
of Europeans as the starting-point for his vision of the New World. He
noted its promiscuous social mix where Europeans intermarried in a way
that was impossible in any other country. What was more, this process of
intermingling made the American into a man who:

> leaving behind him all ancient prejudices and manners, receives new
> ones from the new mode of life he has embraced, the new government
> he obeys, and the new rank he holds. . . . In America individuals are
> melted into a new race of men.
>
> (Crevecoeur 1957: 39)

For Crevecoeur America was the place where migrants would slough
off the burdens of their inherited pasts and create themselves anew in the
liberating conditions of American life. In America rights belonged to the
individual rather than to social or ethnic groups; the openness and mobility
of American society would encourage personal transformation rather than
the reassertion of traditional beliefs and values. Amid all Crevecoeur's
optimism he notes that the 'Indian' falls outside this process of 'melting'
preferring 'his native woods' over the 'best education', 'bounty' and
'riches' offered by Europeans. He admits an admiration for 'their social
bond' over the individualism of Europeans and comments that 'thousands
of Europeans are Indians [but] we have no examples of even one of those
aborigines having from choice become Europeans!' (ibid.: 42). This suggests the peculiar tensions of ethnic difference and in particular the pull
between worlds, traditions and values. In the case of the Native Americans,
assimilation, as Crevecoeur testifies, seemed impossible, and with all
groups it became a dominant feature of American social development and
nation-building. A consideration of ethnicity might, therefore, begin with
the particular situation of the Native Americans and their relationship to
the wider issues of America as a nation, before moving on to consider
other groups and their responses to the centralising demands on identity.

NATIVE AMERICANS: ASSIMILATION AND
RESISTANCE

Turner's 'The Significance of the Frontier in American History' (1893) saw
the Native American as a line of 'savagery' against which 'civilisation' had

collided, an obstacle in the way of America's 'composite nationality', whose 'primitive Indian life had passed away' in favour of a 'richer tide' (in Milner 1997: 16, 8). Assimilation could not, according to this logic, cope with the presence of the Native Americans whose customs and traditions were too alien, too different to become merged into the new American self. Thus, the struggle against the Native American was a fight over ideological differences based on the idea of 'egocentrism, in the identification of our own values with values in general, of our I with the universe – in the conviction that the world is one' (Todorov 1987: 42–3). Americanisation, in this context, was an imperialist imposition of values, seeking in different ways to assert a particular, narrow definition of what it might mean to be American at the expense of others.

White Americans in positions of cultural power defined Native Americans as racially inferior, savage, childlike and in need of radical readjustment to the 'better' life of the dominant culture. These stereotypes formed a way of seeing and speaking about Native Americans, a discourse, that contributed greatly to the consensus for their destruction. James Hall wrote in 1834–5 that Native Americans showed 'systematic anarchy' in their tribal organisations, preferring 'a restless wandering' to settlement and government. To combat this 'un-American' activity they should be controlled by being rounded up and domesticated, since 'an Indian, like a wolf, is always hungry, and of course always ferocious. In order to tame him, the pressure of hunger must be removed' (Drinnon 1990: 208). Similarly, Elwell S. Otis wrote in 1878 that the Native American lacked 'moral qualities . . . goodness . . . virtues' and shows 'not the slightest conception of definite law as a rule of action. He is guided by his animal desires . . . takes little thought except for the present, knows nothing of property . . . and has not . . . any incentive to labor' (Robertson 1980: 108–9). All these 'lacks' are linked to the 'spirit of communism which is prevalent among all tribes' (ibid.) and so seen as opposite to the traits that Turner saw as being created in the 'new product', the American, on the frontier. Native American culture represented a challenge to the emergent national identity; it was already 'un-American', believing in communal lands, tribalism, sacredness of the earth, and being suspicious of private property.

The reservation policy aimed to ensure that Native Americans would be systematically educated and 'civilised' into the American way of life. Social planner Francis Amasa Walker equated the Native American with the madman or the criminal and imagined the reservation as a kind of asylum or prison. Secluded and separated from the mainstream they could be watched over, ordered and trained into habits of respectability, ownership, self-reliance and other similarly authorised values. The reservation was to be 'a rigid reformatory discipline' (Takaki 1979: 186) in which an ideological homogeneity could be instilled in the wayward Indian, just like upon the insane in Michel Foucault's discussion of the asylum where 'a system of responsibilities' (Foucault 1977: 247) became the norm, involving work and education. On the reservation, as in the asylum, the inmates are 'transformed into minors . . . a new system of education must be applied, a new direction given to their ideas; they must first be subjugated, then encouraged, then applied to work' (ibid.: 252). 'Ethical uniformity' (ibid.: 257) was the underlying intention of the reservation system and the establishment of Indian schools, like the Carlisle School started in 1879 with a philosophy of 'Kill the Indian and save the man'. Both worked towards de-Indianisation and the ideology 'one country, one language, and one flag' (Adams 1991: 39).

With the massacre of the Lakota Sioux at Wounded Knee in 1890 the 'primary resistance' of 'literally fighting against outside intrusion' (Said 1994: 252) came to a close. However, the Native American 'ideological resistance' aimed at reconstituting 'a shattered community, to save and restore the sense and fact of community against all the pressures of the colonial system' (ibid.: 252–3) has never ceased its actions. Louis Owens has written of the 'recovering or rearticulation of an identity, a process dependent upon a rediscovered sense of place as well as community' (Owens 1992: 5), through Native American narrative in the twentieth and twenty-first century. The attack on tribalism was an assault upon the culture and tradition of the Native Americans, and as such at its history and its beliefs. The need to rediscover self-belief, or what in the 1960s was known as 'Red Power', has been crucial to the growing authority of the Native American. As Said has written:

> To achieve recognition is to chart and then to occupy the place in imperial cultural forms reserved for subordination, to occupy it self consciously, fighting for it on the very same territory once ruled by a consciousness that assumed the subordination of a designated inferior Other.
>
> (Said 1994: 253)

The Native Americans, like other ethnic groups in America, had to decolonise language for their own uses, through what Said calls 'reinscription'. The task for writers was to 'reclaim, rename, and reinhabit the land' (ibid.: 273) both literally and metaphorically.

REINSCRIBING THE TRIBE: WRITING ETHNICITY

One of the functions of stories in the Native American tradition has always been to unify the tribe and endow it with a communality and continuity. For so long these were attributes diminished by the Indian policies of the successive administrations. Leslie Marmon Silko, a Native American storyteller, explains that telling stories is an essential component of her life since 'one story is only the beginning of many stories, and the sense that stories never truly end' (Mariani 1991: 84) is a reminder of the survivalist character of the people. For her, 'storytelling continues from generation to generation' and 'cannot be separated from ... [the] geographical' because in them the present and living are connected to the past and the dead. For in the telling of the story, in its coherence, 'we are still all in this place, and language ... is our way of passing through or being with them, of being together again' (ibid.: 84, 92). In the 1890s the Ghost Dance Religion was an attempt to reconnect the living with a vision of the next world in which the whites would disappear and all the dead Native Americans would rise up, with the buffalo, to live again in a Utopia. Stories perform a similar function, a circulation of the tribal lifeblood through the act of telling and an assertion of visibility against the dominant culture's denial of native life, against its creation of absence, and much Native-American narrative works against these 'narratives of absence and victimry' (Vizenor 1998: 23).

By the 1960s 'those inner colonized of the First World – "minorities", marginals, women' all began to find 'the right to speak in a new collective voice' and the 'hierarchical positions of Self and Other, Center and Margin [were] forcibly reversed' (Jameson 1984: 181, 188). Alongside the struggle of African Americans within the dominant white culture during the 1960s, there was also a resurgence in many ethnic literatures – Native American, Chicano and Asian American in particular. The 'Declaration of Indian Purpose' (1961) spoke of being 'absorbed' by American society and called for 'a better life educationally, economically, and spiritually' (Josephy 1985: 37) through self-determination, the protection of existing lands, and continued federal aid. Activism in the 1960s, including the National Indian Youth Council (NIYC) and the American Indian Movement (AIM), challenged further diminution of Indian rights. President of NIYC, Melvin Thorn, said in 1964: 'We do not want to be pushed into the mainstream of American life. ... Any real help for Indian people must take cultural values into consideration' (ibid.: 55–6).

By 1969 'the normal expectation on the reservation is that the Indians may not do anything unless it is specifically permitted by the government' (ibid.: 99). Increasingly direct actions, such as 'fish-ins' protesting against the loss of land rights, the occupation of Alcatraz in 1969 to reclaim land, and the confrontations at Wounded Knee in 1973 and Oglala in 1975 showed the growing resistance and anger among the Native Americans. Above all, these protests asserted that 'Indian voices are not lost' in the 'bureaucratic and political maze in which Indians [were] trapped' (ibid.: 135). Alongside political resistance, both passive and active, there grew an ever-more persistent assertion of 'Indian voices' through imaginative and polemical literature. Gerald Vizenor argues that these are 'postindian warriors' in that they have come through the 'Indian' phase of being

Plate 2.1 Native American histories: Newspaper Rock, Canyonlands National
       Park, Utah.
© Neil Campbell, 1995

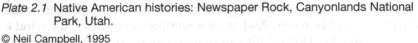

spoken for and controlled by others, and now 'encounter their enemies
with the same courage in literature as their ancestors once evinced on
horses, and they create their stories with a new sense of survivance and
counter the manifest manners of domination' (Vizenor 1994: 4).

He speaks of the 'indian' 'deadeningly imaged in museum displays,
captivity narrative, BIA [Bureau of Indian Affairs] and other documentation, photography, or New Age and other bogus Shamanism' and
how in contemporary culture 'post-indians' must resist such 'static a set
of reductions' (Vizenor and Lee 1999: 15). Vizenor's work in novels and
critical writings aims to overturn the 'linguistic slave name' of 'Indian'
(ibid.) weaving original languages 'to create a new tribal presence in
stories', 'surmount the scriptures of manifest manners . . . [and] counter
the surveillance and literature of dominance' (Vizenor 1994: 5, 12). His
ethnic stories counter those perpetuated by others like Ronald Reagan,
whom Vizenor calls the 'master of . . . manifest manners' (Kroeber 1994:
232), who spoke in 1988 of how 'we', that is the dominant white culture,
had 'humored' the Indian who 'want[ed] to stay in that primitive life style',
but should have been encouraged to 'be citizens along with the rest of us'
(Drinnon 1990: xiii). Vizenor writes of 'tragic wisdom' born out of tribal
power, as 'a pronative voice of liberation and survivance, a condition in
native stories and literature that denies victimization' (Vizenor 1994: 6).

Leslie Marmon Silko's novel *Ceremony* (1977) epitomises such wisdom, beginning with the reminder that stories 'are all we have' and that to 'destroy the stories' is to make Native Americans 'defenseless' (Silko 1977: n.p.). Yet as long as the stories survive and are passed on, the Native peoples retain their traditions, history and identity, reminding them of their roots in the land, which in turn constitutes their sense of self. Tayo, the central character, broken by war and 'trained' in the Indian school to take on the white ways, journeys to a new point of recognition about his construction in the white world so that he might be healed. He remembers his school where science books explained the world to him and contradicted the stories of the tribe and yet 'he still felt it was true, despite all they had taught him in school' since, 'everywhere he looked, he saw a world made of stories, the long ago, time immemorial stories, as old Grandma called them' (ibid.: 95). Tayo must re-learn and be healed in the tribe, and be able to see 'beyond the lie' of a 'nation built on stolen land' (ibid.: 191).

Similarly, in Louise Erdrich's *Tracks* (1988), we find the 'tribe unravelled like a coarse rope' (Erdrich 1988: 2), losing its land to corporate America and government taxes, and consequently losing its traditions and its grip on history. 'Land is the only thing that lasts life to life. Money burns like tinder, flows off like water. And as for government promises, the wind is steadier' (ibid.: 33). Dollar bills cause the memory to vanish (ibid.: 174), Nanapush, one of the narrators, says at one point. Erdrich's concern is that the collective, cultural memory survives, for it provides the strength of what Vizenor calls survivance and tragic wisdom. Echoing a phrase in *Ceremony* – 'vitality locked deep in blood memory' (Silko 1977: 220) – Erdrich writes that 'Power travels in the bloodlines, handed out before birth. . . . The blood draws us back, as if it runs through a vein of earth' (Erdrich 1988: 31). The task of Nanapush's storytelling is to instruct his granddaughter, Lulu, in the history of her family, the tribe and the land. She has been educated off the reservation in the government school and must be re-educated, like Tayo, by the stories. Nanapush says he has 'so many stories. . . . They're all attached, and once I start there is no end to telling' (ibid.: 46). This is not an unqualified positive novel, but it presents a strong image, like Silko's *Ceremony*, of solidarity and ethnic survival through the persistence of tradition, the 'blood memory' of history, and the power of a forward-looking community. In Sherman Alexie's stories and novels it is often humour that provides a source of resistance and a way to reimagine the Native American as complex and ambiguous: 'I wonder if loneliness causes acne. I wonder if being Indian causes acne', his time-travelling hero puts it in *Flight* (Alexie 2007: 4).

The film *Smoke Signals* (1998, directed by Chris Eyre, scripted by Sherman Alexie from his 'novel' *The Lone Ranger and Tonto Fist-fight in Heaven*) is a 'postwestern', produced entirely by Native Americans and deliberately feeding off Hollywood's stereotype of the 'Celluloid Indian' in order to challenge it through irony and humour (see Churchill 1998; Campbell 2008). Echoing Vizenor's call for post-indian warriors who refute the static 'museum' images of the Native American, Eyre's film resists and plays with a reservoir of knowledge about how Indians have been portrayed and have been complicit in their own representation – 'Indians watching Indians on TV', as the film puts it. In this way it is 'post' – that is, *beyond* the classical Western – but nonetheless 'needing' the Western to exist and to draw out new, interesting positions on identity and cultural formation. There are references within it to *Dances with Wolves*, John Wayne and the Lone Ranger, as the film charts the journey of two young men, Thomas Builds-the-Fire and Victor Joseph, towards friendship and reconciliation with family and community. Reservation life is revealed as harsh, troubled (by alcohol and violence), but also warm and engaging, as the film is reluctant to represent any simplistic one-dimensional view; indeed, as Susan Kollin has written, it rethinks and revises the audience's concept of 'what Indians are and what they do and believe . . . creating an insurgent Native American counter-cinema' (Kollin 2000: 142).

The film uses the idea of paternal disappearance and loss as a framing device, starting with the fire that kills Thomas's father, as Thomas himself is saved from the flames by Arnold (Victor's father), who in turn later runs away from his family, the 'rez', to die alone in a trailer home in Phoenix. The road movie that ensues enacts an ironic redemption, returning Arnold to the salmon river of his ancestors from the trailer park and drawing the rebellious Victor towards some sense of his 'native' self redefined as responsible and caring, rather than 'stoic' and mean. *Smoke Signals*'s use of humour, irony, parody and self-deprecation functions to play with the stereotypes of the 'noble' stoic or the New Age Indian, with the romance of tribal memory both parodied ('that was a great example of the oral tradition', says one character after another tale from Thomas) and yet still treasured for its 'tragic wisdom' with stories told, magic sensed, the past's presence felt in the present, and the reiterated need for community and 'survivance' against the pressures of the white world (Vizenor 1994: 12).

In these different patterns of denial and resistance we can learn much about the experience of 'ethnic' Americans who, in different ways, have had to confront the pressures to assimilate and diminish their former traditions. Native Americans faced near genocide in the process of 'nation-building', but have survived to rearticulate and promote their cultures within the United States. In 2006, the US Census Bureau estimated that about 0.8 per cent of the US population was of American Indian or Alaska Native descent. Although always in an uneasy and ambivalent position, their ethnic identity is not invisible and their culture and history continue to develop and inform each generation. As Vizenor has written, 'Natives create their identities in "dialogical relations" with many others, with nature, and with those who must bear the *indian* simulations of dominance' (Vizenor 1998: 22). In so doing, Native Americans can, according to Vizenor, reverse the trend whereby 'they [traditionally] vanish' at the end of Hollywood movies, 'because their absence is better understood than their presence', as long as they seek to show Native peoples in 'all their diversity and contradictions' (Vizenor and Lee 1999: 157–8).

IMMIGRATION AND AMERICANISATION

The experience of Native Americans demonstrates the extreme workings of assimilation theory, or the 'melting pot', and how in many cases it meant 'renouncing – often in clearly public ways – one's subjectivity, who one literally was: in name, in culture, and, as far as possible, in color' (Goldberg 1995: 5). It also shows how ethnic identity can be preserved as an active coexistent element even within the larger 'nation'. Native Americans were seen as beyond assimilation because their ethnicity was too dissimilar to the traditions of Northern European American culture. It was, therefore, to immigrants that attention turned as efforts were made to integrate them into the American cultural mainstream.

The assimilationist metaphor of melting down emerged in a play entitled *The Melting Pot* by an English Jew, Israel Zangwill, in 1908. The play celebrates the possibility of different backgrounds and religions being united in the 'American crucible'. The original set contained a view of Lower Manhattan and the Statue of Liberty outlined against a setting sun, literally an image of the golden land:

> DAVID: (*Prophetically exalted by the spectacle.*): It is the fires of God around His Crucible. (*He drops her hand and points downward.*) There she lies, the great Melting Pot – listen! Can't you hear the roaring and the bubbling? There she gapes her mouth (*He points east.*) – the harbour where a thousand mammoth feeders come from the ends of the world to put in their human freight. Ah, what a stirring and a seething! Celt and Latin, Slav and Teuton, Greek and Syrian – black and yellow –
> VERA: (*Softly nestling to him.*): Jew and Gentile –
> DAVID: . . . Here shall they all unite to build the Republic of Man and the Kingdom of God . . . what is the glory of Rome and Jerusalem . . . compared with glory of America, where all races come to labour and look forward!
>
> (Zangwill 1908: 184–5)

Zangwill's play was first produced in Washington, DC in 1908 at a critical moment in the history of American immigration. The period since the 1880s had witnessed both a massive expansion in the numbers of those leaving Europe and other parts of the world for the United States and a shift in their countries of origin. The net migration to the USA rose from 7.7 million between 1851 and 1880 to 17.7 million between 1881 and 1910. Increasingly migrants from such well-established regions as the United Kingdom, Germany and Scandinavia were being joined by citizens from Italy, Russia and the many different provinces of the Austro-Hungarian Empire. The apparent change in the nature of migrants pouring into the country gave rise to a major debate about the effect they would have on American society and values. Some argued that these 'new' immigrants brought with them cultural, social and political practices which made them far more difficult to assimilate into American life than immigrants of the old-stock who largely came from northern and western Europe.

This concept of the threat of the 'new' was documented in the forty-one-volume Dillingham Commission Report (1911), which investigated the impact of unrestricted immigration on the United States. The report claimed that the 'old' immigrant values and institutions went back to the origins of the Republic, while the 'new' brought with them what appeared to be a challenge to the dominant Anglo-Saxon tradition. Increasingly, the case for restriction took on an explicitly racialist tone. It was not just that new immigrants, in the words of the poet Thomas Bailey Aldrich writing in 1892, were 'a wild and motley throng' carrying to America 'unknown Gods and rites . . . tiger passions . . . strange tongues' and 'accounts of menace alien to our air', but also that they seemed to threaten American racial homogeneity. 'O liberty, white Goddess!' asked Aldrich, 'Is it well to leave the gates unguarded?' (Fuchs 1990: 57). His question was increasingly argued in the negative in the period between the end of the nineteenth century and the early 1920s. Many felt that America's racial as well as cultural identity was threatened by unrestricted immigration and 'mongrelisation' just as it had been by Native American tribes. Such a hierarchical view of white Anglo-Saxon racial superiority ran counter to Zangwill's assumptions that 'all nations and races' were welcome in 'the glory of America', but in the end it prevailed, encouraged by fears of business and labour leaders that unrestricted immigration threatened economic stability, and further enhanced by the debate over national identity which broke out with American involvement in the First World War in 1917. The results were the Immigration Restriction Act of 1921 and the National Quota Act of 1924, which explicitly sought to protect the Anglo-Saxon element in the American population against further encroachment by undesirable groups from Southern and Eastern Europe and Asia. The Immigration Acts of the 1920s contained within them, therefore, assumptions about the desirable national racial mix, and the terms on which immigrants, both past and present, would be expected to adapt to the majority culture.

'Americanisation' and the forging of a 'true' American identity demanded strict adherence to the values of the cultural majority in such key areas as language, religion and manners. The New York Kindergarten Association, in a 1919 survey of educational provision in Manhattan, found that, in one small area, 309 out of 310 children were of foreign parentage and English was rarely to be heard. What could there be of 'an American atmosphere in such homes? What did such children know about the Fourth of July or the Spirit of 76 or Washington or Lincoln?' Taking such children away from the potentially harmful influences of immigrant families and friends and placing them in more secure and controlled environments would 'make Americans of them'. Kindergartens, for instance, could provide in their games, 'wholesome lessons in American-ism' by encouraging immigrant children 'to feel that there is such a country as America and that they are part of it'. There is a curious similarity between this logic and that which created reservations to re-educate and Americanise Native Americans.

The model of the melting pot assumed that everyone could better themselves in American society, despite any ethnic distinctiveness, and improve their position through economic opportunity. There might have been disagreements about how best to maximise that opportunity, but whether it was realised through free-market forces or through federal intervention and social reform, the result would be the same: old ethnic loyalties would diminish in the face of an inexorable process which emphasised those values that Americans held in common rather than those which kept them apart.

One prominent area which has aroused considerable disagreement has been the issue of language. In the period immediately before the Immigration Acts of the 1920s, it was generally assumed that while linguistic diversity might continue at a local level, English would be maintained as the language of the public culture. In the nineteenth century across the country a number of states, counties and local school districts allowed at least some educational provision in languages other than English, but this tended to die out as the campaign for immigration restriction developed in the early twentieth century. In its place came a much greater insistence that English was the necessary basis of a unified culture. This was regularly enforced by both private industry and city and state governments, in a way which reveals the close links between language and expected patterns of social and political behaviour. The International Harvester Corporation, for instance, promulgated English 'Lesson One' for its largely Polish workforce as follows:

I hear the whistle. I must hurry . . .
It is time to go into the shop . . .
I change my clothes and get ready to work.

The starting whistle blows.
I eat my lunch.
It is forbidden to eat until then . . .
I wait until the whistle blows to quit.
I leave my place nice and clean.
I put all my clothes in the locker.
I must go home.

(Gutman 1977: 6)

In a similar vein, the Detroit Board of Education, in 1915, launched a cooperative programme with local industry to transform Detroit from a place in which about three-quarters of the population was foreign-born, of foreign parentage and largely foreign-speaking, into an English-speaking city within two years. Adopted policies included making night school attendance for non-English-speaking workers a condition of employment; preferential employment strategies in which workers who were trying to learn English would be the first to be promoted, the last to be laid off and the first to be taken back; and incentive schemes whereby non-English-speakers who attended night school would receive a bonus in their wages. State governments in the same period emphasised the role of the public school system in the safeguarding of a distinct national linguistic identity. The Americanisation Department of Connecticut, for instance, argued in 1919 that 'America was in danger of being not a unified America, but a polyglot boarding house'. One solution was to promote the school as 'the melting pot of the nation, where Americanism is molded and formed, the great factor of our national life. Our whole fabric and national ideal is here inculcated in the heart and mind of young America, its history, customs, its laws and language' (Circular Letter No. 5, October 1918).

By the 1970s, however, it was clear that the battle for an unquestioned national linguistic identity was far from over. Encouraged by the attempts of African Americans to first recover and then reassert the importance of a black culture, other minority groups sought to articulate their own sense of marginalisation in an English-speaking world by emphasising the continuing vitality of their linguistic inheritance. This process has been affected by further changes in the main sources of immigration to the United States. Since the Second World War, and more particularly since the Immigration Act of 1965, Europe's role as the main supplier of migrants has been taken over by the Americas, Asia, the Middle East and Africa. The 2010 census, for instance, reported that 81 per cent of the foreign-born were of Hispanic or Asian origin, out of an overall immigrant population of c. 40 million. By 2013, about 54 million people of Hispanic background lived in the United States, 18.8 million (38 per cent) of whom were foreign-born. At the same time the variety of recent immigration was emphasized by the fact that the fastest-growing groups in the first fifteen years of the twenty-first century were Asian, Middle Eastern and African. Many government agencies, both at a national and a local level, now existed to help these immigrants adjust to American society and were more sympathetic to ethnic ties in aiding the process of adjustment. Becoming American, it was officially argued, need not be at the expense of older ethnic cultural traditions. One such strategy was the encouragement of bilingual teaching in the elementary classroom for children from Hispanic and other minority groups. But, just as this new sensitivity to cultural difference was encouraged by the emergence of the Civil Rights movement in the 1960s, so the ebbing of enthusiasm for civil rights in the 1970s and 1980s often brought with it hostility to such programmes. In 1981, for instance, Senator Alan Simpson of Wyoming articulated his own fears about the massive rise in the Hispanic population in words which were strongly reminiscent of the language used by campaigners in the early twentieth century: 'A substantial proportion of these new persons and their descendants do not assimilate into our society. . . . If language and cultural separation rise above a certain level, the unity and political stability of our nation will – in time – be seriously eroded' (Dinnerstein and Reimers 1982: 273).

Simpson's concerns were reflected in the move by a number of states (thirty-one by 2015) to make English their official language, and to emphasise the importance of teaching in English in the public school system. In 1986, for instance, California voters amended the state constitution to make English the state language, and followed it up in 1998 with a policy of providing intensive English instruction, in place of bilingual education, to non-English speakers. A new emphasis on English was needed, it was argued, not the preservation of native language and culture as it had been in the heyday of bilingual education. On the other hand, critics of so-called 'immersion' in English continued to argue for bilingual programmes which recognised the cultural context in which the children of immigrants began their formal education (*New York Times* 2009). Schools should become 'authentic culturally democratic sites' so that students from different racial, ethnic and social groups enjoyed educational equality with students from the majority culture. Samuel P. Huntington described these battles over English, 'in terms of both symbol and substance', as 'a major front in the broader war over American identity' (Huntington 2004: 158, 173). Multicultural education 'came at the expense of teaching the values and culture that Americans . . . had in common' and 'represented the culmination of a long erosion of the emphasis on national identity in American education' (ibid.: 173, 174). As a result, continuing high levels of immigration and low levels of assimilation could turn America 'into a country of two languages, two cultures and two peoples' (ibid.: 256).

By 2015, these debates were being given an extra edge by the existence in the country of about 11 million undocumented migrants who had no legal or political status, who lived in the country but were not citizens of it. In the public sphere they were essentially voiceless, silent for fear of imprisonment and deportation. They were regularly accused by anti-immigrant politicians and campaigners of threatening national security in the aftermath of 9/11 and creating an extra burden on the public purse. 'Undocumented' immigrants were, by definition, 'illegal' and should be treated as law-breakers as in the book *The Beast* and the films *Sin Nombre* and the *Golden Dream* discussed below. Behind these charges, however, also lay cultural concerns associated with crime, disease and problems over language, all issues which reawakened the rhetoric of the late nineteenth century. At the heart of these intense debates over immigration's place in contemporary America, John Tirman has charged, lay issues of cultural identity and what it means to be American (Tirman 2015).

Conservative alarmism, however, was partly undermined by evidence that it was the wish of many Latinos themselves to learn English, with an overall majority (87 per cent in 2015) believing that immigrants had to speak English to be able to succeed (Pew 2015). This suggests a realistic attitude towards getting on in America, which reflects the experience of many earlier waves of migrants, though it did not mean that Latino culture had to be discarded along the way. Some 95 per cent of Hispanics in 2015 believed that it was important for the Latino populations to speak Spanish in future (ibid.). The poet and journalist Ed Morales called this 'Living with Spanglish', fusing the North American with the Latin American 'in a way that approaches the former with a healthy scepticism and takes care not to obliterate the essence of the latter' (Morales 2003). But whatever the eventual outcome, the continuing controversy over language has emphasized the recurring tension between the acknowledgement of diversity and concerns for unified national identity which had so marked earlier debates over the role of ethnicity in American life.

THE CRUCIBLE OF DIFFERENCE

Ethnicity in contemporary America is a 'pluralist, multidimensional, or multifaceted concept of self' in which 'one can be many different things, and this personal sense can be a crucible for a wider social ethos of pluralism' (Fischer 1986: 196). Fischer's language harks back to the earlier idea of the 'crucible' in which Americans were forged, melted down from their various ethnicities into a new nation, but alters it with his sense of a crucible for difference and pluralism in which class, race, religion and gender are all interconnected with ethnicity. At a base level, 'ethnicity is a process of inter-reference between two or more cultural traditions' and it is this rich 'reservoir that sustains and renews humane attitudes' (ibid.:

201, 230). Cohering with Werner Sollors's famous comment that ethnic literature is 'prototypically American literature' (Sollors 1986: 8), Fischer goes on to declare the potentiality for 'reinvigoration and reinspiration' at work in the mingling of different ethnicities, with their own traditions, cultural practices and expressions. Rather than a retreat into the past or a separatist mentality, he sees the 'textured sense of being American' as the process through which 'a dialogue generating new perspectives for the present and future' is created (Fischer 1986: 230, 231). For example, the works of Jewish Americans like Roth, Bellow and Malamud act as an 'interference' between the Jewish and the American, preserving, reworking and creating through their language some new considerations, and at the same time, they are 'inter-referencing' between different cultural traditions, mingling and connecting, questioning and accepting. The point here is that ethnic literatures are dynamic and mobile, born out of the traditions of immigration and migration, and they are also the products of tradition and continuity. This duality is productive and enables a richness and diversity in their interactions within American life. As Bodnar has written:

> The point is that instead of linear progression, immigrants faced a continual dynamic between economy and society, between class and culture. It was in the swirl of this interaction and competition that ordinary individuals had to sort out options, listen to all the prophets, and arrive at decisions of their own. . . . Inevitably the results were mixed.
>
> (Bodnar 1985: xx)

Such an atmosphere is apparent in the stories of immigrants, both first-hand and fictional, and in the work of subsequent generations still haunted by these tensions. As Madan Sarup has put it, 'When migrants cross a boundary line there is hostility *and* welcome. [They] are included and excluded in different ways' (Sarup 1994: 95). These are recurrent and potent themes in immigrant and ethnic literature, raising thoughts of home, belonging, memory and forgetting, old and new traditions; and every crossed borderline, real or imagined, brings these questions to mind. Like the migrant person, 'the borderline is always ambivalent' (ibid.: 99), marking the transformative movement between worlds of desire and trepidation, hope and fear. 'In the transformation every step forward can also be a step back: the migrant is here and there' and it is for these reasons of ambivalence that to understand America, in particular, one must wrestle with the migrant experience, for it asserts above all that 'identity is not to do with being but with becoming' (ibid.: 98).

Traditional imaginings of America were of the promised land where the newcomer could undo the sufferings of the Old World. Louis Adamic expressed this as: 'it was a grand, amazing, somewhat fantastic place –

the Golden Country – a sort of Paradise – the Land of promise in more ways than one – huge beyond conception ... untellingly exciting, explosive, quite incomparable' (King *et al.* 1995: 164). Immigrant stories, both 'old' and 'new', respond to and engage with the tensions that arise from such myths in order to demonstrate how ethnic Americans cope with something 'beyond conception'. Myths are present in Jewish American texts, as we shall see, and equally in the work of Chinese Americans, like Maxine Hong Kingston, whose characters leave China in search of 'Gold Mountain' (Kingston 1981: 45), which they 'invented and discovered' on every journey (ibid.).

IMMIGRANT STORIES: JEWISH AMERICANS

You are the promise of the centuries to come. You are the heart, the creative pulse of America to be.

(Yezierska 1987: 137)

A prominent group within patterns of American immigration have been the Jews, who arrived in the country from Eastern Europe as a result of the prejudicial laws and pogroms after 1880. Imagining America as a place where they might be free from persecution and able to practise their religion unhindered, the New World echoed Jewish beliefs about a promised land and seemed to fulfil their greatest dreams. For this reason, much Jewish writing articulates mythic notions of America, typified by stories of hard work, suffering, promise and achievement. Early immigrant accounts and autobiographies like Mary Antin's book *The Promised Land* (1912) typify a celebratory representation of America:

So there was our promised land, and many faces were turned towards the West. And if the waters of the Atlantic did not part for them, the wanderers rode its bitter flood by a miracle as great as any the rod of Moses ever wrought.

(Antin 1912: 364)

She links the religious dreams of redemption and hope with the possibilities of America as a 'second birth' allowing her a creative mixture of two worlds: 'Mine is the whole majestic past, and mine is the shining future' (ibid.). For her, tensions between the old and new, past and future were interpreted as an advantage and a source of possibility, whereas for others, it became the emblem of immigrant dilemmas. How was one to be an American while tied to the Old World through customs, religion and family? Unlike Antin, who found education and the process of 'Americanisation' a source of reinvigoration, many found America a destabilising place without the security of the village and their ancestral past. Handlin calls the village and land the 'pivot of a complex circle of relationships, the primary index of . . . status' (Handlin 1951: 20). Losing this secure base in America and taking up a new life in the city 'was like a man without legs who crawls about and cannot get anywhere' (ibid.). For some, the rootedness of ancient community was threatened by the wrench into the New World and the mixing with others from outside the village. Anzia Yezierska described it as like 'getting ready to tear my life from my body' (1987: 124). However disorientating this experience was for some, for others it marked their freedom and was viewed as a liberating possibility for building a new identity in America. Outside the controls of the village were different challenges which became synonymous with the American Dream of achievement through struggle and industriousness: 'Though a man's life may be sown with labor, with hardship, with blood, a crop will come of it, a harvest be reaped' (Handlin 1951: 102). The immigrant experience thus confirmed and reinforced certain dominant stories of America, an argument asserted in Handlin's grandiloquence: 'The new was not the old. Yet the new and the old are related . . . by the death of the old which was necessary for the birth of the new' (ibid.: 101–2).

For Handlin, America is a place 'in motion', constructed by 'the values of flight' and rooted in the 'experience of being rootless, adrift' (ibid.: 307), and this is vital to the belief, now current in critical thinking, that identity is neither fixed, nor unitary, but fluid and multiple, conditioned and constructed in a variety of changing situations. Thus Carole Boyce-Davies argues that she, as a 'migratory subjectivity', has learned that 'the renegotiating of identities is fundamental to migration. . . . It is the convergence of multiple places and cultures' (Boyce-Davies 1994: 3). Immigrant stories of Jews and others do not together create a harmonised, orchestrated version of America as 'one voice', but instead stress dissonance and variation: a 'dissensus' (Ferraro 1993: 6). In early immigrant voices, with their tense negotiations over old and new, self and other, past and future, America debated its identities and established the cultural contest over the centre and the margin that has characterised so much of its later history. The centre here is the pull to assimilation and acculturation – that is, the Antin school of immigrant culture that veers towards the embrace of an acceptance of Americanisation above the pull back to traditions from the Old World. At the margins are the less settled, migratory forces that feel uneasy in accepting such a positioning and would rather continue to question and contest the cultural meanings provided from the centre. Amid such collisions, 'The migrant voice tells us what it is like to feel a stranger and yet at home, to live simultaneously inside and outside one's immediate situation' (King et al. 1995: xv).

The tensions of immigrant experience are expressed well in the work of Anzia Yezierska, who portrays a woman's struggle between the dreams of 'the new golden country' (Yezierska 1975: 9) and the 'shut-in-ness' (Yezierska 1987: 170) of the ghetto. In her work the Old World is related to the further restrictions of gender and thus is associated with the twin powers of father and Torah (Jewish religious law). For her, the escape to America is also the possibility of escaping these limitations on her self-definition.

In some respects, her largely autobiographical stories embrace America through linking themes such as education (as Mary Antin had too), marriage (into non-Jewish life) and success, but not without careful interrogations of the idealisations of America through immigrant eyes. As a later writer, Bernard Malamud, has Bober say in *The Assistant* (1957), 'Without education you are lost' (Malamud 1975: 77). Education is represented as a key to the creation of a new life. In one of Yezierska's stories she quotes Waldo Frank: 'We go forth all to seek America. And in the seeking we create her. In the quality of our search shall be the nature of the America that we create' (Yezierska 1987: 297). This suggests the twin factors of search and creation that figure in her stories of immigrant life, with her characters longing for America initially through dreams and then tempered by lived experience. It is a 'hunger' to possess the dream, to be taken up by America – often imaged as a lover – and yet Yezierska's stories are not lost in sentiment, for they also reflect the processes of immigrant struggle and de-idealisation. As if deliberately countering Emma Lazarus's words on the Statue of Liberty to 'Give me your tired, your poor, your huddled masses yearning to breathe free', Yezierska's immigrants are trapped in the ghettos of the New World, choking and restricted, struggling to better themselves through education and hard work.

However, Yezierska suggests that America can be remade constantly through the additions and mixtures provided by new groups. Rather than the 'dead grooves' (ibid.: 140) of homogeneity, she proposes the 'power to fly' (ibid.: 137), to resist incorporation into a ready-made America and make it yourself; for as Frank wrote, it is in the seeking that we make her. The 'unused gifts' (ibid.: 283) of ethnic Americans had to be realised in order for the whole nation to benefit, argues Yezierska, and yet the prejudices constantly keep the worlds apart. In one of her best stories, 'Soap and Water', she identifies mainstream American society as the 'laundered world' that she keeps clean as a worker in the laundry itself: 'I, the unclean one, am actually fashioning the pedestal of their cleanliness' (ibid.: 167). Again trapped by economics, class and a lack of power, her character seems hopeless, but education offers her a way out. It is the 'voice', 'the birth of a new religion in my soul' (ibid.: 168), that education might provide, which could enable and empower her to resist those 'agents of clean society' who withheld positions and judged her from the outside only. Unwilling to remain strangled and 'unlived' (ibid.: 173), Yezierska links personal fulfilment and education with the wider possibilities of social change. The individual, improved by work and education, can, in her vision of America, alter the public sphere; as she puts it, 'I was changed and the world was changed' (ibid.: 177).

Such belief in the vitality of ethnic Americans was echoed in the work of Randolph Bourne, whose essay 'Trans-National America' (1916) was published before Yezierska's work, but was connected to her through his mentor John Dewey, who had a brief relationship with Yezierska. Bourne's essay questions the 'melting pot' theory of immigration and the process of assimilation that it presumed, and like Yezierska he felt 'that America shall be what the immigrant will have a hand in making it, and not what a ruling class ... decide that America shall be made' (Lauter et al. 1994: 1733). Bourne argues that Americanisation must not mean that 'these distinctive qualities should be washed out into a tasteless, colorless fluid of uniformity' (ibid.: 1736), for such a loss would weaken and deprive the nation as a whole. Assimilation that was akin to uniformity produced an 'elementary grasping animal' without connection to a strong tradition and was rather part of the 'cultural wreckage of our time' (ibid.: 1736–7). For Bourne, America is summed up in his slogan: 'They merge but they do not fuse' (ibid.). Americans must, he argued, rewrite 'the weary old nationalism' (ibid.) that was tearing Europe apart in 1916, reject the uniform ideology of the 'melting-pot' and reach towards 'a new key' (ibid.: 1738) to unlock the future – a future in which 'America is coming to be, not a nationality but a trans-nationality, a weaving back and forth, with the other lands, of many threads of all sizes and colors' (ibid.: 1742). The effect of such an approach for Bourne was to enliven America, rather than flatten it into uniformity through melting down existing differences, and so 'liberate and harmonize the creative power of all these peoples and give them the new spiritual citizenship' (ibid.) and a real investment in 'the Beloved Community' (ibid.: 1743).

Bourne's American 'Beloved Community' enriched by ethnicity and Yezierska's belief in personal achievement as an emblem of collective social betterment were not persuasive visions for all immigrants, many of whom questioned the possibility of changing anything, especially as individuals. The mistrust felt by others towards immigrants was a reason for this doubt and especially in the strong nativist feelings expressed by the likes of Madison Grant in the same year as Bourne's essay. He wrote of the 'mongrelisation' of America in his *The Passing of the Great Race* (1916), and claimed that immigrants 'adopt the language of the native American [that is the white American], they wear his clothes, they steal his name and they are beginning to take his women, but they seldom adopt his religion or his ideals' (Horowitz et al. 1990: 11).

This kind of racism had been used against the Native Americans too and one of the great perpetuators of this pseudo-science was Theodore Roosevelt, who worried about the 'deterioration in the English-speaking peoples' (ibid.). To counter such views and gain some power, many immigrants became involved in political activism and union movements in attempts to secure collective, organised social change. For example, rather than follow the beliefs of their immigrant parents, awaiting the Messiah, many Jews sought a political 'messiah' in Communism and Socialism condemning the capitalist system that created exploitation and poverty and rewarded the struggling working people. Writer–activists like Michael Gold, who edited the radical paper *The Liberator* in the 1920s and helped to found 'The New Masses', which specifically published left-wing writers, spoke from a Jewish immigrant background, but with the purpose of precise social protest. Gold's major work, *Jews Without Money* (1930), is a hard-hitting description of ghetto life and suffering, and a vehement attack on capitalism as a root cause of the difference in class and status. It is full of questions, anger and exclamatory prose and in Gold's novel, the promised land is 'O golden dyspeptic God of America' (Lauter *et al.* 1994: 1759), a place of destruction that has 'taught the sons of tubercular Jewish tailors how to kill' (Gold 1965: 23). In one scene, Gold emphasises the clash of old and new cultures as the father extols the importance of the Talmud to Jewish faith and life and the son is asked to recite his hymn to Americanisation learned in the public school: 'I love the name of Washington / I love my country too, / I love the flag, the dear old flag, / The red, white and blue' (ibid.: 80). Gold wants to surmount these simple myths of belief and strike out for political change, from a learning rooted not in dreams, but the harsh experience of ghetto life. As the autobiographical novel says, 'It is all useless. A curse on Columbus! A Curse on America, the thief! It is a land where the lice make fortunes, and the good men starve!' (ibid.: 79).

Philip Roth's early work represents a more cynical view of ethnic life in America and his own position is more fluid and less fixed on the issues of ethnicity and community. Using an essay by the critic Philip Rahv, which had discussed America as a nation divided between 'Redskins' and 'Palefaces', and hence split along lines of ethnic ancestry and beliefs, Roth argued that he felt himself to be a 'redface' who 'sympathises equally with both parties in their disdain for the other' (Roth 1977: 76–7). His work explores this position and the confusions of ethnic identities in contemporary America:

> All this talk about 'identities' – your 'identity' is just where you decide to stop thinking, as far as I can see. I think all these ethnic groups . . . simply make life more difficult in a society where we're trying to just live amicably.
>
> (Roth 1987: 305)

This suggests some of the problems in over-emphasising ethnic differences at the cost of living amicably in a community. His work often presents ongoing ethnic divisions and is well demonstrated in a novella that, in part, echoes Michael Gold's curse on Columbus, in its title *Goodbye, Columbus* (1959). His young Jewish protagonist's name, Klugman, means both 'clever' and 'curse' as if to signal again the kind of in-betweenness that interests Roth. He is between two cultures: the old Newark Jews of his childhood and the upwardly mobile Jews of Short Hills. The use of place in the novella articulates the kind of communal tensions over identity and belonging that are explored in the work as a whole. Neil Klugman, existential migrant, crosses a borderline within the Jewish community, proving, as Roth is keen to do, that difference marks all people and there is no identifiable, single Jewish American. 'It was, in fact, as though the hundred and eighty feet that the suburbs rose in altitude above Newark brought one closer to heaven, for the sun itself became bigger, lower, and rounder' (Roth 1964: 14). This environment, with 'regulated . . . moisture' from garden hoses, 'planned . . . destinies of the sons of its citizens' and streets with the names of eastern colleges contrasts with the old community down below 'in the cindery darkness of the alley' and the sweet 'promise of afterlife' (ibid.). Klugman belongs in neither and his life is defined only by 'edginess' because that is where he is positioned, on the edge, between the offered communities.

Roth links Klugman to a black child who visits the library where he works and becomes enthralled by the worlds projected in the paintings of Gauguin. It is as if both ethnic Americans long for something other than the lives they have, but their dreams are as unreal as the Polynesian images in the paintings, distant and out of reach. Roth is also reminding us of the immense difference within ethnic groups and how there can be no single community or determined sense of identity, all is flux and division. Even the assimilation of the Short Hills' Jews does not mean uniformity, but only more division. As Mrs Patimkin asks Klugman, 'are you orthodox or conservative?' to which he naïvely replies, 'I'm just Jewish' (ibid.: 87).

Roth's comic but sensitive awareness of the mixture of American identities reminds us of the current debates about identity as problematic because of the multicultural, hybridised nature of contemporary America. At the end of *Goodbye, Columbus*, Klugman, troubled by his own sense of self and identity, gazes at himself in the library window. What is reflected back is not a single, neat vision of a whole individualised self, but 'a broken wall of books, imperfectly shelved' (ibid.: 131), suggesting the multi-faceted imperfections of the postmodern American identity constituted not by simple ethnic regulations but by difference and contest. He is a reflection of the multiple stories contained in those haphazard books, and not a single self. In this he is like America, constructed of many dissimilar, ill-fitting pieces all of which can coexist and function together. This moment brings to mind a comment from a character in a later Roth book who asks, 'What's so intolerable about tolerating a few differences?' (Roth 1987: 305).

One can see many of these tensions, negotiations and meanings played out too in the films of Woody Allen. In particular, *Radio Days* (1986) articulates the immigrant community as settled and yet still in turmoil, working through its intergenerational desires for different and better lives in America. The family are introduced to the audience through the narrative voice of the main character, remembering his boyhood in Rockaway. He is shown torn between the pull of the radio with its unifying 'American' adventure stories of the 'Masked Avenger' who can magically restore order and put the world to rights, and the 'real' issues presented through Hebrew School and the rabbi as he is encouraged to collect for 'the Jewish homeland in Palestine'. To the boy this means nothing except 'some place near Egypt' and he would rather use the collection to buy the 'Masked Avenger secret compartment ring' – his own object of desire. When found out, the boy is brought before the rabbi in a scene that suggests comically the confusions of the two worlds: the dark, forbidding world of the rabbi in contrast to the brash excitements of the radio adventure; the call for 'discipline' in contrast to the apparent laxity of mainstream America. The boy is literally caught between the parental punishment and that of the rabbi, whom the boy has unknowingly insulted by calling him his 'trusty Indian companion' (in a reference to the Lone Ranger). The rich comic effects do, however, leave us with a sense of cultural tension, especially for the boy for whom America signifies not the disciplined faith, nor the dreamy hopes of his parents, but a radio adventure and the romance of New York.

The traditions of film and television 'Jewishness' have been continued most notably in *Curb Your Enthusiasm* (HBO, 2000–11), in which Larry David 'for all intents and purposes', as one observer has commented, recreates the long-dead world of the Jewish *shtetl* transposed to contemporary Los Angeles (Green 2006), an urban community, yet, in the way David represents it, a place where everyone knows everyone and where all are 'related' – if only by business contacts and rivalry instead of blood. Mixing this sense of anxious community with the conventional Jewish figure of the *schlemiel*, the ordinary man struggling with his everyday problems at the core of much Yiddish literature, the show presents David's comic persona, echoing Roth's Klugman, as engaged in crazy everyday situations of confusion and social mishaps which still reflect, to some degree, the uneasiness many Jewish people continue to feel about their place in multicultural America (see Gillota 2010).

THE FUTURE BELONGS TO THE MIXTURE: MELTING POT, MOSAIC OR HYBRID?

Stuart Hall has written of the fact that 'we all speak from a particular place, out of a particular history, out of a particular experience, a particular culture, without being contained by that position' and goes on to stress that 'our ethnic identities are crucial to our subjective sense of who we are'. Yet such a location is not necessarily based upon exclusivity or 'marginalizing, dispossessing, displacing and forgetting other ethnicities', as older imperialisms had been. Instead, argues Hall, we can achieve a 'politics of ethnicity predicated on difference and diversity', rethinking identity and culture as a series of overlapping routes that accepts 'diasporic' movement as part of the process (Morley and Chen 1996: 447; Massey and Jess 1995).

This is a cultural approach that has emerged as a result of multiculturalism and 'ethnocriticism' (Krupat 1992) in which immigrant and ethnic voices are central, contributing hugely to the 'polyvocality' (many-voicedness) that describes a cosmopolitan, multicultural America. Thus culture is seen like language, hybrid, an encounter that can be familiar and new, different and the same within itself. This possibility recognised in language has a useful parallel in the study of ethnic America, which, as we have suggested, is a culture of encounter and contact, of boundary crossings, and so a place of merging, of tension and contest, in which differences coexist.

Bakhtin, exploring novelistic language, wrote of the 'dialogic . . . [where] two points of view are not mixed, but set against each other dialogically' (Bakhtin 1990: 360). This resembles America, where the impetus to forge a single, American self, a national identity, out of difference, has always existed in tension with a counter-impetus towards separation, distinct communities of interest, religion, race and ethnicity. Bakhtin, however, argues that a certain type of hybridity 'sets different points of view against each other in a conflictual structure, which retains "a certain elemental, organic energy and open-endedness"' (Young 1995: 22, quoting Bakhtin). Thus in Bakhtin's use, hybridity connotes 'an antithetical movement of *coalescence and antagonism* . . . that both brings together, fuses, but also maintains separation' (ibid. – our emphasis). Ethnicity in the United States of America has been and continues to be this blend of antagonism and coalescence, a mix of different voices struggling to be heard, some restricted and silenced, while others dominate, and yet always with the possibility of finding expression and authority.

Postcolonial critic Homi Bhabha has taken these linguistic ideas and extended them to examine relations of power within the colonial situation, and his conclusions too are relevant to the American experience. He argues that hybridity allows the voice of the other, the marginalised, and the dominated to exist within the language of the dominant group, whose voice is never totally in control. As Young puts it:

hybridity begins to become the form of cultural difference itself, the jarrings of a differentiated culture whose 'hybrid counter-energies' in

Said's phrase, challenge the centred, dominant cultural norms with their unsettling perplexities generated out of their 'disjunctive, liminal space'.

(Young 1995: 23)

This is an interesting way of seeing America; hybrid in the sense of permitting challenge, 'counter-energies' and 'unsettling perplexities' to exist in constant dialogue with the dominant norms of established mainstream culture. Hybridity is once again viewed as merger *and* 'a dialectical articulation' (ibid.), characteristic of postcolonial, syncretic cultures which are blends and co-minglings of different voices and traditions; for example, Native American with the mainstream. In this respect, America can be seen as 'postcolonial', with its range of other voices, the 'inner colonized', interrogating the dominant discourses of power with gestures of fusing and of countering – always the double action of hybridity (see Singh and Schmidt 2000).

Hybridization as creolization involves fusion, the creation of a new form, which can then be set against the old form, of which it is partly made up . . . as 'raceless chaos' by contrast, [it] produces no stable new form but rather something closer to Bhabha's restless, uneasy, interstitial hybridity: a radical heterogeneity, discontinuity, the permanent revolution of forms.

(Young 1995: 25)

If the old metaphors for American ethnicity no longer ring true; 'melting pot', 'mosaic', 'salad bowl', then a more fluid representative accumulation of tensions may be found in the ideas of hybridity, which are ambiguous, contrary and processive. Hybridity pulls towards sameness and fusion while also allowing for the importance of difference as a creative, new energy brought to the mix.

What hybridity cannot do is to resolve the differences and tensions between groups or ideologies, but instead it establishes a problematic in which 'other "denied" knowledges enter upon the dominant discourse and estrange the basis of its authority' (ibid.: 114). The emergent histories of ethnic groups within American culture serve to articulate and rearticulate hidden pasts and excluded voices that provide a heterogeneous, multiplicitous remapping of American culture and identity. As a place of encounter, migration, mixing, settlement, colonialism, exploitation, resistance, dream and other forces, America cannot be viewed as a closed culture with a single tradition, but as 'diasporic' because, as Hall puts it, summarising Gilroy's and Clifford's work, 'the connections are not linear but circular. We should think of culture as moving, not in a line but through different circuits' with an emphasis on the different routes that have been travelled to form its complex, unstable ensemble (Hall in Massey and Jess 1995: 207–9).

In re-viewing America from its complex, ethnic 'borderlands', one can see the value of such ideas (see Saldivar 1997) as in the 'circuits' undertaken by Mexican Americans as they move across to work in the USA and return to villages in the south (see Martinez 2001; Boyle 1995). Gloria Anzaldúa, Chicana, lesbian, living on the borderlines, in every sense of the phrase, sees America as 'a place of contradictions' with herself 'at the juncture of cultures' which is 'not a comfortable place to be'. Yet it is still a place of possibility, where 'languages cross-pollinate and are re-vitalized; they die and are born' (Anzaldúa 1987: Preface). Like America itself, the borderlands, unfixed and fluid, permit 'one's shifting and multiple identity and integrity . . . to swim in a new element' (ibid.). Here exists a hybrid place, for the 'new mestiza', as she terms it, where multiplicity is encouraged, rather than curtailed, in the creation of a collage-like new subjectivity.

However, the possibilities of a hybrid America may only be another version of the old migrant dream. The journalist and poet Rubén Martinez writes of his hope that 'the many selves can find some kind of form together without annihilating one another' and that the warring selves within himself might 'sign treaties' (Martinez 1992: 2). And yet, he

Plate 2.2 Mural, El Corrido Del Segundo Barrio, El Paso.

recognises that the reality of contemporary America resists such a coming together, replacing it with something 'like a crucifixion – each encounter signifies a contradiction, a cross: the contrary signs battle each other without end' (ibid.). This is 'anything but a multicultural paradise' (ibid.) with cultures in cities like Los Angeles in violent struggle, but he still longs for some sense of 'new subjectivity', like Anzaldúa. For him, it is signified in the search for 'the home' and for 'a one that is much more than two . . . North and South in the North and in the South' (ibid.: 2–3). Ultimately, as his later work *Crossing Over: A Mexican Family on the Migrant Trail* testifies, in a diasporic American life there can be no idealised, fixed, promised land, but instead an ambivalent 'jumble of objects is as close as I get to "home"' (ibid.: 166).

THE NEW AMERICANS?

> 'Where do you come from?' 'What's the difference, I'm here now.'
> (Woman in Louis Malle's *And the Pursuit of Happiness*, 1986)

Louis Malle, the French film director, made a fictional film in 1985, *Alamo Bay*, about a Galveston Bay fishing community beset by migrant Vietnamese who had fled their war-ravaged country to live in the USA. The film dramatises the problems of new ethnic groups in America and brings out many of the nativist fears that have recurred throughout the nation's history. The white community feel threatened by the competition of Vietnamese fishermen and by the new faces and practices entering their neighbourhood, heightened by the confused aftermath of the Vietnam War. The involvement of the Ku Klux Klan further connects these contemporary events with earlier ethnic and racial conflicts in America and suggests the persistence of deep-seated fears of the outsider and the alien in American life. A year later, Malle made a complementary documentary about new immigration to America called *And the Pursuit of Happiness* in which he emphasised the persistence of the immigrant dream. The film ranges across myriad ethnic groups who straddle various cultures and demonstrates through interviews and reportage their aspirations and their doubts about the country. In one scene, Malle, himself a migrant, meets a group of mixed immigrants who have established their own company in Dallas, Texas. Appropriately the firm is the 'Liberty Cab Company', with drivers from Kurdistan and Ethiopia, and a manager from Ghana, who had established a democratic cooperative with share-ownership among the 130 drivers. Contained in this scene are the persistent signs of the immigrant dream of America as a place of possibility, a vision, it would appear, undeterred by the experiences of others before them who may not have succeeded. Although Malle's film is far from celebratory, it does, however, suggest the resilience of the beliefs that pulled people to America from its very beginnings. In an equally revealing moment in the film, an Asian family are shown with a Hindu temple and a barbecue pit alongside each other in their home, as if to present visually what the father explains on camera, that they 'have two cultures and . . . can choose the best from it' in order to create their new and better lives. Another Asian American, the writer Bharati Mukherjee has made a similar point, arguing that America is a place where she could choose 'to discard that part of my history that I want, and invent a whole new history for myself' (Lauter *et al.* 1994: 3103).

In 2004 Rubén Martinez published *The New Americans* to accompany a television documentary about immigrants in the USA from all over the world (Palestine, Nigeria, India, Mexico) and begins by reviewing how the 'outsider' might be seen differently after 9/11 and the subsequent 'War on Terror'. Despite the increased nativism and the effects of the so-called Patriot Act, Martinez recognised the continued 'pull' of the USA and that 'who and what is an American, has never been resolved', since it is an 'ongoing process' of 'acculturation – an adaptation, not a whole-scale transformation . . . somewhere in-between Old and New worlds, in between languages, mores, and tastes. . . . The in-between space is dynamic and shifting' (Martinez 2004: 24, 208). These comments echo the theoretical ideas of Bhabha, Hall, Gilroy and Clifford discussed throughout this section, and without being over-romanticised suggest the possibility of 'new ethnicities' emerging from the complex processes of cultural hybridity. However, Martinez is quick to recognise the conflict, inequality, racism and division that remain within this process and in migrants: he writes, there is a 'mirror in which we see the best and worst of ourselves, our past and our future. They remind us over and again that there is nothing stable in our world . . . migrants tell us that we are, all of us, always on the move' (ibid.: 225). In this tension, between dynamism and division, is the challenge for America's future:

> A newly emergent American identity must acknowledge and em-power difference without breaking under its weight. In rethinking our complex multicultural past, we need to address issues of distortion and erasure, of shared myths and attitudes, even as they are inter-rogated, separately and together, by race, immigration, and ethnicity.
>
> (Singh *et al.* 1994: 25)

Martinez, following Mexicans on the migrant trail in his *Crossing Over*, recognised that 'they can partake in – indeed, be protagonists of – transnational or "global" culture even as they nurture the vestiges of their roots. In this context, the regional is global and vice-versa' (Martinez 2001: 132). Here he sees a form of 'newly emergent American identity' where

'The kids will be neither Mexican nor gringo but both, and more than both, they will be the New Americans, imbibing cultures from all over the globe' (ibid.: 191).

However, the terrible dangers of migrant travel have been explored in the films *Sin Nombre* (2009, Carey Fukunaga) and *Golden Dream* (2013, Diego Quemada-Diez) where vulnerable, but hopeful teenagers (the nameless) travel north from Central America in search of a new life in the USA. Like Oscar Martinez's book *The Beast* (2013), named after the train used to travel north, both films focus on the struggle and desperation of the migrant experience on the 'la bestia' – 'the snake, the machine, the monster . . . full of legends and their history soaked with blood': 'the metal clanking of The Beast enveloping everything, hardly a moment to think. It's a sensation between the excitement of the ride and the fear of the uncertainty . . . The train is a long series of uncertainties' (Martinez 2013: 53, 50). The dark, closed, almost Gothic world of Mexico in *Sin Nombre*'s Mara Salvatucha ganglands is defined through acts of violence and brutal allegiance to a self-perpetuating system of control and circularity and is held in sharp contrast to the occasional sweeping landscape glimpsed from the crowded, threatening roof of the train heading to El Norte. As Fukunaga (2009) has argued, this is a post-industrial Western recycling of long-held dreams of hope attached to a new land, but now complicated by new uncertainties and different forms of brutality. Yet it is in the quasi-sublime use of landscape, established in the opening shot of the film, when Casper appears to step out into a wondrous (but almost Oz-like) autumnal woodland, where Fukunaga suggests the still-pulsing dream of a New World held in the migrant's heart; the moments of intense promise inherent in the urge to leave home and risk everything. The fantastical visions that appear fleetingly in the film stir these echoes of tragic longing, of a world, for many, like Casper, and many of the other characters in these three examples, always just out of reach.

CONCLUSION: NO BORDER HERE

Frozen River (2008, directed by Courtney Hunt) is set in the north country of New York State, near the little city of Massena on the St Lawrence River and the Mohawk Nation at Akwesasne straddling both the mile-wide river and the US–Canadian border. Melissa Leo plays Ray, a single Anglo mum, struggling to make ends meet after her dissolute Mohawk husband has run off with their savings. To feed her family she forms an unlikely alliance with a young Mohawk woman, Lila (Misty Upham), from the nearby reservation, to smuggle Chinese and Pakistani immigrants across the Canadian border through the tribal lands. This film epitomises the complexity of ethnicities in contemporary America, where cultures collide and exchange both legally and illegally across borders. Hunt saw the film as related to the Western genre because, 'The western is the story of America … the story of migrants, of people moving forward. The original settlers saw the wilderness and thought "That's our backyard" – we just haven't got to the end of it yet' (in Brooks 2009: 4). As Lila puts it in the film, 'There's no border here. This is free trade between nations.'

The 'frozen river' of the title marks the borderline between Canada, Mohawk land and the USA, symbolically suggesting its uncertain status, sometimes fixed and frozen, other times fluid and mobile, while also reminding us of those 'living on thin ice' in surrounding communities. The film explores the contrastive tension between spatial expansiveness, represented here by nature and by the promise of a new life for immigrants still willing to risk everything to come to America, and the claustrophobic, cluttered world of everyday poverty and survival where the two women live.

In stressing the gradual friendship between Lila and Ray, finding common ground in their different struggles over family and work, they appear as parts in a terrible global network of trafficking across borders from the 'snakeheads' who bring desperate people from China or Pakistan, the Quebecois who sell them on, the Mohawks who transport them to the US. This is an ugly frontier America of bleak lives and economic hardship where the remnants of hope have become the 'Yankee Dollar' store where Ray works, the 'Live the Dream' slogan of the mobile home seller, or the 'Pioneer Motel' now the site of human commerce across borders. What survives though, as so often in the ethnic histories that constitute America, is human spirit, epitomised by Ray's willingness to confess her crimes so that Lila can be reunited with her son and become the surrogate mother to her own children. This hybrid 'new family' at the end of the film is a strange vision of hope and expediency, a mixed race group, last seen on a do-it-yourself merry-go-round made of recycled junk, toy horses and saddles ironically pointing backward to another more 'glorious', mythic frontier of Manifest Destiny and forward to a different, if troubled America where cultures come together to survive.

REFERENCES AND FURTHER READING

Adams, D.W. (1991) 'Schooling the Hopi: Federal Indian Policy Writ Small, 1887–1917' in L. Dinnerstein and K.T. Jackson (eds) *American Vistas: 1877 to the Present*, New York: Oxford University Press.

Adiche, C. Ngozi (2013) *Americanah*, London: Fourth Estate.

Alba, R. and Nee, V. (2003) *Remaking the American Mainstream: Assimilation and Contemporary Immigration*, Cambridge, MA: Harvard University Press.

Alexie, S. (2007) *Flight*, New York: Black Cat.

Altschuler, G. (1982) *Race, Ethnicity and Class in American Social Thought, 1865–1919*, Arlington Heights: Davidson.

Antin, M. (1912) *The Promised Land*, Boston: Houghton Mifflin.

Anzaldúa, G. (1987) *Borderlands/La Frontera*, San Francisco: Aunt Lute Books.

Archdeacon, T. (1983) *Becoming American: An Ethnic History*, London: Collier Macmillan.

Bakhtin, M. (1984) *Rabelais and His World*, Bloomington: Indiana University Press.

—— (1990) *The Dialogic Imagination*, Austin: University of Texas Press.

Bammer, A. (ed.) (1994) *Displacements: Cultural Identities in Question*, Bloomington: Indiana University Press.

Bhabha, H.K. (1994) *The Location of Culture*, London: Routledge.

Bodnar, J. (1985) *The Transplanted: A History of Immigrants in Urban America*, Bloomington: Indiana University Press.

Boyce-Davies, C. (1994) *Black Women, Writing and Identity*, London: Routledge.

Boyle, T.C. (1995) *Tortilla Curtain*, London: Bloomsbury.

Brooks, X. (2009) 'In the Hands of the Devil', *Guardian*, 17 July, p. 4.

Campbell, N. (2008) *The Rhizomatic West: Representing the American West in a Transnational, Global, Media Age*, Lincoln: University of Nebraska.

Churchill, W. (1998) *Fantasies of the Master Race: Literature, Cinema, and the Colonization of American Indians*, San Francisco: City Lights.

Clifford, J. (1988) *The Predicament of Culture*, Cambridge, MA: Harvard University Press.

—— (1997) *Routes: Travel and Translation in the Twentieth Century*, Cambridge, MA: Harvard University Press.

Crevecoeur, H. St J. de (1957) (first 1782) *Letters From an American Farmer*, New York: E.P. Dutton.

Deloria, P. and Salisbury, N. (eds) (2001) *Companion to Native American History*, Oxford: Blackwell.

Dinnerstein, L., Nichols, R.L. and Reimers, D.M. (eds) (1990) *Natives and Strangers, Ethnic Groups and the Building of America*, New York: Oxford University Press.

Dinnerstein, L. and Reimers, D.M. (1982) *Ethnic Americans: A History of Immigration and Assimilation*, New York: Harper.

Drinnon, R. (1990) *Facing West: The Metaphysics of Indian Hating and Empire Building*, New York: Schocken Books.

Dublin, T. (ed.) (1993) *Immigrant Voices: New Lives in America, 1773–1986*, Chicago: University of Illinois Press.

Erdrich, L. (1988) *Tracks*, New York: Harper Perennial.

Ewen, E. (1985) *Immigrant Women in the Land of Dollars: Life and Culture on the Lower East Side, 1890–1925*, New York: Monthly Review Press.

Ferraro, T.J. (1993) *Ethnic Passages: Literary Immigrants in Twentieth-Century America*, Chicago: University of Chicago Press.

Fischer, M.M.J. (1986) 'Ethnicity and the Post-Modern Arts of Memory' in J. Clifford and G. Marcus (eds) *Writing Culture*, Berkeley, CA: University of California Press.

Foner, E. (ed.) (1990) *The New American History*, Philadelphia: Temple University Press.

Foucault, M. (1977) *Discipline and Punish: The Birth of the Prison*, Harmondsworth: Penguin.

Fuchs, L. (1990) *The American Kaleidoscope, Race, Ethnicity and the Civic Culture*, Hanover: Wesleyan University Press.

Fukunaga, C. (2009) 'On the Making of *Sin Nombre*', Interview by Scott Macaulay, 20 March, Film in Focus, at http://www.focusfeatures.com/article/cary_fukunaga_on_the_making_of_sin_nombre?film=sin_nombre (accessed 15/9/2015).

Gabaccia D. (2002) *Immigration and American Diversity: A Social and Cultural History*, Oxford: Blackwell.

Gerdge J. and Ngai, M. (eds) (2011) *Major Problems in American Immigration History*, Florence, KY: Wadsworth.

Gillota, D. (2010) 'Negotiating Jewishness: *Curb Your Enthusiasm* and the Schlemiel Tradition', *Journal of Popular Film and Television*, 1930–6458, vol. 38, issue 4, 2010, pp. 152–61.

Gilroy, P. (1993) *The Black Atlantic*, London: Verso.

Gold, M. (1965) (first 1930) *Jews Without Money*, New York: Avon Books.

Goldberg, D.T. (ed.) (1995) *Multiculturalism: A Critical Reader*, Oxford: Blackwell.

Green, M. (2006) 'Curb Your Judaism', *The Jewish Daily Forward*, 3 March, at http://www.forward.com/articles/6641/ (accessed 12/10/2010).

Gunn Allen, P. (1992) *The Sacred Hoop*, Boston: Beacon.

Gutman, H. (1977) *Work, Culture and Society in Industrialising America*, Oxford: Blackwell.

Hall, S. (1995) 'New Cultures for Old' in D. Massey and P. Jess (eds) *A Place in the World?*, Oxford: Oxford University Press.

—— (1996) 'New Ethnicities' in D. Morley and K.-H. Chen (eds) *Stuart Hall: Critical Dialogues in Cultural Studies*, London: Routledge.

Handlin O. (1951) *The Uprooted*, New York: Grosset and Dunlap.

—— (1959) *Immigration as a Factor in American History*, Englewood Cliffs, NJ: Prentice Hall.

Higham J. (ed.) (1978) *Ethnic Leadership in America*, Baltimore: Johns Hopkins University Press.

—— (1981) *Strangers in the Land: Patterns of American Nativism, 1860–1925*, New York: Atheneum.

—— (1989) *Send These to Me: Immigrants in Urban America*, New York: Harper and Row.

Horowitz, D.A., Carroll, P.N., and Lee, D.D. (1990) *On The Edge: A New History of Twentieth Century America*, New York: West Publishing.

Huntington, S.P. (2004) *Who Are We? America's Great Debate*, London: Free Press.

Jacobson, D. (ed.) (1998) *The Immigration Reader*, Oxford: Blackwell.

Jacoby, T. (2004) *Reinventing the Melting Pot*, New York: Basic Books.

Jameson, F. (1984) 'Periodizing the Sixties' in S. Sayres *et al.* (eds) *The 60s Without Apology*, Minneapolis: University of Minnesota Press.

Jones, M. (1992) *American Immigration*, Chicago: University of Chicago Press.

Jordan, G. and Weedon, C. (1995) *Cultural Politics*, Oxford: Blackwell.

Josephy, A.M. (1985) *Red Power: The American Indians' Fight For Freedom*, Lincoln: University of Nebraska Press.

Kidwell, C.S. and Velie, A. (2005) *Native American Studies*, Edinburgh: Edinburgh University Press.

King, D. (2006) *The Liberty of Strangers: Making the American Nation*, Oxford: Oxford University Press.

King, R., Connell, J., and White, P. (eds) (1995) *Writing Across Worlds*, London: Routledge.

Kingston, M.H. (1981) *Woman Warrior*, London: Picador.

Klein, M. (1981) *Foreigners: The Making of American Literature, 1900–1940*, Chicago: University of Chicago Press.

Kollin, S. (2000) 'Dead Man, Dead West', *Arizona Quarterly* 56, Autumn, pp. 125–54.

Kraut, A. (1982) *The Huddled Masses: The Immigrant in American Society*, Arlington Heights: Harlan Davidson.

Kraut A., *et al.* (eds) (2007) *From Arrival to Incorporation: Migrants to the U.S. in a Global Era*, London: Eurospan.

Kroeber, K. (ed.) (1994) *American Indian Persistence and Resurgence*, Durham: Duke University Press.

Krupat, A. (1992) *Ethnocriticism: Ethnography, History, Literature*, Berkeley, CA: University of California Press.

Lauter, P. *et al.* (1994) *The Heath Anthology of American Literature*, vol. 2, Lexington: D.C. Heath.

Lowe, L. (1996) *Immigrant Acts: On Asian American Cultural Politics*, Durham: Duke University Press.

Luedtke, L. (ed.) (1992) *Making America*, Chapel Hill: University of North Carolina Press.

Malamud, B. (1975) (first 1957) *The Assistant*, Harmondsworth: Penguin.

Mann, A. (1979) 'The Melting Pot' in R. Bushman *et al.* (eds) *Uprooted Americans: Essays to Honour Oscar Handlin*, Boston: Little, Brown.

—— (1992) 'From Immigration to Acculturation' in L. Luedtke (ed.) *Making America*, Chapel Hill: University of North Carolina Press.

Mariani, P (ed.) (1991) *Critical Fictions*, Seattle: Bay Press.

Martinez, O. (2013) *The Beast*, London: Verso.

Martinez, R. (1992) *The Other Side: Fault Lines, Guerrilla Saints and the True Heart of Rock and Roll*, London: Verso.

—— (2001) *Crossing Over: A Mexican Family on the Migrant Trail*, New York: Picador.

—— (2004) *The New Americans*, New York: The New Press.

Massey, D. and Jess, P. (eds) (1995) *A Place in the World?*, Oxford: Oxford University Press.

Milner, C.A. (ed.) (1997) *Major Problems in the History of the American West*, Lexington: D.C. Heath.

Morales, E. (2003) *Living in Spanglish: The Search for Latino Identity in America*, New York: St. Martin's Press.

Morley, D. and Chen, K.-H. (eds) (1996) *Stuart Hall: Critical Dialogues in Cultural Studies*, London: Routledge.

Naficy, H. (1999) *Home, Exile, Homeland*, London: Routledge.

New York Times (2009), 'The Best Ways to Teach Young Newcomers' at http://roomfordebate.blogs.nytimes.com/2009/03/11/the-best-ways-to-teach-young-newcomers (accessed 4/11/2010).

Owens, L. (1992) *Other Destinies: Understanding the American Indian Novel*, Norman: University of Oklahoma Press.

Parrillo, V. (2005) *Strangers to These Shores: Race and Ethnic Relations in the United States*, Harlow: Pearson.

Pearce, S. *et al.* (eds) (2011) *Immigration and Women: Understanding the American Experience*, New York: New York University.

Pew Research Center: Hispanic Trends (2015) at http://www.pewhispanic.org/ (accessed 17/05/15).

Reed, U. (ed.) (2011) *A Companion to American Immigration*, Hoboken: Wiley-Blackwell.

Robertson, G. *et al.* (eds) (1994) *Travellers' Tales: Narratives of Home and Displacement*, London: Routledge.

Robertson, J.O. (1980) *American Myth, American Reality*, New York: Hill and Wang.

Roth, P. (1964) (first 1959) *Goodbye, Columbus*, London: Corgi.

—— (1977) *Reading Myself and Others*, London: Corgi.

—— (1987) (first 1986) *The Counterlife*, London: Jonathan Cape.

Said, E. (1994) (first 1993) *Culture and Imperialism*, London: Vintage.

Saldivar, J.D. (1997) *Border Matters: Remapping American Cultural Studies*, Berkeley: University of California Press.

Sarup, M. (1994) 'Home and Identity', in G. Robertson *et al.* (eds) *Travellers' Tales*, London: Routledge.

Sayres, S. *et al.* (eds) (1984) *The 60s Without Apology*, Minneapolis: University of Minnesota Press.

Shenton, J.P. (1990) 'Ethnicity and Immigration' in E. Foner (ed.) *The New American History*, Philadelphia: Temple University Press.

Silko, L.M. (1977) *Ceremony*, New York: Penguin.

—— (1981) *Storyteller*, New York: Arcade.

Singh, A. and Schmidt, P. (eds) (2000) *Postcolonial Theory and the United States: Race, Ethnicity and Literature*, Jackson: University of Mississippi Press.

Singh, A., Skerrett, J.T. and Hogan, R.E. (eds) (1994) *Memory, Narrative and Identity: New Essays in Ethnic American Literatures*, Boston: Northeastern University Press.

Singh, N.P. (2009) 'Rethinking Race and Nation' in J. Radway *et al.* (eds) *American Studies: An Anthology*, London: Wiley-Blackwell.

Sollors, W. (1986) *Beyond Ethnicity: Consent and Descent in American Literature*, New York: Oxford University Press.

Sollors, W. (ed.) (1989) *The Invention of Ethnicity*, New York: Oxford University Press.

Spickard P. (2007) *Almost All Aliens: Immigration, Race, and Colonialism in American History and Identity*, New York: Routledge.

Stam, R. and Shohat, E. (1994) *Unthinking Eurocentrism*, London: Routledge.

Steiner, D. (1987) *Of Thee We Sing: Immigrants and American History*, San Diego: Harcourt Brace Jovanovich.

Takaki, R. (1979) *Iron Cages: Race and Culture in Nineteenth Century America*, London: Athlone.

—— (1994) *From Different Shores: Perspectives on Race and Ethnicity*, New York: Oxford University Press.

Thernstrom, S. (ed.) (1980) *The Harvard Encyclopedia of American Ethnic Groups*, Cambridge, MA: Harvard University Press.

Tirman J. (2015) *Dream Chasers: Immigration and the American Backlash*, Cambridge, MA: MIT Press.

Todorov, T. (1987) *The Conquest of America*, translated by R. Howard, New York: Harper Perennial.

Vizenor, G. (ed.) (1993) *Narrative Chance: Postmodern Discourse on Native-American Indian Literatures*, Norman and London: University of Oklahoma Press.

—— (1994) *Manifest Manners: Postindian Warriors of Survivance*, Hanover and London: Wesleyan University Press.

—— (1998) *Fugitive Poses*, Lincoln: University of Nebraska Press.

Vizenor, G. and Lee, A. Robert (1999) *Postinidian Conversations*, Lincoln: University of Nebraska Press.

Wilkinson, R. (1992) *The American Social Character*, New York: HarperCollins.

Yans-McLaughlin, V. (ed.) (1990) *Immigration Reconsidered: History, Sociology, Politics*, New York: Oxford University Press.

Yezierska, A. (1975) (first 1925) *Bread Givers*, New York: Persea Books.
—— (1987) (first 1920) *Hungry Hearts and Other Stories*, London: Virago.
Young, R.J.C. (1995) *Colonial Desire: Hybridity in Theory, Culture and Race*, London: Routledge.
Zangwill, I. (1908) *The Melting Pot*, New York: Macmillan.

FOLLOW-UP WORK

There are a number of additional resources, assignments and other materials to be found on the website that accompanies this new edition: http://www. routledge.com/cw/campbell/

1   Analyse the film *Frozen River* and show how it represents a contemporary and complex view of US ethnicity.
2   Search the library and Internet for immigrant stories told by different groups travelling to the USA – for example sites like http://library.thinkquest.org/20619/Present.html.

 • Analyse their content for certain patterns and repeated ideas.
 • Are they similar or different to stories recounted in this chapter? Examine why.

3   Examine how the work of EITHER

 (a) Sherman Alexie – as novelist and scriptwriter (see Alexie's official website for a range of useful materials)
 OR
 (b) the artist Gerald McMaster (see http://www.ccca.ca/artists/artist_work.html?languagePref=en&link_id=2)
 has challenged stereotypes with humour and irony, and presented Native American life as complex and ambiguous.

4   Examine the arguments over illegal immigration in the contemporary US. What do they reveal about current debates over national identity?

Chapter 3

African Americans
'I don't sing other people's voices'
(Skip James)

OUT OF SLAVERY

This chapter discusses the issues surrounding African Americans and their struggle for self-definition within the United States of America, through an exploration of a range of assertive modes of expression. In a culture whose dominant historical voice has been white, there is a vital need for African Americans to present their lives, past and future, as of equal importance in the 'American story'. As Werner Sollors writes, 'For this reason, what is called "memory" . . . may become a form of counter-history that challenges the false generalizations in exclusionary "History"' (Sollors 1994: 8). African American 'voices' actively express 'memory', as Sollors refers to it, present 'counterhistories' to resist the tendency to exclude, and articulate African American identities to break the imposed 'silence' inherited from slavery and perpetuated in the written history and social frameworks of the USA.

This chapter will emphasise the dynamic quality of the contest between 'silence' and 'voice' in African American culture and how this process has been integral to a wider struggle for political power and authority in the United States. This concept of expressive 'voices' takes a variety of forms: slave songs, autobiography, fiction, political speech, rap music and film, but together they create an alternative mode of communication through which African Americans both state their own culture and assert their difference, while positioning themselves alongside the often more domi-nant voices of white mainstream culture. These 'repositories of individual memories, taken together, create a collective communal memory' (Fabre and O'Meally 1994: 9) that represents a black counter-historical identity. As cultural commentator Touré has written, there are 'Forty Million Ways to Be Black' and above all, 'there is no dogmatically narrow, authentic Blackness because the possibilities for Black Identity are infinite' (2011: 1, 5). This 'collective construction' of identity includes the vital oral culture from Africa sustained and developed through many expressive modes such as song and story. This was, according to Ralph Ellison, 'what we had in place of freedom' (Ellison 1972: 255), because 'since we were excluded from the cultural mainstream', it was 'only performative spaces we had left' (Hall 1992: 27). In the very first black newspaper, published in 1827, its editor, John B. Russwurm, wrote that for 'too long others have spoken for us' (Ripley 1993: 11) and so put into words the primary concern of African Americans, to speak for themselves and dispel the 'implication ... that only certain Americans can define what it means to be American – and the rest must simply fit in' (West 1993a: 256–7).

To resist definition and speak for oneself is fundamental to the assertion of identity, as bell hooks puts it:

> Moving from silence into speech is for the oppressed, the colonized, the exploited, and those who stand and struggle side by side, a gesture of defiance that heals, that makes new life, and new growth possible. It is that act of speech, of 'talking back' that is no mere gesture of empty words, that is the expression of moving from object to subject, that is the liberated voice.
>
> (Mariani 1991: 340)

In order to examine the ideas of expression, of 'voice' and 'talking back', in all their variety, we will begin with the heritage of slavery in African American culture and its impact on the positioning of people of colour within a framework of values dominated by the mainstream culture of whites who tended to assume the slave was 'a kind of *tabula rasa* upon which the white man could write what he chose' (Levine 1977: 52). The 'master-culture', like the master of the plantation who sought to rule the lives of the slaves, tried to impose its norms and values on the minority group which was derided because of its colour and because of an inherited European view of the African as barbaric, heathen and of a lower order.

> The African was ... defined as an inferior human being. The representation of the African as Other signified phenotypical and cultural characteristics as evidence of this inferiority and the attributed condition of Africans therefore constituted a measure of European progress and civilization.
>
> (Miles 1989: 30)

Defining the African within these limits of representation meant the power and status of the master were increased since, as the quotation suggests, the slave was an Other or a mirror against which whites measured themselves and their value systems; to assume the inferiority of the African thus bolstered the power of white civilisation. The master/slave system was grounded in denials: of black history, identity, humanity, community, knowledge and language. These were all seen as means through which slaves might assert themselves and ultimately question their condition in relation to the dominant group. To deny or erase these was, therefore, a method of control, a device to deny the slaves' identity and history and enforce an impression of being adrift, worthless and devoid of ancestry.

In 1965, during the struggles for civil rights, James Baldwin echoed much of this analysis when he wrote:

> It comes as a great shock to discover that the country which is your birthplace and to which you owe your life and identity has not, in its whole system of reality, evolved any place for you. . . . I was taught in American history books that Africa had no history and neither did I. I was a savage about whom the least said the better. . . . You belonged where white people put you.
>
> (Baldwin 1985: 404)

Baldwin's own writings, by 'challenging the white world's assumptions' (Baldwin 1963: 31), sought to construct a place in America for the black man and to defy being positioned:

> the truth about a black man, as a historical entity and as a human being, has been hidden from him, deliberately and cruelly; the power of the white world is threatened whenever a black man refuses to accept the white world's definitions.
>
> (Ibid.: 62)

The increased political demands for Black Power in the 1960s also followed this argument, claiming that any movement 'must speak in the tone of that community . . . [so that] black people are going to use the words they want to use – not just the words whites want to hear' (Carmichael 1967: 5).

RECOVERING BLACK HISTORY

As a consequence of the Civil Rights movement and the kind of 'refusal' that Baldwin and Carmichael refer to, historians working on slave culture began to question previously accepted versions of history by arguing that the denials, brutality and restraints of slavery did not crush the persistent desire in the slave community to maintain their own identities and their own sense of culture. The work of John W. Blassingame (1972), for example, demonstrated how through various cultural forms, such as songs, stories, dance and religion, the rigors of bondage did not crush the slave's creative energies [and] through these means the slave could view himself as an object, hold on to fantasies about his status, engender hope and patience, and at least use rebellious language when contemplating his life.

(Blassingame 1972: 59)

Slave expression encouraged 'group identification' and therefore argued 'that slaves were not solely dependent on the white man's cultural frames of reference for their ideas and values' (ibid.: 75–6).

Lawrence Levine developed these arguments, claiming that slaves 'were able to create an independent art form and a distinctive voice' (Levine 1977: 30) through vital channels of expression outside the control of the 'master-culture'. The importance of language and of preserving a 'voice' is a recurrent idea in such histories of slavery and its culture. They indicate an important stream of resistance which was conveyed through the arts of expression, especially song and storytelling. Through these means, communities of Africans could articulate and understand their place in the world outside of the immediate horrors and restrictions of slavery. The past was not dead in these oral arts, but very much present through the authority of the singer/teller or 'griot'. As Africans in America, slaves had 'alternatives open to them – alternatives that they themselves fashioned out of the fusion of their African heritage and their new religion' (ibid.: 35). Levine's emphasis on the actions of the slaves themselves is important because it underscores the essential quality of self-definition associated with these creative acts. In them and through them, the self is asserted in a world of constant denial in which the 'definitions belong to the definers, not the defined' (Morrison 1987a: 190).

Levine's idea of 'fusion' establishes a sense of new identity for African Americans, who as slaves still maintained an effective and life-affirming set of values through the power of the voice and its willingness to enter into a dialogue with the dominant culture's own expressions. Levine is clearly seeing in these early examples a pattern in history towards integration wherein black and white cultures could find some point of harmonious contact. In this respect Levine's history is in keeping with a particular set of arguments and interpretations of African American life associated with the stance of Martin Luther King in the Civil Rights movement. The liberal position suggested by Levine is of a distinct and valid 'black culture and consciousness' which 'interacted with a larger society that deeply affected it but to which it did not completely succumb' (Levine 1977: 297).

In contrast to the white historian's liberal perspective offered by Levine, Sterling Stuckey's work argues that the roots of black 'nationalist consciousness' (1987: 30) can be found in slave culture. It was there that different tribes were forced together in slavery into shared experiences through which 'the principal forms of cultural expression [were] essentially the same' helping to mould a 'oneness of black culture' (ibid.: 82, 83).

In all these versions of slavery, the idea of resistance and defiance of the master-culture is paramount and is always connected to the ability of the slaves to hold on to the ancestral past through the internal rituals, songs and stories of the group. Recent scholarship has suggested even more complex and ambiguous relationships between the slave and the master. Slave performance was encouraged by masters as an 'exotic presence' (Abrahams 1992: xvii), but slaves themselves used it as a means of maintaining community and ancient beliefs. Abrahams argues for 'dynamic, expressive interrelations of the two cultures living side by side' (ibid.), acknowledging the persistence of African culture in the expressive, but subversive, lives of slaves.

This passing on is expressed well in two brief fictional examples. In Ellison's *Invisible Man* (1952) Brother Tarp passes on a link from a slave's leg chain, saying 'it's got a heap of signifying wrapped up in it and it might help you to remember what we're really fighting against' (Ellison 1952: 313). An object can voice history and memory, tell a vital story as part of the struggle. Second, in Alice Walker's *Meridian*, the story of Louvinie, the storyteller, is used as a reminder of both the importance of passing on memories, and also of the challenge this poses to white society which fears the rewriting of 'its' versions of history. Her tongue 'was clipped out at the root' (Walker 1976: 33) as a punishment for telling her tales, thus imposing silence and obedience once again.

Levine tells of the ways slaves continued these rituals of telling and passing on despite the ever-watchful eyes of the overseers, and captures the two sides of the 'fearful paradox' (Baldwin 1963: 71). He describes how slaves would contain the sounds of their shouts, songs and rituals by various means, for example, by chanting into a large kettle which muffled their voices so they would not be found out. He comments, 'they could shout and sing all they wanted to and the noise would not go outside' (Levine 1977: 42). The paradox is surely in the slaves' desire to express themselves and yet at the same time their inability to move 'outside', into a genuine, public point of contact with the world beyond the plantation. This encapsulates an important aspect of the struggle for voice and expression in black life. How could the creative spirit, the assertion of a valid, black history, be extended rather than continually stifled by the presence of the more dominant and powerful voice of the white master-culture?

One answer to this had to be the increasing presence of African Americans in the public sphere, through the pre-Civil War abolitionist movement, the ending of slavery and the opportunities for citizenship, limited as they were, and then the growth of movements for civil rights and social justice in the twentieth century. All of these, in different ways, reflected determined efforts by African Americans to take their 'voice' outside, and engage directly with the authorised and official culture. Indeed, the rewriting of black history in the second half of the twentieth century, through its use of sources such as slave testimony and narratives, and its determination to recover a sense of autonomy and identity in African American culture may be seen as part of the same process. One key starting point here which serves to illustrate the need 'to voice or speak the African into existence in Western letters' (Gates 1985: 403) is *The Narrative of the Life of Frederick Douglass, An American Slave Written by Himself* (written in 1845). Unlike Levine's account of the muffling of the voice, Douglass had to find ways out of the imposed silence of slavery in order to tell the world 'outside' of its horrors. In this respect *The Narrative* is a kind of prototype for so many African American literary forms as it charts the journey from slavery by linking it with the assertion and command of language. For Douglass the process of liberation is intimately connected with the ability to express and define oneself in society. Consider, for example, how the narrative begins:

> I have no accurate knowledge of my age, never having seen any authentic record containing it. . . . slaves know as little of their age as horses know of theirs, and it is the wish of most masters . . . to keep their slaves thus ignorant.
>
> (Douglass 1982: 47)

What does this suggest of Douglass's condition under slavery? He goes on in the next few lines to answer this question using negatives such as 'I could not tell . . . deprived . . . not allowed . . . I know nothing; the means of knowing was withheld from me' (ibid.: 47–8). The 'want of information' (ibid.: 47) oppresses him, dehumanises him to the level below a horse by depriving him of basic human facts of identity. He is denied an immediate history, but recognises the importance of finding a means of articulating as a source of self-assertion. It is through songs that Douglass is first stirred:

> They told a tale of woe which was then altogether beyond my feeble comprehension . . . they breathed the complaint of souls boiling with the bitterest anguish. . . . The songs of the slave represent the sorrows of his heart; and he is relieved by them, only as an aching heart is relieved by its tears.
>
> (ibid.: 57–8)

Years later the African American intellectual W.E.B. Du Bois wrote of also being 'stirred' (Du Bois 1965: 378) by the 'sorrow songs' because they were 'full of the voices of the past' and 'the singular spiritual heritage' (ibid.) which together formed 'unvoiced longing toward a truer world of misty wanderings and hidden ways' (ibid.: 380). Writing in 1903, Du Bois saw the 'Negro' as part of a world that yielded him 'no self-consciousness, but only lets him see himself through the revelation of the other world' (ibid.: 214–15). This became Du Bois's famous definition of 'double-consciousness' for the African American, 'always looking at the world through the eyes of others, of measuring one's soul by the tape of a world that looks on in amused contempt and pity' (ibid.: 215). Du Bois wrote of the 'twoness – an American, a Negro; two souls, two thoughts, two unreconciled strivings; two warring ideals in one dark body, whose dogged strength alone keeps it from being torn asunder' (ibid.).

Prompted by slave songs, Douglass and later Du Bois felt the call to resist the *prescribed* world of the master-culture, by which we mean a world already set out, as if literally 'written' for the African American, with its denials, its imposed public silences and its cruel disciplinary system. As Douglass writes, 'To all these complaints, no matter how unjust, the slave must answer never a word. . . . When [the master] spoke, a slave must stand, listen, and tremble' (Douglass 1982: 61).

In another slave narrative, *Incidents in the Life of a Slave Girl* (1861), the female slave–author, Harriet Jacobs, uses almost identical words to identify her master's control over speech and movement: 'I was obliged to stand and listen to such language as he saw fit to address to me' (Gates 1987: 364). Echoing Levine's stifling of the voice, Douglass writes that there evolved a 'maxim' for slaves defined by these boundaries: 'a still tongue makes a wise head. They suppress the truth rather than take the consequences of telling it, and in so doing prove themselves members of the human family' (Douglass 1982: 62). It was as if the only way to be connected to the 'human family' was to 'suppress' speech and expression, and follow the lead of the master who dictated and 'authored' the terms of life in a system of 'no answering back' (ibid.: 65). Douglass states clearly the relationship of expression to freedom: 'What he most dreaded, I most desired. . . . That which to him was a great evil, to be carefully shunned, was to me a great good, to be diligently sought' (ibid.: 79). To have knowledge, to read, write and express oneself was to step outside the master's boundaries and away from the dictated and defined world he established and controlled for the slave. Indeed, any effort to 'talk back' was a blow against a system that denied the African American 'the full, complex ambiguity of the human' and preferred to present the image of the 'oversimplified clown, a beast, or an angel' (Ellison 1972: 26). W.E.B. Du Bois saw the journey to knowledge and expression as essential for the development of a strong culture.

> In those somber forests of his striving his own soul rose before him, and he saw himself – darkly as through a veil; and yet he saw in

himself some faint revelation of his power, of his mission. He began to have a dim feeling that, to attain his place in the world, he must be himself, and not another. For the first time he sought to analyze the burden he bore upon his back.

(Du Bois 1965: 218)

Du Bois's sense of the veil that must be seen through is a valuable image, for it suggests the difficulty of asserting a self in a world that continually seeks to place and determine what you are and can be by prescribing your history and denying you any opportunity to express your thoughts or feelings. Later, James Baldwin wrote, 'The details and symbols of your life have been deliberately constructed to make you believe what white people say about you. . . . Please try to be clear . . . about the reality which lies behind the words' (Baldwin 1963: 16).

In a similar vein, Houston Baker has written that

blacks lay veiled in a shroud of silence, invisible not because they had no face, but rather because they had no voice. Voice, after all, presupposes face. . . . Without a voice, the African is absent, or defaced, from history.

(Baker 1987: 104)

The slave narrative was an essential expressive effort to break this silence, for as Baker adds, 'slaves could inscribe their selves only in language' (ibid.: 105). Expression, through speech, song and, later, writing was a means of resistance, an 'act of creating a public, historical self' (ibid.: 108) and to enable the radical shift of the African American from prescription to inscription and from clownish representation and over-simplification to complex, human ambiguity. The terms are important for they suggest the very politics of the process towards authority in African American culture as prefigured in the author-ing of their own life stories and history. This struggle for voice and identity within African American life can be linked to the postcolonial movements of Africa itself where similar arguments have been made about the need to maintain and develop the languages of resistance. As Ngugi wa Thiong'o has written, 'Values are the basis of a people's identity, their sense of particularity as members of the human race. All this is carried by language. Language as culture is the collective memory bank of a people's experience in history' (Williams and Chrisman 1994: 441). Ralph Ellison, whose novel *Invisible Man* is concerned with the need to break the silence and invisibility that surrounded black life, expressed this idea with characteristic sharpness:

For history records the pattern of men's lives, they say. . . . All things . . . are duly recorded – all things of importance that is. But not quite,

for actually it is only the known, the seen, the heard and only those
events that the recorder regards as Important that are put down, those
lies his keepers keep their power by.

(Ellison 1952: 353)

Slave narratives, like those of Douglass and Jacobs, and later 'autobiographical criticism', as bell hooks has termed it, are concerned with
'sharing the contradictions of our lives, [to] help each other learn how to
grapple with contradictions as part of the process of becoming a critical
thinker, a radical subject' (hooks 1994a: 186). These forms of expression
characteristically are about the transformation of the self from the object
of someone else's control and authority, to the possibility of self-definition
and being one's own subject. As hooks writes, quoting Michelle Cliff, it
is the 'work against the odds to claim the I' (ibid.: 177) from those who
would contain, define and limit black experience and continue to deny
them the full opportunity within the United States.

IMAGINATIVE CULTURAL RETRIEVAL

African American expression provided a means of 'claiming the I'
through telling personal and cultural histories that together formed a vital
strand of black experience not given space in traditional white history
books. As Malcolm X stated in his *Autobiography*, at school when they came
to the section on Negro history, 'it was exactly one paragraph long' and
told how the 'slaves . . . were lazy and dumb and shiftless' (Malcolm X
1985: 110). As a response to the dominant culture's control of language,
African American culture took up the call to re-establish its own history
as a means of political and social assertion, through a diverse 'telling',
using a variety of avenues through which to express its own vision and
to tell its own story rather than the 'whitened' version that Malcolm X
knew. As one person said, 'while you whites have schools and books for
teaching your children, we tell stories, for stories are our books' (Levine
1977: 90). The use of memory has become central to this process for it
allows the inclusion of stories excluded or denigrated or erased from the
versions of white history. African myths, folklore, the communal stories
and tales of slavery and freedom could be passed on orally, as they always
had been, through alternative channels of communication within the black
community. If the books, media and other techniques of the mainstream
dominant culture denied space and access to these stories then other ways
had to be found to express the continuities of black life.

The postcolonial critic Edward Said argued that, 'The power to narrate,
or to block other narratives from forming and emerging, is very important
to culture and imperialism, and constitutes one of the main connections
between them' (Said 1994: xiii). In a world where such power dictates,

authorises and controls what can be said, done and thought, there is a need to intervene in the process and 'un-block' the imperialist grip on a single version, and to 'progress beyond a number of assumptions that have been accepted uncritically for too long' (Levine 1977: 444). For bell hooks this means habits of being that were a part of traditional black folk experience that 'we can re-enact, rituals of belonging . . . [the] sharing of stories that taught history, family genealogy, and the facts about the African American past' (hooks 1991: 39). In this type of alternative education 'memory [is] . . . a way of knowing and learning from the past' (ibid.: 40) so that one might be able 'to accept one's past – one's history – [and] learn . . . how to use it' (Baldwin 1963: 71) in a positive, assertive way.

George Lipsitz calls this 'counter-memory', which he explains as 'not just a rejection of history, but a reconstitution of it' (Lipsitz 1990: 227),

> a way of remembering and forgetting that starts with the local, the immediate, and the personal. Unlike historical narratives that begin with the totality of human existence and then locate specific actions and events within that totality, counter-memory starts with the particular and then builds . . . [it] looks to the past for hidden histories excluded from dominant narratives . . . [and] forces revision . . . by supplying new perspectives.
>
> (ibid.: 213)

In writing, it is like 'literary archaeology' visiting the 'site to see what remains were left behind and to reconstruct the world that these remains imply' (Morrison 1987b: 112) in order to provide a sense of racial continuity in a culture structured on its denial.

A very similar and related project is Julie Dash's *Daughters of the Dust* (1991), a film set at the turn of the century in the South Carolina islands dealing with a Gullah family of slave descendants who have retained their ancestral connections to Africa and yet are being pulled into the world of the 'mainland' with all its new pressures and demands. The film is about storytelling and the importance of passing on the memories of the people as a mode of cultural anchorage. To this end, Dash is concerned with the role of the 'griot' or storyteller who 'will recount the family's history, with the stories going off at a tangent, weaving in and out' (Dash quoted on Argus/BFI video sleeve, 1993). This is how she structures her film too, with many voices in the text, from the past, the future and the present, echoing the work of Walker and Morrison, to whom Dash has paid homage as her inspiration; 'they made me whole' (ibid.) she says, and their techniques were transposed into her own film-making. At a key point in the film, the sense of struggle and the threat of the loss of the past and its traditions are emphasised through the ideas 'recollection', stories and their importance. Nana, the great-grandmother, tells the leaving Eli Peazant: 'It's up to the living to keep in touch with the dead. . . . Respect your elders, respect your family, respect your ancestors. . . . Call on your ancestors Eli, let them guide. . . . Never forget who we is and how far we done come this far.' It is the duty of each generation to connect with its past, to remember the 'wisdom', for it provides a framework of belief and history that is not that imposed by white culture. 'There's a time, a recollection, something somebody remembers, we carry these memories inside of we. . . . I'm trying to give you something to take along with you, along with all your great big dreams.' Dash's film dramatises the process of recovery and invites us to 'undergo a triple process of recollecting the disremembered past, recognizing and reappraising cultural icons and codes, and recentering and revalidating the self' so that African Americans 'consider our positions and our power in the USA' (Bambara 1993: 125).

Dash, therefore, has continued and updated the work of Blassingame, Stuckey, Genovese and others who have reclaimed invaluable aspects of previously buried histories for black culture and expression, and paralleled imaginative writing's efforts to go further. The novels of Toni Morrison, in particular, demonstrate the imaginative reconstruction of black history, using fiction to tell 'a whole unrecorded history' (Ellison 1952: 379). As Michelle Wallace has written:

> we must choose to recount and recollect the negativity, the discount, the loss. In the process, we may, ultimately make a new kind of history that first recalls how its own disciplinary discourse was made in brutality and exclusion, and second, a history that seeks as its starting point the heterogeneity of the present.
>
> (Mariani 1991: 139)

Toni Morrison's fiction, like Dash's film, aims 'to bear witness to a history that is unrecorded, untaught, in mainstream education, and to enlighten our people' (Wisker 1993: 80) through the telling of stories often ignored in conventional sources. Echoing Du Bois, she longs 'to rip that veil drawn over proceedings too terrible to relate' (Morrison 1987b: 109–10). She wishes 'to implement the stories that I heard' so as to 'fill in the blanks that the slave narratives left' and to reposition the African American into 'the discourse that proceeded without us' (Morrison 1987b: 111–12). Like Wallace, she writes of a 'reconstruction of a world . . . [and] exploration of an interior life that was not written and to the revelation of a kind of truth' (ibid.: 115). Through her form of counter-memory, Morrison's fiction aims to reposition African Americans in American life by re-examining their history. In her novel *The Bluest Eye* (1970), she writes:

Being a minority in both caste and class, we moved about anyway on the hem of life, struggling to consolidate our weaknesses and hang on, or creep singly up to the major folds of the garment. Our peripheral existence, however, was something we learned to deal with.

(Morrison 1970: 11)

Morrison combats marginalisation through the reconstructive process of telling African American history to remind her audience, both black and white, of the restrictions imposed on the opportunities of young blacks, as in this section from *The Bluest Eye*:

They go to land-grant colleges, normal schools, and learn the white man's work with refinement: home economics to prepare his food; teacher education to instruct black children in obedience; music to soothe the weary master and entertain his blunted soul. Here they learn . . . how to behave. . . . In short, how to get rid of funkiness. The dreadful funkiness of passion, the funkiness of nature, the funkiness of the wide range of human emotions.

(Ibid.: 64)

Reminiscent of Jacobs and Douglass, this passage posits 'funkiness' as a version of self-expression that needs to find an outlet, for 'Funk is really nothing more than the intrusion of the past in the present' (Gates 1984: 280). What Morrison calls eruptions of funk are the threads of an alternative narrative of African American life that refuse to be veiled behind the master-narrative. Indeed, this is the premise of the novel *Beloved*, wherein the past returns to the present in the form of a family ghost in order to bring others to certain recognitions about their past lives and their racial history.

The community of women is central to this vision of a 'new history', for they pass it on to their children. As bell hooks writes,

We could not learn to love or respect ourselves in the culture of white supremacy, on the outside; it was there on the inside, in that 'homeplace', most often created and kept by black women, that we had the opportunity to grow and develop, to nurture our spirits.

(hooks 1991: 42)

The 'ghost' of the past, Beloved, enters into one such 'homeplace' in Morrison's novel of the same name, and forces the group of women to uncover and discuss their lives. This force of counter-memory surges into the lives of Sethe and Denver to strengthen them against the repressive, dominant power of 'schoolteacher', the overseer on the plantation.

He literally 'writes' the existence of the slaves by charting and recording them in his 'book', with their 'characteristics' divided into 'animal' and 'human', their bodies measured in pseudo-scientific ways, aimed at dehumanisation as a means of social control. Under the gaze of the master who writes only his version of the narrative into his 'notebook' and thereby excludes all other stories, Sethe is contained by his words. 'First his shotgun, then his thoughts, for schoolteacher didn't take advice from Negroes. The information they offered he called backtalk and developed a variety of corrections (which he recorded in his notebook) to reeducate them' (Morrison 1987a: 220). What is 'recorded' by the schoolteacher is indicative of the single, authorised narrative of black history that must be countered by 'funkiness', the 'homeplace' and the other expressions to which the community has access. It is 'voice', 'backtalk' or 'talking back' that provides the resistance to the schoolteacher's master-culture. In the novel, it is through the stories that Denver is, at first, reluctant to hear from her mother, grandmother, Paul D and Beloved that 'backtalk' emerges as reconstructed history. Only through these is Denver released into the world and able to re-engage with the black community in a way that further aids her healing. The novel suggests that remembering is a way forward for the future (Denver), as Baby Suggs, her grandmother, earlier instructs her to 'Know it, and go on out of the yard. Go on' (ibid.: 244). She must listen to her ancestral voice, not so she can dwell in past horrors, but so that she can both know who she is and use this to move forward with greater certainty. The growth of Denver from the sheltered and protected daughter of Sethe to her final position in the novel is shown when Paul D says:

> 'Well, if you want my opinion –'
> 'I don't', she said. 'I have my own'.
> 'You grown', he said.
>
> (Ibid.: 267)

Denver's assertion of independent thought and opinion shows she has indeed 'grown', both from childhood and also into a new knowledge of her self within a community which comes together at the end of the novel to exorcise the ghost of Beloved, a community described as 'voices of women [that] searched for the right combination, the key, the code, the sound that broke the back of words. Building voice upon voice until they found it' (ibid.: 261).

Denver's process is echoed in the words at the novel's end: 'she gather them and give them back to me in all the right order' (ibid.: 272–3), for her growth has depended upon the 'pieces I am' being told and brought out into the open, rather than evaded or hidden from view. Out of the pieces of the (hi)story, memory and wisdom, Denver reconstructs a self which is not reliant upon the schoolteacher's 'story', or indeed even Paul D's, but comes out of her 'familial past' in order to provide her with 'some kind of tomorrow' (ibid.: 273). Denver's going out of the yard is the step into the future based on 'knowing' rather than ignorance, and is her effort to fill 'the space of not knowing' as a positive gesture of resistance and reconstruction of self and community.

LINKS IN THE CHAIN: MUSIC AND SPEECH

If contemporary fiction could play a part in the process of self-definition and the growing confidence of African Americans in the public sphere, then as important, if not more so, has been the role of music. We have already seen that songs played an important part in the preservation of African culture for slaves, and that tradition, like so many others, was passed on as musical forms developed. As Lawrence Levine has written:

> Black secular song, along with other forms of oral tradition, allowed them to express themselves communally and individually, to derive pleasure, to perpetuate traditions, to keep values from eroding, and to begin to create new expressive moods . . . which continued a rich internal life.
>
> (Levine 1977: 297)

The potential of music and language to challenge white power is characterised by this section from Ishmael Reed's *Mumbo Jumbo*:

> Son, these niggers writing. Profaning our sacred words. Taking them from us and beating them on the anvil of Boogie-Woogie, putting their black hands on them so that they shine like burnished amulets. Taking our words, son, these filthy niggers and using them.
>
> (Reed 1972: 130)

To acquire a language seen only as 'white' and seek to 'use' it, and indeed prove that it can be used with power and authority, was a threat to the established order of things. Music had long provided a source of just such powerful expression within the black community. As Brian Ward has commented, 'the most popular black musical styles and artists achieved their popularity precisely because they have dramatized and expressed, but also helped to shape and define, a succession of black consciousnesses' (Ward 1998: 15).

One can see this in Ralph Ellison's description of jazz musicians' 'delicate balance . . . between strong individual personality and the group' which, he goes on to write, had as its goal the desire to express an affirmative way of life through its musical tradition and that this tradition insisted that each artist achieve his creativity within its frame. He must learn the best of the past, and add to it his personal vision.

(Ellison 1972: 189)

Jazz, for Ellison, was 'a definition of . . . identity: as individual, as member of the collectivity and as a link in the chain of tradition' (ibid.: 234) because it permitted full creative expression of the self, in response to the energy of the group, with both relating to a long, and varied tradition of musical forms of articulation. In *Invisible Man* Louis Armstrong's music reveals 'unheard sounds . . . and each melodic line existed of itself, stood out clearly from all the rest, said its piece, and waited patiently for the other voices to speak' (ibid.: 11). And these voices open a journey into an often hidden African American past, with

an old woman singing a spiritual . . . a beautiful girl . . . pleading in a voice like my mother's as she stood before a group of slave owners who bid for her naked body . . . I heard someone shout: 'Brothers and sisters, my text for this morning is the "Blackness of Blackness".'

(Ibid.: 13)

In this, Ellison suggests the capacity of music to carry 'a whole unrecorded history' (ibid.: 379) and to offer the listener and the performer access to emotions and ideas little expressed in the mainstream dominant culture.

August Wilson's play *Ma Rainey's Black Bottom* (1985) makes a similar claim about the blues in a speech given by Ma Rainey, a real-life blues singer from the 1920s:

White folks don't understand about the blues. They hear it come out, but they don't know how it got there. They don't understand that's life's way of talking. You don't sing to feel better. You sing 'cause that's a way of understanding life. . . . This be an empty world without the blues. I take that emptiness and try to fill it up with something.

(Wilson 1985: 194–5)

Black music, in various forms, is about 'talking', 'understanding' and 'filling up' life, for it channels emotions and responses into an affirmative mode of expression. Blues was 'a way of solidifying community and commenting on the social fabric of Black life in America' (Hill Collins 1990: 99)) and as bluesman Skip James put it, refused 'to sing other people's voices' (in Sackheim 1993: 56). A generation later, the rise of soul music developed a sense of 'personal expression and communal celebration' as it accompanied the emergence of the struggle for racial justice in both the north and the south (Ward 1998: 16). Performers like Sam Cooke and

Aretha Franklin took the liberating vision of gospel, and linked it to dreams of social and personal transformation. A good institutional example here was the establishment of the Tamla Motown label by Berry Gordy in Detroit in 1960. Although not overtly political, the fact of a successful black enterprise and the impact of black performers echoed the changes being made politically. Within the wider context of the Civil Rights movement, Martha and the Vandellas' song 'Dancing in the Street' was a call to emancipation: 'Callin' out around the world, are you ready for a brand new beat?' Motown's merging of gospel traditions such as tambourines, clapping, call and response, and advisory lyrics, with the interest in a greater freedom of expression, provided a base for Motown and other soul singers to contribute to the voicing of black culture (Gillett 1983: 211–13). As James Brown sang, 'Say it Loud (I'm Black and I'm Proud)'.

The African American traditions of song, storytelling and preaching found a precise outlet in the politics of the Civil Rights movement and beyond. With the increased importance of the mass meeting, often directed from local churches, expression was a vital component of the political process. The meetings were 'events/places where participants could express fear as well as resolution, anger as well as understanding, make plans and formulate strategies . . . expression became a way of channelling fear and anger into effective collective action' (King 1988: 10). On such occasions expression found a variety of avenues, as it always had in black life: preaching, testifying, passing on stories of the movement and performing 'freedom songs', all of which helped to define the experience of participation in the movement. Richard King calls these expressions 'the new language of public action' (ibid.: 11).

This can also be seen in the oratory of Martin Luther King, who built his speeches upon a diverse background of biblical, folk and slave stories to weave a persuasive, rhythmic song-like pattern which asserted the individual power of the voice, but included the audience in the spectacle of the occasion. This was, as Levine wrote of slave songs and Ellison of jazz, both personal and political, individual and collective. Instead of 'a junkheap of isolated voices, unrelated experiences, and forgettable characters', preachers formed a chain of connections, creating a 'choir of voices', the many in one (Miller 1992: 131, 144). In King's speeches there is a strong attention to 'voice merging', or the bringing together of diverse themes into a harmonious whole, his performance style paralleling the politics of integration for which he stood. Drawing upon concepts which were a part of white American mythology, such as the American Dream, he merged them with a rich black tradition in a manner which sought to integrate the redemption of the oppressor with the aspirations of the oppressed. His most famous speech, 'I Have a Dream' (1963), creates just such a new, inclusive voice for America that unites around Abraham Lincoln – under whose memorial the speech was given – the biblical prophecies of Isaiah and Amos, 'justice rolls down like waters . . .', and the Negro spiritual, 'Free at Last', alongside references to the Declaration of Independence and the alternative national anthem, 'My Country, 'Tis of Thee'.

Politics continued to discover the power of language in other ways. For example, Malcolm X, during his time in prison, saw the relationship between self-expression and liberation, beginning with reading and moving on to the power of speech: 'in the prison, speaking to a crowd, was as exhilarating to me as the discovery of knowledge through reading had been' (Malcolm X 1985: 280). Malcolm X's use of language could be more direct than the 'voice-merging' style of King, and used none of the preaching techniques that King had learned in the seminary. Malcolm's voice comes out of the poverty of the ghetto where he 'learned early that crying out in protest could accomplish things' (ibid.: 86) and he speaks in a direct and forceful manner; more James Brown than Motown:

> I'm speaking as a victim of this American system. . . . I don't see any American dream; I see an American nightmare. These 22 million victims are waking up. Their eyes are coming open. They're beginning to see what they used to only look at.
>
> (Malcolm X in Lauter *et al.* 1994: 2497)

The tone and choice of words show clearly Malcolm's different message but still the vital importance of the voice as the means of communication within the community. For Malcolm X, the voice must carry the 'raw, naked truth . . . to clear the air of the racial mirages, cliches and lies' (Malcolm X 1985: 379). He goes on in the same speech to call for 'a new interpretation' of the Civil Rights movement, for 'black nationalism' to 'enable us to come into it, take part in it', rather than wait for others to give you 'what's already yours' (Lauter *et al.* 1994: 2500–1). As Eldridge Cleaver later wrote, Malcolm X 'articulated . . . aspirations better than any other man of our time . . . he had continued to give voice to the mute ambitions in the black man's soul' (Cleaver 1968: 47). Malcolm X's autobiography explains his own, personal journey towards self-determination, but like so much black autobiography, it also relates to the wider condition of the community's move to political equality. The individual voice must be found so that it can speak out with confidence and self-respect to the group, to 'build up the black race's ability to do for itself' (Malcolm X 1985: 382), within the context provided by the stories and heritage of a meaningful past. In this way the individual life can become a 'testimony of some social value' (ibid.: 497) for it becomes a thread within the larger fabric of black life.

Thus, the push for self-definition, 'the claiming of the I', was only a stage in the political process, which aimed at transforming the 'I' to a 'We': 'We must move past always focusing on the "personal self" because there's a larger self. There's a "self" of black people' (Tate 1983: 134). Alice Walker, who was active in the Civil Rights movement, captures these sentiments in her novel *Meridian* (1976), which shows the struggle of Meridian Hill for self-definition, both as woman and African American, in a white, male-dominated society, while at the same time revealing her growing awareness of the importance of community to the wider struggle. Walker echoes the words of Stokely Carmichael, the Black Power leader, who wrote of the need to 'create in the community an aroused and continuing black consciousness that will provide the basis for political strength' (Carmichael 1967: 6). Walker suggests this in a scene at the end of the novel when Meridian goes to church to hear a politicised preacher, 'deliberately imitating King . . . consciously keeping the voice alive . . . not his own voice at all, but rather the voice of millions who could no longer speak' (Walker 1976: 200). Walker sees the strands of tradition come together: the oral inspiration, the retelling of black history and the empowerment of the group through vital expressivity: 'Focusing on connection rather than separation, transforming silence into speech, giving back power to the culturally disenfranchised, black women writers affirm the wholeness and endurance of a vision that, once articulated, can be shared' (Pryse and Spillers 1985: 5). This 'sharing' is demonstrated in the communality of the gathering at the end of the novel:

> let us weave your story and your son's life and death into what we already know – into songs, the sermons, the 'brother and sister' – . . . 'the church' (and Meridian knew they did not just mean simply 'church' as in Baptist, Methodist or whatnot, but rather communal spirit, togetherness, righteous convergence) . . . 'the kind of ritual you share with us, these are the ways to transformation that we know'. . . . For she understood, finally, that the respect she owed her life was to continue, against whatever obstacles, to live it. . . . And that this existence extended beyond herself to those around her because, in fact, the years in America had created them One Life.
>
> (Walker 1976: 204)

Meridian's revelation connects so many of the strands of black resistance, and emphasises the power of the voice, what she calls the 'song of the people, transformed by the experience of each generation' as the means 'that holds them together' (ibid.: 205) as part of a broad unified view of black life within America, rather than separate from it. Her politics are closer to those of Martin Luther King and the integrationists than to the more extreme views of the Black Muslims who called for separation, or Black Power activists who felt the Civil Rights movement's 'tone of voice was adapted to an audience of liberal whites' (Carmichael 1967: 5).

However, in the later stage of the career of Malcolm X, for so long a voice associated with black nationalism and the Muslims, one sees emerging a position quite close to that expressed in Walker's novel. It is a new universalism, 'committed to survival and wholeness of entire people, male and female' (Walker 1984: n.p.), a call for human rights, not dissimilar from that expressed by Stokely Carmichael, who wrote in 1966, 'We are just going to work, in the way we see fit, and on our goals we define, not for civil rights but for all human rights' (Carmichael 1967: 8). Malcolm X states his goal as, 'truth, no matter who tells it. I'm for justice, no matter who it's for or against. I'm a human being first and foremost, and as such I'm for whoever and whatever benefits humanity as a *whole*' (Malcolm X 1985: 483). There is less talk of separatism and more about joint responsibility between races since 'with equal rights there had to be a bearing of equal responsibilities' (ibid.: 494). By the end of his autobiography, Malcolm X, echoing King, expresses his hopes in terms of the specific contribution he had made to the struggle for human rights in America.

> Sometimes, I have dared to dream to myself that one day, history may even say that my voice – which disturbed the white man's smugness, and his arrogance, and his complacency – that my voice helped to save America from a grave, possibly even a fatal catastrophe.
>
> (Ibid.: 496)

Malcolm X's tone, as ever, is far more direct and assertive in its condemnation of white culture than is King's, but his use of the 'dream' and his recognition that it is his 'voice' that carries his authority place the two together in the struggle for 'what America must become' (Baldwin 1963: 17). It also recognises the interrelatedness of the two cultures, black and white, and echoes Paul Gilroy's work examining how 'double consciousness' involves precisely this interrelationship between black and white cultures within and without America, creating a hybrid sense of identity. The Afrocentric 'roots' were necessarily crossed by the many 'routes' travelled by Africans in their diasporic relations with the world (Gilroy 1993).

NEW BLACK VOICES: RAP

In contemporary American culture, hip hop, in its diverse forms, suggests another medium in which the drive for self-expression can be seen in African American life. Despite the struggles and achievements of those figures and movements discussed in this chapter, the continuing search for fresh ways to articulate social criticism and personal and communal dreams has continued to mark African Americans' efforts to assert identity

in the wider context of mainstream society. Rap music's emergence in the
1980s, in particular, articulated a youthful, vital voice, at once rooted in
the everyday traditions and sources that have been discussed above, but
also which tried to create a new mode of expression. As always, the 'voice'
sought to found a new form, often mixing and 'sampling' from others,
through which to convey its messages of resistance to the dominant
culture. As rapper Melle Mel once said, 'Rap music makes up for its lack
of melody with its sense of reminder. It's linked somewhere into a legacy
that has been overlooked, forgotten, or just pushed to the side among
the glut of everything else' ('Looking for the Perfect Beat', *The South Bank
Show*, ITV, 1993).

   In an interview in 1989 Cornel West (1992: 222) commented that 'music
and preaching' are central to African American communication and that
'rap is unique because it combines the black preacher and the black music
tradition . . . pulling from the past and present, innovatively producing a
heterogeneous product' that links the 'oral, the literate, and the musical'
(ibid.). The essence of what Melle Mel calls the 'reminder' in rap music is
part of that continuing call to an African American history, which has had
to struggle to be heard in a dominant white culture. Like the preacher
calling to his congregation, or indeed King or Malcolm X from their
platforms, the rapper exhorts his audience to listen and to learn from
the words he weaves into narratives of experience and the rhythms of
black life. But as West suggests, the form of the rap intertwines different
modes, extending, sampling, playing with sound and language in an
effort to create something new and communicative. It was, at least in the
beginning, the new '"testimony" for the underclass' providing young
blacks with a 'critical voice . . . a "common literacy" . . . explaining, demanding, urging' (hooks 1994b: 424). Rapper Chuck D (of Public Enemy) called
rap 'media piracy . . . to get a big text to people . . . an information network
of sorts . . . to fuel the mind and the body' ('Looking for the Perfect Beat',
The South Bank Show, ITV, 1993). Rap 'is black America's TV station . . .
and black life doesn't get the total spectrum of information through
anything else' (Ross and Rose 1994: 103). Tricia Rose terms this
characteristic 'polyvocal conversations' (Rose 1994: 2) through which raps
become elaborate stories 'to articulate the shifting terms of black
marginality in contemporary American culture' (ibid.: 3). As the sounds
are 'mixed' in the textures of the 'sonic force' of the music, so too does
the vocal 'cut and mix' different threads of stories and snippets of noise
from the variety of street life experienced by young African Americans.
Chuck D explained the effects of this on his work: 'I'm trying to alert as
many people as possible and that's why on my records I like to put noise
in them. I consider them an alarm for Black-Americans' (*Rapido*, BBC2,
March 1992). 'Noise', like shouting at a congregation or haranguing a
crowd, can be a useful tool for the orator and works together with the

educational passing on of communal stories. As Rose writes, like '"noise" on the one hand and communal countermemory on the other, rap music conjures and razes in one stroke' (Rose 1994: 65), constructing 'oppositional transcripts' as cultural responses to oppression and the stories told from within the closed circle of a preferred, official discourse. Rap provided resistance to 'dominant public transcripts' (ibid.: 100), offering the oppressed a public arena through which to air their 'hidden transcript' and so to give voice to a history not often told: 'a contemporary stage for the theater of the powerless' (ibid.: 101). Hence, a rap like Public Enemy's 'Fight the Power' attacked both lyrically and musically the bastions of the mainstream. Elvis Presley, 'a hero to most', means nothing to the young, urban black man who sees him as a 'racist . . . simple and plain' in a culture that pretends that 'we are the same', when there are vast differences in wealth and power. The rap called for forthrightness: 'What we need is awareness, we can't get careless', and a questioning of the bases of power. A more extreme rap, developed as part of the Los Angeles 'gangsta' rap scene, was that of Ice T's 'Freedom of Speech' of 1990, which challenges those who would censor rap lyrics: 'We should be able to say anything / Our lungs were meant to shout . . . Say what we feel, yell out what's real.' Expression, of various kinds, was still a marker of freedom, 'a form of testimony . . . of social protest' that rap took forward by embracing technology to construct a musical style that pushed African American storytelling into the future (Rose 1994: 144–5). Rap refused to languish in the past, but instead found a method of speaking to the future.

> Rappers . . . are the miners, they are the cultivators of communal artifacts, refining and developing the framework of alternative identities that draw on Afrodiasporic approaches to sound organization, rhythm, pleasure, style, and community. . . . Rap is a technologically sophisticated project in African American recuperation and revision . . . yet another way to unnerve and simultaneously revitalize American culture.
>
> (Ibid.: 185)

Like Morrison's literary archaeology and project to rewrite history, rap from the outset was engaged in 'massive archiving', 'gather[ing] . . . a reservoir of threads' (Baker 1993b: 89) drawn from a range of sources into a new, vital hybrid form. Of course, within this 'archive' were rappers like Snoop Dogg or 50 Cent, whose expression was as much about performing an identity, such as 'gangsta', articulating a different version of self-definition (however ironic and playful) aligned to empowerment through wealth, 'respect', territorialism and sexuality. Put another way, the popular success of rap by the early twenty-first century raised the question of excessive commercialisation, and alarmed those who feared, like Tricia Rose, that this limited what could be said: 'Hip Hop stories should be speaking to the real contours of people's lives, not replacing human connection and self worth with consumption.' What started out as an 'affirmation of collective self' had to find ways of overcoming the limitations on expression imposed by the process of being co-opted into mainstream culture (Rose 2005). Hip Hop had to challenge the ways in which its most commercially successful products were dominated by crude stereotypes about hos and gangstas, and seek to create what Rose describes as a richer public space where issues of cultural identity could be fully discussed and expressed (ibid.). But despite this danger, Baker argues, it is, in the end, 'the voice' that 'catches the consciousness' (Baker 1993b: 91), the voice that refutes homogeneity in favour of the critical mix of the 'sonic soul force', the dialogics of 'edutainment' as KRS-1 termed it: education and entertainment speaking together as the 'updated song of explanation' (Baker 1993a: 46). Hip Hop, as Touré asserts, is part of 'a post-Black era', which means not that the past has been moved beyond or forgotten, but that 'the definitions and boundaries of Blackness are expanding in forty million directions – or really, into infinity' (2011: 12). This is not a naïve 'post-racial' vision, but rather one which looks to America's first black president Barack Obama, who is 'rooted in, but not restricted by Blackness' (ibid.). As Touré puts it, 'post-Black is not a box, it's an unbox. It opens the door to everything . . . It's whatever you want it to be' (ibid.: 12).

NEW BLACK VOICES: *BOYZ N THE HOOD* (1991)

[I]t's you young ones what has to remember and take the lead.

(Ellison 1952: 207)

John Singleton's *Boyz n the Hood* is a rites of passage story dramatising the triangular relationship between the sports star (Ricky), the 'gangsta' (Doughboy) and the boy 'in between' (Tre), all struggling to come to terms with the ghetto life of containment, control, surveillance and oppression. Singleton wanted to give black youth stories an audience in a way that rap had done in music, bringing to the fore familiar themes of self-definition, violence and masculinity with some of the forms of the autobiographical tradition in black writing. As he put it:

Everything in the culture tells him to 'be a man'. Everything has something to do with a dysfunctional rite of passage: You have to be a killer to be a man. And who are they talking about killing? Each other. There are all these insults to a person's manhood. So these guys are growing up in basically a 'baby boy' situation, where they're raised by their [single] mothers and are always trying to define – then defend – their manhood.

(Singleton 1995)

Singleton's film offers various narrative 'codings' and 'recodings' (Harris 2006: 84) of masculinity, from excessive gang violence and misogyny to patriarchal guidance for wayward sons, but its overarching theme is education, from the 'street' and school, as well as from Tre's black nationalist father, Furious Styles, and his successful, but estranged, mother. The drama is then about whether Tre will learn to take responsibility for himself and his community and be empowered to escape the ghetto. Ultimately, despite the perpetual waste and death around him, he does, going on to college and a more balanced life with his girlfriend, Brandi. In this, the film points towards a vision of African American life that understands the value of knowledge, self-awareness and community – the lessons given by Furious – but refuses to be bound only by those ties at the expense of equality and opportunity that may indeed exist beyond or alongside these perspectives. One might see the film, in Touré's terms from above, as beginning to 'unbox' blackness and suggest its multiple identities, always struggling and contested, but present in Singleton's film and continuing in many of his later diverse works such as *Poetic Justice* (1993), *Higher Learning* (1995) and his remake of *Shaft* (2000).

CONCLUSION: A STORY TO PASS ON

Manning Marable has written that:

African American identity is much more than race. It is also the traditions, rituals, values, and belief systems of African American people ... our culture, history, art and literature ... our sense of ethnic consciousness and pride in our heritage of resistance against racism.

(Dent 1992: 295)

This 'collectively constructed' identity is an essential part of the freedom struggle to go alongside the more specific dismantling of the economic, legal and social aspects of racism, for it empowers the black community through expressions of human dignity which assert 'a sense of "being-for-ourselves", and not for others' (ibid.: 302). It has been this ongoing struggle to 'position' oneself rather than be positioned by others that we have followed in African American life, but, as many critics have commented, these processes are unfinished and cannot be ignored in the contemporary world where it remains central to an understanding of cultural contestation in the contemporary United States. A novel like *Americanah* (2013) by Chimamanda Ngozi Adiche demonstrates the globalised struggle is ongoing, as she traces the complex routes of black identity from Nigeria to London to the USA and back again. Trying to understand her adopted home, Ifemelu reads *The Fire Next Time* by James Baldwin and other books gradually comprehending 'America's tribalisms – race, ideology and region' (2013: 136). She reads *Dreams From My Father* and marvels at the possibility of a black president and 'at that moment, nothing was more beautiful to her than America' (ibid.: 361) as she relates his journey to her own (see also Senna 2000).

This is clearly reflected in the political career of Barack Obama and his election in 2008. Obama's dramatic success was undoubtedly a major moment in American history, when for the first time an African American was sworn in as president on the steps of the Capitol building, where the Voting Rights Act guaranteeing African Americans the right to vote had been passed only forty-four years earlier. Our focus here is not so much on the implications of Obama's victory for policy, either at home or abroad, as the ways in which his political career connects with the themes and figures discussed above. Obama's rise to power demonstrates very clearly, for instance, the importance of positioning oneself against cultural expectations and assumptions. His memoir, *Dreams From My Father*, written when he was only thirty-three, and first published in 1995, self-consciously follows in the tradition of African American autobiography stretching from Frederick Douglass through to Malcolm X. Its structure is guided by many of the conventions of the genre, from the search for family and community, through efforts to find a sense of moral purpose in life, to the way in which the quest for self-realisation is paralleled by a series of travels (Remnick 2010: 35). At the heart of this relentless internal and external exploration lies his attempt to discover what it means to be black in contemporary America, twenty-five years after the heyday of the Civil Rights movement. For Obama, of course, there was a specific dimension to his journey. His father, though black, came from Kenya, and left his family to return there when Obama was only one. His mother was white, and for most of his childhood he was raised in a white household.

How then could he discover his identity as an African American, how could he define himself in relation to the black struggle within America? A key strategy was consciously to invent himself. Here he drew directly on Malcolm X, whose 'repeated acts of self-creation' would provide a model, 'forged through sheer force of will' (Obama 2008a: 96). It was not Malcolm's political philosophy he admired so much as his approach to life; 'the blunt poetry of his words, his unadorned insistence on respect' (ibid.). In practice Obama rejected Malcolm's emphasis on separatism and nationalism. As he declared in his breakthrough speech at the Democratic National Convention in 2004, 'there is not a Black America and a White

America and Latino America and Asian America – there's the United States of America' (Obama 2004). His candidacy in 2008 rejected 'a politics based solely on racial identity . . . or victimhood' and disavowed claims that he was in some way the spokesman for black America (Tuck 2010: 415). At the same time, however, in his early career he had sought to find a path for himself which located his blackness within a community which recognised its own past, emphasising the importance of reclaiming memory as a means of providing identity and a sense of social purpose.

In *Dreams From My Father* he recalls the period when he worked as an organiser in Chicago, and the efforts he made to seek out the stories different members of the African American community told each other about who they were and where they came from (Obama 2008a: 155–8). These accounts would help him in his own self-conscious search for a past that would give meaning to his life. As his biographer, David Remnick, suggests, Obama was in this respect involved in the 'social construction' of his own identity. 'He ha[d] to make sense of his circumstances and his inheritances, and then decide what he want[ed] to make of it all and who he wan[ted] to be' (Remnick 2010: 242).

There were potential dangers, however, with this approach for an ambitious black politician. Which aspects of the black tradition would he claim and which would he discard? This was demonstrated during the struggle for the Democratic nomination in March 2008, when the pastor of the church where Obama worshipped, the Reverend Jeremiah Wright, was revealed to have delivered a sermon in which he condemned America for treating her citizens as less than human. 'Not God bless America', he declared, 'God *damn* America . . . for killing innocent people' (Remnick 2010: 518). Obama responded with a speech entitled 'A More Perfect Union' in which he sought to reconcile a condemnation of Wright's radical extremism, with an explanation of the 'despair' which had driven him to preach as he did. As a black man, Obama declared, 'I can no more disown [Wright] than I can disown the black community' (Obama 2008c) but he could not follow Wright into a wholesale rejection of American values and achievements. Progress had been made in the area of civil rights, and would continue into the future within America, as long as white and black united to create that more perfect union. The black cultural critic Henry Louis Gates compared Obama's approach to that of Frederick Douglass in the nineteenth century (cited in Remnick 2010: 539). Both figures, he suggested, sought to 'mediate' an eventual resolution to conflict, conscious as they were of their mixed racial background. However, for Cornel West, another leading black intellectual, Obama's approach smacked too much of compromise. His invocation of 'union' betrayed a reluctance to speak out on behalf of the black poor, and pandered to the concerns of the white majority. West, in contrast, reaffirmed a description of the future based on the cultural politics of difference 'in which differences are not elided, but accepted as healthy expressions of individual and communal energies'. Rather than 'a homogenizing impulse' which suggests that all black people are the same, West called for 'responses that articulate the complexity and diversity of Black practices' and engage with the 'mainstream' and the 'nourishing subcultures', so that they 'cultivate critical sensibilities and personal accountability – without inhibiting individual expressions, curiosities and idiosyncrasies' (West 1993b: 17, 14).

Obama's dream of an America based on 'unity', however, and West's vision of a country which accepted 'difference' based on 'a new language of empathy and compassion' (West 1993a: 260) would both have to come up against the way in which specific events revealed how deeply race continued to be embedded in American society and culture, and how significant it remained that the voiceless find the means to express their views. This was particularly the case with the 'disproportionate racial impact' of Hurricane Katrina on New Orleans in 2005 (Tuck 2010: 408). Some of the most affected areas of the city had large majority black populations and critics charged that the slowness of the Bush administration's response to the disaster revealed a lack of concern for those outside of the norms of middle-class white society. The displaced, from this perspective, were depicted as 'long-suffering, unfortunate multitudes in need of rescue . . . seen but not heard . . . [and] excluded from the rights and protections of full citizenship' (Kish 2009: 688). What helped, however, to stop them being presented simply as helpless victims was the determination from within the dispersed black New Orleans community to 'voice' their own interpretation of the disaster and to critique how it had been represented in the wider culture. Just as blues and jazz had developed a direct, often personal response to previous episodes of black displacement in the 1920s and 1930s, so now a range of musical forms in New Orleans, but particularly hip hop, mounted a determined attempt to articulate the experience of dispossession. 'We were left for dead for vultures all through the city' rapped New Orleans activist Mia X in 'My FEMA People' – an indictment of the Federal Emergency Management Agency, and of the way in which New Orleans had become a war-zone like Beirut or Baghdad (ibid.: 689).

Equally strikingly, despite Obama's elections in 2008 and 2012, it soon became clear that America's race problems had not been solved. A series of events including Trayvon Martin's death in Florida 2012, Michael Brown's shooting in Ferguson, Missouri, in 2014, Walter Scott's shooting in North Charleston, South Carolina, and Freddie Gray's death while under arrest in Baltimore in 2015 dramatically showed enduring problems between police and African Americans. At the same time, the very high levels of incarceration of African American males exposed wider racial failings in the administration of the criminal justice system. Obama's initial response was to deliver an even-handed assessment of the difficulties that had developed between the police and black communities in places like Ferguson (see Plate 3.1). The United States was a nation built on the rule of law, and all Americans needed to accept that the decision not to indict the policeman who had shot Michael Brown was the grand jury's to make. At the same time, he admitted the profound distrust of the police that existed in many black areas across the country. African Americans were right to be concerned, but they needed to demonstrate their feelings in a peaceful manner. Obama's later response was to link Ferguson to the long-term struggle for racial justice, but in a way that emphasised his tendency to speak as a president who happened to be black rather than a black president. The year 2015 marked the fiftieth anniversary of the march from Selma to Montgomery and the passage of the Voting Rights Act. In characteristic tones, he sought to locate the problems of Ferguson in the wider battle for civil rights, but in a way that ended up in the centre-ground of American culture. Tremendous gains had been won by the bravery of the protestors at Selma, and elsewhere. However, racism was not 'inherent to America, and it could be overcome by a renewal of the commitment of all Americans to the principles of equality.' Selma had shown that America was not the project of any one person. 'The single-most powerful word in our democracy', he asserted, was 'the

Plate 3.1 Robert Longo, Untitled (Ferguson Police, 13 August 2014), diptych, 2014, charcoal on mounted paper, 86 x 120 inches (overall).
Courtesy of the artist and Metro Pictures, New York

word "We." "We The People." "We Shall Overcome." "Yes We Can."' In the end it was the people themselves, white as well as black, who had 'to tell the truths that need[ed] to be told' (Obama 2015). For Cornel West, this kind of invocation amounted to a fresh evasion. Obama was 'just another neoliberal centrist with a nice rhetorical flair' at a time when 'America needed new truth-tellers . . . to keep alive . . . memories of when we had some serious, serious movements and leaders' (Frank 2014).

In their very different ways both Obama's search for a usable past and his efforts to link it to a national sense of purpose, West's critique of his position, the songs of marginalised youth in a ruined New Orleans or protestors on the streets of Ferguson, Missouri, suggest the significance of the continuing struggle by members of the African American community to find their own voices within America.

Of course, there is always the warning of the scene in *Invisible Man* when the narrator delivers a speech inadvertently referring to 'social equality' only to be greeted with 'the sudden stillness . . . sounds of displeasure . . . [and] hostile phrases', and the swift reminder 'you've got to know your place at all times' (Ellison 1952: 30). But in contrast, there is also the more positive take of Alice Walker's description in *Meridian* of a voter registration episode: 'It may be useless. Or maybe it can be the beginning of the use of your voice. You have to get used to using your voice, you know. You start on simple things and move on' (Walker 1976: 210). The significance of 'moving on' remains an essential component of a voiced identity rooted in a strong sense of the past, but flexible enough to be used in the context of a world in which there are still many changes to be made.

REFERENCES AND FURTHER READING

Abrahams, R.D. (1992) *Singing the Master: The Emergence of African American Culture in the Plantation*, New York: Pantheon.
Adiche, C.N. (2013) *Americanah*, London: Fourth Estate.
Alexander, M. (2010) *The New Jim Crow: Mass Incarceration in the Age of Colorblindness*, New York: New Press.
Angelou, M. (1984) (first 1969) *I Know Why the Caged Bird Sings*, London: Virago.
—— (1986) *All God's Children Need Travelling Shoes*, London: Virago.
Aronowitz, S. (1994) *Dead Artists, Live Theories*, London: Routledge.
Baker, H. (1972) *Long Black Song*, Chapel Hill: University of North Carolina.
—— (1987) *Modernism and the Harlem Renaissance*, Chicago: University of Chicago Press.
—— (1993a) 'Scene . . . Not Heard' in R. Gooding-Williams (ed.) *Reading Rodney King, Reading Urban Uprising*, London: Routledge.
—— (1993b) *Black Studies, Rap and the Academy*, Chicago: University of Chicago Press.
Baldwin, J. (1963) *The Fire Next Time*, Harmondsworth: Penguin.
—— (1972) *No Name in the Street*, London: Michael Joseph.
—— (1985) *The Price of the Ticket: Collected Essays 1948–85*, London: Michael Joseph.

Bambara, T.C. (1993) 'Reading the Signs, Empowering the Eye: *Daughters of the Dust* and the Black Independent Cinema Movement' in M. Diawara (ed.) *Black American Cinema*, London: Routledge.

Benston, K. (1984) 'I Yam What I Am: The Topos of (Un)naming in Afro-American Fiction' in H.L. Gates (ed.) *Black Literature and Literary Theory*, London: Routledge.

Bhabha, H.K. (1994) *The Location of Culture*, London: Routledge.

Blassingame, J.W. (1972) *The Slave Community: Plantation Life in the Ante-bellum South*, Oxford: Oxford University Press.

Campbell, N. (1995) 'The Empty Space of Not Knowing: Childhood, Education and Race in African American Literature' in E. Marum (ed.) *Towards 2000: The Future of Childhood, Literacy and Schooling*, London: Falmer Press.

Carby, H.V. (1987) *Reconstructing Womanhood: The Emergence of the Afro-American Woman Novelist*, Oxford: Oxford University Press.

Carmichael, S. (1967) *Black Power*, Harmondsworth: Penguin.

Clayton, J. (1993) *The Pleasures of Babel: Contemporary American Literature and Theory*, New York: Oxford University Press.

Cleaver, E. (1968) *Soul On Ice*, London: Jonathan Cape.

Couzens Hoy, D. (ed.) (1986) *Foucault: A Critical Reader*, Oxford: Blackwell.

Dent, G. (ed.) (1992) *Black Popular Culture*, Seattle: Bay Press.

Diawara, M. (ed.) (1993) *Black American Cinema*, London: Routledge.

Douglass, F. (1982) (first 1845) *The Narrative of the Life of Frederick Douglass, An American Slave Written by Himself*, Harmondsworth: Penguin.

Du Bois, W.E.B. (1965) (first 1903) *The Souls of Black Folks*, in *Three Negro Classics*, New York: Avon.

—— (1970) *Speeches and Addresses 1920–1963*, London: Pathfinder.

—— (1972) (first 1964) *Shadow and Act*, New York: Vintage Books.

Early, G. (ed.) (1993) *Lure and Loathing: Essays on Race, Identity and the Ambivalence of Assimilation*, London: Allen Lane.

Ellison, R. (1952) *Invisible Man*, Harmondsworth: Penguin.

—— (1972) *Shadow and Act*, New York: Vintage.

Fabre, G. and O'Meally, R. (eds) (1994) *History and Memory in African American Culture*, New York: Oxford University Press.

Frank, T. (2014) 'Interview with Cornel West', *Salon*, 24 August, at http://www.salon.com/2014/08/24/cornel_west_he_posed_as_a_progressive_and_turned_out_to_be_counterfeit_we_ended_up_with_a_wall_street_presidency_a_drone_presidency/ August 2014 (accessed September 2015).

Gates, H.L. (ed.) (1984) *Black Literature and Literary Theory*, London: Routledge.

—— (1985) *The Classic Slave Narratives*, New York: Mentor.

—— (1987) *Figures in Black: Words, Signs, and the 'Racial' Self*, Oxford: Oxford University Press.

—— (1990) *Reading Black, Reading Feminist: A Critical Anthology*, New York: Meridian.

Genovese, E.D. (1976) *Roll, Jordan, Roll: The World the Slaves Made*, New York: Vintage.

Gillett, C. (1983) *The Sound of the City: The Rise of Rock and Roll*, London: Souvenir Press.

Gilroy, P. (1993) *The Black Atlantic: Modernity and Double Consciousness*, London: Verso.

Gooding-Williams, R. (ed.) (1993) *Reading Rodney King, Reading Urban Uprising*, London: Routledge.

Hall, S. (1990) 'Cultural Identity and Diaspora' in J. Rutherford (ed.) *Identity, Community, Culture, Difference*, London: Lawrence and Wishart.
—— (1991) 'Old and New Identities, Old and New Ethnicities' in A.D. King (ed.) *Culture, Globalization and the World System*, London: Macmillan.
—— (1992) 'What is this "Black" in Black Popular Culture?' in G. Dent (ed.) *Black Popular Culture*, Seattle: Bay Press.
Harris, K. (2006) *Boys, Boyz, Bois: An Ethics of Black Masculinity in Film and Popular Media*, New York: Routledge.
Hill Collins, P. (1990) *Black Feminist Thought*, London: Routledge.
hooks, b. (1990) 'Talking Back' in R. Ferguson *et al.* (eds) *Out There: Marginalization and Contemporary Cultures*, New York: MIT Press.
—— (1991) *Yearning: Race, Gender, and Cultural Politics*, London: Turnaround.
—— (1994a) 'Black Women: Constructing the Revolutionary Subject' in M. Klein (ed.) *An American Half-Century*, London: Pluto Press.
—— (1994b) 'Postmodern Blackness' in P. Williams and L. Chrisman (eds) *Colonial Discourse and Post-Colonial Theory*, London: Harvester Wheatsheaf.
King, A.D. (ed.) (1991) *Culture, Globalization and the World System*, London: Macmillan.
King, R. (1988) 'Citizenship and Self-Respect: The Experience of Politics in the Civil Rights Movement', *Journal of American Studies*, vol. 22, no. 1, pp. 7–24.
Kish, Z. (2009) '"My FEMA People": Hip-Hop as Disaster Recovery in the Katrina Diaspora', *American Quarterly*, vol. 61, no. 3, pp. 671–92.
Lauret, M. (1994) *Liberating Literature: Feminist Fiction in America*, London: Routledge.
Lauter, P. *et al.* (1994) *The Heath Anthology of American Literature*, vols 1 and 2, Lexington: D.C. Heath.
Leovy, J. (2015) *Ghettoside: Investigating a Homicide Epidemic*, London: Bodley Head.
Levine, L.W. (1977) *Black Culture and Black Consciousness: Afro-American Folk Thought from Slavery to Freedom*, New York: Oxford University Press.
Lewis, S. (1990) *African American Art and Artists*, Berkeley: University of California Press.
Lipsitz, G. (1990) *Time Passages*, Minneapolis: University of Minnesota.
Malcolm X (1985) (first 1965) *The Autobiography of Malcolm X*, Harmondsworth: Penguin.
Marable, M. (1985) *Black American Politics: From the Washington Marches to Jesse Jackson*, London: Verso.
—— (1992) 'Race, Identity, and Political Culture' in G. Dent (ed.) *Black Popular Culture*, Seattle: Bay Press.
Mariani, P. (ed.) (1991) *Critical Fictions*, Seattle: Bay Press.
McGuire, D.L. and Dittmer, J. (eds) (2011) *Freedom Rights: New Perspectives on the Civil Rights Movement*, Lexington: University Press of Kentucky.
Miles, R. (1989) *Racism*, London: Routledge.
Miller, K. (1992) *Voice of Deliverance: The Language of Martin Luther King and Its Sources*, New York: Free Press.
Morrison, T. (1970) *The Bluest Eye*, London: Chatto & Windus.
—— (1981) 'City Limits, Village Values: Concepts of the Neighbourhood in Black Fiction' in C. Jaye and A.C. Watts (eds) *Literature and the Urban American Experience*, Manchester: Manchester University Press.
—— (1987a) *Beloved*, London: Picador.

—— (1987b) 'The Site of Memory' in W. Zinsser (ed.) *Inventing the Truth: The Art and Craft of Memoir*, Boston: Houghton Mifflin.

—— (1988) 'Living Memory', *City Limits*, 31 March, pp. 10–11.

—— (1989) 'Unspeakable Things Unspoken: The Afro-American Presence in American Literature', *Michigan Quarterly Review*, vol. 28, Winter, pp. 1–34.

Munslow, A. (1992) *Discourse and Culture: The Creation of America 1870–1920*, London: Routledge.

Neal, L. (1989) *Visions of a Liberated Future: Black Arts Movement Writings*, New York: Thunder's Mouth Press.

Obama, B. (2004) 'Democratic National Convention Keynote Address' at http://www.americanrhetoric.com/speeches/convention2004/barackobama 20 04dnc.htm (accessed 17/09/2010).

—— (2008a) (first 1995) *Dreams From My Father*, Edinburgh: Canongate.

—— (2008b) *The Audacity of Hope*, Edinburgh: Canongate.

—— (2008c) 'A More Perfect Union' at http://my.barackobama.com/page/content/hisownwords (accessed 13/10/2010).

—— (2015) 'Remarks by the President at the 50th Anniversary of the Selma to Montgomery Marches' at https://www.whitehouse.gov/the-press-office/2015/03/07/remarks-president-50th-anniversary-selma-montgomery-marches (accessed 30/03/2015).

Painter, N.I. (2006) *Creating Black Americans*, Oxford. Oxford University Press.

Patterson, O. and Fosse E. (2015) *The Cultural Matrix: Understanding Black Youth*, Cambridge: Harvard University Press.

Pew (2008) *Pew Forum on Religion and Public Life: U.S. Religious Landscape Survey*, at http://religions.pewforum.org/pdf/report-religious-landscape-study-key findings.pdf

Pryse, M. and Spillers, H.J. (1985) *Conjuring: Black Women, Fiction and Literary Tradition*, Bloomington: Indiana University Press.

Reed, I. (1972) *Mumbo Jumbo*, New York: Avon.

Remnick, D. (2010) *The Bridge: The Life and Rise of Barack Obama*, London: Picador.

Ripley, C.P. (ed.) (1993) *Witness For Freedom: African American Voices on Race, Slavery and Emancipation*, Chapel Hill: University of North Carolina Press.

Rose, T. (1994) *Black Noise: Rap Music and Black Culture in Contemporary America*, Hanover: Wesleyan University Press.

—— (2005) 'Interview', at http://www.triciarose.com/commentary.shtm.

—— (2008) *The Hip Hop Wars: What We Talk About When We Talk About Hip Hop – and Why It Matters*, New York: Basic Books.

Ross, A. and Rose, T. (eds) (1994) *Microphone Fiends*, London: Routledge.

Sackheim, E. (1993), *The Blues Line*. Hopewell, N.J.: The Ecco Press.

Said, E. (1978) *Orientalism: Western Conceptions of the Orient*, Harmondsworth: Penguin.

—— (1994) *Culture and Imperialism*, London: Vintage.

Senna, D. (2000) (first 1998) *From Caucasia with Love*, London: Bloomsbury.

—— (2004) *Symptomatic*, New York: Riverhead Books.

Singleton, J. (1995) 'Interview', at www.metrotimes.com/editorial/story.asp?id=1971 (accessed 14/5/2005).

Sollors, W. (1994) 'National Identity and Ethnic Diversity: "Of Plymouth Rock and Jamestown and Ellis Island"; or Ethnic Literature and some Redefinitions of American' in G. Fabre and R. O'Meally (eds) *History and Memory in African American Culture*, New York: Oxford University Press.

Stanley, L.A. (ed.) (1992) *Rap: The Lyrics*, Harmondsworth: Penguin.
Storey, J. (1993) *An Introductory Guide to Cultural Theory and Popular Culture*, London: Harvester Wheatsheaf.
Stuckey, S. (1987) *Slave Culture: Nationalist Theory and the Foundation of Black America*, New York: Oxford University Press.
Tate, C. (ed.) (1983) *Black Women Writers at Work*, Harpenden: Oldcastle.
Terrill, R.E. (2010) *The Cambridge Companion to Malcolm X*, Cambridge: Cambridge University Press.
Touré (2011) *Who's Afraid of Post-Blackness: What It Means to be Black Now*, New York: Free Press.
Tuck, S. (2010) *We Ain't What We Ought To Be*, Cambridge, MA: Harvard University Press.
Wald, E. (2014) *Talking 'Bout Your Mama: The Dozens, Snaps, and the Deep Roots of Rap*, New York: Oxford University Press USA.
Walker, A. (1976) *Meridian*, London: Women's Press.
—— (1984) *In Search of Our Mothers' Gardens*, London: Women's Press.
Wallace, M. (1980) *Black Macho and the Myth of the Superwoman*, New York: Warner.
Ward, B. (1998) *Just My Soul Responding: Rhythm and Blues, Black Consciousness and Race Relations*, London: UCL Press.
West, C. (1992) 'Interview' in P. Brooker (ed.) *Modernism/Postmodernism*, London: Longman.
—— (1993a) 'Learning to Talk of Race' in R. Gooding-Williams (ed.) *Reading Rodney King, Reading Urban Uprising*, London: Routledge.
—— (1993b) *Keeping Faith: Philosophy and Race in America*, London: Routledge.
Williams, P. and Chrisman, L. (eds) (1994) *Colonial Discourse and Post-Colonial Theory*, London: Harvester Wheatsheaf.
Williams, R.Y. (2014) *Concrete Demands: The Search for Black Power in the 20th Century*, London: Routledge.
Wilson, A. (1985) *Fences and Ma Rainey's Black Bottom*, Harmondsworth: Penguin.
Wisker, G. (ed.) (1993) *Black Women's Writing*, London: Macmillan.
Wright, R. (1970) (first 1945) *Black Boy*, London: Longman.

FOLLOW-UP WORK

There are a number of additional resources, assignments and other materials to be found on the website that accompanies this new edition: http://www. routledge.com/cw/campbell/

1   Write a short critical analysis of an African American song or rap explaining the ways in which you feel it expresses ideas explored in this chapter.
2   Visit http://www.noi.org/ – which is the Nation of Islam website – and examine the various statements and documents available. In particular, assess and comment on its political and social agendas.
3   Examine the ways in which black communities developed resources to withstand the impact of either slavery or 'Jim Crow'.
4   African American art has not been examined here, but many of the ideas put forward could be applied and related to the work of an artist

like Romare Bearden (1911–88). MOMA's collection is excellent and explores the Bearden collage *The Block* about one area of Harlem, NY. The Art Institute of Chicago has an excellent guide: http://www.artic. edu/artaccess/AA_AfAm/pages/AfAm_11.shtml – look at its brief discussion of Kerry James Marshall's *Many Mansions* (1994). Then research the artist to find out more.

5   Examine traditions of 'voice' in African American culture through an analysis of Martin Luther King's 'I Have A Dream' speech, looking at his combinations of traditions, intertextual references and modes of address. You could also examine a contemporary rap song such as Grandmaster Flash's 'The Message' or a soul song like Aretha Franklin's 'Respect', for the diverse ways in which they project political points of view through form and content.

6   Explore the contemporary debates about the way in which the criminal justice system operates with regard to race. What do the mass incarceration of African Americans and the relations between the police and African American communities reveal about race relations in Obama's America?

Plate 3.2 Barack Obama giving a speech on the Change Campaign, 2008.
© Alan Freed / Shutterstock

Chapter 4

In God we trust?
Religion in American life

The role played by religious thought and practice is of immense importance to a full understanding of American life. As Anthony Giddens has argued, religion is a 'central part of human experience, influencing how we perceive and react to the environments in which we live' (Giddens 2001: 530). A range of Gallup polls in 2013–14 suggested how importantly this is reflected in the contemporary United States. In 2014, 86 per cent of Americans said they believed in God, 59 per cent said they belonged to a church of some kind, and 50 per cent attended a church service once a month or more. Another 56 per cent believed religion was very important in their lives, and answered their problems (Gallup 2015). In 2011 other Gallup polls showed that 85 per cent of Americans believed in heaven and 75 per cent believed in hell. Most Americans were pretty sure where they were headed: 77 per cent thought their chances of getting to heaven were good to excellent, and only 6 per cent felt they were likely to go to hell (Gallup 2004b, 2015). By comparison 38 per cent of Germans, 44 per cent of Britons and 54 per cent of Italians believed in life after death. Half of the American population claimed they prayed at least once a day. Belief was matched by financial commitment, with contributions to religion estimated at \$105.53 billion in 2012–13 (Giving USA 2014). 'There is no country in the world where the Christian religion retains a greater influence over the souls of men than in America', wrote de Tocqueville in 1835 (1965: 233), but his comment might equally apply to the contemporary republic.

What further complicates the picture today, of course, is that Christianity has been joined by a number of other religions to make the American religious mosaic much more varied than it was in the mid nineteenth century. The great waves of Jewish immigration in the late nineteenth and early twentieth centuries made the United States a major centre of Judaism. In the twentieth century a range of other religions have grown significantly including Islam, and a host of New Religious Movements, incorporating a wide range of cults, sects and other spiritual groups (Giddens 2001: 553). They have also been joined by a host of new ethnic religious groupings stimulated by changing patterns of immigration from Asia and Latin

America. While these trends have not overturned the dominance of Christianity in America, they have contributed to a recent relative decline. By 2014, the Christian share of the population had dropped from 78.4 per cent in 2007 to 70.60 per cent, and the same surveys also suggest a rise in those who are unaffiliated to any religion, particularly among the young. In 2014 22.8 per cent of all Americans described themselves as atheist, agnostic or 'nothing in particular', with that percentage rising to 36 per cent for those aged between 18 and 26.

However, to emphasise statistics about church attendance or denominational membership is to paint only part of the picture. Religious traditions in America have always involved visions of America itself. America was where good and evil would struggle in a continuing battle for supremacy in full view of the rest of the world. It may be that America's divine mission would ensure a victory for light over darkness, but the various narratives of that mission have been frequently aware of the dangers of failure. Jonathan Edwards, in the early eighteenth century, on the one hand, located America as the place where God's plans for the world would be realised, where the 'Sun of righteousness' would shine over a paradise set in the wilderness of the West, but at the same time he could issue apocalyptic warnings about the ever-present threat of hell and eternal damnation (Trent and Wells 1901). The religious dimension to the story of America, where good and evil exist alongside each other, has been a pervasive theme in the country's expressive culture, giving it a powerful resonance beyond the history of specific churches and often endowing its language with special meaning and force. From this perspective, religious imagery and behaviour have had an important part to play in disagreements over how American identity should be defined, and who should be involved in that process. This has been true for much of American history, but it is striking how much religion continues to influence contemporary battles over what it means to be American.

CHURCH AND STATE

The importance of religion in American culture may seem surprising since as part of its historical development the United States of America relinquished the concept of an established church and instead opted for religious freedom, and a system of churches based on the voluntary principle. The words of Article 6 of the Constitution make the point clearly: 'no religious Test shall ever be required as a Qualification to any Office or public Trust under the United States.' This is reinforced by the declaration in the First Amendment that 'Congress shall make no law respecting an establishment of religion, or prohibiting the free exercise thereof.' For Thomas Jefferson, these provisions were intended, as he suggested to a group of Baptists in 1802, to 'build a wall of separation between church and state' which would prevent mutual interference. The principle of the separation of church and state assumed the secular identity of the state and forbade it from the promotion of specific forms of religious belief and practice. In the contemporary world it has often been argued that those societies in which religion has continued to survive as a major force have been those where the church has been an arm of the state. Secularisation, in contrast, went hand in hand with modernisation, which by its very nature offered a series of irresistible challenges to traditional forms of religious influence. Economic growth, technological sophistication, wider educational provision, and the development of new forms of popular culture would all weaken the grip of religion on ordinary citizens, and usher in a society where the blinkers of religious belief would be discarded in favour of rational and self-determined choices about how to live the good life. However, in the USA the decision to avoid established religion on the European model clearly has not demonstrated an inexorable link between modernisation and the decline of religious observance. In his discussion of the links between religion and politics in the United States, Kenneth Wald argued that the United States was 'a conspicuous exception to the generalisation that economic development goes hand in hand with a decline in religious sentiment' (Wald and Calhoun-Brown 2007: 6).

Elsewhere in the Western world, the development of modern societies has been reflected in patterns of religious decline, but in America this does not appear to have happened in quite the same way. Secularisation, of course, can be measured in other ways than formal church membership. Churchgoing does not necessarily imply profound belief, and positive answers in opinion surveys may disguise a fairly low level of genuine commitment. At the same time, too, assessing the impact of secularisation needs to take into account the extent to which religious organisations are able to exercise an influential public role. High levels of church attendance may still be accompanied by a decline in the political and social influence of church groups. Whatever the answers to these questions, it remains the case, as Robert Handy has succinctly put it, that the provisions of the American constitution 'meant that the churches would increasingly become wholly voluntary institutions, dependent on their ability to reach and persuade free people to join and support them, and that religious pluralism would markedly increase' (Handy 1976: 142). This emphasis on persuasion and competition, what has been described as the 'free market of American popular religion', has characterised American religion ever since the late eighteenth century and appears to have encouraged rather than deterred religious activity (Carpenter 1997: 4). Moreover, religious freedom has certainly not meant neutrality about the importance of religion in American life. As the social indicators appear to suggest, religion is clearly of central importance in American culture, even though it is not 'established' in any formal sense through a national church. The motto of the country is 'In God we trust'; the federal Congress has chaplains who watch over its business and pray for its successful conclusion; church properties are able to claim tax exemption; and oath taking in court involves the pledge 'so help me God'. When incoming American presidents make their Inaugural Address, custom and popular expectations demand some reference to God's purpose for America. 'In this dedication of a Nation we humbly ask the blessing of God', declared Franklin D. Roosevelt in 1933. 'May he protect each and every one of us. May he guide us in the days to come.' Dwight D. Eisenhower in 1957 sought 'before all else . . . upon our common labor as a union, the blessings of Almighty God'. The Roman Catholic John F. Kennedy concluded his remarks in 1961 by asking God's blessing and his help, but knowing that here on earth God's work 'must truly be our own' (Wrage and Baskerville 1962: 161, 313–14, 320). In 1985 Ronald Reagan declared:

> For all our problems, our differences, we are together as of old, as we raise our voices to the God who is the Author of this most tender music. And may He continue to hold us close as we fill the world with our sound – sound in unity, affection, and love – one people under God, dedicated to the dream of freedom that He has placed in the human heart, called upon now to pass that dream on to a waiting and hopeful world.
>
> (Reagan 1985)

And in 2009 Barack Obama declared:

> Let it be said by our children's children that when we were tested we refused to let this journey end, that we did not turn back nor did we falter; and with eyes fixed on the horizon and God's grace upon us, we carried forth that great gift of freedom and delivered it safely to future generations.

Since the 1950s presidents have also been expected to attend the National Prayer Breakfast, joining faith leaders from around the country. 'God Bless America', wrote Irving Berlin in 'My Home, Sweet Home', a 1939 song which has come to serve almost as an alternative national anthem.

It is against this background that we want, in this chapter, to look at some of the ways in which religion continues to resonate in contemporary American society, and at how the issues it raises influence debates about such topics as the proper division between the sacred and the secular, the private and the public. Our approach is necessarily selective here and does not attempt to provide a survey of American religious practice as a whole.

Rather, we have chosen areas for discussion which seem to us to offer insights into the continuing debates about the importance of religion in the modern United States, and the part it plays in contributing to the formation of a national identity, in a manner which we hope will connect with themes explored in other chapters, notably Chapters 1, 2 and 3.

'THE EYES OF ALL PEOPLE SHALL BE UPON US'

The fate of America has from the very beginning been entwined with notions of religious destiny, which stretch back to John Winthrop's vision, in the early seventeenth century, of Massachusetts as a 'city upon a hill', with the eyes of the world upon it (see the discussion in Chapter 1). Puritans like Winthrop envisaged a community in which life would be guided by God's will, and there would be close links between civil government and religious authority. Using the biblical precedents of Genesis and Exodus, the Puritans presented themselves as God's Chosen People, searching for the Promised Land. William Bradford, in his journal *Of Plymouth Plantation*, testified at length to the religious significance of the Puritan destiny. Having battled across the Atlantic, the first settlers encountered 'a hideous and desolate wilderness, full of wild beasts and wild men', without 'friends to welcome them nor inns to entertain them or refresh their weather-beaten bodies, [nor] houses or much less towns to repair to, to seek for succour'. All that was left to sustain them was 'the Spirit of God and His Grace' (Miller and Johnson 1963: 100–1). At the beginning of his epic ecclesiastical history of New England, *Magnalia Christi Americana*, first published in 1702, Cotton Mather presented his central theme:

> I write the *Wonders* of the Christian Religion, flying from the Depravations of Europe to the *American Strand*: And, assisted by the Holy Author of that *Religion*, I do with all the conscience of *Truth*, required therein by Him, who is the Truth itself, Report the *Wonderful Displays* of his Infinite Power, Wisdom, Goodness and Faithfulness, wherewith His *Divine Providence* hath *irradiated* an *Indian Wilderness*.
>
> (Ibid.: 163)

Puritanism had begun to lose its energies by the end of the seventeenth century, but it bequeathed to subsequent American culture a sense of the importance of God's purpose for the nation. The Great Awakening of the eighteenth century, which emerged at a time when many colonists had come to believe that religious piety was in decline, provided the opportunity for a fresh reaffirmation of God's role in directing the fortunes of his chosen people. It emphasised the importance of the Millennium, when Christ would return to establish a new kingdom on earth over which he would reign for a thousand years before the Last Judgement. The Millennium, in the words of the evangelist Samuel Hopkins in his *Treatise on the Millennium* published in 1793, would be a time of 'eminent holiness' when there would be 'a great increase of light and knowledge'. It would be a time of universal peace, love and general and cordial friendship, when truth and harmony would prevail over error and conflict. The earth would be marked by 'great enjoyment, happiness and universal joy. . . . All outward worldly circumstances would then be agreeable and prosperous.' Here religious prophecy merged with republican optimism to describe a coming golden age of benevolence, prosperity and righteousness' (Wood 1990: 45–53). The Revolution, while it reinforced the special destiny of the United States in political terms, acted as something of a solvent on traditional forms of religion, by cutting churches loose from government, and by encouraging rationalism and concepts of individual liberty. In the 1790s formal church membership for white adults may have dropped to as low as 10 per cent of the population. However, as in the early eighteenth century, concern over the decline of religious belief was in turn followed by a fresh wave of revivalism known as the Second Great Awakening, which had a profound impact both on the scale of church membership, and on the range of American sectarianism. In the nineteenth century, despite the republican commitment to freedom of religion, Americans themselves as well as external commentators frequently remarked on how important broad religious values were for some sense of national identity.

The most important of European writers on America, Comte Alexis de Tocqueville, wrote in 1835, in his classic text *Democracy in America*, that America's westward progress was providential in that it was 'like some flood of humanity, rising constantly and driven on by the hand of God'. The phrase 'Manifest Destiny', coined in 1839 by John L. O'Sullivan, a New York editor, expressed similar attitudes and encouraged the expansion of American borders, and the spreading of American influence. Henry F. May has discussed how these kinds of attitudes in the early nineteenth century meshed with evangelicalism and revivalism to form what has been described as the religion of the Republic, a national religion which in his words was 'Progressive, Patriotic and Protestant' (May 1983: 179). It was progressive in the sense that it incorporated the belief inherited from the eighteenth-century Enlightenment that mankind had within it the capability to improve its position through the application of reason and science. At the same time it drew on the pervasive popular hope in mainstream evangelicalism about the advent of the Millennium and the establishment of God's kingdom on this earth. As part of this process the world would be converted to Christianity and democracy in a manner which connected America's historic destiny to the full implications of the Protestant Reformation, particularly its belief that salvation would be obtained by faith, and that all believers were members of the priesthood – concepts which May argues worked as well for the secular as for the sacred sphere.

This Protestant worldview also emphasised the importance of personal morality both for individuals and for the success of the national project. All of this would be achieved within America, to which God had given a special purpose in the world. May argues that this discourse prospered during the nineteenth century reaching something of a peak in the late nineteenth and early twentieth centuries, where it was reflected not only in a range of religious activists like Henry Ward Beecher and Washington Gladden but also in political leaders like Theodore Roosevelt, and above all Woodrow Wilson, whose views about America's role in the wider world contained many of these assumptions. What damaged this vision was the disillusionment which followed the end of the First World War. In 1919 a range of American churches launched the Interchurch World Movement, which aimed to convert the whole world to evangelical Christianity through a mighty crusade that would be the 'greatest programme undertaken by Christians since the days of the Apostles'. The movement collapsed, however, without achieving any of its aims, and this, for May, marked at least the end of the hegemony of the progressive, Protestant strand in American religious discourse, though it remained a significant force in the way many Americans thought about their country and its place in the world (May 1983: 163–83).

By that stage, of course, American religion had become much more varied in its make-up. The great waves of immigration of the nineteenth and early twentieth centuries brought with them a massive influx of fresh Christian and non-Christian beliefs which served to dilute the Protestant domination of American religious culture. By the early twentieth century, for instance, Catholicism had become a major force in American religious life, sustained by a highly organised parochial system, and with strong links to the international Catholic Church. At the same time Judaism had become well established, particularly in the major cities of the East Coast, where large numbers of Jewish migrants from Eastern Europe settled in the late nineteenth and early twentieth centuries. Many Protestants were alarmed at the threat these developments posed to 'the American tradition', and threw their support behind such movements as the campaign to end unrestricted immigration, in part because it promised to prevent further erosion of the religious beliefs which had guided the Republic through the first hundred years of its history. By the 1920s, however, it was too late, and much more extensive patterns of religious diversity had become firmly entrenched on American soil.

CHANGING PATTERNS IN AMERICAN RELIGIOUS LIFE

Variety and secularisation

This emphasis on the variety of its religious life continued to characterise the American experience after the Second World War. Against this backdrop, however, a number of important themes emerged. First was the resurgence of religious involvement in the late 1940s and 1950s. At the same time, however, the expansion and diversification of the economy encouraged a continuing shift towards secularisation in terms of the patterns of daily life. Major religious groups gradually found themselves adjusting to the demands of modern culture, in ways which perhaps began the process of diluting their distinctiveness from each other. This was a process that operated at different speeds and at different times across the country, but it was nevertheless far-reaching. The traditional Sunday, for instance, in which patterns of life were lived according to a routine of expected church attendance, and in which there was little opportunity for any other kind of activity outside of the home, came under considerable pressure. Community custom, sometimes reinforced by 'Blue' laws, had ensured that Sunday was very different from other days of the week. Since the Second World War, however, the whole concept of Sunday as a special day set aside for prayer and rest came under attack from a host of rival attractions such as restaurants, shopping malls, supermarkets and cinemas. Norman Mailer put the charge succinctly in *Advertisements for Myself*: 'American Protestantism has become oriented to the machine, and lukewarm in its enthusiasm for such notions as heaven, hell and the soul' (Mailer 1968: 348). To this extent, then, secularisation appears to have had an effect on the way people lived their religious lives on a daily basis. The statistics cited at the start of this chapter may appear to contradict this argument, but seen from this angle they represent the popularity of a diluted, generalised form of religion in which the importance attached to sharply defined matters of theology or dogma has given way to a broader acceptance of what Will Herberg called 'the American Way of Life' (1955: 86–94).

Weakening of denominational loyalty

As part of this process, it has been argued, major religious groups began to lose the qualities which marked them out from each other and, as a result, their traditional hold on their members began to slip. One conventional attribute of religious behaviour in the United States had been the importance of denominational loyalty. Throughout the nineteenth and early twentieth centuries American denominations frequently asserted the supremacy of their own missions as against the errors and apostasies of their rivals. The division was perhaps clearest in the split between Catholics and Protestants, and American history is littered with outbreaks of conflict between the two. As late as the 1950s a leading Catholic churchman – Cardinal Francis Spellman (Archbishop of New York) – could refer to Protestants as unhooded Klansmen. Tensions were also frequently apparent within Protestantism, and encouraged that tendency towards sectarianism which has been such a marked feature of American society. However, in the period since the Second World War, in particular, significant changes began to dilute the firmness of the attachment Americans had to a specific denomination. As late as 1955, a vast majority of church members remained loyal to the denomination of their childhood. By 2000, however, something like one-third of adults had switched from the denomination in which they had been reared. In some of the older denominations this trend has been particularly striking. Presbyterians, Methodists and Episcopalians all have recently witnessed significant loss of members to other denominations of the order of around 40 per cent. What this trend appeared to show, in part, was an increasing tendency for American worshippers to experiment with attending services across traditional boundaries. Almost two-thirds of Americans in the early twenty-first century attended the church services of at least three different denominations, a trend which appears to be encouraged by educational background and intermarriage. At those services, too, they could expect to receive an increasingly warm welcome, as denominations themselves relaxed rules on participation. Surveys in the 2000s suggested that most Protestants were in favour of more cooperation between local churches and generally sympathetic to the beliefs and practices of Protestants in other denominations. Not only has this shift been apparent within the Protestant Churches but also between Catholics and Protestants. The successful participation of Catholics in American political life at the highest level was crowned by John F. Kennedy's election as president in 1960. Marriages between Catholics and Protestants had become far less controversial by the early twenty-first century than they had been in the 1950s. As ecumenism spread throughout considerable sections of the Christian world, Catholics and Protestants frequently cooperated at a local level in a way which would have been unthinkable fifty years before.

Orthodox versus progressives

On the other hand, this weakening of denominational loyalties did not lead to a broad cross-religious consensus on public issues, in opposition to a secular perspective, as the discussion of fundamentalism (see pages 134–7) makes clear. Instead a sweeping ideological realignment took place across denominational boundaries. In place of the traditional division between Catholics and Protestants, for instance, what emerged was a growing affinity between orthodox and progressives within different religious groups. By the 2000s, surveys increasingly found that those who held orthodox views on the theology of their faith, whatever the denomination, often had more in common on a range of public issues with orthodox members of other denominations than with progressive members of their own faith. The obverse was also the case, as progressives of one faith frequently made common cause with progressives of another. Generally, orthodox opinion was sympathetic to what might be described as a right-wing set of political and cultural attitudes, while progressives were more likely to veer towards liberalism. If one takes the example of America's role in the world, for instance, a major 1987 survey found that a considerable majority of the orthodox within Protestantism, Catholicism and Judaism believed that America was a 'force for good' in the world, while a slight majority of progressives believed that her influence was either 'neutral' or a 'force for ill'. The orthodox were far more likely to be suspicious of government programmes like social welfare, while progressives were much more likely to be sympathetic to federal reform programmes. These divisions between orthodox and progressive within denominations were reflected in an increasing number of alliances across what were often in the past unbreachable barriers, as like-minded believers came together to make common cause on the cultural issues that concerned them. Though one way of categorising these alliances was to see them along a conservative–liberal political spectrum, they also reflected a much deeper disagreement over the sources of moral authority. For the orthodox, moral authority came from God's will for the world; for progressives moral authority was to be found in rational attempts to come to terms with the world, without relying on external authority. Two commentators in the 1990s concluded that it was

> these opposing conceptions of moral authority [which] are at the heart of most of the political and ideological disagreements in American public discourse – including the debates over abortion, legitimate sexuality, the nature of the family, the moral content of education, Church/State law, and the meaning of First Amendment free speech liberties.
>
> (Hunter and Rice 1991: 331)

CONTEMPORARY EVANGELICALISM

The weakening of older denominational loyalties has been accompanied by the continuing vitality of evangelical Christianity as a major characteristic of American religion, sometimes, but by no means always, associated with fundamentalist traits. Evangelicalism is a flexible term but generally includes an emphasis on the significance of the conversion experience (being 'born again'), the authority and accuracy of the Bible (but not necessarily its literal truth) and a commitment to religious activism (or evangelism). Probably about 35 per cent of the total population, amounting to as much as 100 million people, were defined as evangelicals at the beginning of the twenty-first century. Evangelicalism is sometimes described as a style of religious practice, which could be found across the religious spectrum, and marked even parts of the Roman Catholic Church, but it was most clearly evident in the popularity of fundamentalists (defined as those who believe in the literal truth of the Bible), Charismatics and Pentecostals. Its most controversial and sensational popular representation could be found in the growth of television preachers since the 1960s, who were able to reach massive new audiences through their exploitation of the electronic media, but despite their undoubted success and the attention which has been paid to them, they were not fully representative of the sheer variety of evangelicalism, particularly at a grass-roots level.

Coming to terms with modernity

Evangelicalism in practice is an extremely varied form of religious expression, which goes beyond the temptation in the media to equate it either with fundamentalism, or with political conservatism. We shall be exploring below the links between evangelicalism and the political right in the period after 1970, but throughout the postwar era there have been other successful evangelical movements which have sought to try to adapt evangelicalism more effectively to mainstream American life, rather than simply call for the restoration of the old ways. One representative figure of this strain in modern evangelicalism has been Billy Graham, who was educated at the stronghold of conservative fundamentalism, Bob Jones University in Greenville, South Carolina, but whose crusades since the 1950s have sought to appeal to many ordinary Americans in a manner that was self-consciously inclusive. At the height of the Cold War he could certainly be described as anti-communist, but also often showed some sympathy for liberal issues. In the late 1960s, he was sometimes criticised by more politically right-wing evangelicals who felt that his willingness to admit that racism and poverty were pressing problems in contemporary America was betraying the cause. This is a reminder that religious conservatism did not always imply political conservatism. Most black evangelicals, as we shall see below, hardly fitted into that equation, and even one of the fastest-growing of all evangelical groupings, the Southern Baptists, contained a significant liberal wing. A number of prominent evangelicals have also been sympathetic to domestic liberal causes, most notably Jimmy Carter, the former Governor of Georgia, who was elected as president in 1976. Carter talked openly during his campaign about being 'born again', about how the experience of conversion had transformed his life, and encouraged a commitment to social justice at home and human rights abroad.

Another feature of postwar evangelicalism has been the attempt to use its influence to try to restore some sense of community in a society which it sees as threatened by increasing divisions between individuals and groups. In a considerable number of American cities the size of many evangelical congregations has encouraged their emergence as alternative communities which offer shops, schools and a whole array of social and cultural institutions alongside their staple religious services. Willow Creek Community Church in South Barrington, in the northwestern suburbs of Chicago, has a regular weekend congregation of 20,000 and its physical appearance is something of a cross between a giant corporate headquarters and a shopping mall. Its services are carefully crafted and choreographed, more like variety shows, with a sophisticated packaging aimed at its mainly white middle-class audience. The church is equipped with extensive lighting and sound systems, and video recording systems which capture on tape every detail of the weekly meetings. Its services and values are based on market research carried out in the 1970s, which discovered that one way to recapture suburban support was to adapt to its surrounding culture. It has a board of directors, and uses the language of business administration to convey its message. Willow Creek is unashamedly based on the premise that religious truth can be packaged and sold in much the same way as any other product. Its supporters insist that this truth is unchanging but its presentation in a form which is congenial to its suburban audience allows it to be communicated in a manner which would otherwise be impossible. Adherence to the literal truth of the Bible and the experience of being born again are presented in the carefully crafted language and form of mainstream popular enter-tainment. There is also a strong emphasis on the church as a source of community in a world where other social institutions are seen as weak or inadequate. Willow Creek, according to its own prospectus, is a centre of activity, fellowship and learning for the hundreds of sports teams, youth groups and children's ministries that meet regularly, a community where families and friends can meet to talk, eat and share each other's lives as they sit in the 750-seat Atrium/Food Court. It also provides a range of support services for its members, which cover such areas as recovery from addiction, financial advice and family counselling, as well as practical workshops teaching basic skills like car maintenance and do-it-yourself (see www.willowcreek.org). Willow Creek's success has made it a model for many other similar community churches across the country, which have also sought to make contemporary evangelicalism much more palatable and accessible (Shibley 1996). As in the 1920s, when attempts to modernise church services aroused criticism from more orthodox sources, the community church has its critics, who have generally argued that it has given in rather too easily to contemporary culture. Market research and adaptation to the demands of modern consumerism are an insufficient guide to what form religious belief and practice should take. To rely on them overmuch is to abdicate the Church's traditional responsibility to give people what faith and doctrine say they need, rather than what people themselves say they want.

Another example of the scope and energy of modern evangelicalism can be found in its cultural activity, as it entered into the popular American mainstream. An early example was the success of *The Late Great Planet Earth*, by Hal Lindsey, which became the best-selling non-fiction book of the 1970s, with its prophecy that the end of the world would come in 1988. By 2000, Christian music was the fifth largest genre in the country with gains of 11.5 per cent in album sales compared to 6.2 per cent for the music industry as a whole. By 2010 it was experiencing the same problems as other genres in terms of record sales but it had successfully managed the switch into online promotions. Even more striking was the growth of popular fiction. The Reverend Tim LaHaye and Jerry Jenkins, authors of the 'Left Behind' series, have reached a huge readership with their ongoing novels about the 'rapture', when, at the end of the world, those who have been born again will disappear and rise up into heaven. The series is estimated to have sold c. 40 million copies since its first publication in 1995, making the pair among the best-selling novelists in the US in the early twenty-first century. Together with children's versions, and audio and comic formats, the series earns $100 million annually and has now moved into video games and films. Using a fast-paced thriller structure, the books portray the struggle between good and evil in the seven-year period from the beginning of the rapture to the Second Coming. The aim of the series clearly is to evangelise as much as it is to entertain. 'I think if you cut us, Jerry and I would bleed red, white and blue', says LaHaye. 'We believe that God has raised up America to be a tool in these last days, to get the Gospel to the innermost parts of the earth' (Safer 2004). At the same time, too, the novels explain the world, by providing a series of answers to perplexing problems both at home and abroad. They also provide an endlessly replayed vision of a happy ending, though one that avoids the trap of specificity in terms of time. The concept of the 'last days' proves sufficiently indeterminate to allow the series to be extended into a number of 'prequels' which have the effect of postponing Armageddon just a little further. The end of the world will certainly come, but just not yet.

Fundamentalism

Fundamentalism is often loosely used as an alternative to evangelicalism, but it is perhaps more accurate to see it as a strand within the wider movement. Fundamentalists may be described as evangelicals, but not all evangelicals are fundamentalists. Part of the problem, as Joel Carpenter has argued, is that it has 'become a word of wide usage and immense symbolic power . . . that represent[s] deep and long-standing cultural conflicts in modern America'. As a result it has often been used in a generic way to describe American religious conservatism, at the expense of obscuring the unique identities of specific American religious groupings (Carpenter 1997: 4–6).

This temptation to describe fundamentalism in generalised terms has also been encouraged by the movement's ongoing attempts to get involved in American cultural politics, as spokespersons for the 'true' American way. Fundamentalism had its roots in a strand of Protestant evangelicalism, which emphasised the saving of the individual soul as against some form of accommodation with the modern world. Hopes for a progressive transformation of society were doomed. In the words of one of its most influential spokesmen, Dwight L. Moody, 'The Earth is going to grow worse and worse' and the distinction between sinners and those who had been saved would become ever-clearer. Men needed to be saved from the world rather than work to change it.

In contrast to the postmillennial beliefs of many late eighteenth- and early nineteenth-century preachers, this tradition, sometimes described as pre-millennial, argued that conditions on earth would inexorably worsen until Jesus returned to establish his Kingdom at the battle of Armageddon. Until then true believers should concentrate on saving their own souls, for only they would not have to suffer the tribulations accompanying the final struggles between Christ and Antichrist. Instead, they would rise into the air to meet Christ in the 'secret rapture' (as described in Tim LaHaye's novels discussed earlier), and thus escape the terrors of the end of the world. The point of religion was to prepare yourself for the rapture. This trend was reinforced by the crusades of the late nineteenth century against vice and alcohol, and the revivalist attempts by figures like Moody to resist the modernising and liberalising forces at work in early twentieth-century America. It was suspicious of the liberal sympathies of the Social Gospel, and of the spread both of other religions, often associated with the immigrant churches, and a renewed rationalism, which sought to come to terms with science and other features of modern society. Between 1900 and 1915, it acquired a newly self-conscious tone with the emergence of 'fundamentalism', a term coined to represent efforts to reawaken evangelicalism to the fundamentals of faith. At the heart of fundamentalism lay a belief in the literal truth of the Bible, and what made it immediately effective was the link between the conviction of its own cause, and the effectiveness with which it spread its message. In a precursor of the direct mailing tactics used so effectively by the religious right since the 1970s, books and pamphlets containing the fundamentals of faith were distributed widely across the country.

By the 1920s a recognisable coalition of conservative Christian groups had emerged, opposed to the teaching of evolution in the public school system and the influence of Catholicism, as well as older targets like alcohol. During the 1930s and the Second World War, however, religious conservatism moved away from the kind of assertive confrontation with the demons of modern, urban America, which had been reflected in the cultural struggles of the 1910s and 1920s over such issues as prohibition and the public school curriculum. Instead it regrouped, preferring to focus on promoting its activities at a local and regional level. However, after the Second World War, it once again emerged into the national arena from its bases in the South and the West as it profited from the religious revival of the late 1940s and 1950s, when it gained a strongly patriotic and anticommunist gloss. An important feature of its success was its capacity to organise effectively. Bodies such as Carl Mcintire's American Council of Christian Churches, and Billy James Hargis's Christian Crusade provided successful examples of leadership and coordination for the Christian right to use in the 1970s and 1980s. By the 1940s a rising generation of fundamentalist leaders had gravitated towards radio broadcasting and new, electronically inspired entertainment (Carpenter 1997: 236). This highlights a paradox in the re-emergence of fundamentalism as an efficient and effective exponent of the use of modern technology. Many fundamentalists inveigh against the innovations of contemporary society and the way they ensnare the unsuspecting into a trap of consumerism and fulfilment of the self. On the other hand, their message frequently is conveyed through sophisticated use of modern media forms and a willingness to confront what they see as the godless manipulators of popular culture on their own ground.

This was revealed in the way fundamentalism's continued success in the late twentieth century was advanced by torch-bearers like Jerry Falwell – pastor at the Thomas Road Baptist Church Lynchburg, Virginia, and founder of Liberty Baptist College – whose task was to train a new generation of fundamentalist ministers to save America. Falwell had risen to national prominence through the success of his Old Time Gospel Hour, which was distributed widely across the country every Sunday morning. Though in the early 1960s Falwell had firmly asserted that churchmen should concentrate on individual transformation rather than social reformation, by 1980 he had changed his mind, and had emerged as the leader of what he called the 'Moral Majority', a movement aimed at pushing back the tide of 'secular humanism' which apparently threatened the stability of American life. It was opposed, among many other causes, to the right to abortion, to the Equal Rights Amendment for women, to legal and social equality for homosexuals, and argued strongly for the protection of the traditional family, and for the spread of religious values into areas of American life from which they had been excluded by the doctrine of the separation of church and state. Particularly important here was the issue of prayer in the public school system, which had been barred by the Supreme Court, but which became an important symbol of the renewed fundamentalist commitment to political action. By 1980 the Moral Majority and other conservative religious groupings had attached themselves firmly to the coat-tails of Ronald Reagan's presidential candidacy, in which issues like anti-abortion and anti-feminism became linked to Reagan's emphasis on the need to revive the free enterprise economy and American military capability.

Whatever the importance of the role played by the Moral Majority in helping Ronald Reagan to gain the presidency, in office he proved to be something of a disappointment, failing to deliver on many of the key fundamentalist issues like abortion and school prayer. It was not surprising then that in 1988 televangelist Pat Robertson decided that if politicians were unreliable it might be more effective for religious leaders to run for office themselves. His bid for the 1988 presidential nomination faltered, but it only reinforced the conviction that if the fundamentalist cause was to prevail it had to enter fully into the political mainstream and, more specifically, play a central role in the organisation and ideological development of the Republican Party (see later).

Another sign of fundamentalism's influence on other evangelicals, and indeed on society more generally, has been its persistence in advocating creationism in opposition to Darwin's theory of evolution. The Scopes trial of 1925 in Tennessee first dramatised this battle on the national stage. Though John Scopes was found guilty of breaking a state law, which banned the teaching of Darwinian biology, the anti-evolution forces were much mocked for their scientific ignorance, and for a while the movement for anti-evolution teaching broke up. Perhaps 'regrouped' would be a more accurate term, for it re-emerged just as strongly at the century's end. This time it took the form of 'intelligent design' (a belief that evolution is not proven and nature is so complicated that it must have been designed by God) as well as biblical literalism. In 2005, 64 per cent of Americans (many of whom normally would not describe themselves as fundamentalists) said they would be open to the idea of creationism being taught in public schools, and 38 per cent said they would like it to replace Darwinian evolution altogether (*Guardian* 2005). Another poll in 2010 indicated that 40 per cent of Americans believed that God created humans in their present form, and another 38 per cent that he guided the process of human evolution (Gallup 2010).

Much of this political and social activism points to an ambiguity in fundamentalist attitudes between a pessimistic doctrine of God-willed world decline and the optimistic advocacy of political action (O'Leary 1998: 173). A central strand in fundamentalist theology had been pre-millennial, emphasising, as we have seen, efforts to save men's souls. The activism of the Moral Majority and the Christian Coalition, however, indicated a move towards the postmillennial position on the Second Coming. It might be possible to avert the worst aspects of Armageddon, by preparing the way for Jesus's return. Christian action now could help in the transition to the establishment of the Kingdom on this earth.

For many Christian activists in the 1980s and 1990s, saving your own soul remained important, but personal salvation must be accompanied by work to establish a truly Christian society. The traditional division between church and state set up by the Founding Fathers had only allowed the spread of humanism and secularism, and therefore disdain for Christian moral values. 'The moral order at the heart of the universe is broken daily in blasphemy, adulterous sex, in lying, disrespect for parents, and coveting', argued Pat Robertson in his tract, *The New World Order*, published in 1992. 'Society encourages, where possible, every imaginable conduct to violate the true moral law' (Breidlid *et al.* 1996: 260). Faced with such a situation, postmillennialism demanded that Christians no longer refrain from political involvement, but commit themselves fully to the task of establishing God's Kingdom. 'It's important for us not to be afraid of political power', declared an Iowa housewife in 1994. 'We have to assume it as it is given to us and God prepares us to take it. Inch by inch, line by line, we move the way God directs us, reviving America to return to her roots.' As these comments suggest, however, this version of postmillennialism looked to the past rather than the future. Preparation for the millennium could be achieved by restoring that older America before a purer past had been sullied by the perils of modern life. As Falwell put it, before his apparent disillusionment with political activism, his aim was a crusade to 'lead the nation back to the moral stance that made America great . . . to bring America back . . . to the way we were' (Combs 1993: 126). In this respect as Carpenter has suggested for millions of ordinary Americans, this movement has been an adaptive way of living with modernity. Fundamentalism has offered ordinary people of conservative instincts an alternative to liberal faith in human progress, a way of making sense out of the world, exerting some control over their lives and creating a way of life they can believe in (Carpenter 1997: 9).

RELIGION AND POLITICS

As the activities of Falwell and Robertson suggest, fundamentalism has played a more overtly political role in American culture since the 1970s, but it is also the case that religion more generally, particularly evangelicalism, has become increasingly prominent in what have been described as the culture wars of recent American politics. During the cultural turbulence of the 1960s, there was a tendency to underestimate its significance, in part because of the attention paid in the national media to voices of dissent on the left, but this apparent silence was misleading. The unravelling of political liberalism and the collapse of left-wing radicalism at the end of the decade provided a space into which religious conservatism could move, as a self-proclaimed alternative to the supposed collapse of moral values. Moreover, as Steve Bruce has argued, the nature of the American political system, particularly the openings it provides at state and local levels, allowed considerable social, political and legislative opportunities for religious pressure groups to promote their causes (Bruce 1988: 159).

What has given conservative political influence an extra dimension has been its sophisticated use of the mass media, in particular television, as well as its increasing effectiveness in terms of organisation and communication. As Michael Lienesch has suggested, one important characteristic of the religious right in action has been the way in which popular preachers have been adept at using the mass media to promote their causes (Lienesch 1993). A great deal of publicity has been given to the electronic church since the 1980s but the kinds of techniques it uses built on the use of radio by such figures as Gerald L.K. Smith in the 1930s, Reverend Carl Mcintire in the 1940s and 1950s, and Billy James Hargis in the 1950s and early 1960s. All three showed how it was possible to use the media to promote conservative messages beyond the confines of the traditional pulpit. By 2015 the National Religious Broadcasters Association was able to claim a membership of more than 1,600 broadcasting organisations, dedicated to 'us(ing) every electronic medium available to proclaim the Gospel of our Lord and Savior Jesus Christ' (National Religious Broadcasters Association 2015). At the same time, building on the initiatives of figures like Richard Viguerie and Paul Weyrich in the 1980s, activists have pioneered the use of computer technology to develop more sophisticated methods of contacting potential supporters and communicating with them through a host of online initiatives.

There has been considerable debate about how much impact this activity has actually had, both in terms of electoral success, or actual legislation. Bruce's careful analysis of a range of specific campaigns at state and federal levels in the 1980s and 1990s shows that many of the political aspirations of religious activists remained unrealised (Bruce 1988: 143–89). In the case of George W. Bush the evidence is mixed. In some ways, Bush was difficult to pin down in terms of his religious beliefs. He openly committed to the evangelical cause in the run-up to the 2000 Presidential Election, but never claimed to be 'born again' as did Jimmy Carter, nor was he a fundamentalist. However, he often spoke about the significance of his faith as an aid to decision-making and the conduct of policy. He revealed the transformation in his life to a gathering of religious leaders:

> I had a drinking problem. Right now I should be in a bar in Texas, not the Oval Office. There is only one reason that I am in the Oval Office and not in a bar. I found faith. I found God. I am here because of the power of prayer.
>
> (Frum 2003: 283)

Bush put forward his view of religion as a means to understand the world at a Presidential Prayer Breakfast in 2003. What faith shows us, he declared, is 'the reality of good and the reality of evil. Some acts and choices in this world have eternal consequences', he continued.

> It is always, and everywhere, wrong to target and kill the innocent. It is always, and everywhere, wrong to be cruel and hateful, to enslave and oppress. It is always, and everywhere, right to be kind and just, to protect the lives of others, and to lay down your life for a friend.
>
> (Bush 2002)

Many of Bush's critics inside and outside America mocked these kinds of sentiments, but Bush's religious mix appeared to conform to the mainstream evangelical *mélange*, rather than any secretive fundamentalist agenda. This was confirmed at his re-election in 2004, when he received 78 per cent of the white evangelical Protestant vote, and clearly profited from the cultural conflicts that had surfaced during the campaign over issues like gay marriage. On the other hand, in terms of legislative achievements, the Christian right's record remained as limited after Bush's two terms as it had been after Ronald Reagan's period in office. This appears to be due both to the centripetal nature of the American political system, which makes it difficult for sectional interests to get their policies realised at a national level, as well as to what Bruce describes as 'the general reluctance of Americans to support theocracy' (Bruce 2003: 423).

AFRICAN AMERICAN RELIGION

As we have seen elsewhere in this book (see Chapter 3), one of the central themes in American history has been the interaction between white and black culture, whether in the nineteenth-century South, or across the nation in the twentieth century. Of no area has this been truer than religion. African American religion has been extremely important both for American religious culture as a whole, and for the black community itself.

Malcolm X used regularly to argue that in America 'the black man ha[d] been robbed by the white man of his culture, of his identity, of his soul, of his self' (1963). Slavery in particular had provided the opportunity for the colonisation of the black mind, through the imposition of white values and beliefs, especially Christianity. Any sense of an autonomous African religion had been destroyed by the horrors of the Middle Passage, and the oppressiveness of the plantation system. We will be returning to the Nation of Islam later in this discussion, but at this stage it is important to note that there is an alternative vision of the part played by the Christian religion in black culture, which has emphasised its significance in encouraging the emergence of black identity and self-worth. This may be traced back to the period of slavery before the Civil War. Under the restrictions of slave society, masters generally assumed control of their slaves' religious behaviour. Christianity was widespread on the plantation, both because many masters encouraged missionary activity and because slaves often converted voluntarily. Slaves generally were expected to worship under white supervision in services held by white ministers, and in the same churches as their masters, though seating arrangements generally were segregated. Nevertheless, despite this emphasis on supervision and control, one of the most striking themes in the slave experience was the way in which the slaves themselves succeeded in developing their own distinctive religious beliefs and practices, in a manner which enabled them to withstand the travails of bondage. What was crucial here was the autonomy they managed to find in the practice of their faith. The evidence culled from their religious behaviour shows that slaves were not simply acted upon, the passive and downtrodden recipients of whatever their master chose to give them but, rather, acted for themselves in a way that was extremely important in encouraging a sense of identity and purpose in their lives. As John Blassingame has put it, 'In religion, slave[s] exercised their own independence of conscience' (1972: viii). Under slavery, African Americans developed many of the features that were to mark black Christianity in the future. Of particular interest here was the way in which slaves meshed African inheritances with the evangelical practices they took from white society.

After emancipation, the freedmen withdrew from the white-dominated churches in which they had been forced to worship before the Civil War, and set up their own religious institutions. For many of them the freedom to leave behind white preachers and their messages of obedience and restraint and to practise their faith in the way that they chose for themselves was an act of immense importance. 'Praise God for this day of liberty to worship God!' declared one ex-slave (Litwack 1980: 465). As a result of this process the new black churches assumed a central position in the lives of African Americans; they quickly became the main social and cultural institutions which blacks made and operated for themselves, and therefore were indispensable in promoting a sense of communal purpose. Black churches provided the organisational framework for most activities of the community: economic, political and educational as well as religious. At the same time, they provided an opportunity for the expression of individual faith in a manner which encouraged a sense of identity, and confirmed God's role in their lives.

In deciding to 'make Jesus their choice', as Cornel West has put it, 'and to share with one another their common Christian sense of purpose and Christian understanding of their circumstances', they created a situation in which their faith enabled them to hope for eventual triumph, however much they were 'seemingly forever on the cross, perennially crucified, continuously abused and incessantly devaluated' (West 1993: 117–18). Within the black churches, their ministers assumed a particular significance, not just as preachers of gospel but also as educators, community organisers and political leaders. W.E.B. Du Bois at the turn of the century would call the preacher 'the most unique personality developed by the Negro on American soil' (Branch 1988: 3).

If one turns against this backdrop to the black experience in post-Second World War America, and in particular to the Civil Rights movement, then the enduring importance of the black church is readily apparent. As civil rights activity developed at a local level across the South in the 1940s and early 1950s, and then assumed national prominence with the Montgomery Bus Boycott, which began in 1955, religion played a crucial role. It provided, among other things, an organisational structure with deep roots in the black community which could mobilise human and financial support in a manner which was largely independent of white society. It also, in the black ministry, provided a ready pool of potential leaders, many of them college-educated, who could draw on a long tradition of testifying on behalf of their congregations. Black preachers brought to the movement a language which allowed them to link contemporary political struggles to the age-old efforts to escape from captivity and reach the promised land.

All of this was reflected in the career of Martin Luther King, who, as figurehead of the Civil Rights movement from 1955 until his assassination in 1968, became the most significant spokesman of his generation for the importance of religion in national public life. This was never an easy task. King faced many critics, both within his own black community, and from the white churches, who argued that his social activism threatened public order, and ran the risk of damaging the spiritual role of the church by dragging it into politics. While it was true, as suggested above, that the black church was an indispensable institutional foundation for the Civil Rights movement, there were nevertheless many individual black ministers who were wary of challenging the racial status quo for fear of awakening white reprisals, and this was reflected in the caution of established church groups like the National Baptist Convention. King found here that it was more effective to use new organisations like the Southern Christian Leadership Conference, which he helped to set up in 1957, to stimulate the black churches into social action. By moving outside the established centres of authority in the black religious community, King encouraged a grass-roots revival which would play an essential role in transforming the face of the South in the 1960s. At the same time, he spoke out against those in the white religious community who argued that episodes like the Montgomery Bus Boycott or the Birmingham Campaign of 1963 brought religion too much into politics. It was the responsibility of politicians to effect political change, not churchmen.

In his *Letter from Birmingham Jail*, King argued that such a distinction made no sense when men were confronted with evil. It was vital for the sacred to inform the secular if God's will was to be realised. No society could ever fully meet the exacting aims laid down in the Bible, but it was always important that committed Christians struggle to achieve them. Put another way, civil law had to be judged by higher principles than those of the state. King argued:

> A just law is a man-made code that squares with the moral law or the law of God. An unjust law is a code that is out of harmony with the moral law. . . . Any law that uplifts human personality is just. Any law that degrades human personality is unjust.
>
> (King 1964: 84)

The Jim Crow Statutes of the South were unjust because segregation distorted the soul and damaged the personality. Drawing on the German theologian Paul Tillich's argument that sin was separation, King indicted segregation because it exemplified man's 'awful estrangement, his terrible sinfulness' (ibid.: 85). Faced with such evidence of sin, the contemporary church had spoken too often in 'a weak, ineffectual voice, with an uncertain sound'. Organised religion had become too wedded to the preservation of the status quo, when it should be a 'headlight leading men to higher levels of justice'. Faced with compromise and complacency, civil disobedience would reawaken the national conscience, and carry it back to 'the sacred heritage of our nation and the eternal will of God, to all the best in the American dream'.

Barack Obama, in turn, had to face many of these issues during his election campaign in 2008, and then in his presidency. In *The Audacity of Hope*, he had talked about his own personal road to 'a deepening religious commitment'. Gradually becoming aware that he had no community or shared tradition in which to ground his beliefs, he found a home in the black church where he could realise his faith 'as an active, palpable agent in the world' (Obama 2008b: 207–8). It was a 'vessel' he declared in *Dreams*

From My Father, carrying the story of a people into future generations and into a larger world.

> Our trials and triumphs became at once unique and universal, black and more than black; in chronicling our journey, the stories and songs gave us a means to reclaim memories that we didn't need to feel shame about . . . memories that all people might study and cherish – and with which we could start to rebuild.
>
> (Obama 2008a: 294)

However, the specific church he found – Trinity United Church of Christ in the South Side of Chicago – was to create problems for him during his presidential campaign when its pastor, the Reverend Jeremiah Wright, was revealed as a bitter critic of America's failings in the area of race (see the discussion in Chapter 3). Obama's response in his speech, 'A More Perfect Union', was to reassert his own belief that religion need not be a force for conflict, but could provide a bridge across racial and social divisions (Obama 2008c). During his presidency, he returned to this theme at an address at the National Prayer Breakfast in February 2011, amid accusations from some religious groups that he was being insufficiently open about his religious commitment. Faith and prayer would 'open our ears and our hearts to our brothers and sisters with different points of view; that such reminders of our shared hopes and our shared dreams and our shared limitations as children of God [would] reveal the way forward that we can travel together' (Obama 2011).

ISLAM

As the example of King's career makes clear, Christianity has been central to the African American experience, but it has been challenged over the last fifty years by the rise of Islam as an alternative form of religious behaviour. By the early twenty-first century Islam had become one of the fastest-growing religions in the United States, raising questions about the predominance of the Judaeo-Christian tradition in the United States, and adding to the diversity of American religious practice. It drew on two broad streams of support. The first was the rise of the so-called Nation of Islam (NOI) in African American communities in Detroit and elsewhere in the 1930s. NOI despite its name, was disdained by many orthodox Muslims, because of its reluctance to believe that Muhammad himself was the last prophet. Instead, it gave that honour to Elijah Muhammad, the former Elijah Poole, who was instrumental in building up the NOI in the postwar era. The second was the growth of mainstream Islam as American patterns of migration began to change after the 1960s, with the arrival of settlers from the Middle East, East and South East Asia, and Africa.

Within the African American community an influential argument has been that Islam was the original religion of those Africans who were captured and brought across the Atlantic as slaves. Whereas the black Christian tradition has emphasised the role it played in giving African Americans a sense of identity and purpose, the Muslim claim that theirs was the true faith has fitted well into the search for African roots in other areas of black life. This argument was given its most forceful and effective statement by Malcolm X, who became the leading American spokesman for the Nation of Islam in the early 1960s. For Malcolm X, Islam provided a means for the recovery of an identity which had been stripped from him by white Americans. In America, argued Malcolm X, the black man has been colonised mentally, his mind has been destroyed, his identity has been destroyed, he has been made to hate his black skin, he has been made to hate the texture of his hair, he has been made to hate the features that God gave him (Malcolm X 1980: 263).

The chief weapon of colonisation had been Christianity, which had been imposed on black slaves to make them pliant and obedient. If African Americans were to restore any feelings of self-worth, then they had to reject the religion of slavery and segregation, no matter how pervasive it was in the black community. In its most radical form, Islam assumed a black nationalist tone in the 1960s, specifically rejecting the integrationist approach of King to America's racial divisions, and calling for a separatist solution to the country's racial problems. In the last years of his life Malcolm X increasingly became drawn to mainstream Islam outside of the United States of America, and under its influence began to admit that some form of cooperation between the oppressed of both the white and the black race might be possible, but his early death in 1965 left the implications of this move unfulfilled. Malcolm X's journey through the particular stages of his life was vividly described in his *Autobiography*, which though it consistently denounces the links between Christianity and racism, itself belongs to a confessional tradition in which the sinner repents of his sins, and through the process of conversion becomes a preacher for his newly found faith. After breaking with the Nation of Islam, Malcolm eventually found some sense of resolution on a visit to Mecca where he joined his fellow pilgrims 'drinking without hesitation from the same glass as others . . . washing from the same little pitcher of water; and sleeping with eight or ten others on a mat in the open' (ibid.: 343–4).

The most recent manifestation of African American Islam in the United States has been the rise of Louis Farrakhan, like Malcolm X also a member of the Nation of Islam. Farrakhan has become a figure of controversy because of the way in which his fervent black nationalism has spilled over into messages of open hostility to white society, and because of his often virulent attacks on American Jews for their historical role as slave traders, ghetto employers and landlords. Farrakhan's fierce invective, however, cannot hide the continuing success of the Nation of Islam. By 2010 the sect had mosques in about 120 American cities, as well as a range of other social and cultural institutions, which increasingly helped to make it a viable alternative to the Christian Church.

An important aspect of the sect is its emphasis on community work of various kinds. It organises its own schools, which are run according to a strict regimen, which emphasises discipline and the virtues of a traditional curriculum. It also operates a range of other community ventures including supermarkets, restaurants, bakeries and bookstores. Recruits have to undergo 'manhood training classes', which underline the importance of good behaviour, a sober dress code and rigorous self-discipline. Within the black community it runs a range of rehabilitation programmes for drug addicts, alcoholics, ex-prisoners and gang members, emphasising self-help and the need for the community to take more responsibility for its own conduct.

As some of this suggests, the Nation of Islam is undoubtedly male in its orientation. Women within the organisation are assigned traditional roles, which emphasise housework, child-rearing and clothing regulations that call for them to be covered. Farrakhan, too, shares white conservative concerns that welfare subsidises single women to have babies out of wedlock. Many of these attitudes were reflected in the Million Man March of 1995, when several hundred thousand black men met in the Mall in Washington, DC under the auspices of the Nation of Islam. The success of the march was a clue to the Nation's increasing appeal. To many African Americans, Muslims are attractive because of the consistency between their message and the way they live their lives.

Black Christianity, from this perspective, cannot help but be weakened by the compromises it has had to make with white society, partly because of a shared commitment to similar religious beliefs and practices. The reason so many white Americans outside the South were sympathetic to Martin Luther King – members of the Nation of Islam have argued – was that his approach did not directly confront their own involvement in an oppressive system. Farrakhan, in contrast, continually underlines two of the most unpalatable facts about contemporary American life: Many African Americans are full of anger at the oppressive nature of white society, and many white Americans are frightened of their black counterparts.

In terms of overall numbers, however, by 2014 mainstream Islam had clearly eclipsed NOI and had become one of the fastest-growing areas of American religion, with over 6 million adherents, and approximately 0.9 per cent of the overall population. This of course meant that it was still dwarfed by Christianity (70.6 per cent), but its dynamism, variety and distinctiveness ensured that it raised important questions about its place in the wider society, particularly at a time when the attacks of 11 September

2001 encouraged an existing tendency within American popular culture to represent Islam in terms of the generalised threat it was seen as offering to American security. Crude stereotypes about Islamic behaviour in television series like 24 only added to this tendency to represent Islam in opposition to the perceived superiority of the West, and to depict it in terms of its difference from the American way. Islam from this perspective was inescapably alien. At the same time, many non-American Muslims had come to see the United States as a direct challenge to their way of life, based on their judgements about the conduct of American foreign policy in the Middle East. Their views could not but influence debates about whether one could be a devout Muslim, and at the same time a loyal American.

These complications, however, cannot disguise the fact that Islam has become an American religion and that the processes of its adaptation to life in America have not been significantly different to those experienced by Catholics and Jews in the nineteenth and early twentieth centuries. Living in America raised questions, for instance, about reconciling the private practice of one's faith with the demands of a secular society. It offered challenges to traditional religious assumptions about the appropriate roles for men and women in patterns of worship, dress and behaviour. More generally it emphasised the problems of identity many faith-based groups had to face in trying to make sense of how they should live in the United States. As one Muslim leader from the Islamic Organizations of North America put it, 'In the old countries we were living in an Islamic culture, here we must create one' (Scheitle and Finke 2012: 188). On the other hand, Asma Hasan, argued, Muslim migrants had to accept that America was now home. 'My attitude is that I, and other Muslims, are figuring out how to live as Muslims, and Americans, not one or the other' (Allitt 2003: 204) (see the discussion on ethnic identities in Chapter 2).

These concerns can be seen if we look at a specific place like Detroit, Michigan, which contains one of the most diverse Muslim populations in the country, including Bosnians, Yemenis, Syrians, Albanians and Iraqis, as well as many others. Its population also includes many non-Islamic Arabs. The roots of Islamic migration here are to be found early in the twentieth century, and the first mosque was founded in 1921. It is now the home to over fifty mosques, including the largest in the country, The Islamic Center of America (ICA) in Dearborn (Plate 4.1). This emphasises the fact that Islam can best be understood, not just in terms of its overall traditions, but in the ways it has grown over time and in specific contexts, much like other religions. From this perspective, the processes of Islamic integration into America were well underway before early twenty-first-century debates about the un-American nature of the religion.

ICA covers some 122,000 square feet and in the scope of its activities, which include social facilities, a bookshop, educational and outreach

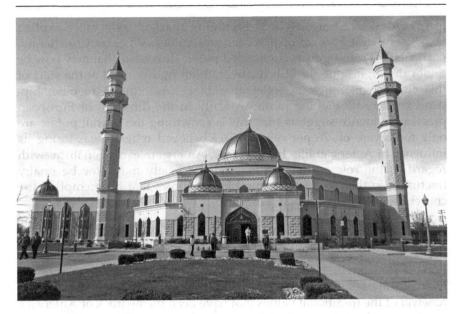

Plate 4.1 Islamic Center of America mosque, Dearborn, Michigan.
© Bill Pugliano / Getty Images

programmes alongside a space for a thousand people to pray at any time, is reminiscent of Christian mega-churches like Willow Creek, discussed earlier in the chapter. Both share a concern for locating themselves clearly in their communities. Both emphasise the importance of integrating social concerns, particularly family and education, firmly into the practice of prayer. Both share a commitment to 'turn irreligious people into fully devoted followers' (Willow Creek 2015). Seen in this light, American Muslims have clearly made their own form of religious practice in America, 'as a vision and a reality on the ground' (Hammer and Safi 2013).

RISE OF THE UNAFFILIATED

The recent decline in American Christianity, and the increasing variety in religious practice, has been accompanied by another significant trend: the rise of the so-called 'nones', people who identify themselves as agnostics, atheists or 'nothing in particular'. In 2014 they numbered 23 per cent of the adult population, a rise of 7 per cent from 2007. This rise was felt across all ages, genders, regions and ethnic or racial groups, though it was most noticeable among the young. Not all of the 'nones' were necessarily irreligious. Some described themselves as believers, but as unaffiliated to a particular church. None the less, this suggests a revealing trend in contemporary American life. Secularism has clearly affected the conduct of everyday life, but now it is becoming marked by a more explicit attachment to it as a set of practices and values. Whereas Christianity, particularly Protestantism, dominated public discourse, that may now be under threat; despite the still relatively high figures cited at the start of this chapter on religious belief attendance and church membership, America may be moving more explicitly in the direction of European practice. Evidence suggests that this is something the overall public are only too aware of: 76 per cent in 2013 believed religion was losing its influence in American life. In this sense, American 'exceptionalism' with regard to the role of religion in modern society may now be finally fracturing in the face of the same kind of forces that have emptied the churches of Western Europe (Pew 2015).

CONCLUSION

Ronald Reagan in his 1983 address to the National Association of Evangelicals talked about a 'great spiritual awakening in America, a renewal of the traditional values that have been the bedrock of America's goodness and greatness'. Americans were far more religious than people of other nations, with 'a deep reverence for the importance of family ties and religious belief'. Americans lived in an imperfect world in which sin and evil existed, but their glory lay in their 'capacity for transcending the moral evils of [the] past'. They would never abandon their belief in God, because it ensured that the source of their strength in the quest for human freedom was not material but spiritual (Erickson 1985: 155–66). Reagan's words, and the support they aroused, testified to the continuing importance of religion in American life, but they also perhaps disguised some of the underlying patterns in religious behaviour which made his picture of a great 'spiritual awakening' in America more complicated than it might at first seem. Religious behaviour and practice had been forced to adapt to the changing conditions of the late twentieth- and early twenty-first-century world, particularly in terms of ethnicity and social change, and a more general weakening in patterns of religious commitment Even where there were apparent strongholds of resistance to modernity, as in fundamental evangelicalism, these were themselves often created with the weapons and techniques of modern society.

REFERENCES AND FURTHER READING

Ahlstrom, S. (1974) *A Religious History of the American People*, New Haven: Yale University Press.
Allitt, P. (2003) *Religion in America since 1945*, New York: Columbia University Press.
Bellah, R. (1988) *Habits of the Heart: Individualism and Commitment in American Life*, London: Hutchinson.

Blassingame, J. (1972) *The Slave Community*, Oxford: Oxford University Press.

Branch, T. (1988) *Parting the Waters: America in the King Years*, New York: Simon & Schuster.

Breidlid, A. *et al.* (eds) (1996) *American Culture: An Anthology of Civilisation Texts*, London: Routledge.

Bruce, S. (1988) *The Rise and Fall of the New Christian Right*, Oxford: Clarendon.

—— (1990) *Pray T.V.: Televangelism in America*, London: Routledge.

—— (2003) 'Religion' in Singh, R. (ed.) *Governing America: The Politics of a Divided Democracy*, Oxford: Oxford University Press.

Bush G.W. (2002) 'President's Remarks at National Prayer Breakfast (7 Feb., 2002)' at http://georgewbush-whitehouse.archives.gov/news/releases/2002/02/text/20020207–1.html (accessed 03/06/2014).

Carpenter, J. (1997) *Revive us Again: The Re-Awakening of American Fundamentalism*, Oxford: Oxford University Press.

CBS (2004) 'Poll: Creationism Trumps Evolution' at http://www.cbsnews.com/stories/2004/11/22/opinion/polls/main657083.shtml

Combs, J. (1993) *The Reagan Range: The Nostalgic Myth in American Politics*, Bowling Green: Bowling Green State University Popular Press.

De Tocqueville, A. (1965) *Democracy in America*, London: Oxford University Press.

Erickson, P. (1985) *Reagan Speaks: The Making of an American Myth*, New York: New York University Press.

Fitzgerald, F. (1987) *Cities on a Hill: A Journey Through Contemporary American Cultures*, London: Picador.

Frum, D. (2003) *The Right Man*, London: Weidenfeld & Nicolson.

Gallup (2004a) 'A Look at Americans and Religion Today', *Gallup Poll Tuesday Briefing* 23 March, pp. 1–7.

—— (2004b) 'Eternal Destinations: Americans Believe in Heaven, Hell', *Gallup Poll Tuesday Briefing* 25 May, pp. 1–4.

—— (2005) 'Religiosity Measure Shows Stalled Recovery', *Gallup Poll Tuesday Briefing* 11 January, pp. 1–2.

—— (2010) 'Evolution, Creationism, Intelligent Design' at http://www. gallup.com/poll/21814/evolution-creationism-intelligent-design.aspx

—— (2015) 'Religion' at http://www.gallup.com/poll/1690/religion.aspx (accessed 4/05/2015).

Garrow, B. (1986) *Bearing the Cross: Martin Luther King and the Southern Christian Leadership Conference*, New York: Random House.

Giddens, A. (2001) *Sociology*, Cambridge: Polity Press.

Giving USA (2014) at http://givingusa.org/ (accessed 14/02/2015).

Guardian (2005) 'On the seventh day, America went to court', 2 October.

Hammer, J. and Safi, O. (2013) *The Cambridge Companion to American Islam*, Cambridge: Cambridge University Press.

Handy, R. (1976) *A History of the Churches in the United States and Canada*, Oxford: Oxford University Press.

Herberg, W. (1955) *Protestant–Catholic–Jew*, New York: Doubleday.

Hunter, J. (1991) *The Culture Wars: The Struggle to Define America*, New York: Basic Books.

Hunter, J. and Rice, J. (1991) 'Unlikely Alliances: The Changing Contours of American Religious Faith' in A. Wolfe (ed.) *America at Century's End*, Berkeley: University of California Press.

Keen, J. (2003) 'Strain of Iraq War Showing on Bush, Those who Know him Say', *USA Today*, 2 April.

King, M.L. (1964) *Why We Can't Wait*, New York: Mentor.

Levine, L. (1977) *Black Culture and Black Consciousness*, New York: Oxford University Press.

Lienesch, M. (1993) *Redeeming America: Piety and Politics in the New Christian Right*, Chapel Hill: University of North Carolina.

Litwack, L. (1980) *Been in the Storm So Long: the Aftermath of Slavery*, New York: Vintage.

Mailer, N. (1968) *Advertisements for Myself*, London: Panther.

Malcolm X (1963) *The Playboy Interview*, at http://www.malcolm-x.org/docs/int_playb.htm (accessed 13/04/2014).

—— (1980) (first 1965) *The Autobiography of Malcolm X*, London: Penguin.

May, H. (1983) *Ideas, Faith and Feelings: Essays in American Intellectual and Religious History*, Oxford: Oxford University Press.

Miller, K. (1992) *Voice of Deliverance: The Language of Martin Luther King and Its Sources*, New York: The Free Press.

Miller, P. and Johnson, T. (eds) (1963) *The Puritans*, New York: Harper & Row.

National Religious Broadcasters Association (2010) at http://www.nrb.org (accessed 23/11/2010).

O'Leary, S. (1998) *Arguing the Apocalypse: A Theory of Millennial Rhetoric*, Oxford: Oxford University Press.

Obama, B. (2004) 'Democratic National Convention Keynote Address' at http://www.americanrhetoric.com/speeches/convention2004/barackobama2004dnc.htm (accessed 17/09/2010).

—— (2008a) *Dreams From My Father*, Edinburgh: Canongate.

—— (2008b) *The Audacity of Hope*, Edinburgh: Canongate.

—— (2008c) 'A More Perfect Union' at http://my.barackobama.com/page/content/hisownwords (accessed 13/10/2010).

—— (2011) 'Remarks by the President at National Prayer Breakfast' at http://www.whitehouse.gov/the-press-office/2011/02/03/remarks-president-national-prayer-breakfast (accessed 18/02/2011).

Pew (2008) *Pew Forum on Religion & Public Life: US Religious Landscape Survey*, at http://religions.pewforum.org/pdf/report-religious-landscape-studykey-findings.pdf

—— (2015) 'America's Changing Religious Landscape' at http://www.pewforum.org/2015/05/12/americas-changing-religious-landscape/ (accessed 14/03/2015).

Reagan, R. (1985) '2nd Inaugural Address' at http://www.yale.edu/lawweb/Avalon/presiden/inaug/reagan2.htm

Safer, M. (2004) 'Rise of the Righteous Army', *60 Minutes*, at http://www.cbsnews.com/stories/2004/02/05/60minutes/main598218.shtml (accessed 17/11/2005).

Scheitle, C. and Finke, R. (2012) *Places of Faith: A Road Trip Across America's Religious Landscape*, New York: Oxford University Press.

Shafer, B. (1991) *Is America Different? A New Look at American Exceptionalism*, Oxford: Clarendon.

Shibley, M. (1996) *Resurgent Evangelicalism in the United States: Mapping Cultural Change Since 1970*, Columbia: University of South Carolina Press.

Singh, R. (2003) *American Government and Politics*, London: Sage.

Trent, W. and Wells, B. (eds) (1901) *Colonial Prose and Poetry*, New York: Thomas Y. Crowell, at http://www.bartleby.com/br/163.html (accessed 4/03/2014).

Wald, K. and Calhoun-Brown A. (2007) *Religion and Politics in the United States*, New York: Rowman & Littlefield.

West, C. (1993) 'The Religious Foundation of the Thought of Martin Luther King' in P. Albert and R. Hoffman (eds) *Martin Luther King and the Black Freedom Struggle*, New York: Da Capo.

Willow Creek (2015) at http://www.willowcreek.org/home1.aspx (accessed 24/11/10).

Wood, G. (ed.) (1990) *The Rising Glory of America*, Boston: North Eastern University Press.

Wrage, E. and Baskerville, B. (eds) (1962) *Contemporary Forum: American Speeches on Twentieth Century Issues*, Seattle: University of Washington Press.

Wuthnow, R. (1988) *The Restructuring of American Religion*, Princeton, NJ: Princeton University Press.

FOLLOW-UP WORK

There are a number of additional resources, assignments and other materials *to be found on the website that accompanies this new edition: http://www. routledge.com/cw/campbell/*

1   How has religious liberty accorded with concepts of secularisation? The principle of the separation of church and state assumes the secular identity of the state, but how far has this been reflected in practice?

2   Cross-refer with Chapter 3's discussion of *Daughters of the Dust* (1991, directed by Julie Dash) and examine the film as a religious text. How does it reveal tensions between Christianity and older African religious beliefs? You might consult Joel Brouwer, 'Repositioning: Center and Margin in Julie Dash's Daughters of The Dust', *African American Review* 29 (spring 1995), pp. 5–16, to help you.

3   How has religion been represented in American cinema? Movies for individual consideration here might include those which treat specific moments/themes in American religious culture, like *Inherit the Wind* (S. Kramer, 1960), which deals with the Scopes trial of 1925 when fundamentalists challenged the teaching of Darwinian biology in the public school system, or *Elmer Gantry* (R. Brooks, 1960), which looks at evangelism, or more recently, *The Apostle* (1997, directed by Robert Duvall).

4   Explore the significance of religion in American political life through an examination of a specific cultural issue like abortion, the teaching of biology or same-sex marriage.

5   What challenges does the growth of Islam in America raise for traditional versions of American religious identity?

Chapter 5

Approaches to regionalism
The West and the South

Michel Foucault has argued that history has excluded too readily 'particular, local, regional knowledge . . . incapable of unanimity', in favour of 'systematising thought', or the official version (Foucault 1980: 82). He calls for the 'subjugated knowledges' 'buried' below to be rediscovered and injected into our perceptions of culture. He calls for a 'genealogy' – a 'painstaking rediscovery of struggles together with the rude memory of their conflicts' – which would combine erudite knowledge and 'local memories' (ibid.: 83) in the understanding of the cultural process. Rather than assume a 'unitary' version of American regions like the West or South, this method insists upon the inclusion of multiple stories of local and regional significance and relates them to a wider inter- or transnational perspective. Such a method takes note of the struggles for power that have marked the burial of certain stories and the elevation of others, and builds them into the analysis. It questions the notion that a particular place or region has a unique or settled set of qualities, and instead argues that stories which have been written about such places have often been written from a perspective that is partial and selective and may even downgrade or omit groups or interests whose experiences or values do not fit with the received version. This is a reminder that we need to take care when we examine the way in which the supposed identity of a place interacts with its history. Generalisations about the character of the South or West may depend upon assumptions about their 'past', which themselves contain untested judgements. This section argues, therefore, for a form of *Critical Regionalism*, a term evolved from the architectural work of Lefaivre and Tzonis and Kenneth Frampton, suggesting a sense of regionalism 'infused with . . . relativity', critical of both imposed universalism and naïve localism, and in a 'constant process of negotiation between local and global' (Lefaivre and Tzonis 2003: 34). The recognition of alternative stories in the form of regional variety and difference asserts diversity and pluralism against any totalising impulse, showing an awareness of complex issues of race, gender and ethnicity, baulking against assumptions of some common identity, and preferring instead the assertion of difference. In this spirit, we would concur with Stephanie Foote's comment:

> The local knowledges that regionalism first helped publicize fracture any monolithic narrative of American literature and . . . identity. Because it held open the meaning of America and Americanness, regional writing helped to create a way to understand and value social differences, and helped to establish a way of imagining communities that interrupted even as they sustained a national culture.
>
> (Crow 2003: 40)

Rooted in the actual varied landscapes of America, regionalism exists as a series of critical dialogues with the centre's official histories and definitions and with the world beyond, while still celebrating local multiplicity and national diversity. Of course, such an emphasis on the regional might become too parochial and inward-looking and so it is vital to stress the term 'critical' in critical regionalism, for it endorses the importance of mediating between the local and the global, seeing relations and connections rather than adopting fixed and rooted positions (see www.critical-regionalism.com for further details of this approach).

CASE STUDY 1: REVISING THE AMERICAN WEST

> All America lies at the end of the wilderness road, and our past is not dead past but still lives in us. . . . Our forefathers had civilization inside themselves, the wild outside. We live in the civilization they created, but within us the wilderness still lingers. What they dreamed, we live; and what they lived, we dream. That is why our western story still holds us, however ineptly told.
>
> (Whipple 1943: 65)

This quotation from Whipple begins Larry McMurtry's epic novel of the West, *Lonesome Dove* (1985), and closes the television documentary *The Wild West* (Burns and Ades 1995). It is both suggestive and ambiguous about the relationship of the 'historic' West to contemporary America's sense of itself. After the transmission of Ric Burns's documentary, one reviewer wrote that, 'Anyone who seeks to understand the United States has first to understand this story, for the West . . . "was the place where we became mythic in our own minds"' (*Observer*, 21 May 1995: 21). Like Whipple's statement, this suggests that the development of American culture and identity and how America has seen and defined itself are linked to the West; and second, it indicates the intertwined relationships between the 'mythic' and the historical, that is, between actual events and how they have been told and retold over time. It reminds us that the West is a 'story' over which there has been an endless contest for 'understanding', and, lastly, it suggests there might in fact be a final understanding, a 'knowing' of the story, which raises the issue of how the 'story' of the West has been produced and received over the last century.

This section will examine how the West, as a region, has been dominant in the way America has imagined itself as a nation. Through representations in different texts we will witness 'a pendulum between a diversity of sectional voices and an ever-new project of unity' (Fisher 1991: xii). By adopting revisionist approaches, we will show the region as dynamic and unsettled instead of one through which a coherent, single American identity emerges. By studying the narratives of place as responses to the West, one acknowledges previously ignored or silenced voices asserting their presence in 'history', just as they have in the culture as a whole. In so doing, they have enriched the whole picture and forced many reassessments of long-held beliefs and assumptions about the formation of the American nation (see the introduction and Chapter 1). In pursuing these threads, we will also show that the construction of the idea of the West reveals certain ideologies that are central to any consideration of American cultural values: exceptionalism, destiny, power, race, ecology, gender and identity. Through examining aspects of this region, one is able to see universal concerns played out in its local and specific representations, tracing the continued significance of the West in the American imagination.

Imagined Wests

In Michael Crichton's film *Westworld* (1973) an organised theme park becomes out of control when illusions take on a frightening and brutal reality. At the heart of the pleasure park is the most popular resort, 'Westworld', in which rich, white middle-class, urban, male Americans take on the personae of Wild West gunfighters, with the guarantee that their fantasies will be played out under a safe and structured set of rules. This is a simulation of a particular version of the West, with all the outcomes pre-arranged and ordered, and a script ready to be followed. When the robot gunfighter (Yul Brynner) breaks out of the neatness of the script, the version of the West is radically altered. Blood, death and fear enter the previously safe and constructed world of 'history'.

In many respects, the film articulates the nature of the American West's relationship to the American cultural memory. The West has too often become a neat script, mixing mythic notions of heroism with stories of the formation of the 'true' character and institutions of the nation forged in its confrontation with 'wilderness'. This orderly vision, as we shall see, has been disrupted since the 1990s by so-called 'New Western History' which sought to revise these 'scripts' of the region and unsettle and challenge the myths that have persisted for so long as central tenets of Americanism. The comforts of such old histories have been disturbed by the intrusive new force, like Yul Brynner's robot, bringing in its wake a new consciousness about the West's past and future. As in the film, once the challenge is made to the bastion of 'reality' that determines the 'world of the West', this new history is a site of struggle and resistance, conquest and death, contention and confusion rather than neat, orderly patterns of existence. *Westworld* is akin to myth because

> Myth functions to control history, to shape it in text or image as an ordained sequence of events. The world is rendered pure in the process; complexity and contradictions give way to order, clarity, and direction. Myth, then, can be understood as an abstract shelter restricting debate.
>
> (Truettner 1991: 40)

In a similar way, Disneyland's 'Frontierland' puts the West at the centre of American history and character as a 'tribute to those hardy pioneers ... [and] frontier way of life ... symbolized by the coonskin cap and the cowboy hat, the calico sunbonnet and the plantation straw' (Fjellman 1992: 73). The assumptions are part of a '"Disney realism", sort of Utopian in nature [which] ... program[s] out all the negative, unwanted elements and program[s] in the positive elements' (Zukin 1991: 222). In E.L. Doctorow's novel *The Book of Daniel* (1971), Disneyland's 'monorail' directs, not just people, but their views, 'like a birth canal', permitting them to participate in 'mythic rituals of the culture', where 'historical reality' becomes a 'sentimental compression ... [a] radical process of reduction', and what remains is 'a substitute for education and, eventually a substitute for experience'. Just as Disneyland reduces history to a simple tale, 'totalitarian in nature', and excludes all elements that do not fit its pattern, it also excludes marginalised people, according to Doctorow, who do not conform to the park's idea of America: 'There is an absence altogether of long-haired youth, heads, hippies, girls in miniskirts, gypsies. ... Disneyland turns away people it doesn't like the looks of' (Doctorow 1994: 292, 294–6). Both Disneyland's representation of the West and its dramatisation in the theme park of Westworld exemplify the dominance of the region in the nation's efforts to define its identity.

An earlier attempt to centralise the importance of the West in the history of the nation was Frederick Jackson Turner's 'The Significance of the Frontier in American History', given as a lecture at the Columbian Exposition in 1893. He argued that on the frontier, a 'line' between savagery and civilisation, American 'traits' and institutions were forged in contact with a variety of forces, of which three were 'free land', nature and the Indian. Turner's 'thesis' attempts to *explain* American progress across the West, as if the complex histories of the region could be organised, like Disney-land, into an identifiable, single shape. 'Turner, in 1893, seemed to have the field of Western American History fully corralled, unified under the concept "frontier".... In fact, the apparently unifying concept of the frontier had arbitrary limits that excluded more than they contained' (Limerick 1987: 21). Turner's 'corral' was constructed to exclude certain views of America and exclude a number of other voices and interpretations which did not match his particular narrative. As Turner had written in 1889, four years before delivering his thesis, 'American history needs a connected and unified account of the progress of civilisation across the continent' (Trachtenberg 1982: 13), and the notion of a 'frontier' provided the opportunity for him to produce a 'coherent, integrated story' (ibid.: 13), a creation story for America.

However, Turner's 'corral' defines America by exclusion, measuring its resilient 'character' against Native Americans, the land and by little or no reference to women or other ethnic groups. It creates a 'cultural myth' (ibid.: 17), controlled like Disneyland: tidy, simple and apparently natural, that is, in a manner which makes its contents appear to be acceptable and 'taken-for-granted'. Turner's language reveals precise ideological readings of the West as a vacant place available, because of its primitive state, to the 'advance' of the urban, sophisticated developments that appeared inevitable and natural. It was a 'wildernesss' to be won by creating 'progress out of the primitive' (Milner 1989: 2) in a movement as 'natural' as glaciation, but predicated upon the diminishment of the Native American, the silencing of women and the 'masterful grasp of material things' (ibid.: 21) implied in a phrase like, 'in spite of environment' (ibid.).

Revisionism and the reassertion of marginalised voices in the West have permitted a critical reassessment of Turner's grand narrative. To borrow from Limerick, 'Exclude women [*Native Americans and their relationship to land*] from Western history, and unreality sets in. Restore them, and the Western drama gains a fully human cast of characters' (Limerick 1987: 52 – our additions in italics). Revisionism can enlarge what the thesis had reduced and show the West not as a 'corral', but an open range of contesting forces, a 'liminal landscape of changing meanings' (Kolodny 1992: 9) in which ethnic, racial, linguistic, gender and geographical diversities have entered the critical arena (see Comer 1999; Robinson 1998; Campbell 2000, 2008, 2013).

Land and the West

The examination of regions is, as we have seen, only partly about geography, but always about place and space. The responses to and representations of the Western landscape have been central to the diverse human interactions within the region, and to study them reveals much about the ecological attitudes prevalent over time in region and nation. One of Kolodny's 'changing meanings' is clearly that of land, and to trace some of these changes is to see how the West's ecology has been interpreted differently by those who lived within it. For Native Americans, the land is sacred, bound up in an intricate web of meaning with all living things, including humankind. The land cannot become property because 'We are the land, and the land is mother to us all' and 'the land is not really a place, separate from ourselves' (Gunn Allen 1992: 119). The abundant wholeness at the centre of this ritual imagery is contained in the metaphorical 'sacred hoop' or circle of being, which is 'dynamic and encompassing' (ibid.: 56):

> In American Indian thought, God is known as the All Spirit, and other beings are also spirit. . . . The natural state of existence is whole. Thus healing chants and ceremonies emphasize restoration of wholeness, for division is a condition of division and separation from the harmony of the whole.
>
> (Ibid.: 60)

In contrast, many Anglo-Americans came to the land 'as possessive individuals pursuing private dreams, trying to fence in their portion of the whole' and 'thought about the land as they thought about each other, in simplifying, fragmenting terms' (Worster 1994: 14–15). As Sitting Bull said, 'healthy feet can hear the very heart of Holy Earth', but the white invaders of his nation's lands had 'a love of possession [which] is a disease with them' and sought to 'claim this mother of ours, the earth, for their own and fence their neighbors away . . . [and] deface her with their buildings and their refuse' (Turner 1977: 255). Thus ecological imperialism was part of the process by which existing Indian attitudes to the land were transformed by the arrival of the settlers.

In the West the capitalist ideology of ownership found a perfect manifestation; it was a 'cultural imperative' (Limerick 1987: 53) to see the land as something to divide, distribute and register. As we have seen, the Turner thesis was based upon the premise that there was 'free land' into which the white settlers came 'winning a wilderness' (in Milner 1989: 2). If it was 'free', it was also 'vacant' and 'virgin' to the white settlers, with strong connotations of the promised land, imbued with a mystical sense in early painted images. This linked it with biblical stories of a new Canaan, suggesting the 'fecundity and promise of the New World and the untold riches that lay in its dark and unexplored corridors' (Greenblatt 1991: 85). Herein lies a constant theme in the history of the West – the conflict between the longed-for possibility of spiritual renewal (fecundity) and the pull to the materiality of wealth (riches). The blurring of distinctions between wealth and spirit is typical of the representation of the West in the minds of many nineteenth-century white Americans.

The Gold Rush of 1849 encouraged the development of new settlements and railroads, but quickly replaced the romantic image of the lone prospector with the large corporations who introduced hydraulic mining, often diverting precious water to blast the ore. As Trachtenberg writes, 'in the path of America's future seemed to lie a natural history' rapidly interpreted as 'natural wealth' to be consumed and used (1982: 18). The Homestead Act (1862) parcelled the land into 160-acre plots to be sold for the nominal amount of $10, and meanwhile the railroad companies were being awarded huge land grants to enable the continued expansion of the railroads across the Plains. Native lands were being divided, buffalo ranges bisected and the once-uncharted wilderness was being surveyed by large corporate interests: railroads, mining and timber companies, driven by profit and loss.

This westward push was imperialist; as George Berkeley wrote in *Verses on the Prospect of Planting Arts and Learning in America* (1726):

Westward the Course of Empire takes its Way;
The four first Acts already past,
A fifth shall close the Drama with the Day;
Time's noblest Offspring is the last.

America was the final act of Time, following its Manifest Destiny, which God ordained, to be the domain of the white settler whose duty it was to 'overspread the continent allotted by Providence' (John L. O'Sullivan quoted in Milner *et al.* 1994: 166), move west, occupy, survey and possess its land. The journalist, William Gilpin, wrote in 1846 that 'the untransacted destiny of the American people is to subdue the continent – to rush over this vast field to the Pacific Ocean – . . . to teach old nations a new civilization – to confirm the destiny of the human race' (Truettner 1991: 101). Paintings such as Leutze's *Westward the Course of Empire Takes Its Way* (1861) or John Gast's *American Progress* (1872) dramatise these urges perfectly (see Plate 5.1). Gast's image, produced to satisfy the needs of publicist George A. Crofutt for a travel guide, performs on canvas Manifest Destiny sweeping aside the Native Americans and buffalo into darkness as the land is contained, farmed and corralled, becoming what Turner would call 'civilization'. Over all hovers the telegraph wire-carrying figure of womanly whiteness, bringing light and education westward from the East, the Old World and the city.

However, images of sexual violence and conquest of the 'virgin land' have often been used to describe the possession of the West, and taken as starting-points for feminist revisions exploring the 'psychosexual dynamic' of the West 'where the material and the erotic were to be harmoniously intermingled' in male language (Kolodny 1984: 3, 4). The land-as-feminine provided a repetitive image of the West as a place of male protection,

Plate 5.1 John Gast, *American Progress*, 1872.
© Fotosearch / Getty Images

possession and assault, in which the woman was held passively as fantasy or ideal. A cluster of images emerged that have maintained their power within American culture to the extent that Chicana feminist Gloria Anzaldúa described the situation in the following way:

> The Gringo, locked into the fiction of white superiority, seized complete political power, stripping Indians and Mexicans of their land while their feet were still rooted in it . . . we were jerked out by the roots, truncated, dispossessed, and separated from our identity and our history.
>
> (Anzaldúa 1987: 8)

The excluded are linked here through the metaphors of violation: women, 'Indians and Mexicans' and the land are all tied to an identity and history that revisionism has sought to reassert.

Masculinity and the land

The dominant image of the land in white American culture is associated with masculinity. From the earliest Western novels, popular narratives circulated and enhanced these beliefs, perpetuating frontier stories of explorers, pioneers and mountain men, developing a powerful mythology of heroic actions while contributing new plots and settings built on existing sources like James Fenimore Cooper's 'Leatherstocking' novels (1823–41) portraying stark contrasts between wilderness and civilisation, red and white, male and female, East and West. In Owen Wister's *The Virginian* (1902) or Zane Grey's *Riders of the Purple Sage* (1912), the West is represented as the testing ground for manhood. The Virginian, for example, evolves from nomadic bachelor to 'foreman', husband and entrepreneur articulating Wister's vision of masculinity and nation; at ease in all company, 'equal to the situation', ruthless and yet always just and fair. However, as part of this process he must kill off Steve and Trampas, purging himself of his wandering, uncivilised self in order to take up his new stable role under the guidance of Molly, the schoolteacher. In this narrative of Manifest Destiny and the 'American Way', mobility becomes social mobility with the Virginian on the side of big business, seeking status, a good woman and wealth, with 'a separate house of his own' and 'a strong grip on many various enterprises' (Wister 1979: 145, 316). For him the land is tamed and controlled as a natural outcome of the management and corporatisation of the West.

In other Western texts, such as the film *Pale Rider* (1985), land is conquered differently. Here the violent process of hydraulic mining is represented as a hellish, phallic vision of the land's destruction. In *Shane* (1949), which *Pale Rider* echoes in many ways, the final resistance of the land is signified by the tree stump which is collectively removed by Joe's and Shane's 'manpower' (Schaefer 1989: 37). In *Pale Rider*, the manpower, now embodied in the machine, is detached and brutal in its destructiveness, but the scene goes further, in juxtaposing the violation of the land with the attempted rape of a young girl. The environmental 'raping' of the land is paralleled to the male subordination and violation of the girl. The scene is crude and problematical, especially as it ultimately becomes a vehicle for the 'saviour-hero' to rescue the girl and the land from their fates, but, however one responds to the film's ideology, this scene does show that even Hollywood mainstream cinema has been touched by revisionism, and has attempted to interlink contemporary concerns about masculinity and its relationship to the feminine and to the environment. This is even more apparent in *Unforgiven* (1992), *The Ballad of Little Jo* (1993) (see Campbell 2000) and more recently in films like *Open Range* (2003), *The Missing* (2003) and *True Grit* (2011) (see Carmichael 2006).

The opening sequences of many classic Western films begin with the hero emerging from the land, as if he is part of its hardness, its severity: 'it says . . . you will become like this – hard, austere, sublime . . . you will have to do without here' (Tompkins 1992: 71). The land is immense, powerful and dominating, but man aspires to its supremacy and so 'men imitate the land in Westerns . . . which means to be hard, to be tough, to be unforgiving' (ibid.: 72–3). This is the chosen landscape of hills and desert, excluding, as myths do so well, the other formations of land that promise 'fertility, abundance, softness, fluidity, many layeredness' (ibid.: 74) for these may be confused with other, feminine qualities. The apparent blankness presents the male hero with a 'tabula rasa on which man can write, as if for the first time, the story he wants to live' (ibid.).

However 'fictional' these images are, they demonstrate the dominant ideology towards the land as testing ground for masculine expression, for simple, unsocial, premodern rituals to take place. In the novel *Shane*, for example, the hero enters 'from the open plain beyond' (Schaefer 1989: 5), his clothes with 'the dust of distance . . . beaten into them', his body with 'the endurance in the lines of that dark figure and the quiet power in its effortless, unthinking adjustment' and his face 'lean and hard and burned' (ibid.: 6). The young observer, Bob, sees in Shane the lone rider, born from the land, that Tompkins writes about, and learns from him a version of masculinity: 'Everything about him showed the effects of long use and hard use, but showed too the strength of quality and competence' (ibid.: 9). But for all his fascination, Shane, like the land he comes from, is no longer suited to the progress represented in the novel by the Starrett family. The 'open range can't last forever', for the future lies with the homesteader and with settlement, and 'the thing to do is pick your spot, get your land, your own land' (ibid.: 13). But Shane, like Ethan Edwards in *The Searchers* (1956), cannot settle or own the land because it is in him and defines his being. Both men need the openness and freedom of the range and cannot exist within a social domain of the feminine, the domestic or the settled. They carry back to the land the central myth of a masculine West.

This myth is examined in Cormac McCarthy's revisionist novel *Blood Meridian, or the Evening Redness in the West* (1985), arguably the first part of his tetralogy of novels (*All the Pretty Horses, The Crossing* and *Cities of the Plain*) where the West is a place of imperialism and Manifest Destiny, not a sacred quest, but a brutal and terrifying assault. At the heart of *Blood Meridian* is Judge Holden, who exemplifies the mythic relationship to the land *in extremis*, wishing to possess the land totally. McCarthy dramatises what Slotkin recognised about the West.

Its ideological underpinnings are those same 'laws' of capitalist competition, of supply and demand, of Social Darwinism's 'survival of the fittest' as a rationale for social order, and 'Manifest Destiny' that have been the building blocks of our domestic historiographical tradition and political ideology (Slotkin 1985: 15).

Holden desires to be 'suzerain of the earth' (McCarthy 1990: 198), a Godlike omnipotent force who acquires all the knowledge contained in nature and stores it in a ledger for himself. At one point, he is seen breaking fossils and minerals from the land because 'he purported to read news of the earth's origins' in them (ibid.: 116), but this is not knowledge to be shared, only to add to his power. The natural objects are 'his [God's] words', since 'He speaks in stones and trees, the bones of things' (ibid.) and Holden is Faust, Ahab, Lear – a terrible vision of mankind's quest for power and control, here played out in the West, the *'terra damnata'* of conquest and imperialism. He must kill to possess, destroy to steal the knowledge and claim it for himself. As D.H. Lawrence wrote,

> To *know* a living thing is to kill it. You have to kill a thing to know it satisfactorily. For this reason, the desirous consciousness, the SPIRIT, is a vampire . . . to *know* any thing is to try to suck the life out of that being.
>
> (Lawrence 1977: 75)

The land is being sucked of all its value for 'man does . . . want to master the secret of life and of individuality' (ibid.: 76). Holden is a dark, rapacious portrayal of the ideology of possession, even to the extent of refuting 'Manifest Destiny' as such and seeking to claim control of it himself: 'Only nature can enslave man and only when the existence of each last entity is routed out and made to stand naked before him will he be properly suzerain of the earth' (McCarthy 1990: 198). Holden's 'claim' is not a patch of land, but the earth itself and all its 'secrets' so that he will have 'taken charge of the world . . . [and] effect a way to dictate the terms of his own fate' (ibid.: 199). He personifies destructive, imperial values where 'the act of destruction itself somehow makes us believe in our manhood and godhood, our Ahab's power to dominate life and to perpetuate and extend ourselves and our power' (Slotkin 1973: 563). Holden is totalitarianism writ large, with his wilful desire for immortality paralleled with the westward quest, which sought to possess the land, destroy the Native American and exclude anything superfluous to this grand design. The West's 'blank page', as Turner called it, offered the opportunity for self-assertion on a massive and terrifying scale. He wrote, 'the individual has been given an open field, unchecked by restraints of an old social order, or of scientific administration of government [and] the self-made man was the Western man's ideal' (Turner 1962: 213).

This rampant, unrestrained individualism epitomises the West as a place of brutal competition, death and horror, where, as William Burroughs wrote, 'all the filth and horror, fear, hate, disease and death of human history flows between you and the Western lands' (Burroughs 1988: 257). How far all this is from the prevalent myths of the golden land and from the 'sacred hoop' of Native American culture. In the extreme revisionism of McCarthy, we are forced to see the repressed of the Western story as he 'rehistoricizes the mythic subject' (Slotkin 1985: 45), not by claiming to give us actual truths about the West, but by creating an imaginative representation that jars the reader into rethinking the old stories and the hollowed-out myths. As John Beck has argued, the consequences of these almost gothic visions appear in McCarthy's later quasi-Western novel *The Road* (2006). It echoes McCarthy's *Blood Meridian* with the 'kid' journeying across a brutal landscape of the West. In the film version (2009) this is more explicit with Viggo Mortensen in flashback as a 'cowboy' with check shirt and horse the first time we see him. The film resonates with the terrible consequences of imperialism and Manifest Destiny, or the 'palpable absence and sense of loss' of promise contained in what Zeese Papanikolas has called 'American Silence': 'a kind of longing, a sense of something lost, lost perhaps even at the moment of gaining it, and possibly irretrievable' (Papanikolas 2007: 19). The dreams of the small farms we see throughout the film, of the broken cities, of families scattered, imprisoned and beaten. It is a cold world 'more poignant, and the wound fresher' since one is conscious always of the 'utopian possibility that we just missed' (ibid.: 21, 22). This is created in the film via the flashback memories of Papa (Mortensen) as much as he tries desperately to erase and block them out for the sake of his son (see Beck 2010).

Women and the West

One of the most important revisions of the American West has been undertaken by feminist critics, who have challenged the conventional histories and representations of the region. Susan Armitage puts it clearly: 'Most histories of the American West are heroic tales: stories of adventure, exploration and conflict . . . their coherence is achieved by a narrowing of focus' (Armitage and Jameson 1987: 10). As Tompkins has argued, such narratives of the West developed as an 'answer' (1992: 39) to the prevalence of domestic, sentimental, female books popular in the East which 'Culturally and politically . . . establish women at the center of the world's most important work [saving souls] and . . . assert that in the end spiritual power is always superior to worldly might' (ibid.: 38).

For Tompkins, the Western is 'secular, materialist, and antifeminist; it focuses on conflict in the public space, is obsessed by death, and worships the phallus' (ibid.: 28). Its masculine representations refer directly to the feminine realms of power: the home, the Church, the family, and seek, as textual reworkings of actuality, to keep the domains apart and allow men the space in which to *imagine* an order in which they can be tested. Thus the Western genre developed a whole set of 'counterrituals and beliefs' (ibid.: 35) to portray masculinity and exclude or marginalise women. The cultural order from which Turner emerged in 1893 permitted him to write of a 'masterful grasp . . . restless, nervous energy . . . dominant individualism' (Milner 1989: 21), always gendered as 'he', and reacting to 'the cult of domesticity' that had dominated American Victorian society.

Even a sensitive, radical poet like Walt Whitman in his 'Pioneers, O Pioneers' (1865) demonstrates through its language and imagery the prevailing idea of the West as the domain of men:

> Conquering, holding, daring, venturing as we go the unknown
>   ways . . .
> We the primeval forests felling.
> We the rivers stemming, vexing we and piercing deep the mines
>   within,
> We the surface broad surveying, we the virgin soil upheaving.
>   (Whitman 1971: 194)

It is a male fantasy of control and domination over both the land and the feminine which comes through this poem, that in so many other ways celebrates the expansionist policies of westward movement. In relationships with women and land, man had to be assertive, to prove himself as superior, to 'tame' them in different ways, and literature offered one method, becoming 'psychosexual dramas of men intent on possessing a virgin continent' (Kolodny 1984: xiii). 'New histories' of the West show the significant roles of women in the region, not just in the permitted, stereotyped roles of 'help-mate', civiliser, whore and mother, but by providing new female viewpoints. One method is to revalue the individual stories of women's lives, their domestic rituals and everyday habits, in contrast to the search for the grand narratives of the West, which sought to identify large trends and 'waves' of settlement.

A 'classic' Western novel and later a film, *Shane*, which has many merits, portrays Marian Starrett in the stereotyped mould of the Madonna of the Prairie, the civilising force for which men struggle. The first words that define her in the text are 'mother's kitchen garden' (Schaefer 1989: 7), and we are soon told: 'She was proud of her cooking. . . . As long as she could still prepare a proper dinner, she would tell father when things were not going right, she knew she was still civilized and there was hope of getting ahead' (ibid.: 11). She is domestic, civilised and yet, strangely, as the novel suggests, capable of being stirred by the sexual threat of the wild Shane. As a woman in the West, she has to be contained by the role, by the house and by the garden, all of which demonstrate the limits of her permitted territory. She may be in the wilderness, but it cannot be in her. It must be repressed and channelled into the healthy domestication that the novel delineates. It was for women, for civilisation, such texts suggest, that men strove to tame the land, remove the wild Indian and drive away the outlaw. In John Ford's classic Western film *My Darling Clementine* (1946), women are firmly rooted in the stereotypes of whore–half-breed Chihuahua and schoolteacher–virgin Clementine, and 'women, the family and the bonds of community can thrive, it seems, only when the West has been tamed. They are the motive that invests the history of western violence with virtue' (Milner *et al.* 1994: 316). In the film, Wyatt Earp is shown to be gradually 'civilised' and in one scene is washed, dressed and perfumed at the barber shop before escorting Clementine to the new town church dance where he is eased into the Fordian ritual of community: the dance. Here, Earp removes his hat and joins the ritual that bonds him, in part, to the new West of town and community, and signals the ultimate settlement and organisation that his violence has enabled. Although finally he cannot settle, the process has been established in the film, as in so many Westerns, and women and the feminine are at its heart, remaining behind in the new order, which has begun to reconcile 'the premodern West and the new, civilized West' (White 1991: 628).

The film echoes the ending of *Shane*, in which the reassuring voice of Marian asserts that Shane has not gone but remains 'here, in this place, *in this place he gave us*. He's around us and in us, and he always will be' (Schaefer 1989: 157 – our emphasis). The civilised, tamed West is the domain of Marian, Clementine and of all the other Madonna-women that masculine mythology created to explain the violence of the country. One image perfectly captures this filmic sentimental ideology in the form of George Caleb Bingham's painting *Daniel Boone Escorting Settlers through the Cumberland Gap* (1851–2). It portrays a Madonna figure being led on a white horse into the Western light by the strong, rugged, begunned Turneresque Boone. The hierarchy of power is apparent in the composition, and the definitions of what women could be in the West are emphasised, bringing light and civilisation into a dark, primitive space (see Plate 5.2).

The ideological elements of these myths serve at least two purposes: first, to gender the West and set definite roles for women and men, and, second, to link this with the wider process of westward expansion as if the two were totally normal and ordained, 'a quality of absolute legitimacy, as if what is being described is natural and unquestionable and therefore a fully sanctioned enterprise' (Truettner 1991: 40). Fortunately, these ideologies can be revealed 'when viewed through a new perspective' and be seen to 'yield [an] agenda' (ibid.), which at the time of their making was masked by their social acceptance and the apparent harmlessness of their intention. Such a 'new perspective' can be seen in the fictional work of Willa Cather, who was prepared to challenge the gendered representations of the West.

Plate 5.2 George Caleb Bingham, *Daniel Boone Escorting Settlers through the Cumberland Gap*, 1851–2, oil on canvas, 36½ x 50¼ inches.

© Washington University, St. Louis, USA / Bridgeman Images

A diverse West: Willa Cather and beyond

In Willa Cather's *O Pioneers* (1913), the traditional, constrained view of the Madonna of the Prairie is countered by answering Whitman's poem, from which she borrows her title, in its portrayal of a capable woman with vision and power, who develops a creative, mutual relationship with the land. Cather's Alexandra Bergson comes from a family whose father saw the land as something to 'tame' (Cather 1913: 20) because 'its Genius was unfriendly to man' (ibid.), an 'enigma . . . like a horse that no one knows how to break to harness' (ibid.: 22). She learns from her father's persistence and industriousness, her mother's sense of heritage and preservation (we see her endlessly preserving fruit in the novel) and above all from the proto-environmentalist Ivar, who lives in harmony with the land. Rather than 'break' the land, Alex learns to live 'without defiling the face of nature any more than the coyote that had lived there before' (ibid.: 36). She has a 'new relation' to the land in which her 'house is the big out-of-doors, and . . . it is in the soil that she expresses herself best' (ibid.: 71, 84). For Cather, the public space is available to women, and they can operate within it without simply imitating men and their mistakes. The Western land is not to be subdued, but to be nurtured and lived with, becoming like an extension of her own body: 'she was close to the flat, fallow world about her, and felt, as it were, in her own body the joyous germination in the soil' (ibid.: 204). Cather proposes a mutual relationship to the land, closer to the Native American view: 'we come and go, but the land is always here' (ibid.: 308). Indeed, in one of the final speeches in the novel, Alex, talking to her future husband Carl, discusses the future of the West and claims 'it is we who write it, with the best we have' (ibid.: 307). The emphasis here is on the 'we', the male and female 'writing' of Western history and the 'writing' of the landscape itself. Elinore Pruitt Stewart, who read and admired Willa Cather, actually lived the frontier life and wrote about it in her letters, seeing homesteading for women as a means of expression and liberation from the ordeals and limitations of the urban East:

> any woman who can stand her own company . . . see the beauty of the sunset, loves growing things, and is willing to put in much time at the careful labor as she does over the washtub, will certainly succeed; will have independence, plenty to eat all the time, and a home of her own in the end.
>
> (Milner 1989: 408)

This 'new perspective' of women's histories is one of the tools by which 'conventional' history can be interrogated and the 'dominant discourse' of white male history be shown to 'close down [effect a closure] on those readings they wish not to run' (Jenkins 1991: 67). As Anzaldúa writes, 'Culture forms our beliefs. . . . Culture is made by those in power – men' (Anzaldúa 1987: 16), but she, like many other women, has begun to question this discourse. Diverse voices have now been empowered by this rethinking of Western history: Chicana, Native American, Anglo, Asian American women have expressed their stories alongside the more conventionally accepted and official versions in a new multiculturalism in the West (see Comer 1999; Campbell 2000).

One example here is the work of E. Annie Proulx, whose Wyoming stories in *Close Range* (1999), *Bad Dirt* (2004), *Fine Just The Way It Is* (2008) and in the novel *That Old Ace in the Hole* (2002) explore versions of the West that deliberately revise conventional stereotypes and modern images of the New West, best introduced by the epigraph to *Close Range*: 'Reality's never been of much use out here.' Her work uses quirky, broken lives, oddball characters and sardonic humour to examine the continued dreams, hardship, disappointment and corporatisation of the region, and in so doing challenges readers' expectations and assumptions.

Her most famous story, 'Brokeback Mountain', is a daring, elegiac story of a homosexual relationship between two cowboys – Ennis Del Mar and

Jack Twist – lasting twenty years and cutting through many of the traditional images and codes of what she calls the West's normative 'stoic life' – family, work and prescribed masculinity (Proulx 1999: 284). In this mythic West 'turned upside down' Proulx explores the 'slow corrosion' of lives in a region whose strict boundaries have been breached so that, as she says, 'everything seemed mixed' (ibid.: 302, 292) and suddenly problematic, no longer under the spell of mythologies and fixed rules. In the story's moving climax Ennis visits the room of his secret lover Jack after his death to find their work shirts hanging inside one another in the closet: 'the pair like two skins, one inside the other, two in one' (ibid.: 316). In many ways this hidden, *closeted* story reminds us of Foucault's call for subjugated knowledges to be heard, and of their necessary interconnection, multiple stories relating to the non-unanimous whole, 'one inside the other', forming the complex, diverse fabric – the 'imagined power' of the West (ibid.). In *Fine Just The Way It Is*, one story, 'Tits-Up in a Ditch', portrays Wyoming as a landscape scarred by loss and death for female army recruit Dakotah Lister returning maimed from Iraq to 'a roll call of grief' where a 'dying sun hit the willows, transforming them into bloody wands . . . a hammered red landscape in which ranch buildings appeared dark and sorrowful' (Proulx 2009: 218). Proulx's tales are miles short of the conventions of the promised land, continuing to show the complex workings of critical regionalism as the local intersects with the global, the national with the transnational (see Hunt 2008).

Conclusion: the contested landscapes of the contemporary West

> The only trouble with the fringe is, it does tend to unravel.
> (Palahniuk 2003: 17)

Revisionism has made accessible more stories about the West than merely the official history or the myths transmitted through popular discourse, and they have demonstrated the intricate relationship between the 'real' and the 'imagined'. Slotkin's 'productive revision of myth' will 'open the system and permit it to adjust its beliefs [and the fictions that carry them] to changing realities' because, if not, the alternative is 'the rigid defense of existing systems, the refusal of change, which bind us to dead or destructive patterns of action and belief that are out of phase with social and environmental reality' (Slotkin 1992: 654–5). Reappraisals 'destabilise the past and fracture it, so that, in the cracks opened up, new histories can be made' reminding us 'that interpretations . . . are aligned to the dominant discursive practices' (Jenkins 1991: 66). Bret Easton Ellis's novel *Less Than Zero* (1985) is a form of this 'new history' whose epigraph is 'There's a feeling I get when I look to the West', and represents an excessive, metropolitan region without any concern for the past. The novel follows the ghostly white Clay, coming home from college in New Hampshire for Christmas to the rich suburbs, nightclubs and drug-fuelled netherworld of Los Angeles. In one respect, it is the classic westward journey of so many Americans, here represented as a shadowy reworking of this Manifest Destiny into the neon West with its scattered remains of once-cherished dreams, now represented by fake tans, dysfunctional families and duplicitous identities. This reminds us of Papanikolas's 'kind of longing, a sense of something lost' no longer accessible to Clay's generation except as ghostly and spectral memories. This culminates in a scene where, driving into the LA hills, Blair, Clay's ex-girlfriend, hits a coyote (with all its rich mythic significance) on the highway and they watch its crushed body convulse and bleed to death beneath the Californian sun. The modern urban West and its cryptic past collide in this scene.

Later, as if to amplify this dramatic collision, in the first of a series of stunning motifs that conclude *Less Than Zero*, Ellis writes of 'a street called Sierra Bonita in Hollywood' where

> people saw ghosts; apparitions of the Wild West . . . Indians dressed in nothing but loincloths and on horseback were spotted, and that one man had a tomahawk which disappeared seconds later, thrown through his open window. One elderly couple said that an Indian appeared in their living room . . . moaning incantations. A man had crashed into a palm tree because he had seen a covered wagon in his path and it forced him to swerve.
>
> (Ellis 1985: 206)

In LA's new urban frontier, history has been overwritten in the headlong rush into the techno future, where environmental destruction and genocide are simply the price paid for the careless life enjoyed by the book's young characters. Yet the past will not 'disappear here' (a recurring slogan in the novel), for it returns, haunting the mind of Clay, as it does the streets of Los Angeles, like these ghostly Indians, or the 'covered wagon' that caused a man to crash his car into a palm tree. The West's past, in all its real and imagined pervasiveness, cannot be repressed, here translated as the Indian *and* covered wagon intervening into the glossy gridlike order of suburban streets and lives.

Other images follow. First, a poster of California 'old and torn down the middle and tilted and hanging unevenly', juxtaposed with 'an old deserted carnival' and a coyote howling (ibid.: 207). This curious, powerful montage spells out the contemporary West, part carnival, part degraded lopsided illusion, part ghostly, natural past. At this moment, Clay, the novel's central character, knows 'it was time to go back' (ibid.), by which he means to the East, to his own personal past, and also into the forgotten past of the West, to understand how his world 'so violent and malicious' (ibid.: 208) was formed. The inner collapse in Ellis's West is reflected in the landscape that intrudes into the human environment like a sinister reminder of the past. The 'houses falling, slipping down the hills in the middle of the night' (ibid.: 114), the earthquakes and the storms suggest the fragility of human existence in the West and remind us of the ever-present environment. As Worster wrote, 'the western lands were not a blank slate on which any identity, old or new, could be arbitrarily written' (1994: 6).

In Karen Tei Yamashita's Californian novel *Tropic of Orange* (1997; see also Chapter 6) the West is not so much apocalyptic as reshaping along new lines of race, language and power, epitomised by one of its characters, Manzanar, who conducts the traffic of LA like a great symphony. It is symbolic of a West full of untapped human potential, with its lines of mobility, living and moving on the highway system; a 'root system' no longer anchored and fixed by notions of historic space, settlement and tradition, but one shifting and writhing with global tensions and flows. But these processes are not removed or distanced from the people living in these Western spaces, for they touch them as global warming, ecological change, toxic pollution, unemployment, border wars, immigration and violence, which all figure in the novel. 'The complexity of human adventure over lines of transit' (ibid.:56) are revealed through Manzanar's emblematic schizoid vision and 'feel' for the city. As an ex-surgeon his job had meant 'careful incisions through layers of living tissue', but now he contributes, as a 'missing person' (ibid.), cast out from the mainstream, capturing the lost sounds and rhythms of the city through its layers of sonic geography. 'There are maps and there are maps and there are maps', we are told, but Manzanar,

> could see all of them at once, filter some, pick them out like transparent windows and place them even delicately and consecutively in a complex grid of pattern, spatial discernment, body politic . . . For each of the maps was a layer of music, a clef, an instrument, a musical instruction, a change of measure, a coda.
>
> (Yamashita 1997: 56)

LA writer and critic Mike Davis has also contributed much in recent years to this 'antimythography' of the New West, developing a specific critique of Western urbanism and environmental abuse that, in a similar manner, remaps the urban West. He shows how the West has become a series of over-developed cities, like Los Angeles and Las Vegas, with surveillance, gated communities, racism and decreased public space. He has drawn attention to the West as a dump for the weapons industry and nuclear waste, and uses the photographs of Richard Misrach as documents of this environmental damage (see Davis 1990, 2002; Beck 2010). Apocalyptic in a different manner that McCarthy's work discussed earlier, these photographs are a 'frontal attack on the hegemony of Ansel Adams', whose awesome photographs of nature in the West have been seen as a final statement of environmental wellbeing. Misrach and others like Peter Goin and Carole Gallagher have 'rudely deconstructed this myth of the virginal, if imperilled nature' and present an 'alternative iconography' (Davis 1990: 57–8) of Western waste, debris and development in order to instigate a photographic equivalent to the work of historians, writers and film-makers discussed earlier. They are 'resurveying' the West (like 'new topographers'), just as it had been originally charted in the 1860s and 1870s, but now in part to demonstrate change and destruction and more generally, as with all revisioning, to alert people to what lies behind the official versions of events. In the words of Mark Klett, one of the 'rephotographers' of the West, the aim was 'to raise questions we might never have thought to ask' (Bruce 1990: 81) about the West as a zone of engagement where different peoples and geographies collide. It is, however, clear that the Turner 'corral' has been opened forever to new and exciting versions of the West, but as Richard White comments, 'this revisioning and reimagining of the West is never complete' and must continue to examine critically the region and its multiple relations with both nation and world (White 1991: 629). Most notably, this can be seen in the increased discussion of the term 'postwestern' to suggest how this critical revision cannot be bound by the mythic past or by the traditional regionalisms embodied in limited understandings of place, race or gender. The word 'postwestern' acts as a reminder to go beyond such conventional tropes and yet simultaneously understand the complex relations that are at play in the composition of the multiple environments of the 'West' and how it lives on as a relevant subject of study even in a globalised world (see Kollin 2007; Campbell 2013).

Tropic of Orange is in many ways a postwestern novel aware of the past and the present as a complex interaction. Hence at one point an African American character, Buzzworm, discusses how maps might better reflect 'the stories of the life surrounding him' (Yamashita 1997: 43). As he ponders a map of LA torn, appropriately, from Mike Davis's book City of Quartz supposedly showing the 'Gang Territories' in 1972 (see Davis 1990: 301; Yamashita 1997: 80–1), 'He shook his head', recognising the limitations of the map's 'thick lines': 'If someone had put down all the layers of the real map', he says, 'maybe he could get the real picture' (Yamashita 1997: 81). This moment returns us to where this section opened; a 'territory', like a region, is not static enough to be accurately mapped by cartographic thick lines, it has to be instead attentive to details and to dynamic change, to the layers that Ellis saw or Klett and Misrach photographed and Manzanar identifies in Yamashita's novel: 'Somebody else must have the big map. Or maybe just the next map. The one with the new layers you can't even imagine' (ibid.: 82).

CASE STUDY 2: THE SOUTH – A WORLD APART?

A key theme in the history of Southern identity has been its supposed difference from the national American mainstream. In the context of the United States, the South has been seen as in some ways 'exceptional' in much the same way that the United States itself has been defined as exceptional in terms of its place in the international order (see the discussion in Chapter 9). A key part of this analysis was the way in which the South was identified for those attributes which set it apart from the North. As W.J. Cash, one of the leading analysts of Southern difference, asserted as late as 1941, 'the South is not quite a nation within a nation, but the next thing to it' and its existence could only really be understood through its relationship with the rest of the country (Cash 1971: vii).

One version of this theme displaced the political and racial divisions of the Civil War through an emphasis on the sacrificial nature of the South's struggle for independence, and the nobility with which it went down to defeat before the superior force of Northern armies. This was enhanced by the construction of the myth of the 'Lost Cause' of the Confederacy, with its emphasis on the truth and goodness of Southern motives. The ending of Reconstruction and Northern attempts to refashion the South were accompanied by a defensive determination of the white majority to regain political control of the region and to reassert its regulation of race relations, and other areas of social and cultural life. In its more sentimental form this was reflected in a passionate attachment to memories of an imagined Old South. As the opening credits of *Gone With The Wind* put it, there once was 'a land of Cavaliers and Cotton Fields' where 'in this pretty world, Gallantry took its last bow'.

However, versions of the past often suppress as much as they recall. The pervasive idealisation of the Old South, for instance, involved passing over the realities of slavery, and constructing a benign image of the plantation system (Brundage 2002: 6). In a similar way to the American West, the South has been a region constructed by many competing narratives, each making claims about how it might be either a part of or separate from other areas of the nation and of the world. As Tara McPherson has argued, though, 'Southern identity comes from somewhere – it has a history and is located in geography – yet it is also in flux, under construction, subject to change' (McPherson 2003: 8).

Rather than seeking to arrive at any precise geographic, cultural or social definitions of the South and its relationship to the rest of the nation, therefore, it may be more helpful to try to approach the problem of Southern identity through the range of attempts to perceive it and how these have changed and developed over time. The South exists because people have seen it as existing, and their efforts to articulate what they have seen, or imagined, carry significance in themselves. Southerners, in this sense, have developed, within a changing historical context, ways of viewing the world that link with their everyday experience. As Richard Gray has argued 'the South is primarily a concept, a matter of knowing even more than being, and, as such, part of the language of our currency and perception' (Gray 1986: xi–xii). Southerners have been 'busy reimagining and remaking their place in the act of seeing and describing it' (ibid.). The 'stories' created constitute the South and can be examined for 'the often ambiguous ways in which Southerners have interpreted and responded to national developments' (Ownby 1993: 3). This approach puts an emphasis on culture as a process in which people are actively engaged and which they make for themselves. However, because they enjoy unequal access to power, this frequently involves conflict. Claims to a distinctive regional identity often hide contests over who controls influential cultural institutions and organisations, and who does not. Historical representation is often closely linked to power and influence. From this perspective, a region is not 'a stable, boundaried, autonomous place' but rather 'a cultural history, the cumulative, generative effect of the interplay among the various, competing definitions of that region' (Reichert Powell 2007: 5). This is as true of the South as of any other region which has made claims to distinctiveness.

Another perspective on the question of 'the South' emerges when the differences between 'region' and 'regionalism' are drawn out as implied in the introduction to this chapter. 'Region' is often defined in apparently objective terms by trying to analyse, say, its dominant economic and social characteristics but often it goes further and turns into 'regionalism', defined as an act of advocacy for a particular set of qualities. One version of 'regionalism' here owes its origins to the early nineteenth-century romantic association between land and culture. Regionalist arguments of this kind have often been conservative in approach, looking back to older traditions and patterns of life, which have been threatened or even swamped by the modern world. In the interwar years, for instance, a group of Southern writers and intellectuals, who came to be described as the 'Agrarians', produced a critique of the urbanising, industrialising forces threatening what they most valued about the South. This 'Southern manifesto' appeared in the 1939 work *I'll Take My Stand: The South and the Agrarian Tradition* (Twelve Southerners 1962); it warned of the threat to individualist and humanist values in a world dominated by the developing power of an economic and political order, which linked centralised government to a productive system based on the machine and the cash nexus.

More recently, however, as suggested in the discussion of the West above, advocates of regionalism have affirmed its usefulness as an assertion of critical difference against both the claims of the centralised state dominated by monopolistic economic and cultural institutions and a nostalgic attachment to the local. Regions, Reichert Powell suggests, 'are not so much places themselves, but ways of describing relationships among places' (Reichert Powell 2007: 10). As such they are always provisional and in transit, and capable of reinterpretation and redirection.

Against this backdrop we want to use examples of the kinds of stories, by a range of insiders and outsiders, that have been told about the South at different stages in its history and to explore some of the ways in which they shed light both on what it has meant to be Southern, and how that difference has been articulated. All the while, it is worth noting David Potter's warning about the difficulties facing historians of the South in trying to come to terms with a region 'whose boundaries are indeterminate, whose degree of separateness has fluctuated over time [and] whose distinctiveness may be in some sense fictitious' (Potter 1968: 182).

One key theme in discussions of Southern identity has been the way in which the 'South' has been defined over time in relation to the concept of the 'North'. A number of commentators have argued that Southern distinctiveness has been much exaggerated and that Southern values and American values have had, and continue to have, much in common. Others went further, asserting that many of the distinctive, often negative qualities of the South, like violence and racism, were only intensified versions of basic American characteristics (Zinn 1964).

At the same time, however, this powerful version of Southern identity was regularly challenged by arguments that the South should adapt itself to change. At the end of the nineteenth century, for example, Henry Watterson, editor of the *Louisville Courier*, wrote that 'the South is simply a geographic expression' and he, along with a number of other editors and politicians, hoped for the disappearance of what they saw as outmoded Southern values and their replacement by national values which would enable the South to become fully integrated into the rest of the country. In the 1880s Henry Grady, the publisher of the *Atlanta Constitution*, defined this 'newness': 'We have sowed towns and cities in the place of theories, and put business in the place of politics. . . . We have fallen in love with work' (Brinkley 1995: 435). Industrial development and material progress on the Northern model would enable the South to resist economic dependency, and regain self-respect after military defeat in the Civil War. In 1895 the black leader, Booker T. Washington, foresaw a 'new heaven and a new earth' in his 'beloved South', as a result of material prosperity and the obliteration of racial animosities.

However, prophecies of transformation were often slow to be realised and old patterns of life remained. For many, the New South foreseen in the late nineteenth century did not appear until after the Second World War, when urbanisation, industrialisation, the decline of cotton agriculture, the rise of mass communications, an integrated mass transport system and air-conditioning came together to effect significant material change. As new businesses moved to Dixie attracted by lower wage rates, and weak unionisation, industrial workers for the first time outnumbered farmers, and a majority of the Southern population became urban. Even then, however, the idealisation of the Lost Cause did not disappear. Though the region opened itself to new economic forces, many of the key features of the old South persisted both in popular culture and the public realm. Cultural references to the past, moreover, often have been reinforced at times when the South has been under pressure from the forces of change. At the University of Mississippi symbols like the carrying of a giant Confederate flag at football games, the singing of Dixie as the school song and the adoption of Colonel Rebel – a white-goateed Southern gentleman of the old school – as mascot, only dated back to the late 1940s and the challenges to the traditional ways of life in the aftermath of the Second World War. Businessmen and politicians in the 2010s sell economic opportunity to foreign investors, but the Confederate flag still flies in the grounds of the Capitol building in South Carolina.

Contested representations of the South have not only come from within the region, but also from without. Southern difference, whether expressed in the romance of the Old South, or the violence of racial oppression, has always had an attraction for outsiders. Alison Graham, for instance, has noted the general infatuation of white Americans for the plantation myth, and the way in which its 'dream of racial purity' exerted 'a powerful pull on the American imagination' (Graham 2003: 20). As a result the temptation for external versions of the South to stereotype the region 'through a lexicon of clichés' has often been in conflict with the ways in which Southerners themselves have articulated their own beliefs and values (ibid.: 2). William Styron caught something of this tension in the arguments about the meaning of the South in his novel *Sophie's Choice* where one character says:

> At least Southerners have ventured North, have come to see what the North is like, while very few Northerners have ever really troubled themselves to travel to the South ... I remember you're saying how smug Northerners appeared to be in their wilful and self-righteous arrogance. .... How can I really have hated a place I have never seen or known?
>
> (Styron 1979: 418–19)

The ambiguous ways in which outsiders have interpreted and responded to the South have become part of the problem of adequately defining what the South is in any clear-cut way. One of the most influential of all versions of the South was Harriet Beecher Stowe's *Uncle Tom's Cabin*

(1852), which was largely written in Maine and was based on very limited direct knowledge of the region. Another Northerner, Stephen Foster, from Pittsburgh, helped to popularise nostalgic views of plantation society with such songs as 'My Old Kentucky Home' and 'Ole Folks at Home', views echoed in the widely reproduced lithographs of Currier and Ives. 'Dixie', the informal anthem of the Confederacy during the Civil War, was written by Daniel Emmett, who was born in Ohio and worked as a black-face minstrel in New York (Cobb 2005: 1). Charles K. Harris, a New York Jew, who wrote, among others, 'Mid the Green Fields of Virginia', had never visited the state, confessed that his version of the South came entirely from the imagination and that he had no idea whether corn was grown in Virginia or whether there were any hills in the Carolinas (Malone 1993: 131). A darker version of Southern difference from outside of the region, emphasised by Cash, described a South benighted by racism, violence and backwardness. This too, however, could be measured against the 'North'; what Kirby has described as Southern 'devilishness' could be juxtaposed against supposed Northern tolerance and liberalism (Kirby 1987: 166).

As this indicates, issues of continuity and change have regularly marked debates about the identity of the region. This has been reflected in Southern historiography as well as in other cultural forms such as literature and journalism. In American popular culture too, Southern 'difference' has been a staple topic. As Shreve McCannon famously urged Quentin Compson in William Faulkner's *Absalom, Absalom* (1937): 'Tell about the South! What do they do there? Why do they live there? Why do they live at all?' (Faulkner 1965: 174). Historian James Cobb urged a sense of caution when regularly asked similar questions about whether the South still existed: 'It depends on who's asking, – and when and why' (Cobb 2005: 8).

A diverse South

These examples suggest some of the difficulties involved in attempts to define the South's apparent difference from the rest of the nation and how this has changed over time: they also warn against assuming a monolithic South and underplaying variations within the region. In geographical terms it has often been defined as the eleven former confederate states, along with Kentucky and a latecomer like Oklahoma perhaps holding marginal positions, half in, half out. But what have these states had in common in terms of their material experience? There are clearly problems with finding objective characteristics, like the weather, which can be quantitatively assessed in a manner that will tell us where one region begins and another ends. Ulrich B. Phillips, writing in the 1920s, believed the climate was the chief agent making the South distinctive because heat and humidity encouraged the cultivation of specific staple crops like tobacco, rice and cotton, which in turn encouraged plantations and a slave labour force (Phillips 1928). *Absalom, Absalom* echoes this link between land, climate and character:

> This land, this South, for which God has done so much with woods for game and streams for fish and deep rich soil for seed and lush springs to sprout it and long summers to mature it and short mild winters for men and animals.
>
> (Cowley 1977: xxv–xxvi)

However, on closer analysis, the concept of a 'solid' South tends to fragment when confronted with the internal variety of the region. To discuss the Appalachian mountain regions alongside the Mississippi Delta, or southern Louisiana alongside Virginia, or Florida alongside anywhere may only expose the fragility of any attempt to provide an objective description of the region as a whole. The South, in geographical terms, has been marked by diverse agricultural patterns, linked to particular types of soil or weather. Recent writers have also pointed out the diversity of the Southern economy over place and time. Even during the South's brief existence as an independent nation during the Civil War, there was considerable tension between different parts of the Confederacy over the conduct of political affairs, which, at least in part, reflected local economic conditions. The Southern up-country, where a majority of white Southerners lived, contained substantial pockets of disaffection with the Confederate cause, and often open and hostile resentment to what many came to see as a rich man's war. Such differences continued to persist in the late nineteenth and twentieth centuries, surfacing with regularity to disrupt the conventional image of the solid white South.

Another set of issues emerge when we link problems of Southern identity to issues of race. Reed has put the question clearly. 'Are Southern blacks "Southerners" in any important sense?' (1982: 3). Deeply held myths about the region, whether they have been held by Southerners themselves or by critics from outside, have assumed that the South is white. The black response to such versions of Southern identity has been varied, with some like Booker T. Washington advocating an acceptance of dominant white values at least as a tactic. In the context of the violence and segregation of the late nineteenth-century South, Washington argued that rather than agitating for immediate equality and integration, black Southerners should concentrate on improving their own communities through education and economic development. Once they had something worthy of recognition, then their place in the South would be acknowledged. On the other hand, many blacks in the first half of the twentieth century rejected the South altogether and simply left it behind, joining the

Great Migration to the cities of the North and West in a search for economic opportunities and a refuge from the restrictions of Southern society. 'Southernness' was something to escape from.

An alternative narrative, however, argued for a remodelling of the South on interracial lines, while retaining a love for the South as a place. The Civil Rights movement of the 1950s and 1960s was largely made up of local black activists who were seeking to remake the South, rather than simply leave it as many of the previous generations had done in the 1920s and 1940s. This attempt to transform the South into a racial democracy and to integrate blacks into the mainstream of Southern life could have ironic consequences as Martin Luther King noted, writing from Birmingham jail in the summer of 1963. 'Virtues so long regarded as the exclusive property of the white South – gallantry, loyalty and pride – had passed to the Negro demonstrators in the heat of the summer's battles' (King 1964: 116).

This sense of pride in being both black and Southern has been a marked feature of many African American writers and commentators around the end of the twentieth century. The poet Nikki Giovanni in her memoir *Gemini* wrote that Knoxville, Tennessee, was 'a place where no matter what, I belong', and that 'Knoxville belongs to me'. Maya Angelou declared a 'sympathy for people who have no Southern roots'. Toni Morrison, though she was born in Ohio, throughout her work (see Chapter 3 for a full discussion) has asserted the importance of remembering the black experience in the South (Cobb 2005: 268–9, 280). Part of that memory was inevitably attached to the suffering of racial exploitation, but another equally significant part emphasised the sense of community and identity that African Americans created for themselves within a segregated world. This sense of the South as home was reflected in the increasing numbers of African Americans who either returned to the South or migrated there from elsewhere in the nation from the 1970s on. This did not mean that the South was now free from racial problems, but it did suggest that those who stayed or returned found it easier to identify with the changes in the South wrought by the Civil Rights movement. A North Carolina poll of 1971 asked a sample of the adult general population: 'Some people around here think of themselves as Southerners, others don't. How about you – would you say that you are a Southerner or not?' Some 82 per cent of whites answered that they were Southerners, but so did 75 per cent of blacks, figures borne out in a range of subsequent polls up until the 2000s. As this suggests, 'Southern blacks have on the one hand re-evaluated their white fellow-Southerners and at the same time laid increasing claim themselves to the label "Southerner"' (Reed 1982: 116–19; Cobb 2005: 263). The 'Lost Cause' revealed that control of the representation of African Americans was a weapon of domination that accompanied the economic and political structures of Jim Crow, but, as discussed in Chapter 3, the legacy of the Civil Rights movement provided an opportunity to open up alternative readings of Southern history and culture.

Another more recent challenge to the concept of a monolithic South has been the impact of globalising forces on the region, particularly as it has been affected by the influx of new migrants from across the world towards the end of the twentieth century. The Vietnamese portrayed in Malle's *Alamo Bay* or the Africans and Kurds in *And the Pursuit of Happiness* (see Chapter 2) are part of this story, but so too are the far more numerous Hispanic migrants who have moved into the region from Central and Southern America. Raymond Mohl has emphasised their significance to the extent of identifying a 'Nuevo' New South stretching from North Carolina to Texas. This latest version of the New South, he argues, has increasingly given the region a multicultural and multi-ethnic character, which has moved it away from its biracial past, and raised a fresh series of questions about its future. Spanish migration to the South, the *Washington Post* reported in 2000, is 'changing forever the old idea of what a southerner is' (Mohl 2005: 70). It has also disrupted the older notion of the South as based on the states in the South East which led the Confederacy, and suggested an increasing commonality with the South West, and then the broader hemisphere of Central America. This latter move has been increasingly related to the term 'Global South' and the concept of a region embedded in a 'larger transnational framework' of shared histories, economies and imaginaries (McKee and Trefzer 2006: 678). One of the functions of such thinking, rather like the project of critical regionalism discussed earlier, is to 'unmap, remap, and demap the U.S. South' in the twenty-first century (ibid.: 688) and place it within a broader context of transnational flows and encounters.

Writing the South

A powerful theme in Southern culture has been the relationship between writers and the region, and this link between writing and place has raised important interpretative issues. Is Southern literature to be valued for the accuracy and depth with which it depicts the geography of the South or, rather, should it be judged as work of the imagination, the authority of which is only diminished by seeking to chain it too closely to some concept of a 'real' world? This tension might be illustrated with reference to the work of a host of Southern writers, but it is most enduringly found in the work and life of William Faulkner. Faulkner lived most of his life in the small Mississippi town of Oxford, where he created the imagined region he called Yoknapatawpha. This was an invented landscape in which he could confront Southern history and society. But in seeking to come to terms with the burdens of the Southern past, Faulkner treated history not just as a collection of factual events, but as an opportunity for reconstructing its dilemmas through the power and scope of his imag-ination. In the stories that make up *Go Down Moses* (1942), for instance, Isaac McCaslin wrestles with the legacy of his family's past as slave-owners, and strains to find ways of liberating himself from its 'curse'. In 'The Bear' he rejects his inheritance since it has been tainted by the sin of ownership, both in terms of land and slaves, and moves into town where he might escape the hold of material possessions. However, later stories reveal that this move does not succeed and Ike returns to the woods where he might realise a genuine freedom, away from the temptations of human corruption. But his vision of the woods as some kind of Eden itself proves an illusion, as they come under increasing pressure from the depredations of 'progress' in the form of logging companies and other economic intrusions.

Southern writers were often concerned with specific themes: family, race, religion, a sense of place and the imperfectability of man and for Faulkner, and others like Robert Penn Warren, Allen Tate and William Styron, these themes were worked out within the context of a Southern history which restricted individual freedom. Ike McCaslin put it mordantly: 'The whole South is cursed, and all of us who derive from it, from whom it ever suckled, white and black both lie under the curse' (Faulkner 1996: 198). In contrast, Bobbie Ann Mason's *In Country* (1985) marks a shift from these traditional concerns, presenting a protagonist, Sam Hughes, who inhabits a world where time is measured by the national popular culture, which colours every part of her existence. Television schedules and music concerts provide markers for particular stages in her life, and this apparent lack of rootedness in communal qualities is reinforced by Sam's restless mobility. In place of Faulkner's contained Yoknapatawpha, we are pro-vided with a South dominated by the road, and by Sam's final trip with her grandmother and her uncle Emmett from Kentucky to the Vietnam memorial in Washington, DC, where she hopes to trace her father's name in the wall. It is not true that Sam is unconcerned with history, but her version of the past comes at the intersection between her personal efforts to make sense of her father's life and the war in Vietnam in which he died, rather than falling under the influence of the older complexities of Southern history. Her past is national rather than regional or local, and her engagement with it is touched by the same popular culture that affects other parts of the country, rather than by any specific Southern values. It is also a short-term past, which only goes back to the early 1960s when the Beatles first came to America, and which makes little attempt to connect the tragedy of Vietnam to deeper themes in the American or the Southern historical experience. C. Vann Woodward once commented that the South, at least up until the Vietnam War, had been un-American in having undergone an experience which no other part of the country had shared: the lesson of defeat and submission after war. He cherished the hope that this might provide a counter-balance to an unquestioned national faith in political progress and 'the conviction that American ideals, values and principles inevitably prevail in the end' (Woodward 1968: 188–9). He was later forced to qualify his position as Southern politicians, like President Lyndon Johnson and Secretary of State Dean Rusk, played an instrumental role in leading America into Vietnam, but he remained convinced that Americans still had something to learn from the experience of the South with history (ibid.: 233). The main characters in *In Country*, however, are notable for their distrust of history: 'You can't learn from the past', declares Sam's uncle Emmett. 'The main thing you learn from history is that you can't learn from history. That's what history is' (Mason 1987: 226). Mason's South of shopping malls, fast-food restaurants, television series and pop songs, with its concomitant distrust of history and tradition, appears to mark something of a break with the conventions of Southern culture. It may also suggest that *In Country* is also different, in that it is about other kinds of Southerners than those who wrote and appeared in earlier Southern fiction. Mason is not writing about the privileged, as older writers had, but about 'the common people' (Hobson 1994: 23). One version of the South is being discarded here, but another may be appearing in its place.

Documentary reportage

Another set of attempts to define Southern identity has been to 'document' it in some way and to uncover through observation and investigation a more accurate picture of the region's life. This goes back to Northern and European travellers to the slave South in the years before the Civil War, and remained a prolific source of material about the region in the twentieth century. The urge to 'document' and just how we should interpret works of documentary remain complex issues. As Paula Rabinowitz has argued, 'documentaries construct not only a vision of truth and identity but an appropriate way of seeing that vision' and so in examining documentary we must interrogate 'what it says, to whom, about whom, and for whom – and how it says it' (Rabinowitz 1994: 7).

In looking at the various forms of documentary which follow it is helpful to bear these considerations in mind: Who has sponsored these specific works? For which kinds of audience are they intended? What kinds of assumptions and expectations would different kinds of audiences have brought to the consumption of these images? How do these assumptions and expectations differ from our own? What kinds of narrative and other formal devices do these works use to gain their effect? These are all awkward questions, but they help to remind us that documentary is a *constructed* form, whose ambiguous meanings need to be as carefully explored as more transparently invented or imagined work. This is crucial when using this material for a history of the South or any other region because documentary works may appear to give us an objective view about different aspects of life in the South, but ultimately they are partial accounts, ideological texts produced according to certain conventions and rules, to communicate what they see as the 'truth' about the period.

Some of the most powerful images of the South in the twentieth century are provided in the work of photographers in the 1930s, who documented the region in a manner which has exercised a considerable hold on how the decade has been remembered. Much of this work was supported by the federal government, through the activities of a photographic section attached first to the Resettlement Administration and then the Farm Security Administration (FSA). Some FSA work celebrated the 'successes'

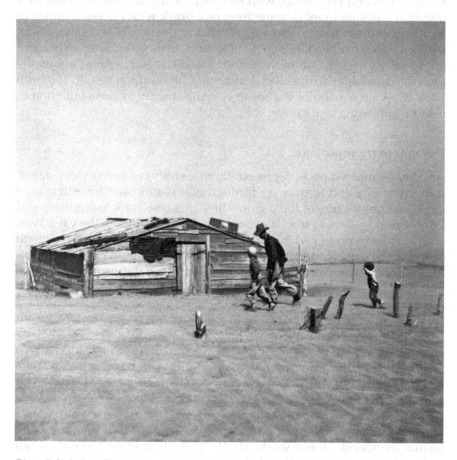

Plate 5.3 Arthur Rothstein, *Farmer and his Sons Walking by Shack in a Dust Storm*, 1936.

© Corbis

of agency programmes, but the pictures which had the greatest impact were those documenting the problems associated with rural poverty. FSA photographs were often used in the news media to illustrate the work of the New Deal in rural America, and, more particularly, the South. Photography's apparent transparency represented a South with 'the dignity of fact' (Orvell 1989: 229), which Dorothea Lange summed up by the quotation from Francis Bacon displayed on her darkroom door: 'The contemplation of things as they are, without substitution or imposture, without error or confusion, is in itself a nobler thing than a whole harvest of invention' (ibid.).

However, in examples of FSA work this emphasis on 'fact' and 'things as they are, without substitution or imposture' is problematic since photographic images 'manipulate the subject in front of the camera' (ibid.: 85). Rather than seeing the photograph as an accurate record of the real world, unchanged by artifice or invention, one must ask: 'What was a "truthful" picture of reality? Was truth to be found in literal exactitude or in artistic generalisation?' Did it matter if a picture was true or if it was convincing? (ibid.: 8). Thus, an FSA photograph by Arthur Rothstein (Plate 5.3) depicts a father and his sons caught in a dust storm in Oklahoma, which the photographer himself admitted was a 'directed' picture arranged for maximum effect. 'Provided the results are a faithful reproduction of what the photographer believes he saw', Rothstein later argued, 'whatever takes place in the making of a picture is justified' (ibid.: 230). Walker Evans, who also briefly worked for the FSA, felt that in work like this Rothstein had violated the tenets of true documentary: 'that's where the word "documentary" holds', he argued, 'you don't touch a *thing*. You manipulate, if you like, when you frame a picture – one foot one way or one foot another. But you're not putting anything in.' Rothstein, however, was unrepentant. For him, a 'factual and true' picture could be gained by exercising an explicit degree of directorial control over his subject. Evans, in contrast, argued that his ideal was to create a 'stark record'. Alteration or manipulation was out of the question, since it would result in propaganda (all in Orvell 1989: 230–1).

Evans put some of these ideas into practice through his and James Agee's documentary book *Let Us Now Praise Famous Men*, first published in 1941, which combined essays and photographs to record the daily lives of representative white Southern tenant farmers. Agee was a particular advocate of the possibilities of popular culture, especially film and photography, and linked them to a hostility to the kind of social and cultural conservatism he saw in the work of the Southern Agrarians. With Walker Evans as his collaborator, Agee approached Southern identity and how it might be documented as a radicalised Southerner who had left home and returned to look again at what he had left behind, but more particularly because he raised so explicitly and emphatically the problems associated with the very process of looking. What authority do we have to record and interpret the lives of others, particularly the poor? For what audiences are our interpretations intended? How can the experiences of our subjects be communicated in a manner that does not demean or marginalise them? In this respect, one critic has suggested that *Let Us Now Praise Famous Men* is not so much a book about sharecropping as a book about the writing of a book about sharecropping. In creating it, Agee raised questions about the contradictions the South faced in the late 1930s, between preserving a past associated with suffering and poverty and at the same time containing immense reserves of resilience and cultural depth, and opting for a future that provided material improvement, but at the expense of communal values. The opening passages of *Let Us Now Praise Famous Men* are concerned with Agee's relentless self-questioning about both the morality of his undertaking, and the technical frailty of the resources at his disposal.

> It seems to me curious, not to say obscene and thoroughly terrifying ... to pry intimately into the lives of an undefended and appallingly damaged group of human beings, an ignorant and helpless rural family, for the purpose of parading the nakedness, disadvantage and humiliation of these lives before another group of human beings, in the name of science, of 'honest journalism' (whatever that paradox may mean), of humanity, of social fearlessness, for money, and for a reputation for crusading and for unbias.
>
> (Agee and Evans 1965: 7)

Agee doubts that language can accurately represent the Southern people and yet he persists in an attempt to capture their spirit. Agee rejects conventional forms of documentary and their concern with 'facts' and objectivity, using different formal devices to overcome concerns about the limitations of the written word. These include extremely detailed accounts of specific topics like work and housing, autobiographical confessions and poetry. Equally important are the sixty uncaptioned photographs by Walker Evans which precede the written text. Standing in juxtaposition to it, they reinforce Agee's concerns with the means of representation. Agee argues that the camera's 'next to unassisted and weaponless consciousness' could overcome the problems he found with words because the camera's ice-cold eye was 'incapable of recording anything but absolute, dry truth' (ibid.).

In Evans's photographs his subjects are aware of their part in the making of the photograph and

> are conscious of the camera, of its manipulator, and of the unknowable audience behind it. They are not taken off guard; on the contrary they

have been given time to arrange and compose themselves for the picture.

(Stott 1973: 268)

In fact, in practice, Evans himself resorted to some of the same strategies as Rothstein, by rearranging furniture in the sharecroppers' houses for aesthetic effect. Nevertheless through the direct, frontal, positioning of his camera he tried to give those whom he photographed a degree of self-respect. At the same time the lucidity of his vision reminds us that, in Alan Trachtenberg's words, his photographs 'transcribe not "reality," but the world as it was seen and recorded' (Trachtenberg 1999: 251). What Agee and Evans in their different ways consider, therefore, is what some historians have also identified as a central issue in seeking to understand the lives of ordinary Southerners, particularly the poor, in the 1930s. Progress here was not always an unmixed blessing. It brought with it the benefits of modernisation such as electrification, improved roads, and scientific farming, bringing the South closer to the American mainstream, but it also damaged a way of life, patterns of living, a culture (Daniel 1987, 2000). Agee and Evans, in constantly calling our attention to the beauty of the sharecroppers' poverty, in asserting the dignity with which they lived their lives, also remind us 'That the world can be improved and yet must be celebrated as it is are contradictions. The beginning of maturity may be the recognition that both are true' (Stott 1973: 289).

Southern music

In a visit to Memphis in 1968, the journalist Stanley Booth recorded meeting Dan Penn, an influential producer and songwriter, at the highly successful American Studios. He spoke of the South as a place where, 'People . . . don't let nobody tell them what to do.' 'But how does it happen that they know what to do?', Booth asked, and Penn 'squinted at me across the desk, "I ain't any explanation for it," he said' (Booth 1993: 78). Penn's laconic style catches something of the unpredictable and often innovative way in which Southern music has developed. Popular music has been one of the most significant cultural forms in the lives of many Southerners, and has been one of the most important contributions the South has made to a wider American and international musical culture. Southern white and black music, as an expression of the values and beliefs of the common people of the South, has had a significant role in the way that ordinary Southerners have thought and felt about the most important themes in their lives such as family, land, work, sacred and profane love. Such music implicitly raises questions about the relationship between popular culture and more traditional notions of Southern culture, linked to the continuing commodification of plantation myth and the genteel traditions of the

Old South. The spread of Southern music, both across the region, and over the rest of the nation, has also been closely connected with the modernisation of the South and arguments as to whether that process has diluted distinctively Southern qualities. Because it is so closely identified with the lives of ordinary Southerners, it also inevitably raises the issue of race, and how that has affected the kinds of musical expression that have emerged from the region.

Country music has been a particularly important form, and can be examined in a number of ways. One approach is to look at it in the context of the modernisation of Southern culture. As Bill Malone has suggested, 'country entertainers were torn between tradition and modernity' because their music 'had its origins in the folk culture of the South – a diverse culture that drew upon the interrelating resources of Europe and Africa', but it was developed and spread, first throughout the South and then the rest of the nation, by the communications revolution of the interwar years, symbolised by the growth of radio and the record industry (Malone 1987: 3). This, of course, was precisely the period in which the rural small-town South was being transformed by the experience of agricultural modernisation. Country music, on the one hand, celebrated many of those virtues that 'progress' seemed to be undermining: a sense of place, community, family, church and motherhood, while on the other hand, it became increasingly popular directly as a result of modernising forces and technological innovation.

This tension between old and new is apparent in the careers of some of the key performers in early country music. The Carter Family, for instance, came from Clinch Mountain in Virginia and their music generally projected a consistent mood, that of the family home, where their 'sound remained that of an intimate singing for a small circle of friends where the values of home and family, decency and modesty, were both assumed and shared as living Christian rural fellowship' (ibid.: 65–8). However, one of the important factors in the popularisation of the Carter Family's traditional music was Mexican border radio. Located just across the Rio Grande, and thus outside federal frequency regulations, these stations broadcast to much of the continental United States, as far as the Canadian border. Border radio programming was extremely varied, but it used country music (or hillbilly music as it was still generally called) interspersed with extensive advertising and religious evangelism.

Another significant figure in the development of country music was Jimmie Rodgers, 'The Singing Brakeman', who celebrated a different image of the South from the settled community of the Carters: the attraction of the open road, of individuals who had left home because of opportunity, homelessness, eviction and crime. He became a decisive influence in 'country music's evolution as a star-oriented phenomenon, with traits increasingly national rather than local in scope' (ibid.: 77), even though he himself never performed in the North, spending his short career criss-crossing the South on vaudeville tours and travelling tent shows. More than was the case with the Carter Family, his commercial success on radio and record helped to bring a romantic stereotype of a certain set of Southern attitudes to a regional, national and international audience. Rodgers's songs about leaving were closely connected to changes affecting the South in the 1920s and 1930s as the Depression, drought, agricultural modernisation and government policies forced Southerners to go on the move. As Pete Daniel has noted, 'the farther they removed themselves from the country, the more alluring country music became' (Daniel 1987: 102).

During the Second World War country music became increasingly national in its appeal as Southerners continued to migrate in ever-increasing numbers to the West and North, and as the appeal of radio spread still further. This boom lasted into the mid-1950s through the careers of such figures as Hank Williams, and the introduction of country music to television, but in the mid 1950s it was severely challenged by an alternative form of Southern music: rock and roll. Elvis Presley was a Southerner, but his early music, while drawing on traditional white (and black) sources, rapidly changed into something fresh and distinctive. Country music responded in two main ways, either by adapting some of the style and instrumentation of 'pop' music, or by periodically reasserting its traditional roots. Since the late 1950s both of these trends have been in existence, sometimes working together, sometimes in opposition to each other. In this sense country music's development has reflected the tension within the concept of regionalism discussed above. On the one hand, it has reflected an attachment to an often sentimentalised version of place, and the way in which it is attached to cultural values as can be seen in the work of artists from the Carter Family in the 1920s and 1930s through to Dolly Parton in the late twentieth century. On the other hand, by providing a voice for ordinary working-class Southerners to express their frustrations and desires it has provided the opportunity for a more implicitly critical approach to what it means to be Southern as can be seen in the work of performers from Hank Williams to Steve Earle. As these four examples suggest, such opposing tensions could regularly be found within the same person.

Another important theme in Southern popular music has been the interplay between black and white cultures; while there have been, and are, predominantly black idioms, like the blues, or predominantly white idioms, like country music, both are impossible to understand without an appreciation of the biracial world from which they emerged. As Edward Ayers has emphasised, 'the presence of black Southerners shaped the private actions and public culture of the white South' (Ayers 1992: 119). Charles Joyner has argued that 'the central theme of Southern history has been racial integration' and that 'cultural styles have always refused to abide by any colour line, however rigidly it may have been drawn' (Joyner 1993: 3–5). This mixing of cultural traditions has been as important as any other factor for the extraordinary richness of Southern music. Despite formal and informal segregation, both races have been heavily influenced by each other. A number of important white musicians both learned from and cooperated with black musicians and vice versa, to create a 'common legacy of musical performance' (Malone 1993: 151). Jimmie Rodgers created 'white blues' in the 1920s and recorded with Louis Armstrong in 1930. Elvis Presley drew on the black rhythm and blues of his home town in Memphis, and his first five singles for Sun Records had blues on one side and country and western on the other. Carl Perkins also picked up on black styles, and his 'Blue Suede Shoes' became the first record to reach the top of the pop, country and rhythm and blues charts. Stanley Booth claims this was more important than the Emancipation Proclamation, which was an edict handed down from above, whereas the success of 'Blue Suede Shoes' among African Americans represented an actual grass-roots acknowledgement of a common heritage, a mutual overcoming of poverty and a kind of redemption (Booth 1993: 14). The Stax label in the 1960s was another cooperative venture whose house band, the MGs, was made up of black and white musicians. Rodgers Redding, the brother of the leading soul singer Otis Redding, praised it in a similar manner to Booth: 'What made it work, the key to it all was black and white working together as a team' (Guralnick 1986: 405).

Just as country music spoke for the concerns of ordinary white Southerners, and soul for a moment articulated the possibilities of black–white cooperation, so rap in turn from the 1980s on expressed different takes on what it meant to be Southern. Emerging from a range of cities across the South like Miami, Houston, Atlanta, New Orleans, Memphis and Virginia Beach, new rap artists articulated the concerns of young black Southerners, in ways that often self-consciously positioned themselves against northern and western styles, and at the same time revealed an openness to transnational influences form elsewhere in the Americas. In Miami, for instance, Matt Miller notes, 'African Americans with roots in the U.S. South formed but one element of a multi-lingual, multi-ethnic, and heavily Caribbean cultural mix' (Miller 2008). In New Orleans it drew on 'deeply rooted traditions of expressive culture, including those related to carnival' to develop another distinctive perform-ance style, sometimes described as 'bounce' (ibid.). One epithet which became attached to these new genres was that of 'Dirty South'. Its origins lay in Goodie Mob's 'Dirty South' (1996), in which the group used its base in Atlanta to express the voices of South's urban black youth against the rest of the country and the world. Although the term became used as a marketing concept to sell Southern rap to national audiences, it neverthe-less offered 'a grounded, oppositional historical consciousness' against the ways in which class and race had influenced conventional notions of Southern identity, associated with racial purity and whiteness (Miller 2008).

Film and the South

Southern identity has also been constructed through film. From its earliest days Hollywood has frequently used the South as subject matter, and in so doing helped to inform the images that Southerners held of their own region, as well as the impressions of non-Southerners, whether in the rest of the country or outside America altogether. Hollywood has often tended to present a range of stereotypical versions of the South, but their resonance and effectiveness have varied according to the era in which they were produced, and the concerns and values of the audiences who consumed them. One of the most influential of these versions is what a number of critics have labelled the 'Southern', as a counterpart to the more widely recognised genre of the 'Western'. For Leslie Fiedler, writing in 1968, the Southern actively sought 'melodrama, a series of bloody events, sexual by implication at least, played out in the blood-heat of a "long hot summer" against a background of miasmal swamps, live oak, Spanish moss, and the decaying plantation house' (Fiedler 1972: 15–16). The Southern has tended to come in two forms: one relatively nostalgic and benign, the other darker and brooding, and the two themes have often been combined in the same film. Traditional versions of the South have been represented in two of the most influential blockbusters in Hollywood history: *The Birth of a Nation* (1915, directed by D.W. Griffith) and *Gone with the Wind* (1939, directed by David Selznick). *The Birth of a Nation* is a difficult film to deal with at the start of the twenty-first century, because its version of Southern history so explicitly endorses white supremacy, and either the childlike or bestial nature of African Americans. Griffith presents a history of the South in which the 'lost cause' of the Confederacy represents all that was best about Southern values and, by implication, those of the rest of the nation. National unity between North and South could only be restored if the virtues of the Southern cause were fully understood and appreciated by 'outsiders'. As one of Griffith's collaborators declared, it was hoped that 'every man who comes out of one of our theaters is a Southern partisan for life' (Kirby 1987: 4).

Scott Simmon has argued that one way to read *The Birth of a Nation* is as part of the sustained Southern argument against Harriet Beecher Stowe's *Uncle Tom's Cabin*. Ever since the novel's original publication in 1852, Southern writers have inveighed against what they saw as Stowe's misrepresentation of the slave South, and the two novels by Thomas Dixon Jr, *The Leopard's Spots* and *The Clansman*, were in part an angry riposte to a popular staging of *Uncle Tom's Cabin* in 1901. Griffith, Simmon argues, used Dixon's material to turn Stowe on her head. 'Whereas Stowe's suffering mothers and violated women served to damn the institution of slavery, the *Birth*'s suffering mothers and violated women damned Reconstruction ideals of equality' (Simmon 1993: 125–6). Family and home were revealingly exploited by Griffith as symbols of morality, with women in particular presented as the epitome of purity, whose reputation and safety it was the duty of men to protect. In one of the key scenes of the film, the daughter of the South Carolinian Cameron family throws herself off a cliff to escape the pursuit of Gus, a renegade black soldier. Death for her is far sweeter than dishonour. The rise of the Ku Klux Klan, inspired by her brother, the Little Colonel, would protect Southern womanhood from such threats, and in so doing regain white supremacy and restore order and harmony in society.

Twenty-four years later, *Gone with the Wind* follows Griffith in representing the plantation South as a kind of Eden, dominated by grace, honour and community, but, fitting the Depression years in which it was produced, shows how that idyll was to be destroyed by social collapse and economic disaster. However, the solution this time is not simply to redeem the South by restoring white rule, though there are affinities between the versions of Reconstruction presented in *The Birth of a Nation* and *Gone with the Wind*, but instead to reassert traditional American beliefs in the virtues of individual effort. Scarlett in the end refuses to stay with Rhett Butler in the privileged and backward-looking seclusion of Charleston and prefers to return to Tara in the hope of restoring both her own and her region's fortunes.

That said, to leave the impression that this kind of treatment of the South on film is the only or even the most dominant one would be misleading. Other influential themes have emerged, particularly since the 1940s. One is the treatment of racial issues, often from a critical or liberal perspective. One of the path-breakers here was *Intruder in the Dust* (1949), based on William Faulkner's novel, but it was followed by such films as *The Intruder* (1962) and *To Kill a Mockingbird* (1963). *In the Heat of the Night* (1967), however, did as much as any other movie of this kind to 'break Hollywood's silence about the contemporary South' by dealing with 'the racism of the Southern legal system' (Graham 2003: 179). By using a plot in which a suspected black criminal, deep in Mississippi, had the false accusations against him cleared after the persistent investigations of a black policeman from the North, it appeared to undermine many of Hollywood's earlier evasions about the nature of race relations in the South. However, at another level, its conclusion worked to redeem much of the Southern system. The small-town police chief eventually joins forces with his black counterpart to track down the real villain, who turns out not to be a local landowner as first suspected, but a feckless redneck. The whiteness of the Southern system is excused by 'projecting the criminality of the race onto its lowest member' (Graham 2003: 181–2). Another more recent trend has been the emergence of films whose protagonists have come from the Southern working class, often as a conscious alternative to the plantation tradition. Sometimes labelled 'hickflicks', these have taken various forms. One popular plot presents restless white male heroes confronting and sometimes overcoming representatives of state authority, often in the form of the police. Characteristically such narratives have often combined comedy and violence, as in the Burt Reynolds *Smokey and the Bandit* cycle (1980, 1983), but they have also on occasion had a more serious purpose, as in a film like *Cool Hand Luke* (1967), where Paul Newman experiences the travails of a Southern chain-gang for a crime which only involved getting drunk and destroying a parking meter. An alternative version of the poor white South, which has allowed more space for women as representatives of what was most important in the culture of the 'common people', and has often presented men as part of the problem, may be found in the recent series of films dealing with Southern music, and particularly country and western. Films like *A Coalminer's Daughter* (1980) and *Sweet Dreams* (1985) portray the lives of singers Loretta Lynn and Patsy Cline and provide a counter to the plantation myth in which such women appear only on the periphery of the action, and may be seen as part of the same process as the democratisation of Southern literature in the hands of writers like Bobbie Ann Mason. Changing attitudes towards the representation of women in the American South is presented in a still more radical form in *Thelma and Louise* (1991). The South here is not represented by a specific, idealised place like Tara, but instead by many of the same developments that Mason writes about in *In Country*: the open road, cheap motels, popular music. The main protagonists do not look to men for their protection, but instead take their own revenge on an uncaring husband by deserting him, and on would-be rapists by exacting their own, violent, form of revenge. And yet by inverting many of the conventions of the Southern way of life, the film still ties in to many of the debates about Southernness, which gives its often turbulent and violent atmosphere an added resonance.

Conclusion

As we have seen, one recent perspective on the South which raises further questions about its future distinctiveness as a region has been the impact of globalising forces on its economy and society. The South has become increasingly open to transnational forces, and has itself entered into the global order through its culture, particularly its music, its products, for instance Coca-Cola, and its values, for instance the example of non-violent direct action as developed by the Civil Rights movement. Of course, the South was never quite as 'separate' from the rest of the nation or the world as mythology suggested, and claims about the imminent loss of Southern identity themselves have a long history. Nevertheless, the pace of change in the region, Fred Hobson suggests, makes the early twenty-first century a 'revolutionary time' in the US South, in which old assumptions about the region have to be discarded, and new participants will play a key role in articulating a very different Southern future (Hobson 2002: 11). This does not mean, however, that the South will no longer generate 'powerful images and complex emotions' (Wilson and Ferris 1989: viii). As Edward Ayers has argued, 'the very story of the South is a story of unresolved identities' – a judgement which chimes with the way in which critical regionalism continues to raise questions about the links between place and identity (Cobb 2005: 337). It may be that modernisation has rendered aspects of the Southern world less distinctive and has destroyed that older notion of a separate monolithic South, set apart from the rest of the country, but somehow Southerners, in all their increasing variety, will still find ways in which to talk about who they are and where they live.

REFERENCES AND FURTHER READING

The West

Allmendinger, B. and Matsumoto, V. (eds) (1999) *Over the Edge: Remapping the American West*, Berkeley: University of California Press.

Anzaldúa, G. (1987) *Borderlands/La Frontera*, San Francisco: Aunt Lute Books.

Appleby, J., Hunt, L., and Jacob, M. (eds) (1994) *Telling the Truth About History*, London: W.W. Norton.

Armitage, S. and Jameson, E. (eds) (1987) *The Women's West*, London: University of Oklahoma Press.

Barthes, R. (1976) *Mythologies*, London: Paladin.

Beck, J. (2010) *Dirty Wars: Landscape, Power, and Waste in Western American Literature*, Lincoln: University of Nebraska Press.

Berkhofer, R.F. (1978) *The White Man's Indian: Images of the American Indian from Columbus to the Present*, New York: Vintage Books.

Berkeley, G. (1726) *Verses on the Prospect of Planting Arts and Learning in America*, at the Berkeley Historical Society website, http://www.berkeleyhistoricalsociety. org/history-notes/bishop-george-berkeley.html (accessed 11/09/2015).

Bruce, C. (ed.) (1990) *Myth of the West*, New York: Rizzoli.

Burns, R. and Ades, L. (1995) *The Wild West*, produced by WGBH Educational Foundation and Steeplechase Films Inc.

Burroughs, W. (1988) *The Western Lands*, London: Picador.

Campbell, N. (2000) *The Cultures of the American New West*, Edinburgh: Edinburgh University Press.

—— (2008) *The Rhizomatic West: Representing the American West in a Transnational, Global, Media Age*, Lincoln: University of Nebraska Press.

—— (2013) *Post-Westerns: Cinema/Region/West*, Lincoln: University of Nebraska Press.

Carmichael, D.A. (ed.) (2006) *The Landscape of the Hollywood Westerns*, Salt Lake City: University of Utah Press.

Castillo, Ana (1994a) *So Far from God*, London: Women's Press.

—— (1994b) *Massacre of the Dreamers: Essays on Xicanisma*, Albuquerque: University of New Mexico Press.

Cather, W. (1913) *O Pioneers*, London: Heinemann.

Chan, S., Daniels, D.H. *et al.* (eds) (1994) *Peoples of Color in the American West*, Lexington: D.C. Heath.

Comer, K. (1999) *Landscapes of the New West*, Chapel Hill: University of North Carolina Press.

—— (2010) *Surfer Girls in the New World Order*, Durham: Duke University Press.

Cronon, W., Miles, G., and Gitlin, J. (1992) *Under An Open Sky: Rethinking America's Western Past*, London: W.W. Norton.

Crow, C. (ed.) (2003) *A Companion to the Regional Literatures of America*, Oxford: Blackwell.

Davis, M. (1990) *City of Quartz: Excavating the Future in Los Angeles*, London: Verso.

—— (1993) 'Dead West: Ecocide in Marlboro Country', *New Left Review*, vol. 200, July/August, pp. 49–73.

—— (2002) *Dead Cities and Other Tales*, New York: The New Press.

Deverall, W. (ed.) (2004) *Companion to the American West*, Oxford: Blackwell.

Doctorow, E.L. (1994) (first 1971) *The Book of Daniel*, London: Pan.

Drinnon, R. (1990) *Facing West: The Metaphysics of Indian Hating and Empire Building*, New York: Schocken Books.

Ellis, B. Easton (1985) *Less Than Zero*, London: Picador.

—— (1994) *The Informers*, London: Picador.

Engel, L. (1994) *The Big Empty: Essays on the Land as Narrative*, Albuquerque: University of New Mexico Press.

Fisher, P. (ed.) (1991) *The New American Studies: Essays from Representations*, Berkeley, CA: University of California Press.

Fjellman, S. (1992) *Vinyl Leaves: Walt Disney and America*, Boulder, CO: Westview Press.

Foote, S. (2003) 'The Cultural Work of American Regionalism' in C. Crow (ed.) *A Companion to the Regional Literatures of America*, Oxford: Blackwell.

Foucault, M. (1977) *Discipline and Punish: The Birth of the Prison*, Harmondsworth: Penguin.

—— (1980) *Power/Knowledge: Selected Interviews and Other Writings 1972–1977*, London: Harvester Wheatsheaf.

Frampton, K. (1983) 'Towards a Critical Regionalism' in H. Foster (ed.) *Postmodern Culture*, London: Pluto Press.

Graulich, M. and Tatum, S. (eds) (2003) *Reading The Virginian in the New West*, Lincoln: University of Nebraska Press.

Greenblatt, S. (1991) *Marvelous Possessions*, London: Routledge.

Gunn Allen, P. (1992) *The Sacred Hoop*, Boston: Beacon.

Hunt, A. (ed.) (2008) *The Geographical Imagination of Annie Proulx: Rethinking Regionalism*, Lanham, MD: Rowman & Littlefield.

Jameson, F. (1984) 'Periodizing the Sixties' in S. Sayres *et al.* (eds) *The 60s Without Apology*, Minneapolis: University of Minnesota Press.

Jenkins, K. (1991) *Rethinking History*, London: Routledge.

King, M.L. (1964) *Why We Can't Wait*, New York: New American Library.

Kitses, J. (2004) *Horizons West*, London: BFI.

Kollin, S. (ed.) (2007) *Postwestern Cultures: Literature, Theory, Space*, Lincoln: University of Nebraska Press.

Kolodny, A. (1984) *The Land Before Her: Fantasy and Experience of the American Frontiers, 1630–1860*, Chapel Hill: University of North Carolina.

—— (1992) 'Letting Go Our Grand Obsessions: Notes Towards a New Literary History of the American Frontiers', *American Literature* vol. 64, no. 1, March, pp. 1–18.

Lawrence, D.H. (1977) *Studies in Classic American Literature*, Harmondsworth: Penguin.

Lefaivre, L. and Tzonis, A. (2003) *Critical Regionalism*, Munich: Prestel.

Lévi-Strauss, C. (1963) *Structural Anthropology*, New York: Basic Books.

Lewis, N. (2004) *Unsettling the Literary West*, Lincoln: University of Nebraska Press.

Limerick, P.N. (1987) *The Legacy of Conquest: The Unbroken Past of the American West*, New York: W.W. Norton.

Limerick, P.N., Milner, C.A., and Rankin, C.E. (eds) (1991) *Trails: Toward a New Western History*, Lawrence: University of Kansas Press.

McCarthy, C. (1990) (first 1985) *Blood Meridian, or the Evening Redness in the West*, London: Picador.

McMurtry, L. (1985) *Lonesome Dove*, New York: Simon & Schuster.

Mariani, P. (ed.) (1991) *Critical Fictions*, Seattle: Bay Press.

Massey, D. (1995) 'Places and their Pasts', *History Workshop Journal*, Spring, vol. 39, pp. 182–92.

Milner, C.A. (1989) *Major Problems in the History of the American West*, Lexington: D.C. Heath.

Milner, C.A., O'Connor, C., and Sandweiss, M.A. (eds) (1994) *The Oxford History of the American West*, London: Oxford University Press.

Misrach, R. (1990) *Bravo 20*, Albuquerque: University of New Mexico Press.

Munslow, A. (1992) *Discourse and Culture: The Creation of America, 1870–1920*, London: Routledge.

Nash Smith, H. (1950) *Virgin Land: The American West as Myth and Symbol*, New York: Vintage.

Palahniuk, C. (2003) *Fugitives and Refugees*, New York: Crown Publishers.

Papanikolas, Z. (2007) *American Silence*, Lincoln: University of Nebraska Press.

Proulx, E.A. (1999) *Close Range*, London: Fourth Estate.

—— (2002) *That Old Ace in the Hole*, London: Fourth Estate.

—— (2004) *Bad Dirt*, London: Fourth Estate.

—— (2009) *Fine Just the Way It Is: Wyoming Stories*, London: Fourth Estate.

Riley, G. (1992) *A Place to Grow: Women in the American West*, Arlington Heights, IL: Harlan Davidson, Inc.

Robertson, J.O. (1980) *American Myth, American Reality*, New York: Hill & Wang.

Robinson, F. (ed.) (1998) *The New Western History: The Territory Ahead*, Tucson: University of Arizona Press.

Said, E. (1994) *Culture and Imperialism*, London: Vintage.

Sayres, S. *et al.* (eds) (1984) *The 60s Without Apology*, Minneapolis: University of Minnesota Press.

Schaefer, J. (1989) (first 1949) *Shane*, London: Heinemann Educational.

Silko, L.M. (1977) *Ceremony*, New York: Penguin.

—— (1981) *Storyteller*, New York: Arcade.

Slotkin, R. (1973) *Regeneration Through Violence: The Mythology of the American Frontier, 1600–1869*, Middletown: Wesleyan University Press.

—— (1985) *The Fatal Environment: The Myth of the Frontier in the Age of Industrialization, 1800–1890*, New York: Atheneum.

—— (1992) *Gunfighter Nation: The Myth of the Frontier in Twentieth-Century America*, New York: Harper Perennial.

Storey, J. (1993) *An Introductory Guide to Cultural Theory and Popular Culture*, London: Harvester Wheatsheaf.

Tompkins, J. (1992) *West of Everything: The Inner Life of Westerns*, Oxford: Oxford University Press.

Trachtenberg, A. (1982) *The Incorporation of America*, New York: Hill & Wang.

Truettner, W. (ed.) (1991) *The West As America*, Washington, DC: Smithsonian Institute Press.

Turner, F.J. (1962) *The Frontier in American History*, (ed.) R. Billington, New York: Holt, Rinehart and Winston.

Turner, F.W. (ed.) (1977) *The Portable North American Indian*, New York: Penguin/Viking.

Twelve Southerners (1962) (first 1939) *I'll Take My Stand: The South and the Agrarian Tradition*, New York: Harper & Row.

Whipple, T.K. (1943) *Study Out the Land*, Berkeley: University of California Press.

White, R. (1991) *It's Your Misfortune and None of My Own: A New History of the American West*, Norman and London: University of Oklahoma Press.

Whitman, W. (1971) (first 1865) *Leaves of Grass*, London: Everyman.

Wister, O. (1979) *The Virginian*, New York: Signet.

Witschi, N. (ed.) (2011) *A Companion to the Literature and Culture of the American West*, Cambridge: Blackwell.

Worster D. (1992) *Under Western Skies: Nature and History in the American West*, Oxford: Oxford University Press.

—— (1994) *An Unsettled Country: Changing Landscapes of the American West*, Albuquerque: University of New Mexico Press.

Wright, R. (1992) *Stolen Continents: The 'New World' Through Indian Eyes*, Boston: Houghton Mifflin.

Yamashita, K. Tei (1997), *Tropic of Orange*, Minneapolis: Coffee House Press.

Zukin, S. (1991) *Landscapes of Power*, Berkeley, CA: University of California Press.

The South

Agee, J. and Evans, W. (1965) (first 1941) *Let Us Now Praise Famous Men*, London: Peter Owen.

Asquith, M. (2014) *The Lost Frontier: Reading Annie Proulx's Wyoming Stories*, London: Bloomsbury Academic.

Ayers, E. (1992) *The Promise of the New South: Life after Reconstruction*, New York: Oxford University Press.

Ayers, E. and Mittendorf, B. (eds) (1997) *The Oxford Book of the American South: Testimony, Memory, and Fiction*, Oxford: Oxford University Press.

Badger, A. (2003) *Race in the American South: From Slavery to Civil Rights*, Edinburgh: Edinburgh University Press.

Baker, H. and Nelson, D. (eds) (2002) *Violence, the Body and the South: A Special Issue of American Literature*, Durham: Duke University Press.

Boles, J. (2000) *The South through Time: A History of an American Region*, London and Englewood Cliffs, NJ: Prentice Hall.

Boles, J. (ed.) (2002) *A Companion to the American South*, Oxford: Blackwell.

Booth, S. (1993) *Rythm Oil: A Journey Through the Music of the American South*, London: Vintage.

Brinkley, A. (1995) *American History: A Survey*, New York: McGraw-Hill.

Brundage W.H. (ed.) (2002) *Where These Memories Grow: History, Memory and Southern Identity*, Chapel Hill: University of North Carolina Press.

Campbell, N. (2016) *Affective Critical Regionality*. London: Rowman Littlefield International (forthcoming).

Carter, M. (2015) *Myth of the Western: New Perspectives on Hollywood's Frontier Narrative*, Edinburgh: Edinburgh University Press.

Cash, W.J. (1971) (first 1941) *The Mind of the South*, New York: Vintage.

Cobb, J. (2005) *Away Down South: A History of Southern Identity*, Oxford: Oxford University Press.

Cobb J. and Stueck W. (eds) (2005) *Globalisation and the American South*, Athens: University of Georgia Press

Cooper, W. and Terrill, T. (1991) *The American South: A History*, New York: McGraw-Hill.

Cowley, M. (ed.) (1977) *The Portable Faulkner*, New York: Viking.

Daniel, P. (1987) *Standing at the Crossroads*, New York: Hill & Wang.

—— (2000) *Lost Revolutions: The South in the 1950s*, Chapel Hill: University of North Carolina Press.

Degler, C. (1977) *Place over Time: The Continuity of Southern Distinctiveness*, Baton Rouge: Louisiana State University Press.

Eagles, C. (ed.) (1992) *The Mind of the South, Fifty Years Later*, London: University of Mississippi Press.

Escott, P. and Goldfield, D. (eds) (1990) *Major Problems in the History of the South*, Lexington: D.C. Heath.

Faulkner, W. (1965) (first 1937) *Absalom, Absalom*, London: Chatto & Windus.

—— (1996) (first 1942) *Go Down Moses*, London: Vintage.

Fiedler, L. (1972) *The Return of the Vanishing American*, London: Paladin.

Foner, E. (1989) *Reconstruction: America's Unfinished Revolution*, New York: Harper & Row.

Frankel, G. (2014) *The Searchers: The Making of an American Legend*, New York, NY: Bloomsbury USA.

Genovese, E. (1974) *Roll, Jordan, Roll*, New York: Pantheon.

—— (1994) *The Southern Tradition*, London: Harvard University Press.

Gerster, P. and Cords, N. (eds) (1989) *Myth and Southern History*, Urbana: University of Illinois Press.

Goldfield, D. (1987) *Promised Land: The South since 1945*, Arlington Heights: Harlan Davidson.

—— (2002) *Still Fighting the Civil War: The American South and Southern History*, Baton Rouge: Louisiana State University Press.

Graham, A. (2003) *Framing the South: Hollywood, Television, and Race during the Civil Rights Struggle*, Baltimore: Johns Hopkins University Press.

Gray, R. (1986) *Writing the South: Ideas of an American Region*, Cambridge: Cambridge University Press.

—— (2000) *Southern Aberrations: Writers of the American South and the Problems of Regionalism*, Baton Rouge: Louisiana State University Press.

Gregory, J. (2005) *The Southern Diaspora: How the Great Migrations of Black and White Southerners Transformed America*, Chapel Hill: University of North Carolina Press.

Guralnick, P. (1986) *Sweet Soul Music, Rhythm and Blues and the Southern Dream of Freedom*, London: Penguin.

Hearne, J. (2012) *Native Recognition: Indigenous Cinema and the Western*, New York: SUNY Press.

Hobson, F. (1983) *Tell About the South: The Southern Rage to Explain*, Baton Rouge: Louisiana State University Press.

—— (1994) *The Southern Writer in the Post-Modern World*, London: University of Georgia Press.

—— (2002) *South to the Future: An American Region in the Twenty-First Century*, Athens, GA: University of Georgia Press.

Jenkins, M. (1999) *The South in Black and White: Race, Sex, and Literature in the 1940s*, Chapel Hill: University of North Carolina Press.

Johnson, M.K. (2013) *Hoo-Doo Cowboys and Bronze Buckaroos: Conceptions of the African American West*, Jackson, MS: University Press of Mississippi.

Joseph, P. (2007) *American Literary Regionalism in a Global Age*, Princeton: Princeton University Press.

Joyner, C. (1993) 'A Single Southern Culture: Cultural Interaction in the Old South' in T. Ownby (ed.) *Black and White Interaction in the Ante-Bellum South*, Jackson: University Press of Mississippi.

Kennedy-Nolle, S.D. (2015) *Writing Reconstruction: Race, Gender, and Citizenship in the Postwar South*, Chapel Hill: University of North Carolina Press.

King, M.L. (1964) *Why We Can't Wait*, New York: New American Library.

King, R. (1980) *A Southern Renaissance: The Cultural Awakening of the American South*, Oxford: Oxford University Press.

King, R. (ed.) (1995) *Dixie Debates: Perspectives on Southern Cultures*, East Haven: Pluto Press.

Kirby J.T. (1986) *Rural Worlds Lost*, Baton Rouge: Louisiana State University Press.

—— (1987) (first 1976) *Media Made Dixie*, London: University of Georgia Press.

—— (1995) *The Counter Cultural South*, Athens: University of Georgia Press.

Lee, A.R. (1990) *William Faulkner: The Yoknapatawpha Fiction*, London: Vision Press.

Malone, W. (1979) *Southern Music, American Music*, Lexington: University of Kentucky Press.

—— (1987) *Country Music, U.S.A.*, Wellingborough: Equation Press.

—— (1993) *Singing Cowboys and Musical Mountaineers: Southern Culture and the Roots of Country Music*, Athens: University of Georgia Press.

Mason, B.A. (1987) (first 1985) *In Country*, London: Flamingo.

Massey, D. (1995) 'Places and their Pasts', *History Workshop Journal*, Spring, vol. 39, pp. 182–92.

McCardell, J. (1979) *The Idea of a Southern Nation*, New York: W.W. Norton.

McKee, K. and Trefzer, A. (2006) 'Preface: Global Contexts, Local Literatures: The New Southern Studies', *American Literature* special issue, 'Global Contexts, Local Literatures: The New Southern Studies', vol. 78, issue 4, p. 678.

McMillen, N. (1997) *Remaking Dixie: The Impact of World War II on the American South*, Jackson, MS: University Press of Mississippi.

McPherson, P. (2003) *Reconstructing Dixie, Race, Gender and Nostalgia in the Imagined South*, Durham: Duke University Press.

Miller, C.J. and Bowdoin Van Pier, A. (eds) (2014) *International Westerns: Re-Locating the Frontier*, Lanham, MD: Scarecrow Press.

Miller, M. (2008) 'Dirty Decade: Rap Music and the U.S. South, 1997–2007', *Southern Spaces* at http://www.southernspaces.org/2008/dirty-decade-rapmusic-and-us-south-1997–2007#section6 (accessed 19/01/2011).

Mohl, R. (2005) 'Globalisation, Latinisation and the *Nuevo* New South' in J. Cobb and W. Stueck (eds) (2005) *Globalisation and the American South*, Athens: University of Georgia Press.

O'Brien, M. (2007) *Placing the South*, Oxford: University of Mississippi Press.

Orvell, M. (1989) *The Real Thing: Imitation and Authenticity in American Culture, 1880–1940*, Chapel Hill: University of North Carolina Press.

Ownby, T. (ed.) (1993) *Black and White Cultural Interaction in the Ante-Bellum South*, Jackson: University Press of Mississippi.

Phillips, U.B. (1928) 'The Central Theme of Southern History', *American Historical Review* vol. 34, no. 3, pp. 30–43.

Potter, D. (1968) *The South and Sectional Conflict*, Baton Rouge: Louisiana State University Press.

Proulx, A. (2009) *Fine Just the Way It Is: Wyoming Stories*, London: Fourth Estate.

Rabinowitz, P. (1994) *They Must Be Represented: The Politics of Documentary*, London: Verso.

Reed, J.S. (1982) *One South: An Ethnic Approach to Regional Culture*, Baton Rouge: Louisiana State University Press.

—— (1986) *The Enduring South: Subcultural Persistence in Mass Society*, Chapel Hill: University of North Carolina Press.

Reichert Powell, D. (2007) *Critical Regionalism: Connecting Politics and Culture in the American Landscape*, Chapel Hill: University of North Carolina Press.

Simmon, S. (1993) *The Films of D.W. Griffith*, Cambridge: Cambridge University Press.

Soja, E.W. (2014) *My Los Angeles: From Urban Restructuring to Regional Urbanization*, Berkeley: University of California.

Stewart, K. (1996) *A Space on the Side of the Road*, Princeton: Princeton University Press.

Stott, W. (1973) *Documentary Expression and Thirties America*, New York: Oxford University Press.

Styron, W. (1979) *Sophie's Choice*, London: Jonathan Cape.

Trachtenberg, A. (1999) *Reading American Photographs: Images as History, Mathew Brady to Walker Evans*, New York: Hill & Wang.

Whisnant, D. (1983) *All That is Native and Fine: The Politics of Culture in an American Region*, Chapel Hill: University of North Carolina Press.

Wilson, C.R. and Ferris, W. (eds) (1989) *The Encyclopedia of Southern Culture*, Chapel Hill: University of North Carolina Press.

Woodward, C.V. (1968) *The Burden of Southern History*, Baton Rouge: Louisiana State University Press.

—— (1971) *The Origins of the New South*, Baton Rouge: Louisiana State University Press.

—— (1983) *American Counterpoint, Slavery and Racism in the North–South Dialogue*, Oxford: Oxford University Press.

Wrobel, D. (2013) *Global West, American Frontier: Travel, Empire, and Exceptionalism from Manifest Destiny to the Great Depression*, Albuquerque: University of New Mexico Press.

Wyatt-Brown, B. (1982) *Southern Honour: Ethics and Behaviour in the Old South*, New York: Oxford University Press.

Zinn, H. (1964) *The Southern Mystique*, New York: Knopf.

FOLLOW-UP WORK

There are a number of additional resources, assignments and other materials to be found on the website that accompanies this new edition: http://www.routledge.com/cw/campbell/

1   Read the different articles and links on Critical Regionalism referenced at the website www.critical-regionalism.com and see how they might relate to your studies of American regions like the South and West. In particular, pay attention to debates about the local versus the global.

2   Examine the images in this section (or accessing others via the website) and discuss what sense of the mythic West they portray. Read Truettner and Barthes (as cited earlier) to help you in your analysis. Explain how certain aspects of the paintings contain ideological significance.

3   Read the brilliant discussion of George Caleb Bingham's painting *Fur Traders Descending the Missouri* (1845) at the opening of Papanikolas's *American Silence* (see earlier) and apply his detailed approach to the Bingham painting reprinted in this chapter.

4   Discuss the use of the term 'postwestern' as a way of understanding how the West 'lives on' as a relevant and meaningful notion today.

5   What might we mean by 'the imagined South'? It is often felt to be a set of images, sounds and narratives that help produce a cluster of influential myths and values which need to be examined critically. Select 'Southern' films or TV that allows this analysis to take place – for example, *The Color Purple, True Blood, Winter's Bone,* or *True Detective.*

6   Read Kathleen Stewart's *A Space on the Side of the Road* (1996) and compare how she develops a portrait of the South ('a lived cultural poetics') following the lead given by James Agee (as discussed above).

Chapter 6

The American city
'The old knot of contrariety'
(Walt Whitman)

CAN WE READ THE CITY?

A popular contemporary perception of the USA is as a vast city recreated from half-remembered fragments of films, television dramas, popular music and a thousand advertising images. Quite simply, American cities appear to be all around us, from the opening sequences of *CSI*'s Las Vegas Strip to the futuristic Los Angeles of *Blade Runner* or the fashionable upmarket lofts and galleries of *Sex and the City*. This is only one aspect of how we imagine America, but it is, for many of us, the most attractive, engaging and threatening aspect of the country. However, despite the constant presence of American cities in our lives, regardless of where we live, they remain mysterious and unknowable, like a familiar text that we seem to possess but whose final meaning evades us as we attempt to read it. This idea may sound rather odd. After all, how can a city be a text? But a city is a gathering of meanings in which people invest their inter-pretations and seek to create their own (hi)story, and therefore resembles a text set out in blocks, lines and grids. A city is constructed like a text, it is 'an inscription of man [and woman] in space' (Barthes 1988: 193), unfolding, challenging, confusing, thrilling and threatening all at the same time. When Joyce Carol Oates asked in 1981, 'If the City is a text, how shall we read it?' (Jaye and Watts 1981: 11), she expressed this fascination with the need to comprehend the very product of our own creation which had somehow become mysterious. It is these different layers of meaning within the city that are hard to fathom, and which vary depending on where you read them from: high and low, inner city or suburb, skyscraper or street level, uptown or the ghetto, inside or out, feminine or masculine, rich or poor and so on. These differing points of view explain the endless possibility of the city for artists and the fascination for historians and sociologists studying its meanings.

This chapter will reflect upon various meanings of the city (including the suburbs), employing an alternative to a strictly historical or sociological methodology. Such approaches are, of course, an important part of how we understand problems of contemporary city life, but it is also revealing and provocative to explore the multifaceted nature of the city from different perspectives. James Donald, for instance, has written, 'By calling this diversity "the city", we ascribe to it a coherence or integrity. The city, is above all, a representation . . . an imagined environment' (Bocock and Thompson 1992: 422). What must concern us then, argues Donald, is how we read the representations of the city and the discourses that express them to us. The idea of discourse is used here (as defined in the introduction) to suggest the manner through which the city is represented to us in language and related frames of reference and definition. Discourses are 'the conceptual frameworks which allow some modes of thought and deny others . . . a body of unwritten rules which *attempt to regulate* what can be written, thought, and acted upon in a particular field' (Storey 1993: 92; our emphasis). These discourses are not about the city, but they constitute it for us as 'readers'/viewers. That is, they do not simply describe, but seek to form our concepts about what the city is and how it relates to life in a wider sense. Discourses organise statements, define texts, promote meanings and position subjects, and any study of urban life has to confront these different formations as they compete for our attention. To what extent the individual can choose between these formations is a matter of intense debate which, indeed, emerges as an issue in many urban texts themselves, for example *Sister Carrie*, as we shall see later. This method derives broadly from poststructuralism, which we have discussed elsewhere. What it offers is one approach and a new way of seeing things that may have been taken for granted before or, indeed, overlooked altogether.

If structuralism looked for the underlying structure upon which rested meaning, then poststructuralism proposes an alternative, in which meaning is always in process and a text is a 'multi-dimensional space in which a variety of writings, none of them original, blend and clash'. The 'text is a tissue of quotations drawn from the innumerable centres of culture' (Barthes 1977: 146). This description conveys an image of city-as-text, and like the perceiver of the city, the reader is the only person that can bring some temporary unity to that text, without, however, fixing it permanently or defining the city totally. It represents it for that moment in the process of signification, with the understanding that meaning is deferred because people will bring various perspectives to that moment and so interpret it differently. The city, seen in this way, is a chain of meanings, each of which is in competition with one another, with certain interpretations emerging at specific points in time with more authority and subsequent power than others. Adopting this approach allows us to interrogate certain established or dominant readings of the city in order to question them and seek alternative ways of seeing. If there can be no guaranteed or fixed single meaning of the city, it does not just signal the fact that 'anything goes' or that everything is relative, but that certain dominant or prevailing discourses and stable meanings have emerged in the city through time and that the contexts within which these readings have arisen need to be re-examined in the light of new theoretical understandings.

COMPETING VERSIONS OF THE CITY

The problem of reading the city can be traced back to the foundation of America. John Winthrop, the first Governor of Massachusetts, gave a sermon on the *Arbella* as it crossed the Atlantic to America in 1630, and spoke of his vision of a new community like 'a City upon a Hill', with 'the eyes of all people . . . upon us'. The ideal of the heavenly city employed here says much about the utopian dreams so often associated with city planning in the future, but it also emphasises the necessity of establishing the city as orderly and godly because the 'eyes' of the world were looking on. He goes on to say 'we shall be *made a story* and a by-word through the world', thereby asserting an early example of the ways in which the city image has been constructed through narrative. The city-story would be watched (and *read*) by the world, noting the good or the bad within it, just as Winthrop, as a Puritan, linked echoes of Sodom and Gomorrah to the possible darker future of the American city, while envisioning in it the strongest beliefs and loftiest aspirations of his community. In part this fits with John Bunyan's *Pilgrim's Progress* (1678), in which he describes the road to salvation as passing through Vanity Fair, with its corruptions and disorder, to the Celestial City and its streets paved with gold.

The dark view of cities can be seen in Thomas Jefferson's comment that cities were 'pestilential to the morals, the health and the liberties of men' and that 'those who labor the earth are the chosen people of God . . . [and] the mobs of great cities add just so much to the support of pure government as sores do the strength of the human body' (Bender 1975: 21). The Jeffersonian warning about the dangers of unrestrained urbanism stressed two broad points: that cities threatened personal morality by encouraging vice, sin and indulgence; and that they might ultimately threaten the Republic itself. These arguments reached a climax in the work of the Reverend Josiah Strong, whose *Our Country* (1885) argued that America was to be God's instrument to redeem the world, but the city stood in the way of that mission since it was a 'storm center' full of 'menace'. The following extract suggests his tone:

> The city is the nerve center of our civilization. It is also the storm center.
> . . . It is the city where wealth is massed; and here are the tangible
> evidences of it piled many stories high. Here the sway of Mammon is
> widest, and his worship the most constant and eager. Here are luxuries

gathered – everything that dazzles the eye, or tempts the appetite; here is the most extravagant expenditure. Here also, is the congestion of wealth the severest . . . here in sharp contrast, are the ennui of surfeit and the desperation of starvation. . . . Here is heaped the social dynamite; her roughs, gamblers, thieves, robbers, lawless and desperate men . . . ready . . . to raise riots for the purpose of destruction and plunder; here gather foreigners and wage-workers . . . especially susceptible to socialist arguments. . . . Thus is our civilization multiplying and focalizing the elements of anarchy and destruction.

(Strong in Glaab 1963: 330–6)

This frames the city as a dark and fearful place in the Jeffersonian tradition, with the overriding threats the new urban masses made to social order. At the same time, however, as Strong interpreted cities in these terms, the poet Walt Whitman defined them in more positive ways, as organic bodies, a 'simple, compact, well-join'd scheme' intimately connecting the individual to the whole, and calling for them to:

Thrive, cities – bring your freight, bring your shows, ample and
    sufficient rivers;
Expand, being than which none else is more spiritual,
Keep your places, objects than which none else is more lasting.

('Crossing Brooklyn Ferry', Whitman 1971: 140)

This essentially positive discourse of the city as vital and dynamic is reflected in William James's appropriation of Strong's 'storm center' image recasting the city as 'the center of the cyclone' producing the 'pulse of the machine', which he found 'magnificent' along with

the heaven-scaling audacity of it all, and the lightness withal, as if there were nothing that was not easy, and the great pulses and bounds of progress, so many in directions all simultaneous that the coordination is indefinitely future [and] give a kind of drumming background of life that I have never felt before.

(James 1920: 67)

James's metaphors, like Whitman's, contributed to an alternative discourse of the city, stressing its dynamic, forward-looking qualities and transformative potential. This kind of discursive conflict is typical of the ways American cities have been read, and is indicative of the city as meaning in process rather than as fixed and static.

This is evident in the ways cities have continued to be represented, for example, in the work of Woody Allen, and particularly his film *Manhattan* (1979), in which the narrator is trying to write the definitive version of the city he loves, but finds the task impossible, reverting instead to a series of complex rewritings, which range wildly from: 'He romanticized it out of all proportion, and to him no matter what the season was, this was still a town that existed in black and white and pulsated to the great tunes of George Gershwin'; to 'He adored New York City, to him it was a metaphor for the decay of contemporary culture . . . how hard it was to exist in a society desensitized by drugs, loud music, television'; to 'He was as tough and romantic as the city he loved, behind his black-rimmed glasses was the coiled sexual power of a jungle cat . . . New York was his town and it always would be.'

At the same time as the voiceover offers us the sense of the city as indefinable, the visual images, in glowing black and white, spread New York's familiar landmarks before us at a distance and with the camera high up in the clouds. This romantic perspective suggests the mystery of the city, without having to confront at 'street level' its awkward and unromantic realities. Because we, as an audience, are at a distance, both physically and formally (Allen uses both black and white photography and a stirring George Gershwin soundtrack), the city shines out as a place of awe and excitement, vitality and wonder. There is little threat in this myth of Manhattan as a gorgeous moment, with all its contradictions reduced into a singular and potent vision. Despite the narrator's comment about it being the 'metaphor for the decay of modern society', the tone and the final swelling music suggest otherwise.

THEORETICAL CITY: THE DESIRE FOR CONTROL AND ORDER

Thus, from whichever era of American life, the city has always been a focus for human desires and dreams, a place of possibility, success and threat. This is echoed in the way many people, like Whitman, think of the city as alive; writing, for example, about its 'heart' and its 'soul', or like Henry James, in his book *The American Scene* (1907), about 'its sharp free accent . . . [and] its loose limbs' (Marqusee 1988: 160). Viewed as human and organic, the city takes on a moral condition too so that its culture is seen to reflect the values, attitudes and mores of the people who breathe within it. Frederick Howe, a believer in the possibilities of the city, wrote in 1905 of society as 'an organism like the human body, of which the city is the head, heart, and center of the nervous system' (Howe 1905: 10). Above all, the American city is a text created, a story written by people who sought to impose their vision of order, their designs upon the world, and to some extent to control the wilderness into a contained and disciplined environment. But at the very same time there was a contrary discourse, which sees control as impossible and where social conflict, crime and corruption flourish. Just as the Puritan Winthrop can be seen as constructing a single discourse for his people, of the city as a testament to their grace, there emerged a counter-discourse that defined the city as the place of recklessness and opportunity, a place of desire, offering the freedom from older, more traditional restraints.

Despite the efforts of people to 'plan' the city, there is a resistance to this form of control and containment, as if the dynamism unleashed in its creation is too immense to manipulate and direct into safe, orderly patterns. Architect Rem Koolhaas's *Delirious New York* (1978) claimed 'the Grid's [pattern of city streets] two-dimensional discipline creates undreamt of freedom for three-dimensional anarchy' (Koolhaas 1994: 20). It is a text we cannot read without difficulties, since it always reaches beyond itself, overflows, contradicts and questions what it is and what it can be. This is the 'archetypal ambivalence of the city' with its 'clashing contradictions', and 'perhaps the central fascination of the city, both real and fictional, is that it embodies man's contradictory feelings – pride, love, anxiety and hatred – towards the civilization he has created and the culture to which he belongs' (Pike 1981: 26). The city is not an easy text to read, but one riddled with contradictions and ambiguities, which account for its mysterious fascinations and its 'new inexplicableness . . . and new unintelligibility' (Trachtenberg 1982: 103).

Trachtenberg's city is *the* modern place where the possibilities of technology, planning, industrialisation and commerce come together in a single environment which thrusts together people, ideas and opportunities in a particular mix of productive kinds of strangeness and distance. The great works of modernist art and literature erupted from this creative mix, reflecting the city itself whose very structures were symbolic expressions of this impulse. As Marshall Berman has written:

> To be modern is to live a life of paradox and contradiction . . . in an environment that promises us adventure, power, joy, growth, transformation of ourselves and our world – and, at the same time, threatens to destroy everything we have, everything we know, everything we are.
>
> (Berman 1983: 14–15)

This sense of the city environment as an 'old knot of contrariety', to borrow a phrase from Walt Whitman, echoes the competing discourses we discussed earlier, and is amplified in an essay by the social theorist Michel De Certeau. For him, New York City seen from a skyscraper is a text 'in which extremes coincide – extremes of ambition and degradation, brutal opposites of races and styles, contrasts between yesterday's buildings, already transformed into trash cans, and today's urban irruptions that block out its space' (De Certeau 1988: 91). It is an ever-changing space/text that 'invents itself from hour to hour' where 'the spectator can read into it a universe that is constantly exploding' and indulge in the 'gigantic rhetoric of excess' that constitutes the urban landscape of America (ibid.). This sense of the whole city spread out like a multidimensional text that can be read, 'grasped', even understood, is questioned as it reduces and 'makes the complexity of the city readable, and immobilizes its . . . mobility' (ibid.: 92) because one is surveying a 'picture', removed and organised by distance so that all one sees are the grids and the blocks, with all the order and control of the city-planners' blueprints. It is the 'theoretical' city because the life of the city, its 'practices', go on below in the hubbub and chaos of the streets and cannot be seen from the remove of the high vantage points. The 'networks of these moving, intersecting writings compose a manifold story that has neither author nor spectator' (ibid.: 93). Years later, when writing of how the suburbs had been misrepresented, D.J. Waldie made a similar point using the concept of aerial photography as a mode of repeated representation that placed suburban reality *at a distance*, showing only the conformity of the grid and not the intimate and differentiated lives of those living within it: 'They report that the grid, briefly empty of associations, is just a pattern predicting itself', failing to see 'the joining of interests, limited but attainable' going on down below (Waldie 1996: 6). In a similar manner, French theorist Henri Lefebvre, writing in the 1990s, argued that to comprehend the 'presence' and 'music' of the city one had to attune to its many rhythms, to feel its 'multiplicity of (sensorial and significant) meanings', like a 'unity of diverse relations' (Lefebvre 2004: 45, 41, 86).

Thus the city's contradictions abound through its rhythms, as Poe charted in 'The Man of the Crowd' (1845; Poe 1975: 169–70), Paul Auster in *The New York Trilogy* (1987) or Karen Tei Yamashita in *Tropic of Orange* (1997) or *I-Hotel* (2010) (see discussion in Chapter 5), and are hard to define or fix, despite the constant efforts of planners and designers to create something like the City Beautiful as a model of order and social control. The design of the city has always been at odds with the way people live within it, as if there is a natural resistance in city life to the desired principles of control and order that seem always to be a significant part of their creation. This theoretical argument can be examined in relation to the earlier comments about representation in Woody Allen's *Manhattan* and its tendency to remove us from the city for specific reasons and effects.

The city planners dreamt of a 'benign coercion' 'to eradicate the communal culture of working-class and immigrant streets, to erase that culture's offensive and disturbing foreignness, and replace it with middle-class norms of hearth and tea table'. This was 'the ordering hand of corporate organization, the values of system and hierarchy asserting itself into the lives of the streets and the bustling neighbourhoods' (Trachtenberg 1982: 111). The potentially unreadable text of the ground-level streets had to be legitimised, ordered and contained within a stable, disciplined text

Plate 6.1 A Nashville skyline.
© Neil Campbell, 1994

and this can be seen as giving rise to what has been termed a clash between 'civic horizontalism and corporate verticality' (Taylor 1992: 52), where the corporation accesses the tower as a symbol of its power and the rest of the city exists down below in its shadow.

Or perhaps, as Waldie notes, this clash might be seen in the tension between the aerial representation of the suburb as mere orderly grid and the living, everyday reality of the lives going on within it. An example of this is the skyline of the booming Southern city, Nashville, which has developed rapidly but still bears the traces of the past at lower levels. Plate 6.1 shows this hierarchical skyline with the foreground of the preserved past, as the city plans into itself a 'historic' simulation of Fort Nashborough, the original settlement of 1779, overshadowed by the dilapidated warehouses of the old riverfront gradually being reclaimed as leisure and shopping sites. Hovering over both is the symbolic skyscraper of the Bell Corporation, epitomising the new economy of Nashville as the financial and insurance centre of the mid-South.

THE UNDIVULGED CITY: POE'S 'THE MAN OF THE CROWD' (1845)

De Certeau's city of levels and networks or Lefebvre's of rhythms suggest intermingling stories as a very exciting way of approaching urban experience, which can be useful to bear in mind as we begin to examine more specific examples of attempts to read the city. Edgar Allan Poe's 'The Man of the Crowd' deliberates upon the meaning of the city and suggests that it is like crime itself whose 'essence . . . is undivulged' (Poe 1975: 179).

The story begins with the warning that 'it does not permit itself to be read' (ibid.) and then conveys the condition of the city as seen through the eyes of a questing narrator following 'the man of the crowd'. It is the classic story of the city, in which the narrator, who sees himself as a man of vision, intellect and reason confronts the 'mysteries which will not suffer themselves to be revealed' (ibid.: 179) in the belief that he can unravel them. As in Poe's later Dupin stories 'The Murders in the Rue Morgue', 'The Mystery of Marie Roget' and 'The Purloined Letter', the belief that the city can be understood and solved is central to this piece. Reading his newspaper in the coffeehouse, he surveys the streets outside, as if he could follow the lines and columns of the urban world in the same manner that he 'amuses' himself with the paper's text and in so doing categorises the 'divisions' he witnesses like the sections of the newspaper. This arrogant detachment permits the city scene to become a neat 'scale' into which he fits all the types he sees in the crowd, enabling him to 'frequently *read*, even in that brief interval of a glance, the history of long years' (ibid.: 183; our emphasis). Poe's narrator echoes the problem described by De Certeau, of the city characterised by those who would try to read its history in a 'glance' and in so doing miss the complex web of relations and practices unfolding there. The urge to define and fix the city as a single thing, like the original and eternal desire to plan and control the life of the city, is suggested here in the actions of the narrator and then rapidly countered by the eruption of 'the man of the crowd' who presents an insoluble dilemma. From the narrator's logical 'analysis of the meaning conveyed', he is altered by the sight of the man, and 'there arose confusedly and paradoxically within [his] mind' a new set of ideas that cannot be so easily reduced to a formula (ibid.). As he follows the man, now engaged himself with the street's 'waver . . . jostle and hum' (ibid.: 184) rather than removed behind the glass, he faces paradoxes and contradictions that defy his 'scale' of meaning and open him up to the street-level city, which 'aroused, startled, fascinated' (ibid.) in equal measure. He is exposed to the multifaceted urban environment, one beyond his simplified and limited categories such as 'poverty . . . crime . . . filth . . . desolation' (ibid.: 186–7), to a complex text 'crossed and recrossed' which 'is a grosser book than the *Hortulus Animae* . . . that *es läßst sich nicht lesen* [it does not permit itself to be read]' (ibid.: 179).

The city, embodied in the story, defies stable meaning, is unreadable and somehow always beyond final comprehension or representation, reinforcing De Certeau's argument that 'Beneath the discourses that ideologise the city, the ruses and combinations of powers that have no readable identity proliferate; without points where one can take hold of them, without rational transparency, they are impossible to administer' (De Certeau 1988: 95). In Lefebvre's terms the city is a 'presence', a 'dialogue' that 'brings forth all its presents' simultaneously (2004: 56–7, 34). As complex as this seems, it theorises what other texts, like 'The Man of the Crowd', *Manhattan*, *The Great Gatsby*, *The New York Trilogy*, *Tropic of Orange* or *The Wire* (see introduction) explore – namely, the problematical nature of defining the city and trying to fix its patterns into a single, identifiable shape. Those who try to do this, planners and reformers, are merely seeking to impose on the amorphous plurality of the city a set order and discipline, like the narrator in Poe's story believing such variety can be read and categorised into a neat 'scale'. The lived experience of the 'migrational city' is in flux and process, unlike the orderly interpretative grid of rational definition that some would try to place upon it. Difference, rather than sameness, is essential to this reading of the city.

THE 'PERSUASIVE LIGHT': COMMERCE AND THE CITY

The tensions inherent within this process can be felt by examining the late 1800s and the specific concerns about the social consequences of the city environment which emerge with rapid urban growth and population increases of extraordinary proportions. In a period between 1870 and 1900, when, for example, Chicago's population multiplied five times and that of New York topped 3.4 million, and when 11 million immigrants arrived in the USA, journalists such as Jacob Riis, with his book *How The Other Half Lives* (1890), and Stephen Crane with his *City Sketches* and *Maggie* (1893) began to question the human costs of such expansion. All these works warrant attention, but we shall examine a novel in which the energies and the consequences of city life are explored in detail and with enormous power. The realist tradition sought to read the city in close-up, paying attention to the street in the hope of exposing its practices and some of the environmental determinants shaping people's lives. Even this project, for all its merits, proved limited as a way of defining the city.

In Theodore Dreiser's *Sister Carrie* (1900), the city has 'cunning wiles' that attract 'large forces which allure . . . the gleam of a thousand lights

... the persuasive light' (Dreiser 1986: 4). It represents the world of urban capitalism as a beacon, pulling into it moths such as Caroline Meeber. She is 'carried' into the glow of money and the urban dynamo in a way which links her journey with the particular view of the city's rapid expansion as a threat to some older order of things in America, connected to rural village life and values. Writers like Stephen Crane and Upton Sinclair used realism as a technique to expose the reader to the details of city life and attempted to convince us of the forces that swept their characters into despair and death. Their work, like that of Dreiser, does, however, suggest a discontent with the promise of the city and questions its cultural dominance and its value systems. This attention to the dark side of the city brought into focus doubts about the rapid growth of industrial, commercial centres and the effects on those living within them. For example, Dreiser's innocent Carrie approaches the city with hope, but the narrator qualifies the reader's impressions with doubts about her destination.

> To the child, the genius with imagination, or the wholly untraveled the approach to the city is a wonderful thing. Particularly if it be the evening that mystic period between the glare and the gloom of the world when life is changing from one sphere or condition to another. Ah, the promise of the night. . . . The street, the lamp, the lighted chamber set for dining are for me. The theatres, the halls, the parties ... these are mine in the night.
>
> (Ibid.: 10)

For Dreiser the city lures with the promise and the mystery, but below the gleam is a well of despair where wealth is disguised in the terrible labours of the poor and exploited, and where the dream of a good life is constructed around the needs of the commercial culture of greed.

> It is like a chemical reagent. One day of it, like one drop of the other, will so affect and discolor the views, the aims, the desires of the mind, that it will thereafter remain forever dyed . . . like opium to the untried body. A craving is set up . . . dreams unfilled – gnawing, luring, idle phantoms which beckon and lead.
>
> (Ibid.: 305)

The city is an addictive drug whose commerce is insatiable, a craving that leads us on into an endless cycle of desire and lack. This echoes Henry Adams's famous comment of 1905, that

> The outline of the city became frantic in its effort to explain something that defied meaning. Power seemed to have outgrown its servitude and to have asserted its freedom. . . . The city had the air of hysteria,

and the citizens were crying in every accent of anger and alarm, that the new forces must at any cost be brought under control.

(Adams 1918: 499)

These writings propose an idea of the city out of control, ruled by forces too powerful for the individual to contend with, and so being swept along in its wake. Adams believed these changes required 'a new social mind' and the 'need to jump' (ibid.: 498) into its rapid accelerations in order to keep up at all, but Dreiser feared the capacity of such change to damage and corrupt. Carrie, he writes, 'had little power of initiative, but nevertheless she seemed ever capable of getting herself into the tide of change where she would be easily borne along' (Dreiser 1986: 321).

In this way Carrie becomes like any other object swept along in the urban tide, and she is 'stared at and ogled . . . in fashions throng, on parade in a showplace' (ibid.: 323–4). It is only when she obtains wealth and power that Carrie can move beyond this condition, but only at the expense of others, for then 'She was capital' (ibid.: 447), thus asserting Stephen Crane's sense of the city as a place of hierarchy and status where alienation, superficiality and selfishness are the norm.

THE SPACES OF THE CITY: ARCHITECTURE, ART AND AMBIVALENCE

However, typical of the ever-contrary nature of the American city, while these versions were appearing there emerged further emphasis upon the need to control this burgeoning environment and an attempt to make it work for people rather than against them. This took various forms: political, social, economic and aesthetic. Upton Sinclair, while railing against the hierarchy of the city, saw within the idea of the new masses a hope for American socialism as an alternative to the cult of the scientific manager. Here, through collective action instead of alienation, the worker might find a new place in a community of strong, shared values. Other aspects of the 'new social mind' can be seen in the City Parks movement of Frederick Law Olmsted, the growth of interest in public hygiene in the 1890s and the development in architectural design within the 'City Beautiful' group. The notion of a hysterical city, posited by Henry Adams, had to be harnessed and brought to order, and these types of social disciplines were attempts to do just that. Once again, the city could be a tribute to human endeavour rather than a mark of its failures, brought about by the assertion of control. As Burnham and Bennett wrote in their 'Plan of Chicago' (1909), 'the time has come to bring order out of the chaos incident to rapid growth, and especially to the influx of people of many nationalities without common traditions or habits of life' (Weimar 1962: 86). And yet, as their language indicates, the most well-intentioned planning has within it precise ideological purposes, in this case to control the immigrant masses and prevent disorder on the streets.

So too the growth of the skyscraper suggested a new vision of the city which was exuberant and triumphant, but which created dark canyons below. As Frank Lloyd Wright commented in 1929, it created 'The overpowering sense of the cell. The dreary emphasis of narrowness, slicing, edging, nicking and crowding. Tier above tier the soulless shelf, the empty crevice, the winding ways of the windy unhealthy canyon' (Marqusee 1988: 165). The ironic relation between these two effects once again reinforces the dominant idea of the city as ambiguous and contrary, what, in 1934, Lewis Mumford would term 'negative energy . . . suicidal vitality' (ibid.: 160). Louis Sullivan, in his essay 'The Tall Office Building Artistically Considered' (1898), wrote,

> It must be tall, every inch of it tall. The force and power of altitude must be in it, the glory and the pride of exaltation must be in it. It must be every inch a proud and soaring thing, rising in sheer exultation from bottom to top it is a unit without a single dissenting line.
>
> (Taylor 1992: 64)

The language and assumptions here are very revealing about the attitudes embodied in the 'tall building' as a masculine, phallic sign of pride, control, authority and no *dissent*. Here, architecture signifies the desire to order and control the urban space through design, and also registers a variety of ideological meanings about how that might be achieved (see Plate 6.2).

Edward Hopper (see Plate 6.3) is an example of an artist whose work was fascinated by the 'raw disorder of New York' (Levin 1980: 22) and its many spaces. This urban space surrounds his subjects, outwardly echoing their inner fears and anxieties, their mix of 'interest, curiosity, fear', which were for Hopper the primary responses to the city (ibid.: 47). In Hopper's art the city takes many forms, moving away from it as a place of elitism and social institutions towards a world of 'mobility and moral relativism replacing the older fixed standards . . . with a new amalgam of its own' (Harris 1990: 25–6). His is a city of streets and everyday practices which we glimpse through the paintings like compelled spectators, before the scene disappears into the rush of the urban whirl. It has a close parallel with the experience of the city recorded in *The Great Gatsby* (1925), written at the time of some of Hopper's finest work:

> There was a *glimpse* of red-belted ocean-going ships . . . a cobbled slum lined with the dark, undeserted saloons of the faded-gilt nineteen hundreds. Then the valley of the ashes opened out on both sides of us, and I had a *glimpse of* Mrs Wilson *straining* at the garage pump

Plate 6.2 Manhattan streets from the Empire State Building.
© Neil Campbell, 2005

with *panting vitality* as we went by. . . . Over the great bridge, with the
sunlight through the girders making *a constant flicker* upon the *moving*
cars, with the city *rising up* across the river in white heaps and sugar
lumps all built with a wish out of nonolfactory money. The city seen
from the Queensboro Bridge is always the city seen for the first time,
in its first wild promise of all the mystery and the beauty in the world.
                                        (Fitzgerald 1974: 74–5; our emphasis)

Fitzgerald's description conveys the frenetic pace, rhythms and mobility
of city life with an edge of sexuality, mystery and a strange mixture of
glamour, wealth and fading glory that is always part of the urban milieu.
This is the environment of 'sugar lumps' and 'garage pumps', where
'anything can happen . . . anything at all'.

Like Dreiser, too, Hopper's attention is given to the sites of popular
culture in the city, to the restaurants, movie-houses, theatres, shops and
to the everyday world of work. Too often these images in Hopper have
been explained too neatly as representative of the modern sensibility, of
alienation and loneliness in the wastelands of urban America. By a closer
consideration of some such paintings, one might see other interpretations,
other readings of the cityscape he portrays. We will examine one painting,
Office at Night (1940), in more depth, in order to suggest this approach.

Plate 6.3 Edward Hopper, *Office at Night*, 1940.
© Heritage Image Partnership Ltd / Alamy

Hopper said this painting was suggested to him

> by many rides on the 'L' train in New York City after dark and
> glimpses of office interiors that were so fleeting as to leave fresh and
> vivid impressions on my mind. My aim was to try to give the sense
> of an isolated and lonely office interior.
>
> (Levin 1980: 58)

Notice the similarity to Fitzgerald's language – 'glimpses/fleeting/
impressions' – and the predominant concern with capturing the moment.
In doing this, the artist takes us into the world of the office, with its objects
and order, its hierarchy and relationships. Although one might sense a
kind of 'estrangement' and 'malaise', words Gail Levin has used about
Hopper, and perhaps most strongly suggested by the white space yawning
at the centre of the picture, other messages about city life are here too.

One significant detail is the repetitive reminder of routine work taking place, through the two figures themselves, but even more so through the pieces of paper positioned around the room. We notice them on the floor, chair, desks, in the man's hand, being filed by the woman; these are signifiers of production, of time filled up, of work completed (there are letters ready to be posted), in an efficient and orderly environment where not even a direct look is permitted. These latter points are suggested by the total arrangement and starkness of the room; for example, the eye is drawn to the umbrella in the corner, the perfectly neat chair and the pure geometry of the man's desktop, all echoed in the rectangles of the screen, walls and window. This echoes the office in Herman Melville's story of Wall Street, 'Bartleby' (1853), with its 'desk close up to a small side window [which] commanded at present no view at all, though it gave some light . . . from far above, between two lofty buildings' (Melville 1979: 67).

And yet, despite all this work, order and control there is something else carried in the picture's focal point – the woman. Her body's shape under the dress echoes the line in Gatsby about Mrs Wilson's 'straining . . . panting vitality', and is in total contrast with the severe, rigid lines of the room, as if her desire for something other than the routinised world of the office is being suggested. Perhaps it is something she links with the man, since Hopper encloses them within the oblong of light cast from the man's desk light, or with the night itself that exists just beyond the boundary of the stark, disciplined office. This may be an image of repressed femininity, caught and held in a masculine world of procedure, paper and routine with a woman powerless to act, 'gaz[ing] speechlessly at nothingness' (Wilson 1991: 82), or it may suggest the tension between the desire to contain the city and the need to express and discover its mysteries, its 'carnival' aspects. As Wilson also reminds us in her feminist study of the city:

[A] place of growing threat and paranoia to men, might be a place of liberation for women. The city offers women freedom. . . . True, on the one hand it makes necessary routinised rituals of transportation and clock watching, factory discipline and timetables, but . . . at every turn . . . the city dweller is also offered the opposite – pleasure, deviation, disruption . . . urban life is actually based on this perpetual struggle between rigid, routinised order and pleasurable anarchy, the male–female dichotomy.

(Ibid.: 8)

The 'male–female dichotomy' that Wilson describes can be seen acted out in the shadowy and tense environments of *film noir* like *Double Indemnity* (1944) and, like Hopper's painting, often creates a sense of ambiguity about life in the city. *Film noir* constructs a claustrophobic, dislocated and paranoid urban world with pools of light under street lamps, muted alleyways, *femme fatales*, murderous desire, criminality, sexual adventure and promise. However, *noir*'s power stems as much from juxtaposing such disruptive yearnings with the mundane and the ordinary, as if existing in a shadowland of desire, always on the edge of becoming some altered and transgressive ambience: 'There's something about the dead silence of an office building at night. . . . Not quite real', says Philip Marlowe in *Murder, My Sweet* (1944) with the street down below and the imminent reflection of Moose Malloy in his neon-inflected window. In the weird disequilibrium these scenes create, *noir*, like the angularity of Hopper's psychological landscapes, defines its dominant forms; unnerving spaces where the past haunts the present, the unfamiliar and the familiar intertwine, and every action has primal consequences somewhere in the night. This sense of the 'not quite real' is ever-present in Hopper and *film noir*, and draws us back to the idea of the city as always complex and mysterious.

COLLAGE CITY

Unlike the ambivalence in Hopper's work and the shadows of *film noir*, the film musical *42nd Street* (1933) culminates in a routine about the street whose lyrics and images record that the city street is 'a crazy quilt' where difference is merged into a harmonious whole, and 'side by side they're glorified, where the underworld can meet the elite, 42nd Street'. This concept of the city as a totality is also registered visually, as we see pedlars close up to play golf and a multicultural New York joining together to create the city skyline itself, at whose summit is not the skyscraper, but the lovers themselves. In this discourse of the city, humanity is in control of a benign and unified environment centred on the image of the quilt with all its pieces coherent and patterned towards the whole. This ideological notion of the 1930s, which sought to provide a unitary resolution for the complex, historical problems of the city, was soon countered by the uncertainties of modernism (see Berman 1983), and beyond that by the fragmentations of the postmodern city.

To contrast this effort at portraying the city as a seamless whole, one might look at Hubert Selby Jr's novel *Last Exit to Brooklyn* (1964), which both belongs to the dark, critical realist tradition of Dreiser, Stephen Crane and Upton Sinclair, and also charts new territory as well. This is not 42nd Street or Broadway, but the Housing Projects of postwar Brooklyn, where the brutalities and deprivations of urban life are expressed without unitary resolutions or hopeful escapes. The power and innovation of the novel lie in its prefiguration of postmodern ideas about the collision of voices in the city, captured in Selby's cacophony of capitalised exchanges where noise seems to replace communication and callousness, care. Selby's nightmare city fragments like his text and the lives of his subjects so that any dream of coherence and possibility is gone. Here, the city is more of a 'collage', with 'the highly differentiated spaces and mixtures' of the contemporary city (Harvey 1989: 40). Just as De Certeau argued, the city can only be totalised and defined from a distance and at the exclusion of the street life within it, and any effort to provide a grand narrative that encompasses the various movements of the city is false and artificial. Postmodernism rejects such attempts, preferring 'a multiplicity and mixing of styles and codes, forsaking modernism's attempts to impose a unifying or over-arching (meta-)theory or narrative' (Hall *et al.* 1992: 227).

Thus seeing the city as a collage/montage where texts intersect with other texts and no single reading can ever be final returns us to the idea of the city as a place of competing discourses in eternal contest for power. Donald Barthelme has written that 'New York City is or can be regarded as a collage' and 'the point of collage is that unlike things are stuck together to make, in the best case, a new reality' (Bellamy 1974: 51). In the postmodern urban space 'unlike things' are thrown together, clashing and colliding, rather similar to the ways in which the elements of collage interact, overlap, cover, layer and so on. No single view is the collage, for it is all the parts at the same time working with and against itself. This creates friction out of the proximity and promiscuity within the space, just as the city does. As Michel Foucault has written, postmodernism 'prefer[s] what is positive and multiple, difference over uniformity, flows over unities, mobile arrangements over systems' (in Harvey 1989: 44). It may be that the city has always been this kind of space and that postmodernism has merely offered a new set of terms with which to describe a much more consistent notion of the city in America.

David Harvey refers to the artist Robert Rauschenberg as one of the 'pioneers of the postmodern movement' (ibid.: 55) and this is, in part, explained by his interest in collage or 'combines' where, as John Cage said, 'there is no more subject than there is in a page from a newspaper. Each thing that is there is a subject. It is a situation involving multiplicity' (Cage 1961: 25). This decentred view of art suited Rauschenberg's portrayal of the city wherein he used its detritus to construct a 'fused metaphor' for urban life (Rose 1967: 217). Later these developed into the 'combine' form, with the artist incorporating three-dimensional objects so that they spill out from the frame and begin to offer back the junk of our world. The artist himself said that 'New York is a maze of unorganized experiences peopled by the unexpected, change is unavoidable' (Conrad 1984: 301).

In *Estate* (1963) (see Plate 6.4), a silk-screen painting, Rauschenberg creates the sense of collage, by colliding images and merging and over-laying a series of urban fragments which seem to mix the politics of housing through a kaleidoscope of colour, time, buildings and slums, as well as the signs of the city: the Statue of Liberty ironically lopsided and

Plate 6.4 Robert Rauschenberg, *Estate*, 1963.

the road sign calling us to stop. It employs certain ironies, a characteristic of postmodernism, to contrast inadequate urban housing with the expensive excursion into space, and simple, natural elements such as birds and water, with the chaos of the city that man has created.

The painting signifies many things, but always the motion and whirl of the city, captured in the close details, and the larger blocks of colour and shape at a distance, which play with our perceptions and constantly alter our point of view. When Joel Rose's novel *Kill The Poor* (1988) was published in Britain, it used this painting on its cover. The novel, like Rauschenberg's painting, centres on housing problems in New York with a playful sense of the irony and absurdity of the postmodern city. This extract shows how Rose conveys the sense of place through the fragments of the city-collage which surround his narrator.

> My daughter goes to daycare across the street from where I live. The butcher shop around the corner was closed down for selling human meat as barbecue. Paul Newman is filming on the corner. All over the neighborhood, homesteaders are rebuilding shells of buildings that have been abandoned by their landlords. No one likes poor people. On the corner heroin is sold for ten dollars a bag. . . . One day there will be a link between the rich section of town and the poor. My grand-mother said they were saying the same thing when she first moved here more than seventy-five years ago. But she doesn't live here now.
>
> (Rose 1990: 18)

Rose's ironic view of his neighbourhood combines the world-weariness of our age with a sharp observant wit and critique of a society where power is in the hands of a few and where image is everything. In some ways, like Jay McInerney, he explores the 'ethic of appearances' in the hope of finding the 'ethic of engagement', despite the seeming despondency embodied in the urban space.

Jay McInerney's *Bright Lights, Big City* (1984) is fully conscious of the tradition of urban texts in which it can be placed. He has written introductions for an earlier novel of the city, *Manhattan Transfer* by John Dos Passos (1986 edition), and for the collection *New York: An Illustrated Anthology* (Marqusee 1988), as well as referring to others like *The Great Gatsby* in interviews and indirectly within his own novel (see McInerney 1984: 180, 'the first Dutch settlers'). His first novel, *Bright Lights, Big City*, remains an extraordinary urban text that asserts the sense of a postmodern city, a 'republic of voices' (ibid.: 6) echoing 'the idea that all groups have a right to speak for themselves, in their own voice, and have that voice accepted as authentic and legitimate [which] is essential to the pluralistic stance of postmodernism' (Harvey 1989: 48). For McInerney, the city is a dialogue where many voices mix and engage in an endless parade and struggle which resists the single dominant discourse and the fixed notions of what a city should be, in favour of a more fluid, processive sense. The novel's unnamed protagonist breaks from a job in which he checks and edits language until it is 'verified' and printable, and thus acceptable to the dominant 'voice', and plunges into a journey of education about values and community.

McInerney captures the city's collage-like, ambivalent quality early on: 'a lone hooker totters on heels and tugs at her skirt. . . . Coming closer, you see that she is a man in drag. . . . Downriver, the Statue of Liberty shimmers in the haze. Across the water, a huge Colgate sign welcomes you to New Jersey, the Garden State' (McInerney 1984: 10). For the protagonist, the city is unlike the magazine he works for; it cannot be verified, ordered and checked because it is always surprising, as his excursions into the street and subway reveal. One brief example reveals this many-voiced city.

> You step into the train. The car is full of Hasidim from Brooklyn. . . . He is reading from his Talmud, running his finger across the page. The strange script is similar to the graffiti signatures all over the surface of the subway car, but the man does not look up at the graffiti, nor does he try to steal a peek at the headlines of your *Post*. This man has God and a History, a Community. . . . At Fourteenth Street three Rastafarians get on, and soon the car reeks of sweat and reefer. Sometimes you feel like the only man in the city without group affiliation.
>
> (Ibid.: 57)

The strange scripts of the city co-mingle, creating a new language in dialogue at all times and curiously unreadable. What McInerney accepts is that the postmodern city is a place of 'competing beliefs, cultures and "stories" . . . [and that] this play of unnerving contrasts and extremes is the essence of the "postmodern" experience' (Wilson 1991: 135–6). To accept this flow is not to give in to chaos, but to find a way of living with multiplicity without seeking to distort it into a fixed and single, dominant discourse. One can find 'community' within this flux of voices because it provides the space for self-expression and the possibility for dialogue, bringing it close to Michel Foucault's concept of the *heterotopia*, which when applied to the city suggests a place capable of juxtaposing in a single locale several spaces, several sites that are in themselves incompatible. It is 'disturbing' because in the heterotopia things do not 'hold together' neatly in order, but are spaces of 'contest', of 'a multiplicity of tiny, fragmented regions' where 'no sooner have they been adumbrated than all these groupings dissolve again' because the city is too unstable and changing to sustain them as fixed and final (Foucault 1966: xviii).

POSTMODERN CITY: LAS VEGAS

Las Vegas, with all its faults, represents a model of the postmodern city, a structure of 'mini-cities' juxtaposing consumption, fantasy and tourism with residential and commercial expansion. It has been called a 'Zeropolis', the 'any place town where everything begins again from zero, touching bottom and coming back up to the surface, with zeros piling up on a screen' (Bégout 2003: 22). Although excessive and larger than life, Las Vegas is a city that refutes any single design principle or meta-narrative, like an urbanised Disneyland, it was first appreciated in Venturi, Scott Brown and Izenour's *Learning from Las Vegas* (1972). They acknowledged its fragmented, commodified surfaces and signs, seeing an urban space that

> *includes*; it includes at all levels, from the mixture of seemingly incongruous land uses to the mixture of seemingly incongruous advertising media . . . a variety of changing, juxtaposed orders, like the shifting configurations of a Victor Vasarely painting . . . 'Chaos is very near; its nearness, but its avoidance, gives . . . force'.
>
> (Venturi *et al.* 1996: 53)

This tension between chaos and order that they found so exciting and postmodern recurs in the long-running television series *CSI: Crime Scene Investigation*, set in a Las Vegas where the chaos, crime, violence and brutality of the glittery pleasure dome is contrasted with the cool, orderly world of reasoned investigation undertaken by the crime lab at the heart of the show. The forensic fragments of Las Vegas crime scenes are reordered, the obscenity of violence is purged and the boiling desert is kept at bay by the actions of the icy Grissom and his fellow officers, and somehow the city itself is placated. *CSI* is a show very much about control, about redeeming a fragile, chaotic world, and reassuring urban audiences that the city can be conquered, or, at least, subdued through the interventions of technology, reason and science.

Las Vegas's simulacrum is like 'a video screen of the national consciousness' (Hess 1993: 123), or more accurately a multiplicity of screens viewed all at once like a frenetic, layered collage and reminds us again of Foucault's 'heterotopia':

> a kind of effectively enacted utopia in which the real sites, all the other sites that can be found within the culture, are simultaneously represented, contested, and inverted . . . capable of juxtaposing in a single real place several spaces, several sites that are in themselves incompatible.
>
> (Foucault 1986: 23–5)

For Mike Davis, however, Las Vegas is already out of control, almost beyond order, 'a hyperbolic Los Angeles – the Land of Sunshine on fast-forward' repeating LA's mistakes by ignoring water issues, fragmenting local government in favour of corporate planning, abandoning public space, embracing the automobile and perpetuating social and racial inequality (in Rothman 1998: 59, 60). Its 'hypergrowth and inflexible resource demand' make the 'need for an alternative settlement model . . . doubly urgent' (ibid.: 71), a model involving Green politics, new urban design and a thoughtful, innovative use of planning. Only in this material action, for Davis, rather than the sleek laboratories solving crimes in *CSI* or in abstract postmodern theories, is there real hope for 'an alternative urbanism, sustainable and democratic' (ibid.).

SUBURBIA: LIVES PLACED SIDE BY SIDE

Perhaps one response to the apparent inexorable growth of the city has been a renewed interest in suburbia (see Waldie 1996; Nicolaides 2002; Beuka 2004; Bruegmann 2005). For so often derided as a blight on the landscape or as the outward manifestation of a postwar containment culture, the suburbs were usually, as Beuka has pointed out, either seen as utopian or, increasingly in the post 1945 USA, as dystopian:

> the grid of identical houses on identical lots, the smoking barbecues, the swimming pool – loaded signifiers that, taken together, connote both the middle-class 'American Dream' . . . and that dream's inverse: the vision of a homogenized, soulless, plastic landscape of tepid conformity, an alienating 'noplace'.
>
> (Beuka 2004: 4)

As discussed earlier, suburbs were represented aerially (see Plate 6.5) and, therefore, appeared empty of life, oddly remote and disconnected from the lives of those who actually lived there. As a consequence it has been easy to dismiss and disregard the significance of suburbia to the study of American culture or to frame it only in these one-dimensional ways. More than hideous images of Sprawl, social breakdown or the debilitating effects of its perceived uniformity and cultural containment, like the world of Richard Yates's novel *Revolutionary Road* (1961) or Sam Mendes's film *American Beauty* (1999), suburbia is worthy of study as a critical space within the modern American city.

D.J. Waldie, author of *Holy Land: A Suburban Memoir* (1996) and *Where We Are Now: Notes from Los Angeles* (2004), claims suburbia is this 'landscape people rarely notice' and responds by constructing a mosaic of memories, gathered stories, observations and other fragments that demonstrate precisely why it is worth noticing and how its multiple

Plate 6.5 Joseph Scherschel, aerial view of rows of modest houses, 1958.
© Joseph Scherschel / Time Life Pictures / Getty Images

narratives, when looked at from the ground up, enmesh us into not just local, but national and international histories (Waldie 1996: 154). Waldie's *Holy Land* cross-cuts the suburban grid revealing historical figures, neighbours, childhood memories and religious rituals; moving seamlessly between stories of Mr H and his fallout shelter built under his garage or Mrs R's dead baby baptised by Waldie's mother in the street, to the implications of geological shifts and water politics in LA and to the racial restrictions on home ownership in the postwar USA. As Waldie writes, 'The critics of suburbs say that you and I live narrow lives. I agree. My life is narrow. From one perspective or another, all our lives are narrow. Only when lives are placed side by side do they seem larger' (ibid.: 94).

THE LIFE AND DEATH OF DETROIT

One consequence of suburban mobility can be seen through the lens of Detroit, Michigan, where the white and middle-class flight to the suburbs accelerated after the 1967 race riots in the city, becoming a contributing factor in the changing demographics of Detroit, which, in turn, depleted

Plate 6.6 Camilo Vergara, *Detroit Skyline*, 1991.
Courtesy of Camilo Vergara

its urban tax base. Detroit spiralled downward from being majority white and a symbol of America's thriving middle class, with a population of 1.8 million in the late 1950s, to being 82 per cent black today, with an average household income nearing the poverty line and a population now under 700,000. At its worst, mortgage foreclosures meant that houses were selling at auction for as little as $500 (see Hackman 2014). Camilo José Vergara, born in Chile in 1944 and a resident of the US since 1965, has produced a body of photographic and textual work that explores some of the implications of such changes (see Plates 6.6 and 6.7).

Yet, rather than the 'ruin porn' that some accuse these photographs of being, Vergara's layered documentation in *The New American Ghetto* (1995) and *American Ruins* (1999) examines 'demise, reuse and replacement' and meditates on progress and decline, as well as renewal and creative rebirth, finding even in this urban 'Smithsonian of Decline' signs of 'soul' and hope (1999: 11, 15, 16). For Vergara, ruins tell stories about American culture, capitalism, race and the resilience of working people to continue against the odds. Thus, his *Firestone Tire Dealership, 1997* (Plate 6.7) illustrates Vergara's concern for the layers of the city as it changes with time and use, charting, as he does, the building's many histories: from its 1940s modernist sleekness supporting the growth of auto-culture, to its later incarnations as garage, hardware store and car wash. In showing these traces on the face of the city, Vergara sees himself as 'a builder of virtual

Plate 6.7 Camilo Vergara, *Firestone Tire Dealership*, 1997.
Courtesy of Camilo Vergara

cities' with his 'images as bricks that, when placed next to each other, reveal shapes and meanings of neglected urban communities' (see Vergara undated a).

As with the photograph of Nashville (see Plate 6.1) Vergara's work records Detroit's (and other cities') growth and decline, as well as its survival and renewal, through photographs, interviews and other research that

> became the beginning of narratives which I hope will help establish a place's changing identity. . . . such as My work asks basic questions: what was this city like in the past, who lives in it and uses it now, and what are its current prospects? . . . Using insights from a variety of disciplines including ethnography, history, and archeology, I uncover patterns shaping the nation's poorest and most segregated post-industrial cities.
>
> (Vergara undated b)

In a way, Vergara's photography echoes David Simon's *The Wire* with its interest in capitalist infrastructures, decline, and also in renewal: 'an abiding faith in the capacity of individuals . . . to somehow endure' (Simon 2009: 31).

CONCLUSION, OR NO CONCLUSION POSSIBLE?

Marshall Berman's provocative book *All That Is Solid Melts Into Air* (1983) spends a good deal of time discussing the nature of the city experience, and his title, with its insistent irony and ambiguity, stands as a fine expression for the problems of trying to grasp the urban condition in any quantifiable way, for as soon as you have it, it disappears or meta-morphoses into something else. In a section of the book he describes an imaginary 'Bronx Mural', which becomes emblematic of the possibility of a city which has learned, however uneasily, to live with itself and with its differences. His description is revealing:

> the driver's view of the Bronx's past life would alternate with sweeping vistas of its present ruin. The mural might depict cross-sections of streets, of houses, even of rooms full of people just as they were before the Expressway cut through them all.
>
> (Ibid.: 341)

In this representation of the city the mural would tell the story of immigration, transportation and neighbourhood history in 'radically different styles, so as to express the amazing variety of imaginative visions that spring from these apparently uniform streets' (ibid.: 342). A close reading of this section suggests Berman's sense of loss, but also his hopes for the future in a city that can be many things, and so, at the very least, retains its capacity for wonder and its essential transformative powers. If the city is an 'imagined' place that we all create for ourselves in the very acts of existing within it, then it is perhaps this changing nature that is its strength, being what Ihab Hassan called 'variousness itself *inscribed* in steel and stone' (Jaye and Watts 1981: 109; our emphasis) and which makes its study so endlessly fascinating. His choice of the word 'inscribed' reminds us of where this chapter began, with the idea of the city-text that we struggle to read, and the signs that surround us in the city that we attempt to navigate. It can be, as Davis asserts, a *noirish* disorder, but as Waldie (1996) and Berman remind us, there is 'disaster and despair ... *but there is much more*' (Berman 1983: 343) in an environment where many voices and discourses coexist in a contest for dominance, authority and spatial justice (see Soja 2010). In fact, returning to the South Bronx in 2005, Berman, like Vergara or Simon above, stressed precisely the possibility inherent within urban and suburban life, the 'resiliency of modern cities, and of the men and women, the people we are: people who have the capacity both to commit urbicide and to overcome it; to reduce their whole civilization to ruins, but also to rebuild the ruins' (Berman 2010: 136).

REFERENCES AND FURTHER READING

Adams, H. (1918) *The Education of Henry Adams*, New York: Houghton Mifflin.
Auster, P. (1987) *The New York Trilogy*, London: Faber and Faber.
Balshaw, M. and Kennedy, L. (2000) *Urban Space and Representation*, London: Pluto.
Barthes, R. (1977) *Image, Music, Text*, London: Collins.
—— (1988) *The Semiotic Challenge*, Oxford: Blackwell.
Bégout, B. (2003) *Zeropolis: The Experience of Las Vegas*, London: Reaktion.
Bellamy, J.D. (1974) *The New Fiction: Interviews*, Chicago: University of Illinois.
Bender, T. (1975) *Toward an Urban Vision: Ideas and Institutions in Nineteenth Century America*, Lexington: University of Kentucky Press.
Bennett, Larry (2015) *The Third City: Chicago and American Urbanism*, Chicago: University of Chicago Press.
Berman, M. (1983) *All That Is Solid Melts Into Air*, London: Verso.
—— (2010) 'Falling' in M. Beaumont and G. Dart (eds) *Restless Cities*, London: Verso, pp. 123–37.
Beuka, R. (2004) *SuburbiaNation: Reading Suburban Landscape in Twentieth-Century American Fiction and Film*, London: Palgrave.
Bocock, R. and Thompson, K. (eds) (1992) *Social and Cultural Forms of Modernity*, Cambridge: Polity Press.
Bridge, G. and Watson, S. (eds) (2003) *A Companion to the City*, Oxford: Blackwell.
Brooker, P. (ed.) (1992) *Modernism/Postmodernism*, London: Longman.
Bruegmann, R. (2005) *Sprawl: A Compact History*, Chicago: University of Chicago Press.
Cage, J. (1961) *Silence*, London: Calder and Boyars.
Cisneros, S. (1984) *The House on Mango Street*, New York: Vintage.
Conrad, P. (1984) *The Art of the City*, New York: Oxford University Press.
Cook, B. (2015) *Flood of Images: Media, Memory, and Hurricane Katrina*, Austin: University of Texas Press.
Davis, M. (1990) *City of Quartz: Excavating the Future in Los Angeles*, London: Verso.
—— (1998) 'Las Vegas Versus Nature' in H.K. Rothman (ed.) *Reopening the American West*, Tucson: University of Arizona Press.
—— (2003) *Dead Cities and Other Tales*, New York: The New Press.
De Certeau, M. (1988) (first 1984) *The Practice of Everyday Life*, Berkeley, CA: University of California Press.
Dos Passos, J. (1986) *Manhattan Transfer*, Harmondsworth: Penguin.
Dreiser, T. (1986) (first 1900) *Sister Carrie*, Harmondsworth: Penguin.
During, S. (ed.) (1993) *The Cultural Studies Reader*, London: Routledge.
Fitzgerald, F.S. (1974) (first 1925) *The Great Gatsby*, Harmondsworth: Penguin.
Foucault, M. (1966) *The Order of Things*, London: Routledge.
—— (1986) 'Of Other Spaces', *Diacritics*, Spring, pp. 2–27.
Glaab, C. (ed.) (1963) *The American City: A Documentary History*, Homewood: Dorsey Press.
Hackman, R. (2014) 'Detroit Demolishes Its Ruins: "The Capitalists Will Take Care of the Rest"', *Guardian*, at http://www.theguardian.com/money/2014/sep/28/detroit-demolish-ruins-capitalists-abandoned-buildings-plan (accessed 8/6/15).
Hackworth, J. (2007) *The Neoliberal City: Governance, Ideology, and Development in American Urbanism*, Ithaca: Cornell University Press.
Hall, S., Held, D., and McGrew, T. (eds) (1992) *Modernity and its Futures*, Cambridge: Polity Press.

Harris, N. (1990) *Cultural Excursions*, Chicago: University of Chicago Press.

Harvey, D. (1989) *The Condition of Postmodernity*, Oxford: Blackwell.

Hess, A. (1993) *Viva Las Vegas*, San Francisco: Chronicle Books.

Howe, F. (1905) *The City, the Hope of Democracy*, New York: Charles Scribner's Sons.

James, H. (ed.) (1920) *The Letters of William James*, vol. II, Boston: Houghton Mifflin.

Jaye, M.C. and Watts, A.C. (1981) *Literature and the Urban American Experience*, Manchester: Manchester University Press.

Joachimides, C.M. and Rosenthal, N. (1993) *American Art in the Twentieth Century*, London: Royal Academy of Arts.

Koolhaas, R. (1994) (first 1978) *Delirious New York*, New York: Monacelli Press.

Kruse, K.M. and Sugrue, T.J. (2006), *The New Suburban History*, Chicago: University of Chicago Press.

Leatherdale, M.-B. (2015) *Urban Tribes: Native Americans in the City*, Toronto: Annick Press.

Lefebvre, H. (2004) (first 1992), *Rhythmanalysis: Space, Time and the Everyday*, London: Bloomsbury.

Levin, G. (1980) *Edward Hopper: The Art and the Artist*, New York: Norton.

Lyotard, J.-F. (1984) *The Postmodern Condition: A Report on Knowledge*, Manchester: Manchester University Press.

Marqusee, M. (ed.) (1988) *New York: An Illustrated Anthology*, introduction by Jay McInerney, London: Conran Octopus.

McInerney, J. (1984) *Bright Lights, Big City*, London: Flamingo.

Melville, H. (1979) *Billy Budd, Sailor and Other Stories*, Harmondsworth: Penguin.

Nicolaides, B.M. (2002) *My Blue Heaven: Life and Politics in the Working Class Suburbs of Los Angeles, 1920–1965*, Chicago: Chicago University Press.

Petry, A. (1986) (first 1946) *The Street*, London: Virago.

Pike, E. (1981) *The Image of the City in Modern Literature*, Princeton, NJ: Princeton University Press.

Poe, E.A. (1975) *Selected Writings*, Harmondsworth: Penguin.

Pratt, G. and San Juan, R.M. (2014) *Film and Urban Space: Critical Possibilities*, Edinburgh: Edinburgh University Press.

Rose, B. (1967) *American Art Since 1900: A Critical History*, London: Thames & Hudson.

Rose, J. (1990) (first 1988) *Kill The Poor*, London: Paladin.

Rothman, H.K. (ed.) (1998) *Reopening the American West*, Tucson: University of Arizona Press.

Sanders, J. (2003) *Celluloid Skyline: New York and the Movies*, New York: Alfred Knopf.

Simon, D. (2009) 'Introduction' to R. Alvarez, *The Wire Truth Be Told*, Edinburgh: Canongate.

Soja, E. (1996) *Thirdspace*, Oxford: Blackwell.

—— (2010) *Seeking Spatial Justice*, Minneapolis: University of Minnesota Press.

—— (2014) *My Los Angeles: From Urban Restructuring to Regional Urbanization*, Berkeley: University of California.

Storey, J. (1993) *An Introductory Guide to Cultural Theory and Popular Culture*, London: Harvester Wheatsheaf.

Tang, E. (2015) *Unsettled*, Philadelphia: Temple University Press.

Taylor, W. (1992) *In Pursuit of Gotham*, New York: Oxford University Press.

Trachtenberg, A. (1982) *The Incorporation of America*, New York: Hill & Wang.

—— (1989) *Reading American Photographs: Images as History*, New York: Hill & Wang.

Venturi, R., Scott Brown, D., and Izenour, S. (1996) (first 1972) *Learning From Las Vegas*, Cambridge: MIT Press.

Vergara, C.J. (1995) *The New American Ghetto*, New Brunswick: Rutgers University Press.

—— (1999) *American Ruins*, New York: Monacelli Press.

—— (undated a) 'Tracking Time', at http://www.camilojosevergara.com/About-This-Project/1 (accessed 08/06/2015).

—— (undated b) 'A Visual Encyclopedia of the American Ghetto: Proposal for an Interactive Website and Book', at http://invinciblecities.camden.rutgers.edu/intro.html (accessed 08/06/2015).

Vermeulen, T. (2014) *Scenes from the Suburbs: The Suburb in Contemporary US Film and Television*, Edinburgh: Edinburgh University Press.

Villa, R.H. and Sánchez, G. (eds) (2005) *Los Angeles and the Future of the City*, Baltimore: Johns Hopkins University Press.

Waldie, D.J. (1996) *Holy Land: A Suburban Memoir*, New York: St. Martin's Press.

—— (2004) *Where We Are Now: Notes from Los Angeles*, Los Angeles: Angel City Press.

Weimar, D. (ed.) (1962) *The City and Country in America*, New York: Appletons, Century, Crofts.

Whiting, C. (2006) *Pop L.A.: Art and the City in the 1960s*, Berkeley: University of California.

Whitman, W. (1971) (first 1855) *Leaves of Grass*, London: Everyman.

Wilson, E. (1991) *The Sphinx in the City*, London: Virago.

Winthrop, J. (1630) 'A Modell of Christian Charity', at http://www.hks.harvard.edu/fs/phall/03.%20winthrop,%20Christian%20Cha.pdf (accessed 11/09/2015), n.p.

Yamashita, K. Tei (1997) *Tropic of Orange*, Minneapolis: Coffee House Press.

—— (2010) *I-Hotel*, Minneapolis: Coffee House Press.

Yates, R. (2000) (first 1961) *Revolutionary Road*, London: Vintage.

FOLLOW-UP WORK

There are a number of additional resources, assignments and other materials to be found on the website that accompanies this new edition: http://www.routledge.com/cw/campbell /

1   Research how the city has been represented in American music. EITHER choose three songs from different genres (e.g. rock, rap, soul) and contrast their sense of the urban, OR write a detailed analysis of how Arcade Fire's 2010 CD *The Suburbs* records growing up in the Sprawl.

2   Read Waldie's *Holy Land* and think about the ways it represents the suburbs as a series of overlapping stories, histories, memories and rituals. Comment on how this mosaic is a particularly appropriate way to represent and evoke the life of the modern suburb.

3   Analyse films which examine city life in different ways, such as *Crash*, *Point Blank*, *Manhattan*, *Double Indemnity*, *Collateral*, *American Beauty* and *Revolutionary Road*; think about how the techniques of the film-makers allow them to create certain feelings about place and space.

4 Compare Baz Luhrmann's film of *The Great Gatsby* with Fitzgerald's attention to the city's different and changing rhythms. Read Lefebvre's *Rhythmanalysis* for some ideas about how to apply theoretical ideas to the film and novel.

5   How is New Orleans after *Katrina* represented in contrasting texts? Use David Simon's television series *Treme* or Spike Lee's *When the Levees Broke* (2012). You might focus on community, corruption, redemption and cultural expression (music, dance, tradition).

Chapter 7

Gender and sexuality
'To break the old circuits'

To break the old circuits.

(Cixous in Marks and De Courtivron 1981: 261)

In his commentary upon the Columbian Exposition of 1893, Alan Trachtenberg describes the special Women's Building as occupying a space between the Court of Honor and the Midway Plaisance, 'at the point of transition from the official view of reality to the world of exotic amusement, of pleasure' (Trachtenberg 1982: 222). This locational irony suggests the position of women in America at the time of the Exposition, since they were, on one hand, revered as the guardians of virtue, the home and the domestic economy, while still seen as possessions, apolitical and, at worst, objects for the male gaze – like the 'exotic' women on display on the Midway. Should women have been integrated into the main body of the Exhibition or should they have had a separate building? If they did not have the latter division, would their activities and achievements be smothered by the dominant presence of masculine displays? These discussions from the 1890s reveal significant arguments about gender, power and identity and have persisted into the twenty-first century. Such interpretations reveal the importance of gender within the politics of culture and begin to show the interrelationships of power, identity, ethnicity and class with issues of gender and sexuality.

The purpose of this chapter is to examine and demonstrate different ways in which 'cultural constructions of sexual difference fundamentally inform history' and how

> the discourses of gender not only regulate the social behaviour of men and women in sexuality, family and work, but they also become ways of ordering politics and of maintaining hierarchies of all kinds . . . describ[ing] a fundamental understanding of difference that organizes and produces other relationships of difference – and of power and inequality.
>
> (Melosh 1993: 5)

Gender, that is the feminine or the masculine, is not born into us but, rather, emerges as we develop and experience life. It is a socially constructed definition created through the various networks of forces that intersect around us as we grow. These cultural discourses, 'unities of theme and shared conventions of knowledge' (ibid.: 4), about gender and sexuality, shape and structure us as subjects within the social order. The privileging of certain discourses over others, as always, will determine which group holds greater authority within the culture at that moment. Thus gender and sexuality are part of the elaborate organisation of power within society, something we must examine in order to appreciate its influence upon the structuring of our lives.

This chapter will explore some examples of the processes and effects of this construction within the American cultural order in the twentieth and twenty-first century. It will also discuss how this order has been questioned in different ways by various groups such as social and radical feminists and male homosexuals. Gender Studies has taken its lead from the questionings of feminism which, in its various forms, challenged assumptions of power based upon the positioning of women in a male-dominated and male-defined society. For example, the tendency for there to be an assumed universal and general address seen as a 'norm' which is, however, male, is an indicator of patriarchal authority. If everything proceeds from this norm then it displaces women from the centre of society, and diminishes their worth and status. Thus, given the limits of space here, the majority of this chapter will examine gender in relation to women, but will also try to emphasise the equally important effects of these challenges to masculinity in America, for this too is constructed within the discourses of gender and sexuality at work in the culture. As Sidonie Smith has written:

> While ... gender ideologies rigidly script identities and differences according to apparently 'natural' or 'God-given' distinctions, these cultural scripts of difference remain vulnerable to contradictions from within and contesting social dialects from without that fracture their coherence and dispute their privileges.
>
> (Smith 1993: 210)

This chapter will identify some of these 'cultural scripts' and show how they have become hegemonic, while demonstrating, as Smith suggests, the possibility for a renegotiation of their dominance and a fracturing of their authority by various means.

NINETEENTH-CENTURY ROOTS: CULTURAL POLITICS

As early as 1837, Angelina Grimké (1805–79), an active anti-slavery campaigner, made important connections between slavery and the oppressed position of women in America. She wrote that 'the mere circumstance of sex does not give to man higher rights and responsibilities than to woman' (Lauter *et al.* 1994: 1866), and so brought into question the assumption that it was 'natural' for women to adopt specific roles in society and for men to assume others. A continual debate in Gender Studies has been over 'essentialism', which is the view that 'objects (including people) have an essential, inherent nature which can be discovered' (Burr 1995: 184). In terms of gender this is often connected with the idea that women, for example, are 'naturally' or 'essentially' homemakers because of their biological link to birth and nurturing. Grimké asserted, however, that 'our duties originate, not from difference of sex, but from the diversity of our relations in life, the various gifts and talents committed to our care, and the different eras in which we live' (Lauter *et al.* 1994: 1866). However, she points out that culture has constructed active 'man', while woman has been taught to lean upon an arm of flesh, to sit

> as a doll arrayed in 'gold, and pearls and costly array', to be admired for her personal charms, and caressed and humored like a spoiled child, or converted into a mere drudge to suit the convenience of her lord and master.
>
> (Ibid.)

The language employed by Grimké emphasises the relation between power and gender, since the woman is subordinated into a variety of roles – doll/child/pet – over which the man has control as 'master'. Such conditioned social thinking concretises the hierarchy so that the woman is 'robbed . . . of essential rights . . . to think and speak and act', becoming a silenced 'appendage of his being, an instrument of his convenience and pleasure, the pretty toy . . . the pet animal whom he humored into playfulness and submission' (ibid.). This advanced thinking was influential within America and provided the impetus and the language for women such as Elizabeth Cady Stanton and Susan B. Anthony, who organised a woman's convention at Seneca Falls in 1848. Its 'Declaration of Sentiments' echoed the American Declaration of Independence of 1776, emphasising the need for woman's rights and recognition within the democratic framework of the USA which had, it stated, established 'an absolute tyranny' over women (ibid.: 1946).

This was a momentous occasion for early American feminism, but within it exist the seeds of a debate, which has raged in different forms within women's groups ever since. That is, whether the demand for equality within the existing system is the correct way forward, or whether the system itself is so strongly biased towards men that it will always favour patriarchy. Patriarchy is a concept at the centre of much theorising and debate within Gender Studies and is best defined as 'a system of social structures and practices in which men dominate, oppress and exploit women' (Walby 1990: 20). Seneca Falls initiated a number of similar events that became the focus for new forms of collective female activity. As Gerda Lerner has written, 'The emergence of female consciousness ... rested on the existence and continuity of woman's clubs movements, and female organizations' (Lerner 1977: 392), which included the anti-slavery organisations, The Woman's Christian Temperance Movement (1870s), Female Labor Reform Association (1844) and many others. Through these collectives, women realised organisational skills, reinforced self-confidence, developed female support networks and became actively involved in a range of political tasks, such as fund-raising, information distribution and petitioning. Elizabeth Cady Stanton, speaking at the 1851 Woman's Convention in Akron, Ohio, said that 'self-reliance is educated *out* of the girl' whereas it was seen as central to the power and authority of men in American society. For her, 'experience comes by exposure' and therefore girls should not be sheltered behind the screen of patriarchy.

> Let the girl be thoroughly developed in body and soul, not modeled, like a piece of clay, after some artificial specimen of humanity. . . . Development is one thing, that system of cramping, restraining, torturing, perverting, and mystifying, called education, is quite another.
>
> (Lerner 1977: 416)

Such a radical call for change and the re-education of women grew during the late 1800s and brought into question the assumptions of patriarchy that women were only represented by the 'cardinal virtues' of 'piety, purity, submissiveness and domesticity' (Norton 1989: 122). Cady Stanton linked, as Grimké had, the woman with the slave, for 'all mankind stands on alert to restrain their impulses, check their aspirations, fetter their limbs, lest, in their freedom and strength, in their full development, they should take an even platform with the proud man himself' (Clinton 1984: 70). Confined by gender definitions, women had to question and challenge this fettering process if they were to play a fuller role in American culture.

At the Columbian Exposition the ambiguities of the 'woman question' were being played out on the national stage. This celebration of America's place in the world did acknowledge women in various ways; for example, with the Women's Building, with a female architect and a Board of Lady

Managers. However, these were compromised by the ever-present linking of women with a particularly limiting sphere – namely, the home. For example, male critics belittled the work of Sophie Hayden, the architect of the Women's Building, describing it as having 'graceful timidity or gentleness ... [which] differentiates it from its colossal neighbours [*that is, male*], and reveals the sex of its author' (Henry Van Brunt, quoted in Banta 1987: 528 – our emphasis and addition). Even Bertha Palmer, president of the Lady Managers, in her speech at the opening of the building, refused to 'discuss ... weighty questions' and assured the audience that 'every woman who is presiding over a happy home is fulfilling her highest and truest function' (Muccigrosso 1993: 139). As if to reinforce this, the building contained a model kitchen and was next door to the Children's Building with its nurseries and childcare exhibits.

However, the Exposition did give rise to some more radical voices that spoke out against these narrow definitions of women, echoing the earlier statements of Grimké and Stanton. One speech, 'The Woman's Sphere from a Woman's Standpoint', given in the Congress of Women by Laura DeForce Gordon, decried the 'system of repression, suppression and oppression practiced toward women', suggesting that,

Woman's sphere in life will be defined and determined by herself alone. Her place in nature, no longer fixed by masculine dogmatism, shall be as broad and multifarious in scope as God shall decree her capacity and ability to accomplish.

(Burg 1976: 240–1)

This more radical approach could be seen in the growth of 'social feminism' during the 1890s, which tried to activate the 'scope' that Gordon spoke of through social involvement outside the male-defined terrain of the domestic. Associated with figures such as Jane Addams (born 1860), who founded Hull House in Chicago as a community for reform and aid for women and families, social feminism has been called 'municipal housekeeping' because of its extension of domestic expertise into the wider arena of the public sphere, and so 'melded traditional charity with intellectual challenge ... [permitted] a dominant leadership role ... [and] excluded family demands' (Woloch 1994: 253). New Women of the 1890s, who questioned their roles, like Jane Addams, and became empowered in this way, extended the 'traditional' gender roles of women into the public domain. The philosophy of 'social feminism' could be summed up in the following speech by Marion Talbot in 1911:

The home does not stop at the street door. It is as wide as the world into which the individual steps forth. The determination of the character of that world and the preservation of those interests which she has safeguarded in the home, constitute the real duty resting upon women.

(Ibid.: 270)

However, to step beyond the street door was to enter the domain of men in a public manner that was controversial, but it became a vital element in the process of emancipation. For example, women's organisations continued to develop throughout this period: the General Federation of Women's Clubs (1890), National American Women's Suffrage Association (1890), National Consumers' League (1899), National Women's Trade Union League (1903) and many others provided 'a living bridge between traditional philanthropy and progressive reform' (ibid.: 299). This accumulation of groups formed a network of women who, together, pushed forward a number of legislative issues, culminating in the 1920 Nineteenth Amendment, which extended suffrage to women.

NINETEENTH-CENTURY ROOTS: LITERATURE AND THE 'FIRST WAVE' OF FEMINISM

Such concerns were also emerging in the literature of the period and provided another important source of discussion and cultural expression. For example, Kate Chopin (born 1851) wrote a short piece called 'Emancipation' in 1869 beginning with images of confinement, 'confining walls ... bars of iron ... a cage', as if to suggest the condition of women caught in the limited, male-defined world of America. The 'animal' that she describes is looked after, but longs for something more, signified by all that exists beyond the cage, and eventually moves out into 'the Unknown'. Now, without the protecting hand of patriarchy, the once-caged animal is awakened to a sensual world: 'seeing, smelling, touching ... all things', 'seeking, finding, joying and suffering' (Chopin 1984: 177–8). Chopin's sense of activated existence is linked to the freedom from the enclosed world of the cage – patriarchy and domesticity – and although the new life involves suffering, it is preferable to the powerless, protected realm which she clearly associates with the situation of women at the time.

Like so much fiction of the time, Chopin's images of confinement are metaphors for the social controls of patriarchy that separated women into very specific, domestic roles and discouraged other expressions or practices. We see this in Charlotte Perkins Gilman's 'The Yellow Wallpaper' (1892), which like her main work of social theory, *Women and Economics* (1898), is concerned with the power relations between men and women. The latter text argues against women as domestic and dependent on men and articulates the 'sexuo-economic' basis of the relationship that 'locks women into their homes and then identifies the work that is done in them as "natural" work for women. Gilman tears away that facade, exposing the reality of the institution as a limiting space' (Lane 1990: 252).

Gilman was a friend of Jane Addams and spent a good deal of time at Hull House and was 'formed ideologically and politically in the burgeoning reform activities of the 1880s and 1890s' (ibid.: 184). In 'The Yellow Wallpaper', Gilman dramatises aspects of her theory of gender relations, showing a woman in an actual 'limiting space', (over-)protected by her husband to the point of being, like Chopin's animal, a prisoner. Ironically, the woman (unnamed throughout the story) is imprisoned in a nursery whose 'windows are barred . . . and there are rings and things in the walls' (Gilman 1990: 43). She is made childlike as a mark of her powerlessness and locked into a torture chamber/nursery/bedroom ruled over by her doctor husband. All she has is the paper she writes on and the paper on the walls that she 'reads', gradually seeing there a version of her own life: 'Behind the outside pattern the dim shapes get clearer every day . . . like a woman stooping down and creeping about behind that pattern' (ibid.: 49). The outside pattern is that of patriarchy, which has shaped her life and defined her as dependent, weak and silent. But the story interfuses the two patterns until 'she just takes hold of the bars and shakes them hard . . . all the time trying to climb through' (ibid.: 53). It is as if the narrator and the 'creeping woman' have become one in the struggle to free themselves from the pattern and its terrible limiting space. Gilman's ambiguous ending leaves John, the husband, fainted and the woman circling around him rather like an animal freed from its cell but not yet equipped for the wild.

As an imagining of gender power relations the story, like Gilman's theory, is provocative and daring, but it was Kate Chopin who wrote an even more dangerous novel in 1899, *The Awakening*. This shows the 'awakening' of Edna Pontellier from the limiting space of a possessive husband to a new sense of identity and ambiguous freedom. She is 'a valuable piece of personal property' to her husband (Chopin 1984: 44), defined by 'a mother's place' (ibid.: 48) to be a 'mother–woman' only. These social definitions fix her by gender into a certain role with which she increasingly is at odds. She thinks of 'the dual life – that outward exist- ence which conforms, the inward life which questions' (ibid.: 57) and this is connected to the tensions explored by Gilman's metaphor of the 'outside pattern'. For Edna Pontellier, the possibility of a life beyond the cage of rigid social expectations is signified by the sea's fluidity, which is 'seductive; never ceasing, whispering, clamoring, murmuring, inviting the soul to wander for a spell' (ibid.). On or in the sea, she feels liberated, 'borne away from some anchorage which had held her fast, whose chains had been loosening . . . leaving her free to drift whithersoever she chose to set her sails' (ibid.: 81).

Myra Jehlen has written of women existing on a border between states, with 'the female territory . . . envisioned as one long border, and independence for women, not as a separate country, but as open access to the sea' (Showalter 1986: 264). Edna's sensual perception of 'independence' is just such fluidity and something that her husband cannot recognise: 'he could not see she was becoming herself and daily casting aside that fictitious self which we assume like a garment with which to appear before the world' (Chopin 1984: 108). At the sea, naked, she casts aside the clothing of pretence associated with the 'man-made' world, to borrow from Perkins Gilman, and in her 'suicide' becomes 'like some new-born creature, opening its eyes in a familiar world that it had never known' (ibid.: 175).

Perhaps in the political arena of Woman's Conventions and the Columbian Exposition such radically imagined alternatives to the gender limitations of late nineteenth-century American culture were difficult to articulate formally. As so often, literature could prefigure later, more overt moves towards feminist questioning of the patriarchal norm. Gilman's and Chopin's work is close to that of French feminist theorist Hélène Cixous, who wrote in 1976 that 'We must kill the false woman who is preventing the live one from breathing' and so 'emancipat[e] . . . the marvelous text of her self' (Marks and De Courtivron 1981: 250). As in French feminism, writers like Chopin and Gilman knew the importance of expression in order to 'break the snare of silence' (ibid.: 251) and to be assertive through the body: 'Women must write through their bodies . . . submerge, cut through, get beyond [patriarchy]' (ibid.: 256). For Cixous, women are akin to birds and thieves (a play on the French word *voler* meaning to fly and to steal), using language stolen from men in order to fly: 'They go by, fly the coop, take pleasure in jumbling the order of space, in disorientating it, in changing around the furniture, dislocating things and values, breaking them all up, emptying structures, and turning propriety upside down' (ibid.: 258).

At the time of Gilman's and Chopin's writing, however, America was unwilling to be 'turned upside down', tending to treat these works as 'scandalous' or eccentric, and peripheral to the mainstream or 'malestream' culture. This is now considered as the 'first wave' of feminism in America, raising important questions about the underlying assumptions embedded in the idea of 'sex-roles' and 'separate spheres' for men and women. However, it is the patriarchal power of the absent Father in Louisa May Alcott's *Little Women* (1868) that typifies the gender authority that must be overcome. His language, delivered through a letter, imposes control over the female household in which Marmee, the mother, becomes his mouthpiece:

> they will be loving children to you, will do their duty faithfully, fight
> their bosom enemies bravely, and conquer themselves so beautifully,

that when I come back to them I may be fonder and prouder than ever of my little women.

(Alcott 1989: 8)

Yet even in such a novel there is the figure of Jo March, who resists the call to duty and repression and seeks, as Cixous says, to 'break the snare of silence' with her body and her writing. She refuses for as long as possible the social construction of her gender, even though, as the novel suggests, it is an inevitable process. She wants to remain young and outside the gender system that makes her fit the role played out by Marmee and her sisters, but she cannot, and must succumb to marriage and to a role close to that of her dead sister Beth. What the novel shows is the extraordinary power tied to gender and the differences that society imposes upon the male and female. When Laurie, Jo's male friend, speaks of his future, his speech betrays his assertive self and the social acceptability of male freedom: 'After I'd seen as much of the world as I want to, I'd like to . . . choose . . . I'm never to be bothered . . . but just enjoy myself and live for what I like' (ibid.: 142). In contrast, Jo's sense of self and future is tentative, qualified and wrapped in fantasy: 'I'd have a stable full of Arabian steeds . . . I want to do something splendid before I go into my castle – something heroic or wonderful, . . . I don't know what' (ibid.: 143). The 'castle' is a metaphor of confinement, of the domestic world that she knows cannot be avoided, but even before this inevitable gender trap, Jo has less certainty than Laurie, fewer options and little access to the world outside her family. This moment is echoed later in the novel with Laurie trying to persuade Jo to run away with him and 'break out of bounds in some way'; but Jo's construction as a 'girl' has convinced her of 'her place': 'I'm a miserable girl, I must be proper, and stop at home' (ibid.: 213). Again and again Alcott reminds the reader of the gender 'civil war' going on in American society while the 'real' battles were being fought elsewhere, and she illuminates the often neglected aspects of power associated with patriarchy and dominance. For example, when Jo sees the fate of Meg marrying John Brooke, she is described as 'enthroned upon his knee, and wearing an expression of abject submission' (ibid.: 232).

During the 1880s and 1890s American women began to organise against such 'abject submission', as we have shown, and their responses were never uniform but formed various strands of feminism, some remaining within the 'family claim' (Rosenberg 1992: 65), while others sought to extend or challenge this notion of the 'woman's sphere' into a wider social dimension. As Rosenberg argues, 'All feminists believed that women should band together to claim personal emancipation, but they disagreed about what emancipation meant and how best to achieve it. . . . In these differences of emphasis lay the potential for much future strife' (ibid.: 68).

With the granting of suffrage to women in 1920, one aspect of the campaign had been achieved, but what became increasingly clear was that this wave of feminism was more than a 'campaign'. It was 'a dimension which informed and interrogated every facet of personal, social and political life' (Eagleton 1983: 150). It was not just about equality of power and status with men within an established and structured system, but rather was more concerned with the 'questioning of all such power and status' (ibid.). Matters of gender were now at the heart of American cultural life and would emerge in a variety of forms in the century ahead.

GENDER AND THE 1950S 'SECOND WAVE'

After the insecurity of the 1930s and the social disruptions of the Second World War, postwar America looked for a return to security, both in social and political ideologies. Gender offered pre-set compartments into which male and female could be arranged so as to create a sense of 'normalcy' and order that were non-threatening and in keeping with precise, uncomplicated versions of an ideal America developed in these years of consensus. However, this 'consensual hole-in-history', as W.T. Lhamon Jr calls it, was an illusion within which many crucial debates were taking place. Indeed, these were 'crucible years [that] forged the succeeding decades' (Lhamon 1990: 3).

In post-1945 America there was a 'new outburst of domestic ideology, a vigorous revival of traditional ideals of woman's place' (Woloch 1994: 493) and yet, at the same time, there were increased demands for women in the workplace too. This suggests what Nancy Woloch calls the 'split character' of the age (ibid.), with its return to notions of domesticity as the core of women's experience and fulfilment, in conflict with the pull of the labour market. One of the implications of this was a fear among males that their 'masculinity' was under threat. In particular, this definition of masculinity was concerned with employment, 'bread-winning', protection and authority, all of which appeared under fire from the potential encroachments of women into these areas. In wartime this had been acceptable, but during peacetime there had to be a return to 'an ideal script against which [women] measured their performance' (Gatlin 1987: 7). The metaphors used here are revealing, for they signal the growing sense of a 'split', resulting in a 'performance' during which women re-conformed to scripts 'written' by men in earlier generations. If women worked, as many did, it was seen as a temporary measure before settling into marriage and raising a family in the suburbs. When Betty Friedan examined this kind of cultural conditioning, she used the phrase 'the feminine mystique' to suggest the script that women had to learn in order to be acceptable within the new suburban middle class:

They learned that truly feminine women do not want careers, higher education, political rights – the independence and the opportunities that the old-fashioned feminists fought for. . . . All they had to do was devote their lives from earliest girlhood to finding a husband and bearing children.

(Friedan 1982: 13–14)

A film like *Rebel Without a Cause* (1955, directed by Nicholas Ray) articulates many of these themes, while ostensibly being a 'youth movie', situating itself in the suburbs with a mobile family in crisis. The roots of the crisis are to do with gender, and in particular the roles of the mother and the father. This was the age in which Dr Benjamin Spock's manual *Baby and Child Care* (1944) warned women against the dual dangers of over-protection and rejection of their children, and generally raised the awareness of models of caring in the public mind. This kind of fascination with raising children, alongside the growing interest in psychology, can be seen dramatised in *Rebel Without a Cause*. After all, if things were unstable at home, if children were wayward and confused, then it must be connected to the roles within the family. When Jim Stark (James Dean) cries out 'you're tearing me apart', he indicates the film's pursuit of familial confusions as its central theme. Dr Spock advised women to stay at home and only 'to leave home . . . for a trip to the beauty parlor, to see a movie, to buy a new hat or dress, or visit a good friend' (Rosenberg 1992: 151), and to guard against over-protection, for it could lead to 'Momism'. This meant adversely affecting the (male) child by smothering and domin-ating them so as to impair their masculine development as individual beings in a competitive society. 'The ideal mother was ever present never controlling' (ibid.), and in order for this to occur, it necessitated a strong husband assuming domestic authority and economic and sexual control in the home so as not to confuse the child.

This was a vision of social order sited in gender, which scripted distinct roles within the family, encompassing power and regulation in specific ways. Edmund White sums up the role of 'manliness' as 'a good business suit, ambition, paying one's bills on time, enough knowledge of baseball to hand out tips at the barbershop' (White 1983: 147). In *Rebel Without a Cause*, the father is weak and 'feminised' – we see him wearing a frilly apron at one point, and Jim mistakes him for his mother – and he is constantly referred to visually as small, imprisoned or indecisive. All the classical masculine traits, according to the cultural stereotype of the strong, individual male figure, are transferred to the mother, who is portrayed as aggressive, dominant and assertive. In the long opening scene of the film in the police station, the father arrives with Jim wanting to make him 'king'. Jim literally enthrones him before our eyes, only to see him 'dethroned' by the authority of the mother and the grandmother who hover like fearsome Harpies in the background. Later, Jim asks his father to advise him, and so take on his ordained position as masculine role model, but when he cannot, the boy is disgusted. At the height of Jim's confusion, just prior to his running away to the mansion, he confronts his parents on the stairs of the family home. It is a wonderful example of director Nicholas Ray's use of the camera, which creates visually a sense of destabilisation, with tilted angles and tight close-ups and editing. Jim is imaged as a crucified figure, unable to identify with the weak father who will not stand up for him against his mother. The boy 'longs for unity – with his parents and with his peers – and is repeatedly and frustratingly blocked from it' (Byars 1991: 128). The scene ends with Jim kicking a portrait of a matriarchal figure, destroying her whole face before he leaves the room.

In a piece written in 1956 for *Woman's Home Companion* the suburbs were described as being populated with 'women . . . like keepers of a prosperous zoo and the men like so many domesticated animals inside of it'. The man, like Jim's father, is 'ill at ease in a world that robs him of his chance at heroism. He wonders, seeing this gap between his dream and his daily life – is he even a man' (Bailey 1989: 103). If masculinity was under threat, then one way of reasserting its traditional 'heroism' was to reinvoke the domestic ideology for women. The 'feminine mystique', the housewife-mother, the suburban goddess, all entwined as a newly written script for postwar women. Appropriately, at the end of *Rebel*, as social order is restored, the father does stand up with Jim ('I'll be as strong as you want me to be') and does silence his wife with a look and a smile before guiding his regenerated family home. Masculinity had to assert itself: 'We must rediscover the art of dominating as the lion dominates the lioness – without force usually, without harshness usually, without faltering always' (ibid.: 105). However, a film like *Rebel*, with its 'tenuousness of resolution' (Byars 1991: 130) and its distorted realism, indicates the underlying discontent with accepted gender divisions and the fact that despite the smoothing over in its narrative closures, society itself was less easily healed.

These examples show that the pursuit of improvements in the lives of women were now being seen as too extreme, and that the social price of such changes of gender role and power could have specific social problems. Resolutions had to be presented even if social trends were themselves more contradictory. Television in the 1950s seemed to be part of this re-masculinisation of America, with its prime-time serials like *Bonanza*, *Gunsmoke* and *Daniel Boone* conjuring up heroic, frontier images of rugged individuals who lived their lives successfully without the intrusion of women, as if to answer the situation comedies that made the 'feminised' man, like Jackie Gleason in *The Honeymooners*, the humorous figure of fun. Women had to be contained if men were to rediscover their masculine authority, and from every source messages came to reinforce the importance of the home, family and marriage. Ironically, it became a 'narrowing of women's sphere' (Harvey 1994: xvi) in which 'their primary focus of interest and activity is the home' (ibid.: 73). After all,

> what profession offers the daily job of turning out a delicious dinner, of converting a few yards of fabric, a pot of paint, and imagination into a new room? Of seeing a tired and unsure man at the end of a working day become a rested lord of his manor?
>
> (Ibid.: 73)

This is the 'cultural script' that had to be recognised and challenged by the gender politics of the age. Betty Friedan's idea of the 'truly feminine woman' as scripted in postwar America is echoed by essayist and poet Adrienne Rich, who felt 'that marriage and motherhood . . . were supposed to be truly womanly', but which left her 'feeling unfit, disempowered, adrift' (Rich 1993: 244). She saw in her own life and writing the kind of 'split' that Woloch commented on as a characteristic of the age. Rich wrote of 'the split I . . . experienced between the girl who wrote poems, who defined herself in writing poems, and the girl who was to define herself by her relationships with men' (ibid.: 171). This conformity to gender expectations and the lines of power channelled through patriarchy forced Rich, like other women of that time, to begin to question this split and the scripts it imposed upon women. Her way forward was to 'use myself as an illustration' (ibid.: 170) and connect her own experiences as a woman in the 1950s with wider 'political' struggles. The two should not be separated, for to do so was to accept the political divisions of gender determined by 'masculine ideologies', which said that women operated in one sphere and that their 'problems [were] trivial, unscholarly, nonexistent' (Rich 1979: 207). This recognition that the 'personal' was the 'political' was central to many of the struggles for 'rights' at this time (see Chapter 3): 'politics was not something "out there" but something "in here" and of the essence of my condition' (Rich 1993: 175).

Thus, out of the 1950s emerged a revived feminism that challenged in different ways the 'script' of domestic ideology being written in the decade: 'Scripts specify, like blueprints, the whos, whats, whens, wheres and whys for given types of activity. . . . It is like a blueprint or roadmap or recipe, giving directions' (Weeks 1986: 57). Such impositions of gender 'scripts' had to be interrogated and challenged by activists, writers and, ultimately, in the lives of ordinary people. If these 'blueprints' did not cohere with individual experience, it was because they spoke from a universalised perspective that did not consider the differences inherent within gender. It has, therefore, always been a characteristic of the excluded and marginalised, like women and homosexuals, that they sought to express their experience in their voice (see Chapter 3 for a similar discussion of

African Americans). To this end, personal autobiographical or semi-autobiographical works have been central to Gender and Sexuality Studies. If the dominant culture assigned a particular normalised image, then part of the struggle was to present a counter-image through a variety of forms. As we shall show, a characteristic of Gender Studies in America has been the proliferation of diverse personal/political histories, stories and accounts determined to demonstrate that 'a person is not simply the *actor* who follows ideological scripts, but is also an *agent* who reads them in order to insert him/herself into them – or not' (Smith 1988: xxxiv–xxxv). The person who 'speaks' for themselves, in whatever arena or form, has been transformed from object, defined by others, to subject through the process of self-definition.

Women since First Wave feminism had begun to connect their personal experience to the wider world of politics, and by the 1960s it had become sloganised as 'the personal is the political'. Using broadly autobiographical experiences, many self-conscious works of subjectivity demonstrated 'new scripts for women's lives . . . being written . . . as oppositional cultural practices trying to change the cultural meanings of gender' (Lauret 1994: 97, 99). They rejected the 'malestream' stories that had privileged certain views of achievement, history and existence, and pointed out that 'they are neither objective, nor value-free, nor inclusively "human"' (Rich 1979: 207). Women's stories intervene in these assumptions, 'offering explorations of the social and psychic construction of female subjectivity' (Lauret 1994: 99) and presenting women as active, articulate beings in the process of becoming and change, rather than as the products of a patriarchal configuration as mother, lover or wife. Instead of the 'careers of domestic perfection', with women defined by 'the suburbs, technology . . . the family' and characterised by 'the sense of drift, of being pulled along on a current' (Rich 1979: 42), women were rediscovering their lives and finding ways to express them.

OUT OF THE 1950s: SYLVIA PLATH, *THE BELL JAR* (1963)

Published in 1963, the same year as Friedan's *The Feminine Mystique*, Plath's novel is an example of 'self-conscious subjectivity' in which her own life is the raw material through which to explore a 'split' self in a split age. Here the central character, Esther Greenwood, is divided between what she is 'supposed to be' (Plath 1972: 2) according to the gender rules of America in the 1950s, and what she wants to be within herself. Early on in the book, she describes herself 'adrift', like Rich: 'I wasn't steering anything, not even myself . . . [I was] like a numb trolley-bus . . . still and very empty, the way the eye of a tornado must feel, moving dully along in the middle of the surrounding hullabaloo' (ibid.: 3). The 'hullabaloo' consists of all the voices and institutions – family, education, work – that seek to define her as 'female' and place her in a specific, pre-ordained category. In particular, Plath uses the world of women's magazines as an example of the formation of such a set of gender guidelines, just as Friedan did in her book and, more recently, Brett Harvey (1994). Esther's self is fixed, with 'the years of my life spaced out along a road in the form of telephone poles, threaded together by wires' (Plath 1972: 129) and all her desires are shrunken and reduced. One of the prominent metaphors in the novel is that of language and writing, which are traditionally denied to women within the framework of patriarchy. Plath asked in her *Journals*,

> what inner decision, what inner murder or prison break must I commit if I want to speak from my true deep voice in writing . . . and not feel this jam-up of feeling behind a glass-dam fancy-facade of numb dumb wordage?
>
> (Yorke 1991: 67)

Marginalised, women do not have access to their own voice and are imprisoned in male language, which 'force[s] us to name our truths in an alien language, to dilute them' (Rich 1979: 207). Toril Moi has termed this 'the ventriloquism of patriarchy' (Moi 1985: 68), with men speaking for women, and Plath uses this precise image of ventriloquism (Plath 1972: 107) in the novel (as does Edmund White later), and in a key section describes how Esther's mother wanted her to learn shorthand, which she resisted because 'I hated the idea of serving men in any way. I wanted to dictate my own thrilling letters' (ibid.: 79). Rather than be 'a slave in some private, totalitarian state' (ibid.: 89), her definition of marriage, she seeks to 'dictate' her own life, write her own script and so reject the limited roles provided by patriarchy:

> The last thing I wanted was infinite security and to be the place an arrow shoots off from. I wanted change and excitement and to shoot off in all directions myself, like the colored arrows from a Fourth of July rocket.
>
> (Ibid.: 87)

To reject the fixed script of wife–mother, with its 'infinite security', is to assert the possibility of self-actualisation and alternatives to this 'norm'; to 'write your self', rather than be a 'scrawled over letter' (ibid.: 21), 'reduced to being the servant of the militant male, his shadow' (Marks and De Courtivron 1981: 250). Plath's novel dramatises, as Chopin's *The Awakening* had a century before, the desire to emancipate the self from the enclosure of patriarchal definition. The transgressive nature of this resistance is articulated using the powerful and violent imagery of suicide, which as Hélène Cixous commented, as discussed above, has a precise function: 'we must kill the false woman who is preventing the live one from breathing' (ibid.). In *The Bell Jar*, Esther severs her 'false' self, 'the smudgy photograph of the dead girl', because it represents the terrible uniformity of gendered society, its impositions and restrictions, buried 'deeper, more secret, and a whole lot harder to get at' (Plath 1972: 154, 156).

The radical cutting away of patriarchal power inherent in *The Bell Jar* does not, however, solve Esther's identity quest, but, like Edna Pontellier and the narrator of 'The Yellow Wallpaper', it unchains her from the 'bell jar' of male definition. Indeed, Esther is, at the end of the novel, full of 'question marks' and 'on the threshold', 'pointing to a yet-to-be determined future' rather than any 'fixed and coherent identity' (ibid.: 257). This is an open reading of identity, which counters the traditional, limited definition of 'woman' by men and by liberal feminists, like Friedan, and presents instead an image of 'subjectivity which is always positional, provisional, or . . . "subject to change"' (Lauret 1994: 101). Plath replaces fixity with flux, adjusting a patriarchal view of woman with, as Rosi Braidotti puts it, 'a knot of interrelated questions' (ibid.), 'as if the usual order of the world had shifted slightly, and entered a new phase' (Plath 1972: 252).

Plath's work, to some extent, relates to a struggle within feminism in the 1960s, between Friedan's National Organization for Women (NOW), formed in 1966, and Women's Liberation, because the novel is concerned with Esther's discovery of her self outside of the control of men. Her difference is important to the book and cannot be found within the existing male structures of power, which appear as 'totalitarian' and brutalising. She has to free herself from male 'colonialism', wherein her body is their conquest, and assert her own agency, through choice and action, at the novel's end. The precise liberation of the body is crucial since for so long it has been the site of restriction and control. Women's bodies apparently defined their lives because they were capable of childbirth and this, as Perkins Gilman asserts, seemed to confine them to the fragile world of the home and the nursery. Plath's fascination with the body typifies the attention given to it in the 1960s and 1970s by feminists who saw it as the lost territory, colonised by men (doctors, teachers, boyfriends, husbands), that had to be rediscovered and repossessed. Writing was a means to this end, for it gave voice to the female body and freed, as Cixous puts it, 'immense bodily territories which have been kept under seal' (Marks and De Courtivron 1981: 250).

What remains suggestive in Plath's work became vital to the growth of radical feminism in the 1970s, with its call for difference and, in some cases, for separatism. This goes back to First Wave feminism's concern for issues such as whether or not women could be included within a system so heavily biased towards men or whether a separate, woman-identified space was needed. Patriarchal values were so ingrained that women had to exist outside them in order to give full voice to a 'female culture' in its own right. This has been seen in French feminism's call for a distinct women's writing, or *écriture feminine*, in which the female body and female difference are asserted in language.

Such gender questioning has enabled other factors of difference to be more openly discussed, and, in particular, those of class, race and sexuality. Women of colour, often excluded from earlier discussions of gender, could now link their oppressions both to gender and to factors such as racism or poverty. The danger of earlier liberal feminism was its tendency to universalise 'woman', and therefore to see her as white and middle class, like Friedan's women in *The Feminine Mystique*. Thus, the broad politics of the Civil Rights movement, including African Americans, Native Americans and lesbians, related to this more open attention to difference in ways that hitherto had been impossible. Such diversity meant that middle-class white feminism was no longer the norm, and other voices contributed fruitfully to debates about the interrelatedness of oppressions across lines of gender, sexuality, class and race. The work of Cherríe Moraga, Gloria Anzaldúa, Maxine Hong Kingston and Alice Walker is of particular importance in challenging the uni-racial model wherein white women appear 'raceless', as though they speak for everyone (Du Bois and Ruiz 1990: xi), rather as patriarchy once did.

Similarly, but going even further, Judith Butler has asserted the importance of 'troubling' accepted categories, refusing to accept any 'single or abiding ground' on which feminism is built (Butler 1990: 33). Any established, fixed notion of 'self' or 'woman' cannot be assumed. Instead, she argues, gender is 'performative' as much as constructed, and any 'rigid regulatory frame' needs to be unsettled by questioning forces – 'mobilization, subversive confusion, and proliferation' to undermine any idea of a feminist 'we' as anything other than a fantasy (ibid.: 34). Butler's ideas are explained further with this much quoted passage:

> Gender ought not to be construed as a stable identity or locus of agency from which various acts follow; rather, gender is an identity tenuously constituted in time, instituted in an exterior space through a *stylized repetition of acts*. The effect of gender is produced through the stylization of the body and, hence, must be understood as the mundane way in which bodily gestures, movements, and styles of various kinds constitute the illusion of an abiding gendered self.
>
> (Butler 1990: 140)

For Butler gender is created by being performed as bodies compose or order themselves in a performative process that functions within certain 'scripts', to use our earlier term, or regulated 'viable roles' through which norms can be established (see Loxley 2007: 119). It is, she argues, 'a ritual reiterated under and through constraint, under and through the force of prohibition and taboo, with the threat of ostracism and even death controlling and compelling the shape of the production, but not, I will insist, determining it fully in advance' (Butler 1993: 95). However, within these normalising processes, there are opportunities for 'dissonant or disruptive gestures' (Loxley 2007: 123) running against expectation in the 'not fully determined' creation of an identity. One way of analysing and discussing Butler's ideas is through the photography of Cindy Sherman, whose early black and white images 'Untitled Film Stills' draw attention to performance, stereotype and identity through a creative reuse of 1950s television and film gender roles drawn from horror, *film noir*, teen movies and soft porn. Sherman's careful re-creation of familiar images forces the audience to look again and to interrogate why such images have held sway in terms of 'normalising' gender attitudes (see http://www.tate.org.uk/ art/artworks/sherman-untitled-film-still-48-p11518). Thus Sherman challenges us as viewers by encouraging certain expectations of roles within her images (the naïve college girl, the housewife, the movie icon, etc.) and then deliberately shocks us by violating those expectations, most notably in her 'Untitled Film Stills' where identities break away from such stereotypes by suggesting alternative, transgressive or, later in her narratives, 'horizontal'/centerfold images where we are confronted by difficult and ambiguous images of women that do not simply confirm stable meanings. This opening-up and 'troubling' of Gender Studies, within the larger frame of Cultural Studies, has given rise to what Toni Cade Bambara calls a 'gathering-us-in-ness' (Moraga and Anzaldúa 1983: vi), in which factors of oppression might be analysed and transformed from different perspectives, but with similar liberative goals. One radical group claimed that 'we are actively committed to struggling against racial, sexual, heterosexual, and class oppression and see as our particular task the development of integrated analysis and practice based upon the fact that the major systems of oppression are interlocking' (ibid.: 210).

SEXUALITY AND GENDER

The introduction of difference into Gender Studies has opened up the discussion of sexuality as a key factor in the way that identity is constructed and reconstructed. It is no longer possible to pretend that there is a 'unitary erotics' (Merquior 1985: 133) or a 'normal' sexuality but, rather, there exists a diversity of sexualities. These may not represent the views of official reality or be seen as acceptable within the mythical notion of the consensus, but they exist and are part of the cultural order. Plath's Esther Greenwood is circumscribed by gender distinctions, played out in the field of sexuality. For example, masculinity is represented as active and aggressive, like Lenny's place, with its 'great white bearskins . . . antlers and buffalo horns . . . [and] cowboy boots echoing like pistol shots', while women must be passive, 'the place the arrow shoots from' (Plath 1972: 15, 74). Esther is caught in the sexual 'double standard' of the age in which women were expected to balance sexuality with marriage and children, or risk being ostracised by society. Thus, heterosexuality was part of the 1950s consensus, the uniform response to sexual desire that gave approval to one particular mode of sexual expression and marginalised others. Adrienne Rich calls this 'unexamined heterocentricity' (Rich 1993: 203) and views it as ideological for it limits expression and choice and bolsters a patriarchal system that discourages autonomy and choice. What Rich calls for, like Butler, is a rethinking of such norms, of 'compulsory heterosexuality', so as to permit wider discussion and prevent 'the retreat into sameness . . . and a renewed open season on difference' (ibid.: 204; see also Butler 1990).

Homosexual rights groups came to the fore in 1969 following a police raid on the Stonewall Inn in Greenwich Village, which turned into a protest riot during which gay men and lesbians made a stand against prejudice and harassment. The Gay Liberation movement was a product of this event, and began to coordinate protest actions, which ranged from direct action to broader critical discussions of the problems of a centralised blinkered view of sexuality. Lesbianism became a decisive factor in the development of radical feminism, with some believing it was the only true expression of feminism, rejecting the patriarchal conventions of family, marriage and reproduction. Some viewed female biology as 'essential', a determinant of being, and thus it was women who knew women's bodies best, and they were naturally nurturing and non-aggressive. Rich called for a 'lesbian continuum' that is not primarily sexual but to do with 'woman-identified experience' set against 'male tyranny', a 'form of naysaying to patriarchy, an act of resistance' (Rich 1993: 217) based upon the ideal for a truly 'woman-centred' culture.

Although clearly not an issue confined to the 1950s, sexuality was discussed greatly alongside feminism at this time. Indeed, connections were often made between the two, claiming that mothers who were veering away from sexual norms influenced their children in favour of homosexuality or promiscuity (see Friedan 1982). A film like *Rebel Without a Cause*, discussed earlier and again in Chapter 8, also connects with a prevalent theory of the time, namely, that 'all parents of homosexuals apparently had severe emotional problems' (Bergman 1991: 190). This is portrayed by the figure of Plato, who attaches himself to Jim and is the product of a broken home. It is significant that Plato has to die at the end of the film, because in one respect he is the dangerous 'rebel' who threatens the status quo of the family and the masculine boundaries of society. Just like women who stand outside the frame of definitions provided by patriarchy, gays and lesbians have to be excluded so that 'order' can be resumed. The film's closure, with its salvation of the family and its pre-figuration of the 'new family' of Jim and Judy, testifies to the social drive, the consensus to marginalise or 'kill off' the outsider. 'Heterocentricity' is, therefore, reinforced.

Edmund White's loose 'trilogy' *A Boy's Own Story* (1983), *The Beautiful Room Is Empty* (1988) and *The Farewell Symphony* (1997) begins in the 1950s and describes the challenges for gay men from a boy's collision with this heterocentric culture to the coming of AIDS in the 1980s. The link between White's novels and Plath's is an important one, and there are many similar-ities between the two, but, in particular, they demonstrate the pernicious effects of gender and sexual construction upon the individual. White's 'boy', who is never named in the novel, is surrounded, as Esther is, by pressures to conform:

> in the mid-fifties . . . there was little consumption of culture and no dissent, not in appearance, belief or behaviour. . . . Everyone ate the same food, wore the same clothes. . . . The three most heinous crimes known to man were Communism, heroin addiction and homo-sexuality.
>
> (White 1988: 7)

White's linking of homosexuality with matters of national security was typical of Cold War paranoia in America, where any threat to the family and to 'normal' sexual behaviour was viewed as potentially anti-American. Plath's novel begins in June 1953, on the day the Rosenbergs were executed for being suspected Soviet spies, and clearly parallels her own 'shock treatment' with their deaths in the electric chair. Women's roles and sexuality were policed and controlled to ensure social order and anyone not conforming was forced into a hidden life. As 'boy' comments, his life was a 'dumb show in which I played such a decisive role – it was merely a simulacrum of actual feelings' (White 1983: 70), causing him to take on a false identity, as Esther had, to be 'the wolf cub in lamb's skin' (ibid.: 79), divided and silenced.

Like Esther, 'boy' desires expression and to be able to write his own existence and not have to follow the script of the aforementioned 'dumb show'. Contained within the discourse of heterosexuality, he sees writing as a way to 'dictate', to use Plath's word, his own subjectivity, with 'language as a site of resistance to the production of gendered meanings and . . . the perpetuation of heterosexually normative taboos' (Easthope and McGowan 1992: 135). He is still, however, caught between two forms of expression:

> I thought that to write of my own experiences would require a translation out of the crude patois of actual slow suffering . . . a way

of at once elevating and lending momentum to what I felt. At the same time I was drawn to. . . . What if I could write about my life exactly as it was?

(White 1983: 41)

To do the latter would require breaking through a level of social taboo and role-playing that is similar to that seen in Plath's work and which is called 'the screen of representation' by French theorist Luce Irigaray (Yorke 1991: 88). White, in the spirit of the age, sees 'the hidden designs other people were drawing around [him]' (White 1983: 104), one of which tells him that homosexuality is a sickness that can be cured by education, psychiatry, religion – all of which become prominent in the novel. But like Esther, he must pass through the 'treatments': confess to his father, betray his teacher and reject the church, before gaining something of his dream of power over the adult world that had circumscribed him. Luce Irigaray has written that women are

> stuck, paralysed by all those images, words, fantasies. Frozen. Transfixed . . . dividing me up in their own best interests. So either I don't have any 'self', or else I have a multitude of 'selves' appropriated by them, for them, according to their needs or desires.

(Yorke 1991: 88–9)

How similar this is to readers of both gay and feminist literature, for it expresses precisely the tensions that underpin their identities in a world that privileges a patriarchal, heterocentric existence. To be 'beyond . . . the screen of their projections' (ibid.: 88) is to be a danger, an outsider and a threat to social order and normality.

In gay male literature, early examples were provided by William S. Burroughs's *Naked Lunch* (1959), John Rechy's *City of Night* (1963) and Christopher Isherwood's *A Single Man* (1964), who all, in very different styles, presented gay perspectives and themes. The latter novel, written by an Englishman and filmed in 2010 by Tom Ford, is set in California in 1962, where George Falconer lives in uneasiness with his gayness. At one point, at the gym, he presents a vision of a more openly accepting culture: 'If only one could spend one's entire life in this state of easygoing physical democracy! . . . Nobody is too hideous or too handsome to be accepted as an equal. Surely everyone is nicer in this place than he is outside it?' (Isherwood 2010: 86).

The consciousness-raising towards such a culture has been continued in the work of writers like Edmund White as well as other writers such as in David Leavitt's *The Lost Language of Cranes* (1988), Gary Indiana's *Horse Crazy* (1990) or *Rent Boy* (1994), Dennis Cooper's *Frisk* (1992), Armistead Maupin's *Tales of the City* (1978), *Dancer From The Dance* (1978) by Andrew Holleran, and *Flesh And Blood* (1995) by Michael Cunningham. This writing explores the dilemmas of gender and sexual identity formation with an intensity, in part due to the discussion and consequences of HIV and AIDS in America. The need to speak openly about homosexuality has been an offshoot of the media's representations of HIV/AIDS and in particular the association of the disease as a 'gay plague'. Gay lifestyles were thrust into the full light of media attention, to the extent that in 1979 *Time* magazine's cover would show two males holding hands (and two females) and ask 'How Gay is Gay?'

It became increasingly important that gay people presented their own images to America to counter the scare being conducted in the media. In contrast to the media's single view of marginal, deviant practices that produced the 'plague', many gays wished to present various counter-views, stressing such values as pride, community and identity that surrounded their sexual preferences. Films like *Longtime Companion* (1990, directed by Norman René) depicted gay lives as close, loving and multifaceted in their dealing with the AIDS crisis, while activist movements like ACT UP (AIDS Coalition To Unleash Power) produced powerful slogans: 'Act-Up! Fight back! Fight AIDS!' and 'Silence = Death'. A writer like Gary Indiana, who represents a more radical gay style, wrote of the 'ideological conformity' and 'large totalitarian capacity' of America and the fact that it necessitated gays be wary of '*how we present ourselves to our executioners*' (Mariani 1991: 23; emphasis in original). This debate about self-representation is as alive in the gay community as it has been in feminist movements. In many respects the solution is representational variety and diversity, what Indiana calls 'a plurality of consciousnesses' (ibid.) and what lesbian feminist Audre Lorde expressed as 'the very house of difference rather than the security of any one particular difference' (Lorde 1982: 226).

Perhaps the best example of this kind of 'plurality' is symbolised by the AIDS Memorial Quilt founded in 1987, coordinated by the NAMES Project, as a memorial to those – male and female, gay and straight – who have died as a result of the disease (see www.aidsquilt.org). Its slogan is 'Remember. Understand. Share the lesson', and each of the 40,000 panels that make up the Quilt memorialises the life of a person lost to AIDS, emphasising the individuality of the person in stark contrast to the media representations that often classify and universalise the sufferers. It does, however, link the individual panels into a whole, to stress unity and diversity while creating an AIDS history to set against the myths constructed elsewhere. The quilt becomes a symbolic text, a reading of an invisible history, connecting the condition of AIDS with earlier minority struggles, of women and African Americans in particular:

> he who possesses the rhetoric also possesses the power . . . the Quilt
> provides an opportunity for People with AIDS (PWA) to repossess

the rhetoric and thus inscribe their stories so that they can claim dignity and status for themselves rather than be marginalized into mere victims.

(Elsley 1992: 190)

Tragically, HIV/AIDS provided a rallying point for gay activism, community and for concerns about representation – about how 'straight' society projected its images of AIDS and gay life into the homes of America. Controversies abounded, like those surrounding HIV/AIDS in advertising, and in particular the use of activist David Kirby, dying of AIDS, in the 1992 Benetton advertisement. It offended 'straight' society, not just because it portrayed death, but because it showed a gay man in relations with a family and suggested an almost Christ-like demeanour. By 1994, Jonathan Demme's film *Philadelphia* had brought together Hollywood studios, box-office stars like Tom Hanks and Denzel Washington and rock stars like Bruce Springsteen as a way of dramatising AIDS for the mass market. *Philadelphia* normalised gay life, via Tom Hanks, and, perhaps, reduced the complexities surrounding AIDS, but it proved that the issues were at the heart of American life and not confined to the margins of private lives. Philadelphia, the City of Brotherly Love, the cradle of democracy, was the site for a new struggle, one that was no longer simply a gay problem. The AIDS crisis was also dramatised with immense power and controversy in the play and later film of Tony Kushner's *Angels in America* (1993).

By the mid 1990s matters of gender and sexuality were centre-stage, in part because of HIV/AIDS, but also as a result of years of discussion arising from feminism, gay rights and new social movements. In some respects, Americans learned that they were plural, made up not only of different colours, ethnicities and classes, but also of different sexualities and genders, typified by the emergence of a spectrum of lesbian, gay, bisexual and transgender (LGBT) representations. This is most notable through the emergence of New Queer Cinema of Gus Van Sant, Todd Haynes and Greg Araki in the 1990s, the publication of books like Leslie Feinberg's extraordinary novel *Stone Butch Blues* (1993), about 'he–shes' and the world of 'passing' and transgendering, or controversial films such as *Boys Don't Cry* (1999, directed by Kimberly Pierce), the dramatised true story of the life of Brandon Teena, a transgendered teenager who lived and performed a male identity until being brutally raped and murdered, and even the various debates that exploded following Ang Lee's so-called gay Western *Brokeback Mountain* (2005). One might argue that the 'centre', with its closed vision of itself as white, heterosexual and male, although still powerful and dominant, had been challenged on a number of fronts; 'the old narratives, stories, scripts, mythologies [have] become transvalued, re-presented in different terms' (Yorke 1991: 1).

These challenges had their most dramatic impact in the rise of the movement to recognise same-sex marriages. In 1996 a Republican-dominated Congress had passed the Defense of Marriage Act (DOMA), which sought to prevent the federal government from recognising marriages between gay couples and gave states the right to refuse recognition to marriages conducted outside their own borders. At that point polls suggested 68 per cent of the wider public believed same-sex marriages should not be recognised by the law as valid, with the same rights as traditional marriages (Gallup 2015). Gradually, however, DOMA was confronted at state level by legal challenges which sought to show that it denied equal rights to gay couples. At the same time, conservative groups sought to shore up support for traditional marriage by seeking to add constitutional amendments to state constitutions, which declared that marriage was for heterosexual couples only. By 2004, the whole issue had become a significant factor in both federal and state elections, where it clearly demonstrated the passions which struggles over cultural identity could arouse. Gay and lesbian advocates increasingly saw gay marriage as a litmus test for equal rights, while opponents identified it as a threat to traditional social and religious values. Gradually, however, the balance of opinion swung towards recognition of same-sex marriage. By 2012 a majority of Americans (53%) now approved of legal recognition, supported by Barack Obama's decision in 2012 to become the first president to back such a move. Interplay between the increasing visibility of gay rights and the courts added to the shift. Key elements of DOMA were struck down at a federal level by the Supreme Court in 2013, and in an increasing number of states appeals through the courts against local laws which sought to deny gay marriage were successful.

Edmund White suggested that 2013 could be declared the Year of the Gay in terms of the number of states which moved to accept gay marriage (White 2014). By January 2015, gay marriage had been recognised in thirty-six states and Washington DC, and nearly 70 per cent of Americans were living in areas where gay marriage was allowed. The final achievement was the majority decision of the Supreme Court in June 2015 that the Constitution guarantees a right to same-sex marriage through the commitment to individual liberty laid out in the Fourteenth Amendment. White gave a typically nuanced reading of the transformation in public sentiment and institutional approval. Clearly this was a cause for celebration in that it brought gays and lesbians more directly into the national mainstream and recognised them as 'normal, loving, decent members of (American) lives and . . . communities' (Boies and Olson 2014: 310). On the other hand, he wondered whether acceptance into the institution of marriage, meant that something 'discordant', different, was being lost (White 2014).

ROSEANNE: THE WORLD BLOWN APART

You get what you settle for.

(Thelma and Louise, 1991)

In Betty Friedan's The Feminine Mystique one of the women interviewed says, 'I'm desperate. I begin to feel I have no personality. I'm a server of food and a putter-on of pants and a bedmaker, somebody who can be called on when you want something. But who am I?' (Friedan 1982: 19). Although a voice from the 1960s, such a statement could have come from the more recent past, for women still struggle against this kind of desperate limitation of their identities in a domestic, patriarchal world. A popular cultural text such as Roseanne shows how this 'despair' and its associated cultural contests can be played out in a different realm of representation with powerful results.

The popular television programme Roseanne, first screened in 1988, is an example of how mainstream culture has integrated aspects of the contests over gender and sexuality into itself. The show adopts the genre made famous in 1950s shows like Leave it to Beaver or The Honeymooners, but 'is a conscious fracturing of the myth of the happy suburban family', becoming instead, it has been argued, 'a vehicle of resistance' (Dines and Humez 1995: 471) with its deliberate disturbance of gender expectations and sexual norms. Roseanne is 'woman-centred', with a 'subversive potential as a source of resistance and inspiration for feminist change' (ibid.: 474), subverting the norms of the sitcom genre which traditionally reduces the influence of the woman along pre-set gender lines. Roseanne has said that humour related to life can have a decisive effect: 'I found a stage, where I began to tell the truth about my life – because I couldn't tell the truth off the stage. And very quickly, the world began to blow apart' (Bonner et al. 1992: 286).

Like many other texts we have examined in this chapter, Roseanne is concerned with 'lifetelling' and using these experiences within the 'fiction' of the show. For example, the fictional Roseanne longs to write, just as the 'real' Roseanne did. Writing, as always, signifies the desire for self-expression and authority. However, the show 'blows the world apart' by upsetting the conventions of sitcoms in every way: she is fat, loud, appears disrespectful of her husband, indifferent to her children and slovenly in her domestic duties. Indeed, 'she built her act and her success on an exposure of the "tropes of femininity" [the ideology of 'true womanhood', the perfect wife and mother] by cultivating the opposite [an image of the unruly woman]' (Rowe 1990: 413). The show examines female relationships across generations, races and regions and has chosen to explore varieties of female community or 'woman-space' (Dines and Humez 1995: 473) in different series (the home, the hair salon, 'The Lunch Box', etc.). In a celebratory episode, Roseanne's kitchen is occupied by a group of quintessential middle-class television housewives who stayed at home to rear children, clean their houses and cook, like June Cleaver (*Leave it to Beaver*), Donna Reed (*The Donna Reed Show*) and Norma Arnold (*The Wonder Years*). As if to remind the audience of her subversion of their 'norm', Roseanne educates them in her liberated ways and frees them from the 'script' that they have followed in their fictional incarnations.

The show made the point, however, as we have within this chapter, that there has been a script of gender and sexuality established in postwar America that has in recent years come under increased questioning. The self-conscious use of these 1950s 'moms' in a 1990s show makes one conscious of the constructedness of the roles and how they might be interrogated with humour and irony. Roseanne has written that her mission was 'to break every social norm . . . and see that it is laughed at . . . because the people I intend to insult offend me horribly' (Rowe 1990: 414). The show has developed beyond this first-level 'unruliness', with its deconstruction of the 'mom' myth and that of the American sitcom family, to introduce several other issues such as class, race and sexuality into its gender framework. For example, it has two regular, overtly gay characters: Nancy (Sandra Bernhard) and Leon (Martin Mull), who are permitted airtime in which to express their sexuality, both visually and verbally. Neither is seen as a 'freak', although, like everyone in the show, they are a source of humour. They are workers, managers, lovers who have power, relationships and emotions, just like all the characters in the comedy.

In an infamous episode, Roseanne's overt heterosexuality is challenged by a lesbian relationship, and a screen kiss, with Mariel Hemingway, which deliberately confronted social fears and taboos through the comic medium of the show. Roseanne's control over the show, her 'authority', ensures a diversity in issues and in characterisation that has resisted the conventions and stereotypes of American television and extended debates about family life and 'values'. Her manic laughter, signalled in the opening title sequence of the show, resembles Cixous's Medusa, whose subversive power unhinged and disturbed, or Freud's Dora, whose hysteria 'undoes family ties, introduces perturbation into the orderly unfolding of daily life, stirs up magic in apparent reason' (Gallop 1982: 133). What a show like *Roseanne* has enabled is a questioning of definitions of gender and sexuality, in particular around the female image, and offered its audience a series of alternative, competing visions of what have so often appeared as fixed and certain categories within American culture. In the past, the 'unruly' woman could be comically assimilated back into the genre, her outrageousness controlled and tempered by the family group. One thinks of Lucille Ball or *Bewitched*, but in *Roseanne* this is never quite the case. The family is not destroyed by her, but it is questioned and decentred while she remains 'unambiguously non-assimilable' (ibid.: 134) and so is challenging and subversive.

In its own way, the show does assert differences between genders and sexualities, and points towards what we might term postmodern gender and sexuality in the spirit of Judith Butler. This 'rejects all versions of essential femininity or masculinity ... [and] suggests that there is no singular, true [gender definition] ... to reclaim', but instead it is 'fractured, contradictory and produced within social practices' (Jordan and Weedon 1995: 203). The show demonstrates constant negotiations over gender relations, sexualities and power-lines within and outside the family. However, if *Roseanne* has elements of this postmodern sentiment, it is also highly conscious of how these power relations underpin differences in class, race and gender and how they affect the public validity of the negotiations. The show no longer hides behind the 'screen of projections', but revels in display and spectacle, using the body as a source of identity and strength and is constantly 'intervening in oppressive identity per- formances, troubling culturally authorized fictions' (Smith 1993: 162) with its carnival spirit. Gender and sexuality are at centre-stage and are part of the show's cacophony of voices, which went on to have a major influ- ence on the kinds of representations that would follow in shows as different as *Ellen*, *Ally McBeal*, *Sex in the City*, *Will and Grace* and more recently in *Girls* (discussed in Chapter 8) and *Orange is the New Black* (discussed below).

CONCLUSION: *NURSE JACKIE* AND *ORANGE IS THE NEW BLACK*

The subversive spirit of *Roseanne* lives on in *Nurse Jackie* (Showtime, 2009–) one of whose writers, Liz Brixius, told the New York *Daily News* that 'Guys' stories

> tend to be about conquests – getting the job, winning the Olympics, whatever. Women stories aren't as immediately climactic so they need to play out over the course of three months. . . . And every medical show out there has been about doctors. Doctors are absolutely unable to do what they have to do without nurses. We want to tell those stories.
>
> (Kinon 2009: n.p.).

It has strong female characters and gay-inclusive storylines partly because its co-creators Linda Wallem and Liz Brixius are 'out' lesbians and wanted a hospital comedy-drama to respond to America's changing relationship with gender and sexuality. To this end the show represents a professional woman, who is mother, friend, lover *and* addict in the figure of Jackie

Peyton (Edie Falco), a flawed women juggling all the parts of her life and just about managing to hold it together: 'Jackie overextends herself. People try to be good mothers, and be good nurses and be good people. But the reality is, we're all really flawed', says Liz Brixius (interview at website *After Ellen*). At times funny and tragic, *Nurse Jackie* is a counter-narrative to the 'normalised' medical dramas like *ER* and *House* ('doctors' stories') in that it is edgy and transgressive, daring to offer us one central character we are supposed to admire, who is a drug addict and unfaithful to the family she clearly loves, or another, Dr Coop, who turns out to have two gay mothers. But the show's social themes are ever-present as well: the crumbling health care system, the class divides of doctors and nurses, and the various tensions over power and authority. At its heart though is Jackie, a wonderfully articulated plurality of selves, a twenty-first-century 'chipped' icon; performative and yet always promisingly unruly at the same time.

Another 'institutional' television comedy-drama to explore the 'unruly' and transgressive is *Orange is the New Black* created by Jenji Kohan and first released on Netflix on 11 July 2013. Here a women's prison provides the focus for a darkly humorous exploration of sexualities, race and power with the advantage of a serial format in which characters change, regress, appear and disappear across time allowing a more honest and ambiguous sense of character and action to emerge (see discussion of serial, long-form television in the introduction). As Kohan has said,

> I'm always looking for those places where you can slam really disparate people up against one another, and they have to deal with each other ... We talk about this country as this big melting pot, but it's a mosaic. There's all these pieces, they're next to each other, they're not necessarily mixing. And I''m looking for those spaces where people actually do mix – and prison just happens to be a terrific one.
>
> (Kohan 2013)

So the show creates drama through juxtaposition and mixing, testing prejudices, both of its characters and its audience, in an effort to create an alternative, and, at times, amazingly touching, new 'unruly' social order that once again asserts that gender and sexuality are not essentialised but rather 'fractured, contradictory and produced within social practices'.

REFERENCES AND FURTHER READING

After Ellen: Interview with Linda Wallem and Liz Brixius at http://www.after ellen.com/TV/2009/7/wallem-brixius?page=0%2C0 (accessed 25/01/2011).
Alcott, L. (1989) (first 1868) *Little Women*, Harmondsworth: Penguin.

Bailey, B. (1989) *From Front Porch to Back Seat: Courtship in Twentieth Century America*, Baltimore: Johns Hopkins University Press.

Banta, M. (1987) *Imaging American Women: Idea and Ideals in Cultural History*, New York: Columbia University Press.

Barber, S. (1999) *Edmund White: The Burning World*, London: Faber and Faber.

Bergman, D. (1991) *Gaiety Transfigured: Gay Self-Representation in American Literature*, Madison: University of Wisconsin Press.

Boies D. and Olsen T. (2014) *Redeeming the Dream: The Case for Marriage Equality*, New York: Viking.

Bonner, F., Goodwin, L., and Allen, R. (eds) (1992) *Imagining Women: Cultural Representations and Gender*, Cambridge: Polity Press.

Burg, D.F. (1976) *Chicago's White City of 1893*, Lexington: University of Kentucky Press.

Burr, V. (1995) *An Introduction to Social Constructionism*, London: Routledge.

Butler, J. (1990) *Gender Trouble: Feminism and the Subversion of Identity*, London: Routledge.

—— (1993) *Bodies That Matter: On the Discursive Limits of 'Sex'*, New York: Routledge.

Byars, J. (1991) *All That Hollywood Allows: Re-reading Gender in 1950s Melodrama*, London: Routledge.

Castro-Borrego, S.P. and Romero Ruiz, M.I. (eds) (2014) *Identities on the Move: Contemporary Representations of New Sexualities and Gender Identities*, New York: Lexington Books.

Chafe, W.H. (1974) *The American Woman: Her Changing Social, Economic and Political Roles, 1920–1970*, Oxford: Oxford University Press.

Chopin, K. (1984) (first 1899) *The Awakening and Selected Stories*, Harmondsworth: Penguin.

Chou, R.S (2015) *Asian American Sexual Politics: The Construction of Race, Gender, and Sexuality*, New York: Rowman & Littlefield.

Clinton, C. (1984) *The Other Civil War: American Women in the Nineteenth Century*, New York: Hill & Wang.

Daniel, R.L. (1989) *American Women in the Twentieth Century*, New York: Harcourt, Brace, Jovanovitch.

Dines, G. and Humez, J. (eds) (1995) *Gender, Race and Class in Media: A Text-reader*, London: Sage.

Du Bois, E.C. and Ruiz, V. (eds) (1990) *Unequal Sisters: A Multicultural Reader in U.S. Women's History*, London: Routledge.

Eagleton, T. (1983) *Literary Theory*, Oxford: Blackwell.

Easthope, A. and McGowan, K. (eds) (1992) *A Critical and Cultural Theory Reader*, Buckingham: Open University Press.

Elsley, J. (1992) 'The Rhetoric of the NAMES Project – AIDS Quilt: Reading the Text(ile)' in E.B. Nelson (ed.) *AIDS: The Literary Response*, New York: Twayne, pp. 186–90.

Friedan, B. (1982) (first 1963) *The Feminine Mystique*, Harmondsworth: Penguin.

Gallop, J. (1982) *Feminism and Psychoanalysis: The Daughter's Seduction*, London: Macmillan.

Gallup (2015) 'Marriage' at http://www.gallup.com/poll/117328/marriage.aspx (accessed 13/03/2015).

Gatlin, R. (1987) *American Women since 1945*, London: Macmillan.

Gilman, C.P. (1990) (first 1892) 'The Yellow Wallpaper' in C. Griffin-Wolff (ed.) *Four Stories By American Women*, Harmondsworth: Penguin.

Habell-Pall'an, M. (2005) *Loca Motion: The Travels of Chicana and Latina Popular Culture*, New York: New York University Press.

Harvey, B. (1994) *The Fifties: A Women's Oral History*, New York: Harper Perennial.

Isherwood, C. (2010) (first 1964) *A Single Man*, London: Vintage.

Jordan, G. and Weedon, C. (1995) *Cultural Politics: Class, Gender Race and the Postmodern World*, Oxford: Blackwell.

Kinon, C. (2009) 'Nurse Jackie', *NY Daily News*, at http://www.nydailynews.com/entertainment/tv/2009/02/16/2009–0216_nurse_jackie_star_edie_falco_marylouise_.html (accessed 23/01/2011).

Kohan, J. (2013) '"Orange" Creator Jenji Kohan: "Piper Was My Trojan Horse"', 13 August, at http://www.npr.org/2013/08/13/211639989/orange-creator-jenji-kohan-piper-was-my-trojan-horse (accessed 18/09/15).

Lane, A.J. (1990) *To Her Land and Beyond: The Life and Works of Charlotte Perkins Gilman*, New York: Pantheon Books.

Lauret, M. (1994) *Liberating Literature: Feminist Fiction in America*, London: Routledge.

Lauter, P. *et al.* (1994) *The Heath Anthology of American Literature*, Lexington: D.C. Heath.

Lerner, G. (ed.) (1977) *The Female Experience: An American Documentary*, Oxford: Oxford University Press.

Lhamon, W.T. Jr (1990) *Deliberate Speed: The Origins of Cultural Style in the American 1950s*, Washington, DC: Smithsonian Institute Press.

Littauer, A.H. (2015) *Bad Girls: Young Women, Sex, and Rebellion Before the Sixties* (Gender and American Culture), Chapel Hill: North Carolina Press.

Lorde, A. (1982) *Zami: A New Spelling of My Name*, London: Sheba.

Loxley, J. (2007) *Performativity*, London: Routledge.

Mariani, P. (ed.) (1991) *Critical Fictions*, Seattle: Bay Press.

Marks, E. and De Courtivron, I. (eds) (1981) *New French Feminisms*, London: Harvester Wheatsheaf.

Melosh, B. (ed.) (1993) *Gender and American History Since 1890*, London: Routledge.

Merquior, J. (1985) *Foucault*, London: Collins.

Meyerowitz, J. (ed.) (1994) *Not June Cleaver: Women and Gender in Postwar America, 1945–1960*, Philadelphia: Temple University Press.

Moi, T. (1985) *Sexual/Textual Politics: Feminist Literary Theory*, London: Routledge.

Moraga, C. and Anzaldúa, G. (eds) (1983) *This Bridge Called My Back: Writings By Radical Women of Color*, New York: Kitchen Table Press.

Muccigrosso, R. (1993) *Celebrating the New World: Chicago's Columbian Exposition of 1893*, Chicago: Ivan R. Dee.

Mulvey, L. (1991) *Visual and Other Pleasures*, London: Macmillan.

Norton, M.-B. (ed.) (1989) *Major Problems in American Women's History*, Lexington: D.C. Heath.

Oldmixon, E.A., Blackstone, B., and Watson, W.L. (2015) *Queer Politics: Identity, Culture, and American Democracy (Routledge Series on Identity Politics)*, London: Routledge.

Plath, S. (1972) (first 1963) *The Bell Jar*, London: Faber and Faber.

Rich, A. (1979) *On Lies, Secrets, and Silence: Selected Prose, 1966–1978*, New York: W.W. Norton.

—— (1993) *Adrienne Rich's Poetry and Prose*, New York: W.W. Norton.

Rosenberg, R. (1992) *Divided Lives: American Women in the Twentieth Century*, New York: Hill & Wang.

Rowe, K.K. (1990) 'Roseanne: Unruly Woman as Domestic Goddess', *Screen*, vol. 31, no. 4, Winter, pp. 408–19.

Showalter, E. (ed.) (1986) *The New Feminist Criticism*, London: Virago.

—— (1992) *Sexual Anarchy: Gender and Culture at the Fin de Siècle*, London: Virago.

Smith, P. (1988) *Discerning the Subject*, Minneapolis: University of Minnesota.

Smith, S. (1993) *Subjectivity, Identity and the Body in Women's Autobiographical Practices in the Twentieth Century*, Bloomington: Indiana University Press.

Trachtenberg, A. (1982) *The Incorporation of America: Culture and Society in the Gilded Age*, New York: Hill & Wang.

Walby, S. (1990) *Theorizing Patriarchy*, Oxford: Blackwell.

Weeks, J. (1986) *Sexuality*, London: Routledge.

White, E. (1983) *A Boy's Own Story*, London: Picador.

—— (1988) *The Beautiful Room Is Empty*, London: Picador.

—— (1998) (first 1997) *The Farewell Symphony* London: Vintage.

—— (2014) 'I Do, I Do', *New York Review of Books*, 14 August, at http://www. nybooks.com/articles/archives/2014/aug/14/i-do-i-do/ (accessed 12/09/ 2015).

Woloch, N. (1994) *Women and the American Experience*, New York: McGraw-Hill.

Yorke, L. (1991) *Impertinent Voices: Subversive Strategies in Contemporary Women's Poetry*, London: Routledge.

FOLLOW-UP WORK

There are a number of additional resources, assignments and other materials to be found on the website that accompanies this new edition http://www.routledge.com/cw/campbell/

1   Examine Debra Granik's film *Winter's Bone* (2010) and analyse how the 'heroic' quest of central figure Ree traverses the county to confront her kin, breaks their silent collusion and tries to hold her family together. How does the film reassess female identity?

2   The focus in this chapter has been largely on female identity. How is masculinity constructed in Clint Eastwood's film *Gran Torino* (2008)? In what ways does the film gradually ask questions of certain, traditional masculinities? One blogger has written that

> In order to tell its story, *Gran Torino* relies on the most typically racist and sexist notions of helpless and dangerous Asian immigrants/Asian Americans, juxtaposed against white male saviours that have been presented in American film over and over and over for decades.
>
> (http://thegrumpysociologist.blogspot.co.uk/2009/06/
> hegemonic-masculinity-run-amok-in-gran.html)

Debate this point of view.

3   Survey any American edition of a fashion or lifestyle magazine to analyse how either men or women are represented in the twenty-first century.
4   Examine in detail an episode of *Orange is the New Black* to analyse how the show juxtaposes class, race and sexuality as a means of challenging the viewer. How does it surprise us, shock us and draw us to points of unusual empathy?
5   Go online to explore Cindy Sherman's photography, especially her 'Untitled Film Stills', and think about how they work to both use and then subvert 1950s gender stereotypes.

Chapter 8

Representing youth
Outside the sunken nursery

Late in Douglas Coupland's *Generation X* (1992), the idea of youth is dwelt upon and a particular metaphor stands out: 'youth really is . . . a sad evocative perfume built of many stray smells' (ibid.: 134). To see youth as something built up, or constructed, of many 'stray smells' is to recognise it as a complex, differentiated 'conjunction point for various discourses' (Acland 1995: 10), all informed by race, class, power, gender and sexuality. Youth is one of the sites where these forces cross, mix and clash: 'at a splendid crossroad where the past meets the future in a jumble of personal anxieties and an urgent need for social self-definition' (Fass 1977: 5). The nature of this collision has given rise to much debate and discussion of youth, its representations and its expressions, and this chapter will examine some of the issues raised by these arguments. What this chapter cannot do is to survey the field and examine youth from all viewpoints, but many of its arguments connect to other chapters in this book. The diversity of youth cultural practices and texts is a testament to the differences within the constructed label 'youth', and this chapter will reflect and explore some of these diverse responses.

If youth is viewed as a 'crossroad', it provides an appropriate spatial metaphor that locates the concerns of this chapter within the extent to which youth challenges social direction, follows the path dictated for it or gravitates across both positions. We will employ spatial images, as youth texts do themselves, as a means of exploring the idea of social boundaries and how these are both transgressed and reinforced by such texts within American culture. As Meyer Spacks has written, youth can be seen 'as violators or precursors of system' (Meyer Spacks 1981: 296), and this chapter will examine the tensions inherent in this duality. These tensions are poetically expressed by the social scientist Edgar Z. Friedenberg's assessment that 'human life is a continuous thread which each of us spins to his own pattern, rich and complex in meaning. There are no natural knots in it. Yet knots form, nearly always in adolescence' (Friedenberg 1963: 3). Youth texts are concerned with the tensions between the desire for a self-generated 'pattern' – 'to be oneself'

– and the 'knots' that fix and bind youth into someone else's definition (see Campbell 2004).

YOUTH/HISTORY/REPRESENTATION

America's historical formation has always drawn special connections between itself as a nation and the concept of newness and youthfulness (see Chapter 1):

> We are young, vigorous, unique; 'on the cutting edge of history'. Since we are new, what is young, or vigorous, or unique is good to use prima facie. . . . All people, everywhere, value youth . . . but America is the 'fountain of youth'.
>
> (Robertson 1980: 348)

This metaphorical language emphasises a perception of the New World as a place of renewal, literally a rebirth in which the energy of childhood and of youthfulness represents the chance to begin again and undo the corruptions of the Old World. 'Americans sought their lost innocence increasingly in their children. A psychic primitivism of youth replaced an accompanied geographical and cultural primitivism' (Sanford 1961: 112). The idea of 'psychic primitivism' means that adult-America endowed its children with the hopes of a new future, for they were untarnished and could develop society from the struggles of their parents, who had been touched by the corruptions of the Old World. The investment and the vision were thrust upon the youthful future. This paradigm relates to the view of the Old World as a 'parent culture' that had grown authoritarian in its power, persecuting and alienating certain groups within it, and the rebellious 'children' had to oppose them in a classic confrontation between the past and the energetic, new future.

> To follow blindly the footsteps of past masters was to remain forever a child; one should aim to rival and finally to displace them. Inherited wisdom should be assimilated and transformed, not simply revered and repeated.
>
> (Lowenthal 1985: 72)

The past, linked as always with the Old World, 'like a parent' (Lawrence 1977: 10), has to be 'transformed' by the energies imbued by the child of the New World, who is unafraid to rebel, to question and to challenge. Ironically, this rhetoric, which had a genuine purpose in the days of colonial rebellion, later presented problems for the newly forming social system in America because each generation could not be continually challenged by the next without destabilising the established order. This 'certain tension' (ibid.: 11) in the way youth has been viewed in America is central to this chapter, which will explore the ambiguities and complexities that emerge through the continued obsession with youth in the culture. At once desired as a generalised notion, as a sign of vigour and energy, America had to temper and control youth to avoid clashes with the mature culture being formed.

America saw itself as the 'Good Bad Boy', a phrase coined by Leslie Fiedler, because it signified a youth who was 'authentic . . . crude and unruly in his beginning, but endowed by his creator with an instinctive sense of what is right' (Fiedler 1960: 265). Youth then became a site of 'sanctioned rebellion' (Fetterley 1973) because the original rhetoric of protest, challenge and opposition to the established order was tempered and channelled by the accepted practices of the given social powers. That is, the 'boy' may be 'bad', but only temporarily, before resorting to the 'good', to the socially reinforced and approved, or 'sanctioned'. In this analysis, youth is defused and made safe, representing a natural, but contained outpouring of 'spirit', but one that cannot be permitted to challenge the hegemony of the adult/parent culture. The order remains and the youth is incorporated into the whole society. Many youth texts, that is, books, films, television shows, songs and so on, are microcosmic workings through of this larger cultural picture, demonstrating the necessity for renewed, coherent social/adult order.

A very good example of this in action is the film *The Blackboard Jungle* (1955, directed by Richard Brook), which was made at a crucial period in the development of a visible youth culture in America. It was the same year that *Rebel Without a Cause* was released, McDonald's opened, Chuck Berry released 'Maybellene', Little Richard released 'Tutti Frutti' and Elvis Presley signed for RCA Records. The film chose as its subject the efforts of a city schoolteacher, Mr Dadier (Glenn Ford), to reach a group of disaffected male students. It set the mould for many 'problem youth' films from this period, even being the first film to use a rock 'n' roll soundtrack: Bill Haley's 'Rock Around the Clock'. Yet for all its spectacle of violence, anti-authoritarianism and social divisions, the film ultimately aims to reassure and to reassert the power of righteous adult order. The film, like the later middle-class reconciliation movies of John Hughes, plays out cathartically the terrors of Dadier at the hands of his student tormentor, the manic West, until the film can resolve and reorganise society around a new 'pact' at the end. Dadier, nicknamed 'Daddyio', re-establishes the law of the father at the end by confronting West and rallying the collective conscience of the class, and in particular the black student Miller (Sidney Poitier). In a wonderfully surreal scene, filmed from a high angle, we see West prowling around the walls of the classroom looking for support to usurp Dadier's power, but visually it is made clear that he has been contained by the teacher's space and authority, and is eventually stopped by the American flag, used to hold him back from attacking the father figure. The scene is followed by one of Miller and Dadier leaving the school with their 'pact' established and a new, hopeful order asserted, which is both the rule of the 'parent/teacher' Dadier and a racial bond wrapped up in the Red, White and Blue. By the 1950s youthful exuberance was read as dangerous and as something that had to be curbed and channelled into 'pacts' of this kind or else excluded permanently, like West, so as to prevent social disorder. Images of youth had to be managed just as youth on the streets had to be watched and controlled.

Thirty years later John Hughes's *The Breakfast Club* (1985) rekindled a similar set of concerns about youth and education. Some of the differences are, however, instructive and relevant to the way youth has been represented and managed. Hughes's films employ adolescent narrators to suggest they are not adult-driven, but do still assert distinct values, moral lessons and return the audience and the characters to a harmonious sense of order and justice – but not before youth has been paraded as full of possibility and inventiveness, as well as cunning and deviousness. Hughes's films, in their own way, demonstrate reconciliation and the incorporation of youth into the mainstream, but also acknowledge the variety (to an extent), resourcefulness and vitality that have to be admitted into that cultural stream. *The Breakfast Club* begins with five students divided along the lines of class, popularity and gender, arriving for a detention with the task of writing an essay entitled appropriately 'Who do you think you are?' Brian, the narrator, tells us 'You see what you want to see. In the simplest terms, the most convenient definitions', and the film's goal is to alter these simple views. The film's closure is a reconciliation of differences into a workable social mix, an ideological vision of America that harks back to the search for fidelity and sincerity at the heart of so many youth texts, as we shall discuss later. The film suggests you can be anything as long as you are honest, have integrity and don't succumb to those who would 'brainwash' you. The final 'club' is a version of the 'pact' at the closure of *The Blackboard Jungle*, a democratisation of youth that harmonises it with the adult world, in Hughes's work, often represented by the family or school. They are both individuals and a club, united and separate, a classic vision of America as the space for all.

In the nineteenth century, children were often viewed as being 'untainted by social artifice' and possessing innocence and emotional spontaneity 'which seemed increasingly absent from the public realm' (Lears 1981: 146). This emphasis upon nostalgic sincerity endowed youth with regenerative powers capable of replenishing the corrupt 'public realm' through a 'vision of psychic wholeness, a "simple, genuine self" in a world where selfhood had become problematic and sincerity seemed obsolete' (ibid.: 146). These romantic, Rousseauesque versions of childhood indicate a certain aspect of nineteenth-century attitudes which saw childhood as an expression of values being undermined or lost in the industrial development and urbanisation of America. Childhood could be the receptacle for adult dreams of innocence and hope. Authors such as Alcott and Twain, however, suggested a complex relationship between competing versions of youth which present a more interesting social pattern than the 'sickly-sweet child' (ibid.: 146) often imagined in nineteenth-century representations. Their work, especially *Little Women* and *Tom Sawyer*, explores tensions within the imagined vision of what youth might be and recognises that youth is a border territory where power and authority are contested and space is won and lost.

BOUNDARIES AND YOUTH SPACES

The concept of youth is 'a term without its own center' (Grossberg 1992: 175), difficult to define, covering many social differences and perceived in a variety of ways depending on the individual's point of view. Youth is part of culture's contested space and any 'unity is an ideological fiction' (Acland 1995: 20). The signifiers that we might try to 'read' in order to define youth are mobile and unfixable, and our attempts to gather them together underline the fact of youth's multifaceted and complex presence as a concept within American culture.

In *Rebel Without a Cause* (Nicholas Ray, 1955), in which youth is the central focus, Ray makes use of place and space throughout the film to delineate and suggest the 'fields of power relations' (Foucault 1986: 247) within which youth exists. Near the end of the film is a particularly relevant sequence of scenes played out in an abandoned mansion, in which Jim (James Dean), Judy (Natalie Wood) and Plato (Sal Mineo) gather. The film's use of space up until this point is dominated by official, adult, public spaces that seem to constrain and trap the young characters: the school, the home, the police station, the planetarium. Only occasionally does the film permit youth to step beyond these defined and controlled spaces, and the abandoned mansion represents the most powerful example. It is an excessive family home which is empty and absent of family, father and all the immediate connotations of control and sur-veillance that the film associates with parental/adult culture. At its heart is an image of this vacancy – a vast, deep, empty swimming pool, which Jim refers to as a 'sunken nursery'. The scene dramatises the film's contention that, like *The Blackboard Jungle*, youth is in crisis in the 1950s and that children are better seen but not heard, for to articulate is to possess a voice which might question the emplacement of the child/youth within the space ordained by adult authority. The wild abandon in the 'abandoned mansion' temporarily carnivalises the adult control and parodies the dominance of the family and its values. Jim and Judy act out roles as a parody family, exaggerating, for comic-ironic effect, the consumerism and narrow-mindedness of the suburban restraint of the family. Judy asks, in her 'role' as Mother, 'What about children?', to which Plato replies, 'You see we really don't encourage them, they're so noisy and troublesome.' Indeed, the controlled space of the 'sunken nursery' provides the answer to troublesome youth, for 'if you lock them in you'll never have to see them again, much less talk to them'. Judy answers that 'no one talks to children, no, they just tell them'. In this powerful scene the parody plays out the concerns of the film with youth and permits its young characters to voice their darkest fears through the veil of the 'play'. For our purposes, it demonstrates the way in which space, its control and ordering indicate the social pressure and authority exercised on youth so as to mould and shape them to the will of the adult world.

The film itself reflects many aspects of youth's relation to American mainstream culture, for it fluctuates between representations of resistance and acceptance of parental–authoritarian hegemony. Youth desires its own space outside the adult/public sphere, beyond the surveillance of the authorities and institutions that dominate their lives. This is characteristic of the way youth uses space, as Grossberg writes:

> youth could construct its own places in the space of transition between these institutions: in the street, around the jukebox, at the hop (and later the mall) . . . spaces located between the domestic, public and social spaces of the adult world. What the dominant society assumes to be no place at all.
>
> (Grossberg 1992: 179)

Youth texts resonate with these marginal spaces where youth finds domains outside of the 'already defined place within a social narrative that was told before it arrived' (ibid.). A nineteenth-century novel like *Little Women* (1868) presents Jo March's space as her 'garret' where she writes, keeps pet rats and wears an ink-stained shirt, all of which run contrary to the expectations of the age for both gender and youth. Only here, *within* the house of her powerful, absent father whose 'law', like the law of society, she will finally accept, does she have some temporary control. By the time of *Rebel*, youth cannot bear to remain in the family house and can find no freedom within it. The film is full of dramatic exits by Jim, most memorably when he has his climactic row with his parents and disappears into the night, stopping only to fight with his father and destroy a family matriarchal portrait. Contested space dramatises and represents the tensions over conditioning and socialisation that occur during childhood and youth and which take a variety of forms, but a predominant example is the domestic control of the house as opposed to Grossberg's notion of the marginal space outside.

HOUSING THE SELF

The house, as a metaphor for adult-parental space, is often linked to the Father, the representative of the dominant social order, and is a powerful visual image of established, solid, economic territory that surrounds and contains youth, acting as a constant reminder of their subordinate position in the hierarchy of familial and social power. It represents responsibility, order, stability and predictability, the very things that youth is supposed to find itself opposing. In *Shampoo Planet* (1993) Douglas Coupland refers to the joy at finding a space he terms 'the antidote to my father's house' (ibid.: 218). In *Ferris Bueller's Day Off* (1986, directed by John Hughes), Ferris's rebellion begins and ends in the family home, as if to remind the audience that his adventures are only a rite of passage, literally a 'day off' from the charted life his parents desire for him, rather than acts of total denial and rebellion. At the end of the film he is happy to return and be 're-housed' in the womb-like cosiness of the bed and to receive the approving words and kisses of his parents.

In Joyce Chopra's film *Smooth Talk*, released in the same year as *Ferris* and based on the Joyce Carol Oates story 'Where Are You Going, Where Have You Been?', the house is the central motif in the film, representing the domain of the mother, who spends her life decorating it, and the father, to whom it signifies the pinnacle of his achievements. In a brief scene with his dissatisfied daughter, Connie (Laura Dern), he speaks of the pleasure the house gives him, providing the freedom to sit and smoke 'all night if I want to' on his own 'lawn chair'. Both the mother's and the father's attitudes, embodied in the house, are viewed by Connie as sedentary, lifeless and banal, in contrast to her 'trashy day-dreams' of escape, sexual exploration and of the world beyond the boundaries of the house. Again, the visual use of the house makes this set of ideas very clear to the audience. Near the opening of the film, Connie is seen in long shot walking down the hallway of the house, in shadow, leaning against the walls as if they were the bars of a cage. Just before she exits the house and the shot, she glances through an open doorway at her mother who, as always, is seen contemplating the decor of the house, holding up a floral wallpaper onto the very walls that seem to enclose and limit Connie. Boundaries can be real, physical forces, but can also be used to represent a wider range of psychological or social determinants that shape and construct youth within the larger cultural framework. In the story, Oates writes that 'Everything about [Connie] had two sides to it, one for home and one for anywhere that was not home' (Lauter *et al.* 1994: 2060–1) and this inside–outside tension is explored in film and story. The attractions of the outside – of men, sexuality and self-identity – become threatening through the figure of Arnold Friend, her seducer, who says at the end of the story: 'This place you are now – inside your daddy's house – is nothing but a cardboard box I can knock down any time' (ibid.: 2170). The house that Connie desires to escape is now her very fragile protection against the presence of Friend, who has brought the seductive outside terrifyingly to life in a manner that reminds Connie of the crossroads of youth. Ironically, at the point of fear she longs to retreat to the safety of her 'daddy's house'.

Coupland's *Generation X* reflects playfully on the significance of the house:

> When someone tells you they've just bought a house, they might as well tell you they no longer have a personality . . . they're locked into jobs they hate . . . they're broke . . . they no longer listen to new ideas. . . . What few happy moments they possess are those gleaned from dreams of *upgrading*.
>
> (Coupland 1992: 143)

In Terrence Malick's film *Badlands* (1973), the house marks the boundary to be transgressed by its young runaways, who see in it Coupland's sense of constraint. Kit (Martin Sheen) invades the house of the father, kills him, burns his house and steals his daughter. The sequence ends with a long scene in which the house burns as a loud religious choral soundtrack underpins the sacrificial act that has taken place. This film's extremity contrasts with Chopra's *Smooth Talk*, on one level, but resembles it in its fascination with images of rebellion and the rejection of adult authority.

In *Badlands* the father guards and watches his daughter, Holly, before his authority is destroyed by her lover, Kit, who wants to liberate them from his control. As Michel Foucault asserts, 'In the first instance, discipline proceeds from the distribution of individuals in space' (Foucault 1977b: 141), and youth is constantly monitored by types of discipline and surveillance. Foucault discusses the ways in which 'enclosure' functions on the subject so that three elements can be ensured – 'knowing, mastering and using' (ibid.: 143). For Connie in *Smooth Talk*, as long as she is in the house of her parents, she cannot be what she wants to be and feels her own identity is compromised. Through the insistence of limits and sanctioned activities within these limits, subjects are correctly trained and normalised, to use Foucault's terms, and take up their places within the social order of adulthood. Youth texts in America have constantly entered into a dialogue with these sanctioned spaces and their circumscribing boundaries, testing out the social order, to offer a sense of 'Otherness' to the ordained and acceptable 'norms' and at the same time, through their incorporation, reinforcing and sustaining the hegemonic, adult framework. Connie's entrapment as feminine and youth within the expectations of her culture echo Jo March in *Little Women*, who says she was tired of care and confinement, longed for change, and thoughts of her father blended temptingly with the novel charms of camps and hospitals, liberty and fun. Her eyes kindled as they turned wistfully toward the window, but they fell on the old house opposite, and she shook her head with sorrowful decision.

(Alcott 1989: 213)

The contrast between the outside and inside is marked here and suggests the precise limitation to which Jo knows she must conform. The outside world, linked to 'liberty and fun', is contrasted with the 'house' and Jo 'must be proper, and stop at home', whereas Laurie, her male friend, 'was possessed to break out of bounds in some way' (ibid.) and move into the world beyond. Youth is constructed differently for feminine and masculine, as *Little Women* shows, for boys are permitted some boundary breaking before being brought back into the fold. Thus, gender is a further boundary that restricts what young females may do within a society in which rules and boundaries are governed and maintained by adults 'whose presence limits the unlimited' (Foucault 1977b: 81).

Foucault's concepts of 'surveillance' and 'panopticism' explain how one group holds power over others and transforms human beings into subjects. The Panopticon, as described by Foucault, ensured a circumscribed world of surveillance in which the practices of the socially dominant group were instilled,

subject to a system of rewards for good behaviour, but . . . viewed at all times by a guard at the centre of the circle whom they could not see. . . . All their acts came under official regulation and inspection.

(During 1992: 156)

The Panopticon is 'power reduced to its ideal form' (Foucault 1977b: 205) instilling itself into the lives of people as if they were prisoners. That is, not knowing if they were being watched, they assumed they were and so conformed to the rules of the space. Such social control can be extended beyond the prison to all social institutions and 'render visible those who are inside it . . . to provide a hold on their conduct, to carry the effects of power right to them, to make it possible to know them, to alter them' (ibid.: 172). This kind of surveillance internalises control, transforming real walls and bars into the spatial boundaries of everyday life.

The surveillance, control and normalising power of the adult society represents a set of forces for conformity and repetition that are resisted by youth, who seek their own space for expression and definition. Contained and delimited by the space that adults, parents and other institutions of control (school, church, law) have prescribed for them, youth struggles to find ways beyond these 'panoptic' forces.

A MODEL YOUTH TEXT? *THE ADVENTURES OF TOM SAWYER*

In Mark Twain's *Tom Sawyer* (1898), Judge Thatcher represents the panoptic forces, standing for the laws of the adult community which eventually incorporate Tom, through a process in which the 'individual is carefully fabricated' (Foucault 1977a: 217). It is the fabrication of the subject, the 'rightly constructed boy's life' (Twain 1986: 152) and the institutions that seek to mould Tom – family, school, church and law – with which the novel is concerned. Twain dramatises judgement as an active communal control working on Tom. As Foucault has written:

> the judges of normality are present everywhere . . . the teacher-judge, the doctor-judge, the educator-judge, the 'social-worker'-judge; it is on them that the universal reign of the normative is based; and each individual, wherever he may find himself, subjects to it his body, his gestures, his behaviour, his aptitudes, his achievements.
>
> (Foucault 1977a: 304)

It is through such means that youth is trained, fabricated and managed, just as in *Tom Sawyer* tokens reward the assiduous Churchgoer able to recite the language of prayer and School uses the Examination as a repetitive, machine-like process aimed at training the young (Twain 1986: 137–8).

As a model of youth texts, *Tom Sawyer* contains the alternative impulse towards the transgressive and to all that exists outside the disciplined and controlled precincts of an adult society's rules and boundaries. Twain suggests this with an image rather like those discussed earlier, with the children contained in the church, 'under supervision' but looking at 'the open window and the seductive outside summer scenes' (ibid.: 37). Tom, like so much of youth, is caught between the pull of the outside and the comforting controls of supervision from the community. To actually transgress into the 'seductive outside' would be to move closer to Huck Finn's world of the 'lawless . . . outcast' (ibid.: 45–6) and ultimately into the world of Injun Joe, who exists at the social margins. Tom, however, knows the boundaries and is never prepared to transgress them in any genuine way. Indeed, Tom's awareness of the limits and transgressions are interrelated and his skill is in keeping the two in balance for most of the novel. Twain's language repeatedly emphasises Tom's concern for boundaries: 'Tom drew a line in the dust with his big toe, and said: "I dare you to step over that, and I'll lick you till you can't stand up"' (ibid.: 13). He is defending communal territory, its rules and codes of behaviour from the 'enemy' (ibid.: 14) outside and so acknowledges again the social space within which he moves. Thus, when really tested, Tom opts for the known, choosing to decorate the fence that encloses his world rather than to break it down. Similarly, at McDougal's cave, a psychological space where 'it was not customary to venture much beyond this known portion' (ibid.: 177), all the elements that structure and order the discipline of Tom's society are replaced. It is a representation of youth's dilemma and Tom opts for the world of 'security' (ibid.: 203) where the norms are clear, rejecting the 'bloody-minded outcast' and true transgressor Injun Joe, who lies dead *in the cave*. Unlike Huck, who loathes being the 'target of everybody's gaze', Tom relishes being 'the spectacle' at its heart to the extent that he is willing to become the surrogate son to the community's controlling force, Judge Thatcher, who compares him with George Washington, Father of his Country, the very figure of America's sense of honesty, truth and goodness. The hegemonic enclosure of Tom into the world of the Judge continues with the programme for his future as 'a great lawyer or a great soldier . . . trained in the best law school in the country, in order that he might be ready for either career or both' (ibid.: 217).

Tom accepts willingly 'the bars and shackles of civilisation [that] shut him in and bound him hand and foot' whereas Huck Finn resists since 'wealth . . . protection . . . society' threaten his need to live *outside* the community. Huck has to be 'dragged . . . [and] hurled . . . into it' (ibid.) and into all its disciplines and routines. To emphasise Tom's total conformity, it is he who takes on the policing parent role with Huck and 'urged him to go home' (ibid.: 218). By becoming the shadow of the Judge, Tom has undergone his fabrication into masculinity and the dominant social order.

> The boy makes peace with his father, identifies with him, and is thus introduced into the symbolic role of manhood. He has become a gendered subject . . . [and] will now grow up within those images and practices which his society happens to define as 'masculine'.
>
> (Eagleton 1983: 155)

Twain suggests that youth can function in direct relation to the dominant adult culture, but as an Other, who tests out the boundaries of that social order, and through this process reinforces its rules. Within this pattern, rebellion is inherently vital to the way culture works because youth interacts, challenges and criticises the adult world, only to be incorporated into it in some form. As Acland writes, 'youth acts as an Other, distanced, yet inseparable, from the social order . . . always dependent upon disgust and desire' (Acland 1995: 19). Just as Tom Sawyer is disciplined for his mischief, he is also a source of fascination for the townsfolk, who desire the freedoms and adventures that he has and the fun he enjoys on the margins of their adult-determined boundaries. Acland argues that 'youth . . . is simultaneously transgressive and revered' (ibid.), a tension, as we have argued, that can be seen in most representative youth texts.

THE DREAM OF EDEN

J.D. Salinger's novel *The Catcher in the Rye* (1951), which has been read as a passionate study of youth alienation, longs for a vision of America that has been lost in the postwar rush into consumerism and technology. For Salinger's hero, Holden Caulfield, the adult world is 'phoney', with the panoptic forces moulding and training the young to imitate the society they have created. Early on in the novel, Holden reports ironically his school's mission of 'moulding young boys into splendid, clear-thinking young men' (Salinger 1972: 6), but he sees through the advertising image to the phoniness below. However, Holden's journey into the adult world of New York only confirms the fear he has that no one else can see the false values that he so detests, and it is he that is driven mad by their dominance.

Holden wants to 'hold on' to other values and, as in *Rebel Without a Cause*, at the centre of *Catcher* is a plea for sincerity, honesty and decency, which for Holden is associated with the past, indeed, with the dead and with the static. The psychologist Erik Erikson termed this the search for 'fidelity', for 'disciplined devotion in youth's roles as 'renewers of ethical strength, as rebels bent on the destruction of the outlived' (Friedenberg 1963: 10). In *Rebel*, Plato says that Jim 'doesn't say much, but when he does you know he means it, he's sincere' and Judy replies, 'Well that's the main thing.' Later, Jim's inadequate father tries to persuade his son to lie rather than tell about the fatal crash on the 'chicken run' – 'that's the main thing', he says. The film suggests that the gap between these versions of 'the main thing' is significant, contrasting youth's desire for sincerity with adult expediency and duplicity. Jim's father says 'You can't be idealistic all your life, Jim', but this is exactly what the film suggests youth wants to be. The phoney world, without trust and courage, is what Jim is confused by, just like Holden who clings onto his dead brother's memory and his catching mitt as if they contain the magic to connect him to a better, now lost, world of innocence and trust. Holden resists overt sexuality for it represents a movement into adulthood and phoniness, responsibilities and choices, preferring instead that the world stand still, in an imaginary time of innocence, like the world he associates with his sister Phoebe and the museum that both she and he have visited. The museum typifies a certain tendency in youth texts towards a celebration of the past and a desire for an unchanging reality. In one respect the museum is Holden's space outside of the rush of adult life, the place where 'everything stayed right where it was. Nobody'd move. . . . Nobody'd be different' (Salinger

1972: 127). In *Rebel*, this is the space of the abandoned mansion before it is disrupted by the arrival of the gang and then the police. The sense of continuity is vital, replacing the rapid change of adulthood with a secure and predictable calm. For Holden the thought that Phoebe is repeating his experience is reassuring, but he knows that although the museum remains the same, she will 'be different every time she saw it' (ibid.: 128): 'Certain things they should stay the way they are. You ought to be able to stick them in one of those big glass cases and just leave them alone. I know that's impossible, but it's too bad anyway' (ibid.).

Texts like *Catcher* and *Rebel* transgress adult social codes because they believe them to be false and desire instead 'lost' values and an authentic world, which is, as Holden admits, 'impossible', because of the inevitability of time and change. Holden's dream of being the 'catcher in the rye', saving children from their 'fall' over the 'crazy cliff' into adulthood, is part of his longing to remain in the imaginary, timeless innocence of childhood.

This specific tendency is repeated in the novel *The Outsiders* by S.E. Hinton (1967), written when she herself was in her teens. Like Salinger, but without his humour and irony, the novel's 'family' of boys without parents is a mythic, surrogate community fulfilling one of the central fantasies of youth texts, namely, to exist in a space beyond the adult world. For Hinton, though, the seeming fantasy is inadequate and imbalanced, producing troubled and violent youths who long for another kind of family. As with Holden Caulfield, it is the desire to return to a simpler, womb-like continuity beyond the class-ridden society of gangs and school: 'It seems like there's gotta be someplace without greasers or Socs, with just people. Plain ordinary people. . . . In the country' (Hinton 1972: 39). Again the imagery of the 'seductive outside' is prominent, with the country representing a natural space beyond the confining world of the social institutions that mould and impose their values on the youthful characters. In *The Outsiders*, this new imagined space permits the rebirth of the dead parents: 'I brought Mom and Dad back to life. . . . Mom would bake some more chocolate cakes and Dad would drive the pick-up out early to feed the cattle. . . . My mother was golden and beautiful' (ibid.: 39–40). A static, golden world without death and change is once again the ideal, as in Francis Ford Coppola's film of *The Outsiders* (1983), where the utopian country is rendered visually in golden and bright colours, both echoing Ponyboy's memory of his mother and also linking to one of the central motifs in the book, a poem by Robert Frost. Its refrain of 'nothing gold can stay' is a reminder, just like Holden's recognition that the static dream of the museum is impossible, that the boys cannot avoid adulthood and 'stay gold' and yet simultaneously celebrates the belief that 'you're gold when you are a kid' (Hinton 1972: 127). As Johnny says, 'Too bad it couldn't stay like that all the time' (ibid.: 59); they know change is inevitable and adulthood will claim them with all its divisions and falsities. This dream of 'Eden', as the Frost poem calls it, is precisely the dream of return to a continuity akin to the womb, to the relationship of unborn child to the Mother where everything coexists and is part of a whole, total sense of being. Holden longs to be free of New York and fantasises about a cabin in the woods (Salinger 1972: 137–8, 205) that he and Jane would go to while they were young and before everything was 'entirely different' (ibid.: 138). Jacques Lacan, the French psychologist, termed this the Imaginary, pre-Oedipal phase, in which the child is undivided, coterminous with the mother and untroubled by the crises of sexuality (the Oedipal phase) and the institutions of the social order (Symbolic Order). It is no surprise that in all Hinton's novels mothers have important, however minor, roles and are often linked with the past and a sense of better times.

In *The Outsiders*, as in *Catcher*, there is a scene in which children are saved. In the case of Hinton's novel it is an actual event in which Johnny saves children from a burning church, while in *Catcher* it is Holden's fantasy of being the 'catcher in the rye'. However, they both represent the belief that childhood is a time of sincerity and goodness, one worth preserving, 'saving', from the 'fall/death' of adulthood. Johnny says, 'It's worth saving those kids. . . . When you're a kid everything's new, dawn. It's just when you get used to everything that it's day' (Hinton 1972: 127). It's appropriate that Holden's favourite novel is *The Great Gatsby*, whose eponymous hero wants only to 'repeat the past' and reinvoke a lost dream of love, as the idea is at the heart of both Salinger's and Hinton's novels. A further reference to Fitzgerald comes later in the novel when Holden keeps trying to erase the words 'fuck you' from the walls so that the children will not be corrupted by the language, thus echoing Nick Carraway at Gatsby's mansion at the end of that novel attempting to preserve his friend's reputation. Both gestures are 'impossible' (Salinger 1972: 208) efforts to forestall time and change and cling to the 'capacity for wonder' (Fitzgerald 1974: 188).

Salinger's final scene is a powerful condensation of youthful desire for sincerity set against this terrible sense of inevitable change and corruption that eats away at the dream. Holden watches Phoebe on the carousel, going round and round in circles, in a perfect unchanging moment: 'I was sort of afraid she'd fall off. . . . The thing with kids is, if they want to grab for the gold ring, you have to let them do it' (Salinger 1972: 218). Although he prefers the security of her circularity, he recognises the inevitable reaching for the future, for adulthood, and her incorporation into the world he detests and he is resigned to do nothing except retreat into his own madness.

Douglas Coupland has a metaphor that captures this problematic desire in youth texts to halt time and keep the future at bay: the 'Kodak snapshot'.

Looking at old photographs he sees that point at which 'the future is still unknown and has yet to hurt us, and also for that brief moment, our poses are accepted as honest' (Coupland 1992: 17). The association of honesty with static, unchanging points in time is redolent of Holden's and Ponyboy's desire to retain their youth. As the high school valedictorian put it in the film *Say Anything* (1989, directed by Cameron Crowe): 'I have something to tell everybody. I've glimpsed our future, and all I can say is – go back.'

THE SPACES OF SELF-CREATION

If one response of youth texts to the onslaught of the social order and adulthood is to hold onto a dream of return and to an Eden beyond its grasp, another has been to seek a measure of control and authority in a world that seems to deny youth this. Texts and cultural practices explore ways by which the young struggle to find a space for individual or group expression outside or alongside the adult mainstream. This has been achieved in many different forms – music, fashion, gangs, subcultural actions, writing and so on – all of which create a 'language' outside the immediate control of the adult world. As W.T. Lhamon Jr writes, the blues had long invented a 'vernacular doubletalk' to overcome the 'force fields of complex surveillance' (Lhamon 1990: 59), and youth culture learned much from oppressed communities elsewhere in America. In a famous scene in the film *The Wild One* (1953, directed by Laslo Benedek), an old barkeeper is bemused by the 'bebop' language of the motorcycle gang who 'jive-talk' to him. The sense of separation and difference is immense and suggests the emergence of youth 'languages' in the 1950s that permitted youth to 'reside in that excluded middle area which resists concrete interpretation' (ibid.: 62). In this 'middle area' youth created its own 'space', one outside the adult world and beyond its comprehension, often characterised by fluidity and forms that celebrate change and motion, for example, dance, graffiti art and video games. As Donna Gaines comments about suburban 1980s youth, they 'fought back symbolically; articulating their dissent culturally, in their clothes, language, music, and attitudes . . . created autonomous spaces for self-expression, carved out a place for themselves on their own terms, and they survived' (Gaines 1992: 254).

Lhamon argues that youth culture disrupts temporarily 'polite culture' (Lhamon 1990: 106) and interacts with it through such things as laughter, critique and rage, effecting adjustments and change. He puts this well, writing that young people 'asserted the principle of public self-definition, and made space for themselves and their idiom in prestigious discourse' (ibid.: 108). In literature this has become a popular youth theme, wherein young narrators aspire to be writers, reluctant to spout the established language of their parents, but anxious to construct a world in their own language. Ponyboy 'writes' the narrative that we read as *The Outsiders*, Holden longs to write, as do Jo March, Edmund White's narrator in *A Boy's Own Story* and Esther Greenwood in *The Bell Jar* (see Chapter 7). The French critic Julia Kristeva recognises this as a major factor in the 'adolescent novel', with the urge for 'a genuine inscription of unconscious contents within language . . . [and] utilizing, at last and for the first time in his life, *a living discourse*, one that is not "as if"' (Kristeva 1990: 9; our emphasis). The 'dead' handed-down discourse of the adult world, Holden's 'phoniness', has to be cancelled out by the living expressions of a new, youthful language, whatever the mode of expression. Although Kristeva writes about the novel, her observations are useful as ways of seeing the various youth texts 'that facilitate . . . the ultimate reorganization of psychic space, in the time before an ideally postulated maturity' (ibid.: 10). Youth texts 'represented values and inculcated legends in the uninscribed places of minds looking for their own values' (Lhamon 1990: 109) and seek their own authority within a world that constantly tells them to keep quiet. The idea of 'authoring' the self, a common desire in oppressed groups (see Chapter 3 on African Americans), is a response to all those who would speak for you and dictate the terms of existence. To articulate is to order the world, to exercise power and to control aspects of reality, and this is why youth texts clamour to express themselves, to be heard rather than be trapped in an 'already defined place within a social narrative that was told before it arrived' (Grossberg 1992: 179). To write is to control material and empower the self and for powerless, unvoiced youth this is an attractive possibility. For Jo March in *Little Women* this is expressed when she says 'Oh, don't I wish I could fix things for you as I do for my heroines' (Alcott 1989: 157) and 'I hate to see things going all criss-cross, and getting snarled up, when a pull here, and a snip there, would straighten it out' (ibid.: 205). If life were like the fiction she controls, she could adjust and edit reality until she had a script she approved of, but in truth others have charge and construct the acceptable world of youth.

Rock music is an example of youth articulation. Emerging from a hybridisation of oppressed culture's musical forms – blues, jazz and country – it offered the possibility for self-expression in a new language. Rock could allow youth to 'live out its alienation in ways that would increase its own sense of control over its everyday life' (Grossberg 1992: 179). Youth music is a means of speaking a 'living discourse', of expressing a counter-voice to the adult society usually presented as the ideal. This was another route to the 'seductive outside', beyond surveillance, authority and control, through the creation and articulation of 'temporary differences' (ibid.: 180). These acknowledge what Ponyboy, Holden and others come to see, that youth is brief and soon consumed, but that in the moments between childhood and adulthood differences can be signalled, pleasure achieved and challenges made. Music could become 'the space of "magical transformations" in the face of youth's own necessary transformation into its own other, adulthood' (ibid.: 180).

Likewise, dancing, losing oneself to the beat and the motion, 'opens up a social space that is quite different from the public and private boundaries that hold our identities all too tightly in place' (Ross and Rose 1994: 11). Youth music, and its associated areas of dance and style, liberate the body to express itself in a manner that counters the social controls of adult society. A scene in the film *The Blackboard Jungle* marks this precise disjunction between the music of the adult and the new voice of youth culture when a teacher attempts to engage the class with his treasured record collection. He pleads with them to appreciate the clarinet in one piece when they desire only to 'feel' the music, thus confirming the gap between them as unbridgeable. They destroy his collection and herald a new tradition and the very 'dislocation between the cultures of two generations' (Gillett 1983: 16) that Chuck Berry would focus upon in 'Roll Over Beethoven'. Berry's songs read like a saga of youth anthems, intensely critical of established forms of adult life, with appeals to the road, to young love, to free the body and to resist 'penned adolescence' (ibid.: 81).

Rock criticised the institutions, such as school and the family, that were central to the limitations and boundaries that checked and curbed youth, and expressed an 'antidomesticity', attacking 'the place in which its own youth is constructed' (Storey 1993: 188). Rock constructed a space in which a new language could speak differently about the world and 'tell the teenage story' (Gillett 1983: 101), like the attack in Eddie Cochran's 'Summertime Blues' (1958) on parents, work and government, who exist only to stand in the way of youth desiring 'somethin' else'. As Gillett has written, 'adolescents staked out their freedom in the cities, inspired and reassured by the rock and roll beat' (Gillett 1983: viii), which they could now listen to on small transistors rather than in the company and surveillance of the family on the living-room radiogram.

The intimate fantasies of rock 'n' roll transformed by this youth space enhanced the articulation of a new language. The mirror in the bedroom, the dance and the look all became inextricably linked to the performance of rock in the youth world, so that the sounds of the 1950s, the youth films and the development of street culture began to mingle in a way that produced new styles and voices. The integrative process of rock into youth culture had begun and established lines of power that would emerge and alter through the 1960s counter-culture and into 1970s punk and new wave, as expressions capable of 'rocking the boat of culture and everyday life' (Grossberg 1992: 156). Even if rock could not change the world, it gave voice to protest, desire and pleasure and through that provided a 'disruption of everyday stability' (ibid.: 156). As with other youth texts, this was not necessarily a full rejection of social values but a temporary halt on them, a space for other questions and expressions to surface, and for an 'identification and belonging' (ibid.: 205) to take place in which youth could map out its own sense of values. It was, as Grossberg argues, the very same desire for authenticity that emerged as a core value in rock, providing a means by which youth could stake out a space for themselves in a world governed by others' boundaries, wherein the music 'spoke' or 'felt' about things that mattered, 'private but common desires' conveyed through performer to audience as an open, true channel of communication.

Youth music, in many forms, answered the surveillance and authority of the dominant culture with 'a counterculture of conspicuous display' that 'found a way to contest their erasure, to reintroduce themselves to the public by "throwing out" a new style that made other people take notice' (Lipsitz 1994: 20). Existing 'underneath the authorised discourses, in the face of the multiple disciplines of the family, the school and the workplace', youth music lingered in 'the space between surveillance and the evasion of surveillance' (Hebdige 1988: 35), making a deliberate spectacle of itself, flaunting its style. As Connie feels in 'Where Are You Going, Where Have You Been?', 'the music . . . made everything so good: the music . . . was something to depend upon' (Lauter *et al.* 1994: 2161).

This belief in music as an articulation of youth protest is central to the film *Pump Up the Volume* (1990, directed by Allan Moyle), the central character of which, Mark (Christian Slater), expresses his anxieties about the contemporary sterility of his dull, Arizona suburb through the medium of rock, transmitting secretly on a pirate radio station. The idea of the secret articulation, of stealing air-time from the official 'authorised discourse' (Hebdige 1988: 35) of adults is an interesting metaphor in itself, but the fact that the pirate DJ uses a disguised voice and rock to present his message suggests the power of the official culture to control alternative expression and force it underground.

The film articulates the 'secret histories . . . lived histories shared in places coded with secret meanings' (Gaines 1992: 47) of teenage suburban life in a society that professes to be concerned about standards, but only speaks in the place of the young themselves rather than allowing them any actual say. 'Hard Harry's' radio 'station' expresses the obverse to a social order built around the precepts 'make the grade, win the prize, play the game' (ibid.: 9) and combines speech, music and form to tell youth stories like those described in *Generation X* as the equivalent to coughing up a piece of diseased lung: 'People want that little fragment, they need it. That little piece of lung makes their own fragments less scary' (Coupland 1992: 13).

AT THE EDGE: THE DARK MOOD

Donna Gaines's *Teenage Wasteland* (1992) is a study of 'suburbia's dead end kids' who find few comforts in a reimagined past, or in the possibility of claiming authority over the self through expression, and who are much more cynical about its position in the world. As Gaines writes, 'These kids were actively guarding their psychic space because the adults controlled everything else' (ibid.: 38). Their options appear to be withdrawal and brooding or violence, destruction and pathology.

Youth is, however, even in the darker materials we will examine here, never in total despair, even when certain channels of articulation and self-definition seem limited and receding rapidly. In the darkest scene in *Rebel Without a Cause*, the chicken run, Jim says to the ill-fated Buzz, 'This is the edge . . . that's the end', as he gazes into the abyss below. In *Less Than Zero* (1985), written thirty years later in the midst of the Reagan years, Bret Easton Ellis's disaffected youth inhabit clubs called 'The Edge' and 'Land's End', and in one scene two characters stand, like Buzz and Jim, looking down into a canyon at the cars wrecked below. In the subsequent conversation, the sense of nihilism which emerges in many of these dark texts is established:

> 'Where are we going?' . . .
> 'I don't know . . . Just driving.'
> 'But this road doesn't go anywhere' . . .
> 'That doesn't matter.'
> 'What does?' . . .
> 'Just that we're on it, dude,' he said.
>
> (Ellis 1985: 195)

One of the refrains in Ellis's novel is 'disappear here', as if to stand as a reminder of the emptiness of the world that surrounds these young characters. All values are gone, even the memory or dream of values, and the only trust in this society is on an Elvis Costello promotional poster tacked to the wall. But the refrain takes us back to *The Catcher in the Rye* in which New York's pavement is like an abyss and Holden is going 'down, down, down, and nobody'd ever see me again' (Salinger 1972: 204). His 'saviour' is his dead brother, Allie, to whom he appeals, 'don't let me disappear' (ibid.). Whereas Holden still believes he can be saved, by the time of *Less Than Zero* 'Gloom Rules' (Ellis 1985: 107), and as Gaines explains, 'The world "out there" is shrinking. The possibilities of suburbia are exhausted, and your capacity to dream has reached a dead end' (Gaines 1992: 54). To 'disappear' in Gaines's 1980s America was to 'burnout', to become 'atomised', with each person suffering in isolation until 'you are lost – to those around you, to your loved ones, even to yourself' (ibid.: 101). Ironically, Gaines's youth find some level of 'self-preservation' (ibid.: 102) in 'disappearing' because it allows them to 'numb out . . . by shutting down, denying access to your feelings' (ibid.: 101) so that they are alive and yet dead to the world around them: 'shut down, tuned out; you're gone' (ibid.). Phil LaMarche's stark, pared-down novel *American Youth* (2007) has been referred to as a coming-of-age story for the post-Columbine era, portraying 'boy' (Teddy) struggling with a moral dilemma over gun violence, who finds himself drawn into an underground fascist gang called American Youth. Its dark heart is summed up when one of the gang says 'You don't have to be ashamed. . . . We're all red-blooded Americans here. We like guns too' (LaMarche 2007: 72). The book's epigraph is from Cormac McCarthy: 'Scars have the strange power to remind us that our past is real' from *All the Pretty Horses*, and this relationship of a haunting past is central to the novel. Plagued by the scars of the past 'boy' self-harms as a way of reminding himself of his guilty actions and his mother's cover-up: 'It hurt, somewhere inside, to see his body so abused. But there was something else in him that said he deserved it . . . it wanted to cover his whole body with burns, it wanted worse' (ibid.: 171).

Earlier, *Badlands* (1973) set in motion a genre of film now much imitated by Hollywood (*Natural Born Killers*, *True Romance*, *Kalifornia*), but one that clearly belongs to the dark cinema of youth. Terrence Malick's film contains archetypal images suggestive of rebellion, discontent and psychic amputation, commencing with the killing of the authoritarian father. It is appropriate in the scheme of youth texts that the father is a sign-painter by trade, that is, the outward manifestation of Holden's 'phoniness'. Erasing the father not only 'frees' the children to wander the badlands, but also strikes at the social order and the lies it creates for itself. When we are told that Kit, the central character in the film, desires 'a magical world beyond the law', he is an extreme version of youth's wish for the seductive outside, beyond the father, the signs and the boundaries of adult laws. Kit's name suggests his efforts throughout the film to construct himself from the debris all around him, and his failure to assemble a coherent 'self' indicates the accommodated prototype that he represents in this dark tradition. There is no father to integrate Kit at the end of the film, since all that remains is the law sent to enclose him and impose its definitions upon his ambiguous personality. As Holly says, 'We lived in utter loneliness, neither here nor there.' Kit's arrest marks his end, for he can no longer construct himself in motion, as he has been doing throughout the film, but has been reclaimed by the realm of the law to be what it wants him to be (the criminal). A prototype for many youth-outsiders, Kit resembles those youths Gaines wrote of in 1980s suburbia: 'disengaged, adrift, alienated. Like you don't fit in anywhere, there is *no place for you*: in your family, your school, your town – in the social order' (Gaines 1992: 253 – our emphasis). As the film ends, Kit flies off into 'no place' and with none of the comforts afforded to Tom Sawyer, who is embraced back into the Judge's world. Having transgressed the boundaries of social space and social order, Kit's final destination is the incarceration of 'no place', where surveillance, control and limit are total, awaiting death itself. His last words suggest his misunderstanding of America as a place that values individualism:

> *Policeman*: 'You're quite an individual, Kit.'
> *Kit*: 'Do you think they'll take that into consideration?'

The extreme individualism exercised by Kit throughout the film is way beyond the acceptable limits of social definitions of self-expression and has to be brought under control, disciplined and punished (see Campbell 2003).

'I can't be what I want to be any more than you can', says Motorcycle Boy at the end of *Rumble Fish*, as if to reinforce Kit's tragic misreading of America. To be young is not to express your own sense of self; instead it is about learning to be what others have scripted for you. *Rumble Fish* (1983, directed by Francis Ford Coppola) was made back-to-back with Coppola's other S.E. Hinton adaptation, *The Outsiders*, in 1983, but represents the opposite, dark side of youth movies in contrast to the more optimistic and romanticised view of the latter film. *Rumble Fish* is a distorted, brooding film that emphasises certain aspects of the original novel through the character of the Motorcycle Boy (Mickey Rourke). In particular, all heroism and light are drained from the film, which is shot in iridescent black and white with a slow surreal quality to it. Whereas *The Outsiders* is like a 1950s remake, *Rumble Fish* is a meditation upon Hinton's major themes but produced with a sinister and menacing edge. One of these central concerns is the theme of time, but here it takes on a terrible threat, akin to the work of Ellis. In one scene in the film, a voiceover from the diner owner Benny (Tom Waits) comments that 'Time is a funny thing. Time is a very peculiar item. See when you're young you've got time, nothing but time . . . throw away a couple of years here . . . and there it doesn't matter.' For Motorcycle Boy, time is running out, just like his health – he is colour-blind and growing deaf – and the film constantly reminds the audience of time's influence. In a key scene Motorcycle Boy, echoing a Gaines 'burn-out', tells his adoring brother Rusty-James that he is 'tired' of being seen as a hero, a Robin Hood or a Pied Piper, because 'if you're going to lead people you've got to have somewhere to go'. This is reinforced in the following shots by a scene in which the brothers stand in front of a huge, surreal, armless clock-face that towers over them as a reminder of their fragility. With echoes of T.S. Eliot's 'The Waste Land', Coppola's film indicates a powerful sense of lost dreams and no salvation with its 'maimed king', the Motorcycle Boy, who will not be healed and whose 'kingdom' is a post-industrial urban desert with no prospect of renewal. Motorcycle Boy 'is living in a glass bubble and watching the world from it' (Hinton 1975: 69), isolated and detached from any hope from the past, and through him Coppola 'problematizes the teen film' (Lewis 1992: 148) by upsetting and dislocating the audience's expectations and denying familiar elements, presenting instead only darkness, death and ambiguity.

One effect of the film is to oppose a romantic, mythic world of gangs and youth violence and to replace it with a slow, brutal recognition of change that pulls the young out of any sense they might have of immortality or staticity and into time's realm. As the novel says of Motorcycle Boy, 'He had strange eyes – they made me think of a two-way mirror. Like you could feel somebody on the other side watching you, but the only reflection you saw was your own' (Hinton 1975: 27). The film reflects back not the golden images of *The Outsiders* with its darkness dispersed by hope and family, but figures that can barely remember a better time and certainly cannot reclaim it. As the film ends, Motorcycle Boy's last gesture is to free the 'rumble fish' from the pet store into the river, an act completed by Rusty-James, since his brother has been shot by the police. In his last speech, the Boy tells Rusty-James to take his bike and go, 'to leave . . . to go clear to the ocean . . . follow the river, clear to the ocean'. Rusty-James is, therefore, connected to the dream of freedom and a return to the primal ocean while his brother cannot be free and must die in the squalor of the claustrophobic city. The film closes with a brief sequence at the ocean, but leaves Rusty-James in the ambiguity of the threshold moment, on the edge of land and ocean contemplating his future, which may be no future at all.

Motorcycle Boy's plea to his brother to follow the river suggests that the movement and fluidity might be a kind of freedom in an otherwise desolate and limiting world, but by *River's Edge* (Tim Hunter, 1987), any sense of liberation has been qualified by the use of the word 'edge', connoting both the marginal and precarious. Like *Badlands* and *Rumble Fish* the film employs images of waste and debris to suggest the futility of young lives being dramatised in the films themselves. In the case of *River's Edge* a human body is signified as waste, dumped by the side of the river with other detritus from this bleak, careless society. Although the familiar youth sub-texts of authenticity and sincerity are employed in the film, they have become threadbare and worthless. Lane says, 'We have to deal with it [the murder]. We've got to test our loyalty against all odds. It's kind of exciting. I feel like Chuck Norris.' As this suggests, loyalty has become unreal, like a movie itself, and within this film the group cannot maintain any loyalty in the face of the overwhelming tedium of their lives. All they have is the marginal space at the river's edge, a space beyond their fragmented, almost non-existent families and the depressing nostalgia of their school, and yet 'this place that is no place is theirs' (Acland 1995: 131).

This despair is present in the work of Larry Clark, whose photographs of youth in Tulsa, Oklahoma (1971) had been very influential on Coppola's *Rumble Fish*. In particular, Clark claimed his raw and uncompromising film *Kids* (1995) aimed to answer the unreal and cynical films, like *Clueless* (1995), that Clark saw as 'bullshit . . . [and] made by grown-ups who just don't know'. Instead, he employed a semi-documentary style with a script by teenage skater Harmony Korine 'to make a movie that shows, from the kids' point of view, what kids are like when they're out of the house, when the parents aren't around' (Clark 1995: 12). Clark's comments return us to *Badlands, River's Edge* and to Oliver Stone's *Natural Born Killers* (1995) which, in effect, explore youth 'out of the house, when their parents aren't around', engaged in transgressions that exist at the extremes of this idea, out beyond the edge of established social order.

GENERATION X/GENERATION Y

When Kurt Cobain killed himself in April 1994 one fan commented: 'He was the one man who sung a message that made me understand who I am' (reported in the *Observer*, 10 April 1994). In some respects his band, Nirvana, have come to epitomise a generation who had grown up without any sense of who they were or wanted to be. Youth identity had found temporary moorings in the 1960s counter-culture, in 1970s punk and as resistant to the 1980s yuppies, but into the 1990s there seemed to be new conditions prevailing. These were first charted and named by Douglas Coupland in his book *Generation X* (1992), but some of the sentiments were prefigured in the film *Pump Up the Volume* (1990, directed by Allan Moyle). The teenage pirate DJ 'Hard Harry' says: 'Consider the life of a teenager. You have teachers and parents and TV and movies telling you what to do – The terrible secret is that being young is sometimes less fun than being dead.' He claims to be part of the 'why bother generation' since 'all the great themes have been used up, been turned into theme parks'. Coupland's later novel, *Shampoo Planet* (1993), actually imagines an America where everything might be a theme park, epitomised by the vast 'HistoryWorld', with its motto 'INSTANT HISTORY'.

Coupland's work examines youth who have 'preferred not to', to borrow from Herman Melville's story of non-conformity 'Bartleby', turning their backs on the Reaganite economics and the yuppie competitiveness to live a subcultural existence 'neither simply affirmation nor refusal, neither "commercial exploitation" nor "genuine revolt" . . . [but] a declaration of independence, of otherness, of alien intent, a refusal of anonymity, of subordinate status. It is an insubordination' (Hebdige 1988: 35). Like Bartleby, who reminds the complacent narrator of his reliance on his workers and of his own dubious values, *Generation X* acts to remind the adult, dominant culture that 'all you're doing with your life is collecting objects. And nothing else' (Coupland 1992: 11), and that its 'traditional templates' (Rushkoff 1994: 7) are no longer valid.

As if to displace these narratives of the official culture, the 'structured environments' (ibid.: 27) that society creates, Xers instigate a 'policy' of storytelling aimed at cutting through the overload of history that has accumulated like a huge burden on the shoulders of youth. As Rushkoff puts it, the Xers are 'encumbered' with a 'legacy' from a past in which baby-boomers had transformed themselves from hippie to yuppies and in so doing had run a society 'on financial credit and social debt', leaving 'a huge lump in the snake's digestive tract called American history' (ibid.: 3). This weight of expectations led Xers to demand 'less in life. Less past'; to step outside history and 'read the letter inside me' instead of the scripts handed down from others (Coupland 1992: 59). Coupland's characters are like computers overloaded with information from a tired 'accelerated culture' who must 're/con/struct/' themselves by erasing or 'downloading' their history and the materials that fill their lives up, so as to 'decomplicate' life (ibid.: 77).

This would become a central theme in his later novel *Microserfs* (1995), which examined the dishevelled lives of Silicon Valley Xers made good in the computer age. The Xers have not become blind to all history, just to its devaluation, having seen it 'turned into a press release, a marketing strategy, and a cynical campaign tool', preferring to desire 'a connection to a past of some importance' (Coupland 2004: 151). To replace a manufactured 'history' with the stories of lives and dreams is part of the 'connection' for Coupland, a way in which youth might inscribe itself into history and create 'a remarkable document and an enchanted space' (ibid.: 150). Yet unlike the darker texts discussed earlier, Xers face the world with irony and an attitude of playfulness that allows them to exist among the debris of postmodern America, its advertising, TV, muzak and McJobs (part-time, non-career jobs). Rather than whine, Xers have adapted and 'celebrate the recycled imagery of our media and take pride in our keen appreciation of the folds within the creases of our wrinkled popular culture' (Rushkoff 1994: 5). Fully aware of the cynicism of marketing and the marketplace, they make an aesthetic out of 'slacking', that is, of living on the distanced edge of the dominant culture and engaging in 'grass-roots cultural hacking' in order to resist, like Bartleby, by 'apathy' 'the mind-numbing Muzak-intoned hypnotic demagoguery' of the adult world (ibid.: 8).

Richard Linklater's film *Slacker* (1992) demonstrates this with humour and observation, and like Coupland seems to be answering Gaines's call to break out of the 'psychic holding pen for superfluous young people' (Gaines 1992: 254) into a new, ironic space for survival. *Generation X* begins in the 1970s with the 'darkness and inevitability and fascination', the mood 'held by most young people since the dawn of time' (Coupland 1992: 4), and suggests that by the mid 1980s the Xers have moved to the 'periphery' and chosen not to participate in a world that 'confuse[s] shopping with creativity' (ibid.: 11), preferring instead the silence and space of the desert. Here, outside the restrictive spaces of the 'veal-fattening pens', Coupland's image for city workplaces, they erase the history and expectations of the baby-boomers that burden them and rewrite their own lives through their own stories, in their own space. In the mode of so many youth texts, creativity and expression take on massive significance, for it is through their stories that they reassess their own selves in opposition to those constructed by others. They long for 'a clean slate with no one to read it' (ibid.: 31). For example, Dag's ex-job in advertising is described as 'not creation . . . but theft' (ibid.: 27) for he feels he is stealing life through deceit, replacing human emotion and desire with simulation.

In a postmodern world, the novel suggests, the grand narratives have become worthless and what can stand in their place are the stories from lives actually lived, of people speaking for themselves in order to 're/con/struct' meanings in everyday terms. As Claire says in the novel, 'Either our lives become stories, or there's just no way to get through them' (ibid.: 8). The Xers might reject the imposed burden of the past, but they seek 'to make [their] own lives worthwhile tales in the process' (ibid.). However, the next generation, the so-called Y generation, born from somewhere around 1976 to around 2000 and sometimes called Echo Boomers as children of baby boomers or the Millennium Generation, grew into a world of total commercialisation of 'stories': 'They dream in Hi definition and Sony sound. Their signs and wonders are the bright logos that line the avenues and shopping malls . . .' (Quart 2003: xxv). Alissa Quart criticises the 'pretty vacant teen movies' she associates with Generation Y in 'makeover' films, like *She's All That* or *Clueless*, which promise 'a new self is merely a new slip dress or lip gloss away' and 'claim that girls being powdered and primped and branded are becoming their "true" selves' whereas they are 'in fact, testifying to the power of constructed and artificial selves' (ibid.: 115–16). Teen films can be, according to Quart, commodities that 'brand' youth and deny opportunities to 'become', to learn 'how to be' and to tell their own stories (ibid.: 124). Instead of youth spaces of edge and possibility they give only 'bounded and superficial versions of their lives' – 'empty vessels slathered with beauty products' (ibid.: 125).

One film that examines this Y anxiety is Catherine Hardwicke's *Thirteen* (2003), which is summed up in the director's comment: 'I think popular culture gives a confusing message to kids: You should not be thinking about sex, but there's a huge Calvin Klein billboard with a stuffed package. How do you navigate?' In the film Tracey, a geekish outsider, falls into the High School 'in-crowd' led by Evie ('alluring, but toxic') and becomes transformed at a cost of disconnection from family, friends and school work, spiralling into a brash world of sex, drugs and consumption. In deconstructing Evie's Y-world the film examines self-harming, anorexia, teenage sexuality and family crisis, and offers only an unsettling and ambiguous conclusion that sees Tracey on a roundabout in slow motion with the likelihood that she has not overcome the decline she has begun. As Hardwicke put it, 'There are crazy influences and pressures on these girls, that they're dealing with, and trying to navigate, figure out what to do with their bodies and their lives' (in Hoover 2003: n.p.). One pressure is the commodification of youth through advertising with the slogan 'Beauty is Truth' haunting the film.

Texts like *Generation X* and films like *Thirteen* offer no easy conclusions about youth or how its ideals might survive in the murkiness of contemporary culture; instead they leave us with the 'stray smells' of youth with which we started this chapter. Deliberating upon yet another story, Dag and Claire in *Generation X* are left with a frustratingly open ending of a young man whose 'fate remains a cliff-hanger' as he 'roams the badlands' (Coupland 1992: 173). Self-consciously or not, Coupland echoes earlier texts we have examined: *The Catcher in the Rye* and *Badlands* and prefigures Tracey in *Thirteen*, with images of staticity (the 'crazy cliff', the roundabout) and rebellion (badlands), before providing Andy's dream of a harmony beyond consumerism, where humanity and nature coexist with 'grace' (ibid.: 173). The 'seductive outside', much cherished in youth texts, re-emerges here as an antidote to the world adults have created, replacing it with 'an instant family' of 'mentally retarded teenagers' (and so fixed in time), unafraid to show genuine emotion to Andy in an overwhelming 'crush of love . . . unlike anything [he] had ever known' (ibid.: 179). The surreal ending emphasises the novel's ultimately ambiguous idealism and counters only some of the darkness associated with *Generation X*, rekindling a sense of wonder at the radiance of youth and its capacity to replenish and to save, while simultaneously, as so often in youth texts, retaining a shadow presence of threat and the possibility of imminent decline. Such a shadow presence can be found in films like *Donnie Darko*, *Igby Goes Down* and *Elephant*.

THE *TWILIGHT* EFFECT

Following *Thirteen*, Catherine Hardwicke directed the first *Twilight* film in 2008 following the phenomenal success of Stephenie Meyer's first volume of her *Twilight Saga* (2005). Meyer's *Twilight* is a hybrid genre built from vampire and youth texts – teen angst high school drama meets *Dracula* (or *Pretty in Pink* meets *Carrie*). It partakes of many of the conventions described throughout this chapter that have evolved in American culture over centuries, while retrofitting them with the gothic fantasies of vampires and werewolves. The word 'twilight' is significant in a number of ways: it is a time between states – day/night – when things are less clear, when vision is indistinct but expectant of change and the emergence of something new. It is an *in-between* condition, a liminality that forces the reader to think across/between expectations of the vampire story, the Gothic story, the modern love story and the youth cultural text. Its themes too work between a series of struggles around choice and action, sexuality and abstinence, familiar and unfamiliar with its central female protagonist, Bella Swan, always torn, lacking the agility and strength of the undead she contrasts with them; awkward, unsure, uncool, clumsy and self-conscious – the Everygirl of many previous youth texts (see Campbell 2015). Through her contact with Edward Cullen and his vampire family and with Jacob Black, the Native American werewolf, she is tested as a human and as a woman. Because of this we are confronted by contrary feelings about Bella, as an independent-minded young woman from a broken home trying to make it in a new community, or an indecisive victim of continued patriarchal infantilisation. This is in keeping with some of the trajectories of the contemporary Gothic as defined by Catherine Spooner, who writes of how

> Teenagers . . . are now as likely to be the source of horror as the victim of it. This . . . reflects a two-edged trajectory: on the one hand teenagers, particularly girls, are being presented as more powerful and in control . . . on the other, teen Gothic capitalizes on real-life moral panics about teenage violence . . .
>
> (Spooner 2006: 107)

Through Bella's struggle over her feelings for Edward in *Twilight*, Meyer's morality tale examines what humanity is through its collision with its 'others'. 'Without the dark', the novel claims, 'we'd never see the stars' (Meyer 2007: 204). To keep Bella human is to allow her the 'beautiful thing about being human', that 'Things change' (ibid.: 416), and save her from the endless immortality of vampire life wherein, as Edward knows, there is deep, troubling torment, the 'crypt' of pain and the 'mask of ancient sadness' (ibid.: 232) as it is called. This is a self-conscious intertextual mix of *Romeo and Juliet*, *Wuthering Heights* and *Pride and Prejudice* for the iPhone generation, with Bella, Edward and Jacob embroiled in a youthful love triangle across the various novels following *Twilight* (*New Moon*, *Eclipse*, *Breaking Dawn*).

Meyer's moral position is clearly about restraint and waiting, with the emphasis on love and romance in an age of acceleration and hyper-sexuality. Almost as a direct response to the forwardness of Generation Y texts, Meyer's popularity suggests the 'abstinence' message ('denying my thirst'; ibid.: 236) along with the intensity of Bella and Edward's love affair has enormous appeal: 'I wrestled all night, while watching you sleep, with the chasm between what I knew was right, moral, ethical, and what I wanted' (ibid.: 265). The risk of sexual contact in this vampire realm is the risk of death after all and Meyer uses this as a mechanism for examining relationship themes, issues of choice and the pressures of growing up. For Bella is like 'heroin' to Edward (ibid.: 234) – an addiction that he has to fight or 'abstain' from (ibid.: 235).

However, one of the most interesting aspects of the *Twilight* phenomenon are the spin-off activities associated with it, which really demonstrate the powerful media landscape it has created in the twenty-first century. From a Facebook site, to endless fansites, to the impressively cavernous *Twilight* Fanfiction sites eager global participants interact with the stories to create their own additions, variations and extensions of the plots (see http://www.fanfiction.net/book/Twilight or Twifans.com). Whatever the debates about the novels' merits or demerits, it is without doubt that they provide an extraordinary development in American Youth Studies, recycling and reworking old themes for a new generation and conveying these across an ever-expanding interactive mediascape. In many ways this characterises the new 'youth spaces' of the twenty-first century, no longer just about writing, music or dance, but increasingly operating in the complex unbounded universe of social media where chat rooms, blogs, fansites and wikis define alternative sources of engagement and dialogue.

CONCLUSION: *GIRLS*

Girls (2012–), written, directed by and starring Lena Dunham, explores post-recession USA from the perspective of a group of girlfriends in New York City: Hannah (Lena Dunham), Marnie (Allison Williams), Jessa (Jemima Kirke) and Shoshanna (Zosia Mamet). Decidedly self-reflexive, the show accepts its limitations as an all-white, middle-class vision and manages as a result to examine the self-centred worlds of the privileged inheritors of Second Wave feminism and girl power. With a direct nod to Helen Gurley Brown's 1962 bestseller *Sex and the Single Girl*, the television series expands on Brown's assertion that single girls should seek pleasure and fulfilment on their own terms. *Girls's* critical self-reflexivity is present from the very beginning when Hannah says 'I am busy trying to become who I am' or grandiosely to her parents, 'I don't want to freak you out, but I think I may be the voice of my generation. Or, at least, a voice. Of a generation' (season 1, episode 1). In this sense, as Maša Grdešic, has put it, 'the series acknowledges the expectations set by the media' to be a ground-breaking study of millennial youth and at the same time 'confesses its own inability to meet them' (2013: 356–7). Hannah is an aspiring writer whose work is clearly limited and yet she cannot see this. Of course, in this sense she comes in a long tradition of American girl would-be writers struggling to find a voice amid patriarchy, from Jo March in *Little Women* to Esther Greenwood in *The Bell Jar*, except in Hannah's case she is a dislikeable selfish person and certainly no role model for a generation. In a sense, however, this is the show's point, for it never intends to speak for all, even though its title suggests otherwise! Instead it offers a glimpse of lives being lived as 'part of a "third wave" of feminism, which has had to respond to a changed set of economic, political and social circumstances' of insecurity, anxiety and doubt (Kaklamanidou and Tally 2014: 2). The world of *Girls* is unsettling and fragile mediated by the gains of earlier generations and the uncertainty of their own. Despite everything they have attained, this new generation remain strangely hesitant because of the 'explosion of social media as well as more conventional forms of media (film and television)', through which they are exposed to a wide range of conflicting gender ideals, and yet remain 'able to craft a subjectivity that both converges with conventional images of femininity while at the same time possibly subverts them' (ibid.: 2). Scenes of sexual experimentation and drug use flirt with styles of freedom that challenge conventional images and yet the show often portrays women who are still determined by their reliance on men to shape and give structure to their lives. The ambivalence of *Girls* is ultimately what makes it uncomfortable viewing, moving its audience, both male and female, through extremes of repulsion and recognition in perplexing ways that, at its best, 'demonstrates promise and invites dialogue' around the social and cultural experience of young women in a postfeminist USA (Bell 2013: 366).

REFERENCES AND FURTHER READING

Acland, C. (1995) *Youth, Murder, Spectacle: The Cultural Polities of 'Youth in Crisis'*, Boulder, CO: Westview Press.

Alcott, L.M. (1989) (first 1868) *Little Women*, London: Penguin.

Bardola, N. (2009) *The Twilight Phenomenon*, London: Piccadilly Press.

Bell, K. (2013) 'Obvie, We're the Ladies!': Postfeminism, Privilege, and HBO's Newest Girls', *Feminist Media Studies* special issue, vol. 13, no. 2, pp 363–6.

Bernstein, J. (1997) *Pretty in Pink: The Golden Age of Teenage Movies*, New York: St. Martin's Griffin.

Brickman, B.J. (2014) *New American Teenagers: The Lost Generation of Youth in 1970s Film*, London: Bloomsbury.

Brode, D. (2015) *Sex, Drugs & Rock 'n' Roll: The Evolution of an American Youth Culture* (Popular Culture and Everyday Life), Berlin: Peter Lang.

Campbell, N. (1994) '"The Seductive Outside" and the "Sacred Precincts": Boundaries and Transgressions in *The Adventures of Tom Sawyer*', *Children's Literature in Education*, vol. 25, no. 2, pp. 125–38.

—— (2003) 'The Highway Kind: Youth, the Road and the West in Malick's *Badlands*' in H. Patterson (ed.) *Poetic Visions of America: The Films of Terrence Malick*, London: Wallflower Press.

—— (ed.) (2004) *American Youth Cultures*, Edinburgh: Edinburgh University Press.

—— (2015) 'Popular Vampires: The Twilight Effect' in C. Berberich (ed.) *The Bloomsbury Introduction to Popular Fiction*, London: Bloomsbury.

Clark, L. (1995) in D. Witter, *New City* (Chicago), 27 July.

Clayton, J. (1993) *The Pleasures of Babel: Contemporary American Literature and Theory*, New York: Oxford University Press.

Coupland, D. (1992) (first 1991) *Generation X*, London: Abacus.

—— (1993) *Shampoo Planet*, London: Simon & Schuster.

—— (2004) (first 1995) *Microserfs*, London: Harper Perennial.

During, S. (1992) *Foucault and Literature*, London: Routledge.

Eagleton, T. (1983) *Literary Theory*, Oxford: Blackwell.

Ellis, B.E. (1985) *Less Than Zero*, London: Picador.

Fass, P. (1977) *The Damned and the Beautiful: Adolescence in the 1920s*, New York: Oxford University Press.

Fetterley, J. (1973) 'The Sanctioned Rebel' in D. Kesterson (ed.) *Critics on Mark Twain*, Coral Gables: University of Miami Press.

Fiedler, L. (1960) *No! In Thunder*, New York: Stein and Day.

Fitzgerald, F.S. (1974) (first 1925) *The Great Gatsby*, Harmondsworth: Penguin.

Foucault, M. (1977a) *Discipline and Punish: The Birth of the Prison*, Harmondsworth: Penguin.

—— (1977b) 'Preface to Transgression' in D.F. Bouchard (ed.) *Language, Counter-Memory, Practice: Selected Essays and Interviews*, New York: Cornell University Press.

—— (1986) *The History of Sexuality: The Use of Pleasure*, London: Penguin.

Friedenberg, E.Z. (1963) *Coming of Age in America: Growth and Acquiescence*, New York: Vintage.

Gaines, D. (1992) *Teenage Wasteland: Suburbia's Dead End Kids*, New York: Harper Perennial.

Gillett, C. (1983) *The Sound of the City: The Rise of Rock and Roll*, London: Souvenir Press.

Grdešic, M. (2013), 'I'm Not the Ladies! Metatextual Commentary in Girls', *Feminist Media Studies* special issue, vol. 13, no. 2, pp. 355–8.

Grossberg, L. (1992) *We Gotta Get Out of this Place: Popular Conservatism and Postmodern Culture*, London: Routledge.

Hebdige, D. (1988) *Hiding in the Light*, London: Methuen.

Hinton, S.E. (1972) (first 1967) *The Outsiders*, London: HarperCollins.

—— (1975) *That Was Then, This is Now*, London: HarperCollins.

—— (1977) (first 1975) *Rumble Fish*, London: HarperCollins.

Hoover, T. (2003) 'Thirteen Days: Interview with Catherine Hardwicke', at http://www.filmfreakcentral.net/notes/chardwickeinterview.htm (accessed 11/02/2011).

Howe, N. and Strauss, B. (1993) *13th Gen: Abort, Retry, Ignore, Fail?*, New York: Vintage.

Kaklamanidou, D.-B. and Tally, M. (eds) (2014), *HBO's Girls: Questions of Gender, Politics, and Millennial Angst*, Newcastle: Cambridge Scholars.

Kristeva, J. (1990) *Abjection, Melancholia and Love: The Works of Julia Kristeva*, edited by J. Fletcher and A. Benjamin, London: Routledge.

LaMarche, P. (2007) *American Youth*, London: Sceptre.

Lauter, P. *et al.* (1994) *The Heath Anthology of American Literature*, 2 vols, Lexington: D.C. Heath.

Lawrence, D.H. (1977) *Studies in Classic American Literature*, Harmondsworth: Penguin.

Lears, J.L. (1981) *No Place of Grace: Antimodernism and the Transformation of American Culture, 1880–1920*, New York: Pantheon.

Lebeau, V. (1995) *Lost Angels: Psychoanalysis and Cinema*, London: Routledge.

Lewis, J. (1992) *The Road to Romance and Ruin: Teen Films and Youth Culture*, London: Routledge.

Lhamon, W.T. Jr (1990) *Deliberate Speed: The Origins of Cultural Style in the American 1950s*, Washington, DC: Smithsonian Institute Press.

Lipsitz, G. (1994) 'We Know What Time It Is: Race, Class and Youth in the Nineties' in A. Rose and T. Ross (eds) *Microphone Fiends*, London: Routledge.

Lowenthal, D. (1985) *The Past is a Foreign Country*, Cambridge: Cambridge University Press.

Meyer, S. (2007) (first 2005) *Twilight*, London: Atom Books.

Meyer Spacks, P. (1981) *The Adolescent Idea*, New York: Galaxy.

Pomerance, M. and Sakeris, J. (eds) (1996) *Pictures of a Generation on Hold: Selected Papers*, Toronto: Media Studies Working Group.

Quart, A. (2003) *Branded: The Buying and Selling of Teenagers*, London: Arrow.

Rabinow, P. (ed.) (1984) *The Foucault Reader*, London: Penguin.

Robertson, J.O. (1980) *American Myth, American Reality*, New York: Hill & Wang.

Ross, A. and Rose, T. (eds) (1994) *Microphone Fiends: Youth Music and Youth Culture*, London: Routledge.

Rushkoff, D. (ed.) (1994) *The Generation X Reader*, New York: Ballantine Books.

Salinger, J.D. (1972) (first 1951) *The Catcher in the Rye*, Harmondsworth: Penguin.

Sanford, C. (1961) *The Quest for Paradise*, New York: AMS Press.

Shary, T. (2003) *Generation Multiplex*, Austin: University of Texas Press.

Shields, R. (1991) *Places on the Margin*, London: Routledge.

Spooner, C. (2006) *Contemporary Gothic*, London: Reaktion Books.

Storey, J. (1993) *An Introductory Guide to Cultural Theory and Popular Culture*, London: Harvester Wheatsheaf.

Twain, M. (1986) (first 1898) *The Adventures of Tom Sawyer*, London: Penguin.

Witter, D. (1995) 'Teen Spirit' in *New City* (Chicago), 27 July, pp. 10–12.

FOLLOW-UP WORK

There are a number of additional resources, assignments and other materials to be found on the website that accompanies this new edition: http://www.routledge.com/cw/campbell/

1   Jocks, cheerleaders, nerds, goths and stoners – the American teen movie seems peopled with stereotypes. To what extent, using any 'teen' film, can you argue that they speak more critically about hopes, dreams and anxieties that do not have just to do with going to the prom or making out?

2   'Vampires, Nina Auerbach argues, change according to their time: "each feeds on his age distinctively because he embodies that age".

The vampire reflects national moods and, hence, tells us who we are' (T. Goddu, Review Essay, 'Vampire Gothic', *American Literary History*, alh.oxfordjournals.org). How and why might *Twilight*, *Buffy the Vampire Slayer* or *True Blood* relate to Goddu's assessment?

3   How does the film *Juno* (2007) address the theme of family, pregnancy and growing up in innovative ways? Consider its use of style and soundtrack in your answer.

4   Read online the various essay on *Girls* in the *Feminist Media Studies* special issue of 2013 (vol. 13, no. 2), and then examine an episode from the series. Discuss the ways in which the show can be seen as a 'postfeminist' youth text.

Chapter 9

The spread of freedom

'From the birth of our liberty', Barack Obama declared in his introduction to the National Security Strategy of 2010,

> America has had a faith in the future. . . . To fulfil that promise, generations of Americans have built upon the foundation of our forefathers – finding opportunity, fighting injustice, and forging a more perfect Union. We have also created webs of commerce, supported an international architecture of laws and institutions, and spilled American blood in foreign lands – not to build an empire, but to shape a world in which more individuals and nations could determine their own destiny, and live with the peace and dignity they deserve.
>
> (National Security Strategy 2010)

Obama's link between America's achievements at home and its role abroad emphasises a significant theme in American culture, and an important aspect of the way in which American identity is constructed. The complex interaction of internal forces is important in helping to understand how America has changed over time but these forces also need to be related to the ways in which different elements in the country have sought, at particular moments, to construct their own versions of 'America' in relation to their perceptions of the outside world. In this respect, 'the conduct of foreign policy plays a central role in the construction of nationalism . . . (as) one of the ways in which nations speak for themselves; it defines not only the boundaries of the nation but also its character, interests, its allies and its enemies' (McAlister 2001: 5–6). From this perspective identity is not something natural or given; rather it is constructed in ways which emphasise difference in relation to others, and which, as a result, helps to create specific discourses about America's role in the world. These discourses or sets of ideas in turn help to shape policy, and their articulation becomes a process which we can analyse in order to understand the sources of foreign policy actions. In this chapter we want to explore some of the implications of this judgement for an understanding of American's position in the world in the early twenty-first century, and how it connects with persistent themes in American history and culture.

Many of these issues were thrown into stark relief by the range of responses by the administration of George W. Bush to the terrorist attacks on the United States of America of 11 September 2001, particularly the wars in Afghanistan and Iraq, and by the ongoing series of debates which have surrounded American foreign policy since then. One place to start here is Bush's first Inaugural Address in January 2001 when he inserted his presidency into a developing American narrative:

> We have a place, all of us, in a long story – a story we continue, but whose end we will not see. It is the story of a new world that became a friend and liberator of the old ... the story of a power that went into the world to protect but not possess, to defend but not to conquer.
> (Bush 2001a)

The identification of the spread of freedom with America's international purpose was a central component of his vision. His language in many ways fitted with the conventional expectations of American inaugural rhetoric (see Chapter 1) but only a few months later both the meaning of his words and the nature of his presidency would be dramatically tested by the attacks of September 11th. America now had to 'go forward to defend freedom and all that is good and just in our world', he declared in his televised address to the American people that night (Bush 2001b). It soon became clear, however, that this commitment highlighted issues of immense significance for America both at home and abroad which would prove difficult to resolve, both for Bush himself, and for his successor, Barack Obama. What responsibility did the United States have to advance freedom beyond its borders? Should it seek to promote democracy in the wider world? Should it seek to advance its values in partnership with others or should it be prepared to go it alone if necessary? How should it balance liberty and security in seeking to protect itself against future attacks? How should America act in the world? President Bush himself gave a range of answers to these questions over the next days and months, but at the heart of them was his assertion that his job was 'to lead this nation into making the world a better place' (Bush 2004b). The course his administration had taken in prosecuting a 'War on Terror' would make America more secure and the world freer and more peaceful. What was at stake here was· a version of American patriotism which was closely connected to a vision of America's historic destiny.

The following sections explore a range of different perspectives on Bush's assertion of America's transparent 'goodness' and commitment to 'freedom', and Obama's 'faith in the future'. They examine assessments of American power, and then look at a number of key themes in the ideology of American foreign policy. As a coda, this chapter also includes discussion of the implications of recent policy for America at home. The domestic and the foreign are always closely connected. What have been the consequences of September 11th, and the debates about the direction of American foreign policy they have encouraged, for American politics and culture? In reviewing these issues, it also takes into account a wide-ranging debate within and without the United States about the extent to which contemporary American strategy is marked by change or continuity. A number of observers have argued that change characterised the Bush presidency, particularly if the focus is on the implementation of policy, rather than its rhetorical justification. The War on Terror, it is suggested, marked a significant departure in the conduct of American foreign relations, by encouraging a willingness to use military power unilaterally in a way which disrupted previous practice. On the other hand, it is striking how much continuity there is between the actions, language and cultural assumptions of both the George W. Bush and Obama presidencies and those of earlier administrations. An over-emphasis on the impact of September 11th as a catalyst for transformation can disguise the way in which assumptions about America's role in the world stretch back to the founding of the nation and have been regularly replayed in different settings.

AMERICAN POWER: RISE AND DECLINE

At the heart of this discussion lies a debate about American power. Henry Luce famously called on the twentieth century to become the 'American' century, and so in many ways it did in the aftermath of the Second World War (see Chapter 10). Whether measured in economic power, military strength or the 'soft' power of cultural practice and political values, America after 1945 seemed to be realising Luce's vision. It is the case that for forty-five years or so this was challenged by the Soviet Union and its allies, but that threat to American preponderance eventually disintegrated with the end of the Cold War in the late 1980s and early 1990s. The United States, so it seemed, was now left as the world's only superpower and the collapse of the Soviet Union left it without the constraints of significant challenges from other rivals. However, over the next twenty-five years, this apparent pre-eminence would be increasingly questioned, as a significant debate emerged whether the United States was not by 2015 a power in relative decline.

By 2000 the United States was responsible for 43 per cent of world military expenditure, six times larger than that of the second highest spender, Russia. In 2005 it had 969 official military bases at home and 725 abroad, as well as an unspecified number of secret bases. The US navy circled the world. The decline of the Russian nuclear arsenal left the United States as far and away the world's most potent nuclear power; agreements in the 2002 Treaty of Moscow and the 2011 START Treaty to reduce its stocks were qualified by maintenance of tactical weapons at Cold War levels and continuing modernisation of a range of delivery systems. The Cold War, in particular, it is argued, had 'nurtured an ideology, a set of leaders, a network of bureaucratic and economic interests, and a cluster of habits . . . which maintained the momentum for military strength' (Eisenberg 2005: 415). Moreover, the size of the American military establishment was grounded in broad popular and bipartisan political support. Respect for the military was anchored in its serving as an avenue of social mobility for lower classes (Pieterse 2003: 76) and also enhanced by its pervasive presence in Hollywood's output of feature films and in public ceremony. In economic terms also, although there was more of a debate here, American power appeared to prevail. Its position in the international economy was clearly less dominant than at the end of the Second World War, when it was responsible for about half of global GNP and controlled 70 per cent of world financial resources, but in 2005 its economy remained nearly 40 per cent bigger than that of any of its rivals. This allowed it, despite its huge military outlays, to spend a percentage of its GDP on defence comparable to that of other nations. It also had significant influence over the regulation of the sources and supply routes of the vital energy and raw material needs of even its most successful economic competitors (Cox 2005: 25).

This was the context in which the attacks on New York and Washington of September 11th took place. The nature of the reaction to these events – the decisions to go to war in both Afghanistan and Iraq – displayed both the size of America's military capacity, as well as its willingness to use it in specific settings. As an essential component of this strategy, Congress approved a marked increase in the military budget, from $310 billion in 2001 to a projected $441.6 billion in 2006. In 2004 President George W. Bush asserted that as the greatest power on the face of the earth, America had 'an obligation to help the spread of freedom' (Bush 2004b). An implicit part of this argument was the assumption that the United States had the military and political capacity to turn this kind of rhetoric into effective practice. American power would ensure that the world could actually be changed for the better. It was in this context that arguments about American empire took place (see below) both in terms of those who sought to justify American power and its use in the world, and those who criticised its arrogance and excessive use of its military might.

However, as George W. Bush's presidency came to an end in 2009, that confidence in the ability of the United States to deliver significant change in the world had been severely challenged. The country found itself still ensnared in two protracted and messy wars in Iraq and Afghanistan, both of which undermined the administration's optimism about 'victory', amid widespread international criticism about the direction of American policy. At the same time the collapse of the international economy in 2007–8, and the severity of recession in America itself, seemed to show that the American economic model was in serious long-term decline. By 2008, the United States had become the world's largest debtor, and faced increasing challenges from China in particular, which in 2011 moved into second place in world rankings, amid prophecies that it would become the world's largest economic power by 2025.

Theories of American decline, of course, have a long history, from concern in the 1950s about falling behind the Soviet Union to arguments in the 1980s about American over-extension of its military and economic resources. Anne-Marie Slaughter has argued that these kinds of anxieties are part of 'a recurring cycle in the American psyche', and that the country has always managed to reinvent itself, when faced with serious internal and external challenges, but it nevertheless remains that the scale of the problems the country faces are very significant (BBC 2011). Others have argued that the scenario of the significant decline of the United States and a decisive power shift to China, Brazil, India and Russia has been much exaggerated. In terms of its continuing economic, financial and technological advantages, its military strength and its 'soft' power, the United States still retains significant advantages (Cox 2012). Henry Luce's 'American Century' may have ended, but the United States still retains a pre-eminent, if no longer dominant, place in what has followed. The Bush administration's real difficulties in successfully using its strength to achieve its policy aims were a consequence of its specific policy divisions, rather than something more long-term and systemic. Nevertheless, even if prophecies of American decline were by no means guaranteed to come true, Barack Obama, and his successor in 2016, would still face difficulties in trying to find appropriate strategies to deal with a world where the old certainties no longer existed, and where a key part of his inheritance was the relative decline of American power, 'with the inevitable effect of America's diminishing influence and capacity to lead' (Niblett 2010: 6). Elected on a platform of 'Change We Can Believe In', he soon found it hard to disentangle his administration from the issues left by his predecessor. This was evident in a less adventurous foreign policy, which reflected a more sober assessment of America's capabilities in an increasingly uncertain world. The final withdrawal of American troops from Iraq in December 2012, with the country still in a turbulent state, only emphasised the scale of the problem. In his 2015 National Security Strategy Obama re-emphasised that 'America must lead' in the world and reiterated its enduring commitment to the advancement of democracy, but stressed supporting 'democratic transitions' rather than crusades to transform the world. American policy should be guided by strategic patience. (National Security Strategy 2015).

Plate 9.1 Soldiers from the 3rd Brigade, 1st Cavalry Division board a C-17 transport plane to depart from Iraq at Camp Adder, now known as Imam Ali Base, near Nasiriyah, 17 December 2011.

© POOL / Reuters / Corbis

EXCEPTIONALISM AND THE MISSION OF FREEDOM

America's rise to international power had been accompanied by an enduring set of arguments about its destiny in the world, and they remained as important influences on the construction of American foreign policy into the twenty-first century. In his State of the Union address in 2004, for instance, President Bush declared that America was a nation with a mission, which stemmed from its most basic beliefs: 'We have no desire to dominate, no ambitions of empire.' Rather America's aim was a democratic peace – a peace founded upon the dignity and rights of every man and woman. 'America acts in this cause with friends and allies at our side, yet we understand our special calling: This great republic will lead the cause of freedom' (Bush 2004a). This vision, with all its attendant ambiguities, has deep roots in American culture, and taps into a range of myths about the nation's values. It connects with a much noted theme in American history, a tendency to emphasise what is supposed to be exceptional about the national experience. America, from this perspective, has followed a different path from other countries, in which the signposts have been its own professed ideals. 'What happens within its borders' has been often seen to 'be of deeper importance than what happens within the space of other, lesser nations' (Cox 2005: 15). It is this exceptionalist sense of mission that lies at the heart of what Michael Hunt describes as the ideology of American foreign policy, and may be traced back to the early days of the Republic (Hunt 1988). The Americans, wrote Alexis de Tocqueville in 1835, 'have grown up unnoticed, and whilst the attention of mankind was directed elsewhere . . . have suddenly placed themselves in the front rank among nations'. They were proceeding 'with ease and celerity along a path to which no limit can be perceived' and were 'marked out by the will of Heaven to sway the destinies of half the globe' (De Tocqueville 1965: 286–7).

De Tocqueville's prophecies about future American greatness and his invocation of America's missionary role in the world tapped into a vein of political rhetoric which was well established by the 1830s and which survived to influence American foreign policy into the twenty-first century. 'We have it in our power to begin the world all over again', wrote Thomas Paine in his pamphlet 'Common Sense' on the eve of American independence in January 1776. The overthrow of British rule would be the occasion of 'the birthday of a new world', through which the American continent would become 'the glory of the earth' (Hunt 1988: 20). Paine drew on a tradition of religious and republican thought in making his appeal, which only added to the force of his language. The idea of America as a nation with a strong sense of mission leant on such early statements as John Winthrop's famous sermon on the *Arbella* as it sailed across the Atlantic to the New World in 1630. Winthrop's invocation of America as a special place, where the holy commonwealth of Massachusetts would be as 'a city upon a hill', a model for the rest of mankind, underlined the importance of America's role in the world, from the earliest days of colonial foundation. Winthrop emphasised the exemplary purpose of the American experiment, but others who followed gave it more of a missionary slant, in a way that foreshadowed Paine. The Puritans, in Walter LaFeber's formulation, soon stepped down from the hill and began to take their values outside into the world where the irreligious might be subdued and their own territory extended (LaFeber 2002: 551). This process is also well illustrated, for instance, in John Adams's diary entry of February 1765:

> I always consider the settlement of America with reverence and wonder, as the opening of a grand scene and design in Providence for the illumination of the ignorant and the emancipation of the slavish part of mankind all over the earth.
>
> (Donoghue 1988: 229)

America from this perspective had a special purpose, one that was closely tied to the process of redemption. America would banish darkness with light, bring freedom in place of slavery and save the world from condemnation. Not only would America exemplify the virtues necessary for long-term success, but it would also apply those same virtues to other peoples and to the way in which nations dealt with each other on the international stage in the future. The general claims Paine made for America's historic role in the world would be amplified as the country grew rapidly during the nineteenth century in terms of territory and economic power and influence. Expansion across the American continent was justified because it would bring with it republican institutions and practices, in a way that made the spread of American borders qualitatively different from the expansionist policies of other nations. Throughout the process of the acquisition of new lands during the first half of the nineteenth century, from the Louisiana Purchase of 1803 to the capture of California and the southwest from Mexico in the war of 1846–8, many Americans assumed that such a process was both benevolent and natural. These views were most vividly displayed in the rhetoric of Manifest Destiny: 'America', declared John L. O'Sullivan in 1839,

> had a blessed mission to the nations of the world ... to smite unto death the tyranny of kings, hierarchs, and oligarchs, and carry the glad tidings of peace and good will where myriads now endure an existence scarcely more enviable than that of beasts of the field.
>
> (O'Sullivan 1839)

This way of thinking about America's role in the world emerged during the nineteenth century, but it remained an abiding influence as the growth of American power more regularly involved the nation in European and Asian politics in the opening years of the twentieth century. Woodrow Wilson led the United States into the First World War with the declaration that right was more precious than peace, and that America would fight for the things it always carried nearest its heart:

> for democracy, for the right of those who submit to authority to have a voice in their own Governments, for the rights and liberties of small nations, for a universal dominion of right by such a concert of free peoples as shall bring peace and safety to all nations and make the world itself at last free.
>
> (Brinkley 2007: 630–1)

When he campaigned in 1919 for American membership of the League of Nations he described the American soldiers who had died in the First World War as crusaders. They were not going forth to prove the might of the United States but to prove the might of justice and right. This would be their transcendent achievement. 'America', Wilson declared, 'had the infinite privilege of fulfilling her destiny and saving the world' (LaFeber 2002: 551).

In defending American involvement in Vietnam in the 1960s Lyndon Johnson argued that America wanted nothing for itself, 'only that the people of South Vietnam be allowed to guide their own country in their own way' (Johnson 1965). Concepts of mission were also a repeated part of the argument in the build-up to the war on Iraq in 2003. The National Security Strategy statement of 2002 emphasised the duty of the United States to 'defend liberty and justice because these principles are right and true for all people' (National Security Strategy 2002). The war in Afghanistan was in part justified as an effort to rescue women and children from the grip of male Taliban oppression. 'At long last, efforts to protect and advance women's rights are where they belong – in the mainstream of American foreign policy', declared the State Department in 2002. As Emily Rosenberg has argued, this chimed with the concept of a 'social imaginary dominated by a masculinized national state that cast itself in a paternal role, saving those who are abused by rival men and nations' (Rosenberg 2002: 457, 464). When President Bush visited London in 2003, in the aftermath of the Iraq War, he explicitly justified the American mission to advance freedom in the world, with reference to Wilson's idealism in search of justice and right (Bush 2003).

Barack Obama's presidency has continued to show the importance of 'exceptionalism' in American political culture. Although giving his language a more inclusive dimension than George W. Bush, Obama also echoed both Paine and Wilson. America, in conjunction with the people of the world, must remember its history, answer its destiny, and 'remake the world once again' (Obama 2008a). America, he asserted before an audience in Strasbourg in 2009, had 'a continued extraordinary role in leading the world towards peace and prosperity'. At the same time, however, he sought to play down the distinctiveness of American exceptionalism. All countries liked to think they were different. Leadership lay through partnerships because the world's problems could not be solved by America on its own (Obama 2009). For this kind of qualification of America's destiny, he would be bitterly criticised by conservatives. Sarah Palin, for instance, attacked Obama for believing 'that America is not the greatest earthly force for good the world has known' (Easley 2010) while Congressman Mike Pence, from Indiana, declared that Republican victory in the House of Representatives in the 2010 elections offered the opportunity to 're-establish American exceptionalism rather than denying or apologising for it' (Pence 2010). As these arguments suggest, American policy in the future would have to overcome an apparent contradiction between fresh calls for a renewal of American leadership, and a more flexible and open set of attitudes towards international cooperation (Niblett 2010: 2).

Obama himself would find this tension difficult to resolve. In 2014 he emphasised his commitment to a vision of American leadership in the world, and insisted that he believed in American exceptionalism 'with every fiber of (his) being' (Obama 2014b). The United States was still the strongest nation in the world, both militarily and economically. At the same time, however, the world was changing fast and American actions had to take into account human dignity, international norms and the rule of law.

CULTURAL SUPERIORITY

During the nineteenth century the commitment to the mission of freedom was often given an added gloss, as many Americans developed a way of thinking about other peoples and nations which linked the spread of liberty to assumptions about cultural superiority, sometimes couched in terms of racial supremacy. Such attitudes from the earliest days of the Republic were an integral part of debates about America's proper role in the world, and frequently affected specific foreign policy decisions. Throughout the nineteenth century and well into the twentieth, American leaders often justified an expansionist foreign policy on grounds that assumed a hierarchy of race, arguing that the future of international civilisation depended on the spread of Anglo-American values and institutions into less fortunate parts of the world. Many Americans, for instance, assumed that skin colour and physical typology carried with them distinctive moral, spiritual and behavioural qualities. At the top of the racial order came whites or Anglo-Saxons, who embodied such attributes as leadership, energy, perseverance and independence. It was this race, Josiah Strong argued at the end of the nineteenth century, which was becoming 'more effective' in the United States than Europe, and which, with its unequalled energy, would spread itself over the earth (Ions 1970: 72). These attitudes had a powerful influence on the making of foreign policy, as Michael Hunt has argued: 'by its grip on the thinking of the men who debated and determined these policies, by its influence over the press, and by its hold on the electorate, race powerfully shaped the way the nation dealt with other peoples' (Hunt 1988: 52). Race, from this perspective, provided an apparently clear and effective way to categorise other peoples both inside and outside the North American continent. It offered a link between attitudes towards Native Americans and African Americans at home, and policies towards the peoples of Asia, Europe and Latin America. At the same time it flattered the assumptions of those who made American policy, since most of them came from the Anglo-Saxon tradition within the United States, at the same time as it fitted in with the views of many ordinary citizens, who were susceptible, for a number of reasons, to appeals that took for granted the historic destiny of the white race. Many of these attitudes may be seen clearly in the relentless progress of the American nation to the Pacific Ocean in the first half of the nineteenth century, and the subsequent settlement of the interior of the continent in the second half of the century (see Chapter 5). The defeat and dispossession of Native American tribes were justified by arguments that, as part of an inferior race, they were doomed to 'vanish' in the face of a superior form of civilisation. Towards the end of the nineteenth century, as it became clear that pacification and reservation policy had assured the defeat of Native Americans, there was a temptation to give their demise a tragic dimension. Images of feckless and incapable Indians were accompanied by a more sentimental vision of noble savages who had failed to survive, not so much because they were inadequate, but because their simplicity, valiant as it might sometimes be, was bound to give way before the progressive march of a superior race.

Attitudes towards Native Americans were repeated in encounters with other peoples as the United States advanced West. In the 1830s, as Americans came into open contact with Latin Americans in the Southwest, a range of stereotypes emerged that provided a mix of justifications for the appropriation of territory or for intervention in Latin American affairs. Latin Americans were, like Native Americans, backward-looking in their bigotry and corruption, and unfitted for the exercise of political responsibility, or essentially childlike and untutored, and thus in clear need of the training and education that Americans could provide. Both perspectives emphasised American superiority and Hispanic inferiority.

Such attitudes, while they have become progressively tempered by the way in which explicitly racialist thought has come under scrutiny throughout the twentieth century, nevertheless continued to act as a filter through which foreign policy leaders and many ordinary citizens saw foreign interventions, as well as how those interventions were represented in a range of cultural forms. During the Second World War, despite both official and unofficial American hostility to the legacy of European imperialism, many American politicians, military commanders and ordinary soldiers found it difficult to divest themselves of a racialist perspective, both with regard to their enemies in Asia, as well as those whom they were trying to protect against aggression. Christopher Thorne has commented that the Pacific War of 1941 to 1945 was to a considerable degree a racial war, not so much because of its immediate causes, but in the sense that Western suspicion of Japanese behaviour, both before and during the war, fed off a hundred years of explicitly racialist arguments about the characteristics of the Japanese people. American policy in an area like East Asia was often significantly affected by perceptions and prejudices, which need to be examined alongside its long-held commit ments to liberty and equality (Thorne 1979: 5–9). Americans brought to Vietnam, as they had brought to much of Asia in their dealings with the region throughout the twentieth century, an ethnocentrism that frequently bordered on the explicitly racialist arguments for American power which figures like Strong had voiced in the nineteenth century. It is true that during the 1940s and 1950s American officials were cautious about being dragged into a 'white man's' colonial war in Vietnam, but under the pressure of events in late 1950s and early 1960s these concerns were often forced to give way to the more basic assumption that Americans knew what was best for the region. Richard Slotkin, among others, has argued that there have been strong continuities between the language and attitudes of Americans in Vietnam and the assumptions, which lay behind Western expansion in the nineteenth century. American soldiers frequently called their Vietnamese enemies Indians, and the jungle in and out of which they moved quickly became Indian Country. Similarly, their use of terms like 'slopes' and 'gooks' served to dehumanise their enemies in a manner which drew on the racial epithets used against the Japanese in the Second World War (Slotkin 1998: 494–6). As Christian Appy has argued in his analysis of combat troops during the war, 'The point was not to know the enemy but to despise him.' Military training encouraged hostility towards all Vietnamese, whether members of the Viet Cong or non-combatants. As one veteran recalled, 'the only thing that they told us about the Vietnamese was that they were gooks; they were to be killed. Nobody sits around and gives you the historical and cultural background. They're the enemy' (Appy 1993: 107).

The presentation of the case for the War on Terror by the George W. Bush administration frequently drew on images of the Arab world which framed policy as the patriotic defence of civilisation, and tended to generalise about negative attributes of Islamic identity. Representative strategies included demonisation of America's enemies as 'evil'. The photographs taken of Iraqi prisoners at Abu Ghraib in 2003 in a range of humiliating poses clearly fit into the same kind of pattern. Their use of physical coercion and sexual degradation in an effort to gain more intelligence about the insurgency explicitly revealed assumptions of racial and cultural supremacy. As Fred Halliday has noted, it was because the victims were from a subordinate people that they were subjected to their tortures (Halliday 2005).

AMERICA AS A MODEL

Alongside notions of mission and cultural supremacy, Americans often assumed, when assessing the status of other nations, that the American pattern of development had some kind of general application. As Emily Rosenberg has suggested, 'To many Americans, their country's economic and social history became a universal model' (Rosenberg 1982: 7). If other countries, particularly those outside Europe, wanted to follow the path to modernisation, then they should seek to emulate the American experience. To those who guided American policy, this meant, among other things, a suspicion of radical political change of a kind that threatened the stability deemed necessary for economic growth. Although the United States had been born out of a revolutionary struggle, this did not mean that all revolutions were of themselves good things, since they might undercut those conditions which would supposedly promote modernisation, such as private enterprise, plentiful cheap labour and unrestricted access to land development. Particularly after the Russian Revolution of 1917, when American forces had briefly intervened on the side of anti-Bolshevik forces, many American officials came to see revolutionary activity as a barrier to American influence, even when they might be in sympathy with, say, the anti-colonialist ambitions of those who were tempted to join such struggles. This, of course, raised policy problems. As Rosenberg has put it: 'How could foreign countries who resisted American-prescribed "development" (often called "civilisation" or "modernisation") be handled without violating their "liberty" to try out competing ideas or techniques?' (ibid.: 234).

One way around this dilemma was to argue that the United States could help such countries to see the light, and discard the blinkers which restricted their vision. American belief in the supremacy of its own missionary role would justify persuading peoples to accept American ways. Allan Bloom revealingly argued in his best-selling work *The Closing of the American Mind* (1987) that what he called 'the American project' was not just for Americans: 'When we Americans speak seriously about politics, we mean that our principles of freedom and equality and the rights based on them are rational and everywhere applicable.' The Second World War was for Bloom not simply a struggle to defeat a dangerous enemy. It was 'really an educational project undertaken to force those who did not accept these principles to do so' (Bloom 1987: 153). The American occupation of Germany and Japan after the Second World War can be seen in this light. Both societies had to be cleansed of aggression and militarism and reconstructed along American lines. President George W. Bush himself justified nation-building in Iraq by referring to both examples:

> Following World War II, we lifted up the defeated nations of Japan and Germany and stood with them as they built representative governments. We committed years and resources to this cause. And that effort has been repaid many times over in three generations of friendship and peace.
>
> (Ferguson 2004: 69)

There was, however, another less positive precedent for the problems nation-building might entail. In the 1950s and 1960s considerable efforts had been made to create a viable state in South Vietnam that would provide a bulwark against communist expansion. It failed, in part, as Robert McNamara, one of its key architects, later argued, because Americans viewed the people and leaders of South Vietnam in terms of their own experience, with a thirst for – and a determination to fight for – freedom and democracy. Americans, he concluded, 'did not have the god-given right to shape every nation in [their] own image as [they] chose' (McNamara 1999: 322–3). Graham Greene put it more mordantly in his indictment of the early stages of American involvement within Vietnam in his novel *The Quiet American* (1955), where an English journalist delivers a damning judgement on Alden Pike, the CIA operative at the heart of the story: 'I never knew a man who had better motives for all the trouble he caused' (Greene 1955: 63).

The concept of America as a model that needed to be implemented across the world was also reflected in 'The Statement of Principles' of the Project for the New American Century, the leading neo-conservative think tank, which argued in 1997 that the country needed 'to accept responsibility for America's unique role in preserving and extending an international order friendly to our security, our prosperity, and our principles'. Among its signatories were future key members of the George W. Bush administration, such as Secretary of Defense Donald Rumsfeld, Vice-President Dick Cheney and Deputy Secretary of Defense (and later president of the World Bank) Paul Wolfowitz (Project for the New American Century). Perhaps unsurprisingly, the introduction to the National Security Strategy of 2002 was couched in similar language: 'The great struggles of the twentieth century between liberty and totalitarianism ended with a decisive victory for the forces of freedom – and a single sustainable model for national success: freedom, democracy, and free enterprise' (National Security Strategy 2002).

However, assertions about the 'victory of freedom' raised as many questions as they answered. As Eric Foner has pointed out, the meanings that Americans attach to the model of freedom have regularly changed over time. Freedom has not been a fixed concept, but one that has been continually debated and contested throughout American history. The rhetoric of American freedom could disguise profound disagreements about what the term actually implied, in the context both of the country's domestic history, and its relationships with the outside world. This has been clear throughout Henry Luce's 'American Century', as encounters with a range of foreign 'others' have emphasised specific attributes of 'freedom' at one time and downgraded others. During the Second World War, for instance, Franklin D. Roosevelt's rallying cry of the Four Freedoms – freedom of speech, freedom of worship, freedom from want and freedom from fear – began the process of committing the United States to a different kind of internationalist role, one that involved constructive engagement with the world. His vice-president, Henry Wallace, in 1942, emphasised that this vision involved a strong element of social justice when he called for the twentieth century to become 'century of the common man'. During the Cold War struggle against Soviet Communism, while 'freedom of speech' remained important, 'freedom from want', perhaps because it sounded too socialistic, gave way to the freedom to consume as a dominant concept that would ensure prosperity and happiness. Right at the end of the Cold War, Ronald Reagan regularly intoned the American mission to spread the idea of freedom, but by now it incorporated limited government and free enterprise, along with anti-communism (Foner 2000). Obama, in his 2008 campaign, talked about advancing 'a common humanity which would join together, through constant cooperation . . . to meet the challenges of the twenty-first century' (Obama 2008b: 276). All people shared America's aspiration to 'live free from fear and free from want' (ibid.: 280). Giving his remarks a more nationalist slant, he declared in his 2011 State of the Union Address that (Americans) do big things. 'From the earliest days of our founding, America has been the story of ordinary people who dare to dream. That's how we win the future' (Obama 2011). In all these cases, however, clarification of what freedom might mean could be found in attempts to apply it in specific historical circumstances and would frequently reveal that ongoing tension between a commitment to American leadership and multilateral cooperation.

PRE-EMPTION AND UNILATERALISM

September 11th (2001), with its profound impact on America's sense of its own security, highlighted many of these themes in public debate. For many Americans the attacks destroyed the sense of relative geographical safety they had enjoyed for much of their history. '9/11', recalled Condoleeza Rice two years later, 'crystallized our vulnerability . . . [It] changed the lives of every American and the strategic perspective of the United States' (Leffler 2005: 406). In his introduction to the National Security Strategy of 2002, President George W. Bush emphasised that 'in the new world we have entered, the only path to peace and security is the path of action' (National Security Strategy 2002). By that time, he had already gone on the offensive. First, he determined not only to pursue al-Qaida, but also to confront Afghanistan, which provided support and bases for the group. No distinction would be made between the terrorists who committed the September 11th attacks and those who harboured them. In his address to Congress on 20 September 2001, Bush went further:

> We will pursue nations that provide aid or safe haven to terrorism. Every nation, in every region, now has a decision to make. Either you

are with us, or you are with the terrorists. From this day forward, any nation that continues to harbor or support terrorism will be regarded by the United States as a hostile regime.

(Bush 2001b)

This argument was reflected in the decision to invade Afghanistan in 2001, but it would also be used in the subsequent justification to attack Iraq in 2003. At the heart of this strategy lay the conviction that concepts of deterrence would be insufficient to guarantee America's security in the future. Instead, any future threat had to be pre-empted by offensive action (National Security Strategy 2002). From the administration's point of view this meant not only seeking to destroy terrorist groups themselves, but also acting militarily against those states that sheltered them. At this point, John Lewis Gaddis has argued, the concept of pre-emption became entangled with the concept of prevention. Preemption involved the right, accepted under international law, to take action against a state about to attack. Prevention, far less accepted, involved a war against a state that might be a threat in the future. The National Security Strategy of 2002 talked about the right of the United States to act pre-emptively 'to forestall or prevent ... hostile acts by adversaries' but in a world where it was becoming increasingly difficult to foresee when terrorist attacks might occur, it became tempting to go after the states that might be helping them (ibid.) This conflation of prevention and pre-emption, however, was profoundly unsettling in an international order built on the key principle of national sovereignty. As Gaddis puts it, 'For the world's most powerful state suddenly to announce that its security requires violating the sovereignty of certain other states whenever it chooses cannot help but make all other states nervous' (Gaddis 2005: 3).

Former Secretary of State Henry Kissinger put it more directly: 'It cannot be either in American national interests or the world's interest to develop principles that grant every nation an unfettered pre-emption against its own definition of threats to its security' (Kissinger 2002). This was clearly revealed in the war on Iraq, when the United States failed to gain the support it hoped for in its efforts to overthrow what it saw as an aggressive and destructive dictatorship, which threatened not only its own people but also the international community. Foreign suspicion of its motives was encouraged by what was seen, once again, as the arrogance of American power, and the apparent willingness of the administration to act unilaterally if necessary, without either the approval of the United Nations or a broad-based international coalition. President Bush's assertions about the need to promote freedom, and America's essential goodness, however deeply felt they may have been, appeared as a simple cover for American self-interest. This was only reinforced by subsequent revelations that the justification of intervention in Iraq was based on intelligence information about both Iraq's links with al-Qaida and its capacity to threaten American security with weapons of mass destruction that was at best flawed.

One influential set of arguments holds that these events of Bush's first term amounted to a revolution in American foreign policy, not so much in terms of long-term goals, but more in the methods used to achieve them. It was this aspect in particular that alarmed many of America's allies and antagonised international opinion. The revolution, clearly outlined in the National Security Strategy, consisted of a reliance on the unilateral exercise of American power rather than international law, the championing of a proactive doctrine of pre-emption at the expense of deterrence and containment. It turned away from treaties as a means of trying to control the proliferation of weapons of mass destruction, and instead opted for military strikes and the promotion of more sophisticated missile defence systems. It resorted to regime change, as in Afghanistan and Iraq, at the expense of direct negotiations. In seeking to achieve its aims, it depended less on existing formal alliances than on ad-hoc coalitions which it used to support an essentially unilateralist strategy (Daalder and Lindsay 2003a). James Maan argues that the Strategy's emphasis on pre-emption involved 'an entirely new set of ideas and principles', which created 'a new conception of American foreign policy' of the same kind of significance as the Truman Doctrine of 1947 (Mann 2004: 329–30). At the extreme, it is argued,

> these notions form a neoimperial vision in which the United States arrogates to itself the global role of setting standards, determining threats, using force and meting out justice. . . . America is to be less bound to its partners and to global rules and institutions while it steps forward to play a more unilateral and anticipatory role in attacking terrorist threats and confronting rogue states. The United States will use its unrivalled military power to manage the global order.
>
> (Ikenberry 2002: 49)

On the other hand it has been equally strongly argued that President Bush's ideological vision was marked by continuity as much as radical change, and that it contained strong links with the perspectives of previous administrations, not only in the twentieth century but stretching back to the beginning of the Republic. For Walter LaFeber, American policy had always been characterised by unilateralism, in a way which allowed for 'freedom of action for diplomacy and military operations . . . over two centuries of American foreign policy' (LaFeber 2002: 558). Much of the language of the National Security Strategy enunciated in 2002 was very similar in tone to many earlier statements about America's role in the world, including, for instance, proclamations by the Clinton administration about American policy. Melvyn Leffler, too, argues that 'unilateralism is quintessentially American', pointing out that pre-emption had a significant strategic role in American history, stretching back to intervention in the Caribbean and Central America during the early twentieth century. Although the Cold War involved the creation of multilateral alliances and institutions, American presidents always retained the option to take the unilateral road should the situation demand it. 'Allied reluctance to act should not inhibit the United States from taking action including the use of nuclear weapons, to prevent Communist territorial gains when such action is clearly necessary to U.S. security', declared the Eisenhower administration in the mid 1950s (Leffler 2005: 398–9, 405). In 1994, Madeleine Albright, American Ambassador to the United Nations, and later Secretary of State for President Clinton, declared that the United States would behave multilaterally when it could and unilaterally when it must.

Another approach to understanding both the difficulties the United States faced in Iraq, and its reputation in the world, is Leffler's argument that at times of national crisis, when the nation's security appears to be under threat, values and ideals tended to be asserted in ways that override a realistic assessment of interests. This is particularly the case when power appears to indicate that the means exist to realise those values. One consequence is a temptation to formulate policy in terms of overarching goals linked to deeply held beliefs, but without always appraising the full implications of what a specific policy might involve (Leffler 2005: 395–6). An example here was the presentation of the War on Terror in terms of opposing binaries – 'good' versus evil, 'liberation' versus 'oppression', 'progress' versus 'the past', 'freedom' versus 'tyranny' – which were difficult to achieve and encouraged 'over reach'. In June 2002, for instance, President Bush emphasised the importance of 'the language of right and wrong'. There could be 'no neutrality between justice and cruelty, between the innocent and the guilty'. America was in 'a conflict between good and evil' (Bush 2002). The phrase 'War on Terror' itself encouraged a sense of open-ended commitment without a clear sense of specific aims that might indicate when the war had been successfully prosecuted. One result was to assume that military victory in Iraq would quickly lead to the realisation of the goals enunciated in pre-war rhetoric, and to underestimate the scale of reconstruction that would be needed after war was over. Undue emphasis on values and beliefs, of the kind discussed earlier in this chapter, blinded policy-makers both to the long-term dangers of unilateralism and to the potential problems involved in spreading freedom and democracy in the aftermath of war.

EMPIRE

Whether the underlying unilateralism of American interventions in Afghanistan and Iraq marked a decisive change or not, it helped to encourage a growing disaffection with American policy in the wider world. To many outside the United States, the administration's apparent determination to go its own way, without either the approval of the United Nations or the support of a number of its allies, only seemed to demonstrate according to one representative critic, the former German Chancellor, Helmut Schmidt, that it was moving in an increasingly imperialist direction (Steinmetz 2003). This perspective chimed with a renewed debate, both within the United States and without, as to whether 'empire' might not be the most appropriate way of describing both America's rise to world power and contemporary American dominance, particularly as a way of undermining the traditional emphasis upon American exceptionalism. The experience of the United States, it is argued, has to be assessed using the same criteria as apply to other nations. Americans may say that they are different but that claim has to be understood as part of an articulation of national identity rather than as an empirical description of American power. Exceptionalism argues that America has somehow 'escaped' from history; what matters, many of these critics insist, is that America be reclaimed for history, be dragged 'into the historical mainstream' (Cox 2005: 26). For exceptionalists, of course, empire was the one thing America was not. When asked in an interview on the Arabic satellite television network Aljazeera whether the United States was 'empire-building' in the Middle East, Secretary of Defense Donald Rumsfeld replied, 'We don't seek empires. We're not imperialistic. We never have been' (Daalder and Lindsay 2003a: 361). As this reveals, Americans have often disliked the term 'empire' because they feel it has derogatory implications and contradicts the official beliefs of the Republic as articulated in the Declaration of Independence and other founding statements of the new nation. Anti-colonialism, as Melani McAlister has argued, 'formed the heart of American national origin stories' and allowed policy-makers to advocate an international order led by a benevolent United States committed to liberalism and democracy (McAlister 2001: 47). 'Empire' involved succumbing to the temptations of power in a way that threatened civic virtue. The great historical example here was Rome, whose fate had to be avoided at all costs if republican political and cultural ideals were to prevail in the United States. For Americans to admit to empire would be to signal the end of the Republic. Critics have charged, however, that it is precisely such 'denial and disavowal of empire [which] has long served as the ideological cornerstone of U.S. imperialism and a key component of American exceptionalism' (Kaplan 2004: 3). Even a sympathetic advocate of American power has recently suggested that America is 'an empire in denial' (Ferguson 2004: 6–7).

As these last comments indicate, use of the concept of empire comes from a number of different directions as part of an internal debate within America about the country's past, present and future. One set of arguments insists that American power is a threat both to the world and to America itself. Another argues that what the world needs is more sustained and effective American involvement. For a critic of America's international role like Chalmers Johnson, the American empire is 'based on the projection of military power to every corner of the world and on the use of American capital and markets to force global economic integration on our terms, at whatever the costs to others' (Johnson 2002: 7). Although he defines this empire as 'informal', and different in kind from empires of the past which are based on territorial domination, it is nevertheless marked by covert operations, secrecy, the indiscriminate use of violence and regular support for dictators (ibid.: 8–34). Disguising the direction they were taking, American leaders cloaked their foreign policy in euphemisms such as 'lone superpower', 'indispensable nation', 'reluctant sheriff', 'humanitarian intervention' and 'globalization'. 'However, with the advent of the George W. Bush administration in 2001, these pretences gave way to assertions of the Second Coming of the Roman Empire.' The result of this hijacking of the Republic would be 'endless war, the loss of Constitutional liberties, and financial ruin' (Johnson 2004: 1–13). 'America today *is* Rome', agreed Andrew Bacevich, in a thoroughgoing indictment of American militarism (Bacevich 2004: 244).

On the other hand Max Boot, a neo-conservative journalist close to the Bush administration, while accepting the concept of empire, made a very different claim. Compared with the grasping old imperialism of the past, America's 'liberal imperialism' pursued far different, and more ambitious, goals. It aimed to 'instil democracy in lands that have known tyranny, in the hope that doing so [would] short-circuit terrorism, military aggression, and weapons proliferation' (Boot 2003: 361). Where European imperialism fought to subjugate 'natives', Americans 'fight to bring them democracy and the rule of law' (ibid.: 366). From this perspective American empire was a positive virtue, one which would be of immeasurable benefit to the rest of the international community. Niall Ferguson agreed that an American empire had a positive role to play in encouraging stability and the advancement of freedom. The world needed an effective liberal empire and the United States was the best candidate for the job. He was, however, less confident than Boot about the country's willingness to undertake the heavy personal and economic burdens such a role implied (Ferguson 2004: 301).

One way of circumventing this kind of debate may be to employ the term 'empire' in a more dispassionate sense. A helpful formulation comes from John Lewis Gaddis in his reassessment of the imperial rivalry of the Soviet Union and the United States after 1945, where he defines empire as 'a situation in which a single state shapes the behaviour of others, whether directly or indirectly, partially or completely, by means that can range from the outright use of force through intimidation, dependency, inducement, and even inspiration' (Gaddis 1997: 27). From this kind of perspective it is difficult to deny that America has frequently acted in an imperial manner for much of its history, but it does allow for more considered judgements about the extent, nature and effect of that activity. One problem with aspects of the polemical debates about the American empire as a force for good or for harm is that they assume that American influence actually works. In terms of Johnson's critique of American empire, for instance, almost every aspect of American involvement in the world is taken as a sign of America's ambition for imperial domination. However, as Michael Cox points out, 'under modern conditions, it is extraordinarily difficult for any single state to exercise preponderant influence at all times', even for one as powerful as the United States (Cox 2005: 25). Describing those aspects of American power which are imperialistic, but being aware of the qualifications necessary in using the concept of empire, may be a more helpful approach when assessing the operation of American power than is allowed either in the exceptionalist argument or in wholesale denunciations or affirmations of American policy. The United States may have acted in an imperial manner in the run-up to the Iraq War, but despite its explicit power it still failed to persuade some of its allies to join it against Saddam Hussein. Following its difficulties in Iraq, it had marked problems in influencing events in the way it would have liked whether in Iran, North Africa or Egypt. Both the American political system and American public opinion also work to undermine empire. Every 'imperial' president has to leave office within a specified time, along with his imperial advisers, while public opinion has proved reluctant to support military adventures for very long, particularly when positive results are not immediately achieved. The attacks of September 11th had encouraged an unprecedented degree of national solidarity, but it was not clear whether this amounted to a long-term mandate for interventionism or that the American people would not tire of the War on Terror before it was won, whenever that would be. Only two years after the end of the Iraq War, 42 per cent of Americans believed the United States should 'mind its own business internationally and let other countries get along the best they can on their own' (Pew 2005).

IMAGE

The emphasis on values and beliefs could also backfire from another perspective. As a number of commentators noted, September 11th transformed Bush's image as presidential leader. His approval ratings quickly soared to an unprecedented 90 per cent, as he put himself at the

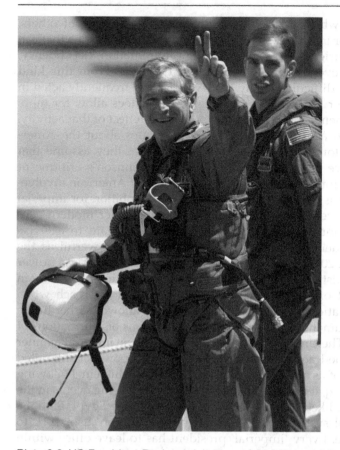

Plate 9.2 US President Bush ready to board S3 Viking Jet in San Diego, 2003.
© Reuters / Corbis

forefront of the national response to the attacks, through a series of dramatic images like his impromptu speech with a bullhorn in the ruins of the World Trade Center and his subsequent televised addresses to the nation. As commander-in-chief at a time of national crisis, he would provide the heroism necessary to inspire the American people. Television and the other media could deliver the means to transmit the implementation of his idealistic vision of advancing freedom. David Holloway, for instance, has shown how much of an effort was made by the administration to present its foreign strategy, particularly the war in Iraq, in a positive light, to the extent of staging spectacular events for media consumption (Holloway 2008: 58–74). As Jon Roper has argued, however, while television can often elevate presidential leadership, it can also help to undermine it (Roper 2005: 132–40). The warning here had been provided by Vietnam, where the television networks had relayed back into the nation's living rooms a devastating mix of American casualties, civilian suffering and North Vietnamese/Viet Cong resistance, in a manner which did a great deal to damage the positions of both Lyndon B. Johnson and Richard Nixon. The Gulf War of 1991, in this respect, was constructed as part of a determined attempt to avoid the 'Vietnam syndrome', particularly through its presentation as a controlled and regulated media spectacle. This was achieved through limiting the war to the specific short-term objective of pushing Saddam Hussein out of Kuwait and back into Iraq, and restricting its duration to 100 days, in comparison to the 10,000-day conflict in Vietnam. In the case of the War on Terror that degree of control would prove far harder to achieve, because of the open-ended nature of the war aims and the sheer difficulty of reaching a satisfactory outcome within a time-scale acceptable to opinion back in America. The carefully orchestrated image of President Bush preparing to fly to the USS *Abraham Lincoln* to announce the end of combat operations in Iraq was clearly an attempt to reinforce a particular version of American masculinity. Dressed as a USAF pilot in the manner of Tom Cruise in *Top Gun*, Bush was tied to a sense of heroic but modest leadership, and restrained strength. However, this version of American victory was quickly challenged by the televised pictures of relentless suicide bombings in the streets of Iraq's cities, not to mention the photographs from Abu Ghraib prison a year later. It was also undermined by the failure to find Saddam Hussein's weapons of mass destruction and sustained investigation of the accuracy of intelligence justifications for the war in the first place.

In February 2004 Bush declared in an interview: 'I am a war president. I make decisions here in the Oval Office in foreign policy matters with war on my mind' (BBC 2004), but by the end of his administration it had become clear that maintaining the image of a successful war leader was extremely difficult, whatever the attempts of his administration to manage the presentation of events.

ANTI-AMERICANISM

Another feature of the early twenty-first century has been the attention paid to the apparent rise of anti-American feeling (see also the discussion of Americanisation in Chapter 10). In terms of international opinion, surveys suggested that American efforts to 'make the world a better place' received a cool and often hostile response. In 2008, in much of Western Europe, with the exception of Britain, less than half of those canvassed had a favourable opinion of the United States. Even in Britain, positive ratings had declined from 83 per cent in 1999–2000 to 53 per cent. Elsewhere ratings were even lower. In Islamic countries such as Pakistan, Jordan and Turkey under 20 per cent viewed America in a positive light.

Polls also indicated a strong feeling that the United States pursued a unilateral foreign policy, with large majorities in both Europe and the Middle East believing that the United States did not consider their countries' interests when making foreign policy decisions. Many people outside the United States saw administration rhetoric as evidence that their views did not count. Of those countries that were part of the US-led coalition during the war in Iraq only in Holland did majority opinion still support intervention. In countries that had refused to participate in the Iraq War, huge majorities in Europe and the Muslim world continued to believe that their governments were wise to stay out of the conflict (Pew 2010). Faced with similar criticism in 2001, President Bush had professed his amazement 'that there is such misunderstanding of what our country is about. Like most Americans, I just can't believe it. Because I know how good we are' (Daalder and Lindsay 2003b: 73).

At one level this kind of suspicion of America's role has deep historical roots. Just as the beginnings of American exceptionalism can be found as early as the seventeenth century, so too has America's growth been accompanied by the regular rise and fall of anti-Americanism. Hostility to the United States might also reflect not just criticism of a particular set of actions, but also a deeper resentment of what the country seemed to stand for in the world. America itself was the problem, not just its policies. Anti-American feeling could transmute into anti-Americanism, defined as a set of assumptions about American identity, against which other countries or groups could assert themselves. American critics of the phenomenon, particularly from the right, have drawn attention to what they see as its 'irrational' qualities (Hollander 1995). That, however, evades the issue too easily. Dismissal of any criticism of American behaviour as unjustified only echoes Bush's assertion of America's innate 'goodness'. Nevertheless, despite the results of public surveys, anti-Americanism has been notoriously hard to pin down; the sheer range of reactions to American culture and political behaviour have made it difficult to find any single overarching explanation for them all. A more appropriate response is to note the widespread nature of anti-Americanism in practice, and to seek to understand how it has often been 'inflected according to histories and traditions of individual nations' (Crockatt 2003: 57). As Robert Singh has noted, 'Its intensity, coherence, and expressions [have varied] tremendously across the non-American world' (Singh 2006: 44–5). It is also the case that the complexity and variety of American society and culture itself has invited a widespread range of responses. As one recent discussion concludes,

> the persistence of anti-Americanism, as well as the great variety of
> forms that it takes, reflects . . . the polyvalence of a complex and
> kaleidoscopic American society in which observers can find whatever

they don't like – from Protestantism to porn. The complexity of anti-Americanism reflects the polyvalence of America itself.

(Katzenstein and Keohane 2006).

At the same time, however, the emergence of anti-Americanism at specific historical moments has also been influenced by American power. As George Herring has argued, 'the greater a nation's global influence, the greater its capacity to provoke envy and anger' (Herring 2008: 10). In this respect, anti-Americanism has often drawn on reaction to specific foreign policy choices such as War on Vietnam in the 1960s and 1970s or the invasion of Iraq in 2003, which seem to show a disjunction between the kind of rhetoric discussed earlier, with its open-ended commitment to freedom and democracy, and the realities of American behaviour in practice. These might provide evidence that it was America itself which was 'wrong', but it also drew attention to the decisions of individual administrations. Changing an administration or a policy might result in a decline in anti-American feeling. This could clearly be seen in the international reaction to Barack Obama's election in 2008, and the widespread hope that this signalled a significant shift to a different set of foreign policies. An example here was the decision in October 2009 of the Norwegian Nobel Committee to award Obama its annual Peace Prize, even though he had spent less than a year in office. He had, it declared, 'created a new climate in international politics' which emphasised dialogue, negotiation and multilateral diplomacy. He had captured attention by promoting a more constructive role for the United States in the world, through an emphasis on democracy and human rights, and a willingness to face climate change (Nobel Foundation 2009).

This emphasis on Obama's image, before the implementation of any of his policies, resulted in a surge in favourable poll ratings in 2009, and even though there was a slight falling away, by 2014 65 per cent of a global survey retained a positive view of what the Pew Research Center described as 'the American brand' (Pew 2015). Obama's own rankings, however, had declined from 2009 when they stood at 62 per cent in global terms to 55 per cent in 2014, which showed how difficult it was to maintain a favourable image in a turbulent environment. It also suggested the significance of Jessica Gienow-Hecht's observation that 'the challenge for the United States today is how to live and act conscientiously in a world where people will always blame the Americans' (Gienow-Hecht 2006).

WAR AT HOME: SECURITY AND LIBERTY

As in the case of the war in Vietnam, the War on Terror had consequences for the domestic front in a number of ways, which raised questions about the balance between security and liberty. An important aspect of the reaction to September 11th was the proliferation of a range of new security measures at home designed to provide a degree of protection against possible attacks in the future. The sense of danger the nation faced from abroad, was inextricably linked to anxiety about challenges from within. A central feature here was the introduction of a new Department of Homeland Security which was given responsibility for leading a unified national effort to secure America. At the same time, Congress passed the USA Patriot Act on 21 October 2001, to give the FBI and other agencies more investigative and surveillance powers with regard to forms of communication such as mobile phones and the Internet. It also extended the authority of the Attorney General to detain immigrants considered to be a potential threat, a move taken without approval from the courts. In November 2001, President Bush also signed an executive order legalising the trial of alien terrorists in military tribunals, outside the jurisdiction of criminal law. This approach was symbolised by the appointment of John Ashcroft as Attorney General. Ashcroft, a right-wing evangelical Christian, quickly developed a reputation as a robust defender of the need for security at all costs, even if it meant some restriction of civil liberty. Although these measures at first had more or less complete support across the party political spectrum and in terms of public opinion, they also gradually revealed splits within the wider culture. The online conservative magazine, *Front Page*, charged that 'most of the groups that adamantly oppose the USA Patriot Act are oriented toward worrying more about terrorists' civil liberties than their murderous intentions' (Weinkopf 2003). President Bush himself strongly defended the Patriot Act during the 2004 election.

> Inside the United States, where the war began, we must continue to give homeland security and law enforcement personnel every tool they need to defend us. And one of those essential tools is the Patriot Act, which allows federal law enforcement to better share information, to track terrorists, to disrupt their cells and to seize their assets.
>
> (Bush 2004a)

Such attitudes persisted into the 2010s. After the Republican success in the 2010 Congressional elections, one of the party's first moves was to use the House Homeland Security Committee to accuse the American Muslim community of not having done enough to demonstrate its loyalty by working to prevent the radicalisation of its members.

From an opposing perspective, it was equally strongly argued that the crisis had led to an attempt to establish political conformity and the stifling of dissent. The US media had been negligent in failing to assess the strategies and rhetoric of the president and his advisers more carefully and their reporting was characterised by docility and compliance. It was not helped by the imposition of stringent restrictions on the press in terms of reporting on overseas campaigns (LaFeber 2002: 558). The *New York Times* admitted in 2004 that its coverage in the run-up to the Iraq War had not been 'as rigorous as it should have been' (Younge 2004). The relationship of the media with the administration, it was argued, could be seen as part of a military–industrial–entertainment complex that provided propaganda and legitimation for US military intervention. Furthermore, protecting 'homeland security' involved

> a highly illiberal rightwing law and order program of unleashing government agencies to surveil, arrest, and detain those suspected of being terrorists in what many saw as the most outrageous assault on civil liberties and the open society in U.S. history.
>
> (Kellner 2003: 40)

The American Civil Liberties Union charged that the responses to dissent by many government officials threatened the underpinnings of democracy itself (ACLU 2005). For one critic this amounted to 'a Jihad on civil liberties, a systematic assault on democracy and constitutional balance of powers', headed by a 'Talibanesque Attorney General' in John Ashcroft (Kellner 2003: 101). The Bush administration was seeking to create 'a dictatorial police state where TV channels were becoming equally subservient to the wishes of the Texas Fuhrer as the fascist media had been to the dictates of the Third Reich' (ibid.: 102).

Amy Kaplan argued that the use of the term 'homeland', as in the Department of Homeland Security, had revealing connotations about the implications of the War on Terror for American society. Homeland, she suggested, 'appeals to common bloodlines, ancient loyalties, and often to notions of racial and ethnic homogeneity . . . a reliance on a shared mythic past engrained in the land itself' (Kaplan 2004: 8). In such a world, distinctions were inevitably drawn between those who could claim America as their birthright and those who might hold a less secure place within the country, because of their status as recent immigrants with shared loyalties to other cultures, other places. The holding of almost 700 prisoners, mainly captives from the war in Afghanistan, at the US naval base at Guantanamo was also taken as evidence of the dangerous implications of the way in which the War on Terror had repercussions for human rights at home. It was a 'mobile, ambiguous space . . . between the domestic and the foreign', which America controlled, but where the courts had limited power to protect the rights of prisoners. It reflected the 'authoritarian incursions [of the Bush administration] against civil liberties, the rights of immigrants, and the provision for basic human needs' (ibid.: 13–15).

One of the most popular indictments of the Bush administration's strategies in its first term was Michael Moore's film, *Fahrenheit 9/11* (2004). Independently funded after Disney withdrew its initial backing, Moore used the documentary format to mount a sustained assault on what he presented as the betrayal of republican values in the War on Terror. Bringing together an extensive range of sources including news footage, extracts from TV shows and Hollywood movies, and the direct testimony of citizens opposed to the administration, Moore sought to create the opportunity for mass audiences to engage in debate about where the country was heading. Moving beyond conventional notions of documentary as 'objective' and 'detached', he developed what Holloway describes as a 'performative ' approach, through which he explicitly sought to confront the administration's claims to 'truth' by exposing the construction involved in any form of representation (Holloway 2008: 100–1). Critics charged that this approach, supported by Moore's own central role in the film, ran the risk of sensationalising his argument, and succumbed to the manipulation of witnesses and supporting evidence. On the other hand this needs to be weighed against Hollywood's wider reluctance to engage in any similar kind of discussion about the impact of 9/11.

Just as the rhetoric of President Bush echoed earlier themes in American attitudes towards the outside world, so too this kind of dissent had plenty of precedents. Generally these kinds of arguments sought to resist the claim that liberty and a full role in world affairs could go hand in hand. Pursuit of some kind of interventionist or imperialist role abroad would threaten the stability of the republic at home and endanger those virtues which distinguished the American experiment from the experience of other nations. The acquisition of empire would mean the development of a more powerful army, a stronger executive and a larger bureaucracy in a manner that would threaten the democratic and egalitarian nature of the American way of life. 'Militarism is an evil from which it has been our glory to be free', the American Anti-Imperialist League had declared in 1899, in opposition to the acquisition of the Philippines in the aftermath of the Spanish–American War. Randolph Bourne, in 1918, had warned that, 'War is the health of the State. It automatically sets in motion throughout society those irresistible forces for uniformity, for passionate cooperation with the Government in coercing into obedience the minority groups and individuals who lack the larger herd sense' (Bourne 1992: 360). Martin Luther King, in his speech 'Beyond Vietnam: A Time to Break Silence' given in 1967, spoke of the ways in which the injustice of the war in Vietnam was spilling out onto the streets of America's cities, with corrosive effects for America's values (King 1967).

During the 2008 election Barack Obama had spoken about the need for change in the conduct of foreign policy and for the way in which national security at home should not compromise America's commitment to civil liberty and freedom of expression. Such a promise would prove far harder to deliver after his inauguration. In a number of different areas critics charged that his administration was continuing as many of his predecessor's policies as it discarded. In 2011, the American Civil Liberties Union could still charge that there was 'an urgent need to restore individual freedoms, due process rights and our system of checks and balances' (ACLU 2011). Obama, for instance, had promised to close Guantanamo Bay as a symbol of the excesses of the war against terrorism, but two years into his presidency it still contained over 150 inmates. 'Ideological exclusion', or refusing visas to foreign nationals with supposedly radical views, continued from the Bush years. Perhaps the most striking example of the tension between liberty and security came with the disclosure by a whistle-blower, Ed Snowden, that the National Security Agency had used the authority of the Patriot Act to undertake mass surveillance programmes on both American citizens and those of other nations. Methods used included the collection of telephone records, tracking of online communication through tapping into a range of Internet companies including Facebook, Google, Yahoo and Microsoft, and eavesdropping on the phones and offices of foreign politicians. These activities took place in both the George W. Bush and Obama administrations. In 2011 Obama signed a four-year extension of the Patriot Act, though as a senator he had been a critic of its provisions, on the grounds that it was unnecessary to protect the country against terrorism. He later admitted, though, in a speech in 2014, that 'the risk of government overreach, the possibility that we lose some of our core liberties in pursuit of security [had] also become more pronounced' and that there needed to be more scrutiny of surveillance activities (Obama 2014a). One limited result was the Freedom Act of 2015, which sought to end mass collection of phone records by the NSA, though anti-surveillance critics charged that it did not go far enough in restraining the organisation's activities.

CONCLUSION

If we return here to President Bush's rhetoric about America's purpose in the world cited in the first part of this chapter, it is clear that 'advancing the cause of freedom' contained with it a range of difficulties and ambiguities, both for effective policy and for America's reputation. The gap between idealised rhetoric and the harsher world of policy implementation leaves the United States open to charges of hypocrisy and double standards (Cox 2005: 29). As a number of critics have pointed out, to dismiss these accusations is almost certain to be counter-productive. 'The more that others question America's power and purpose and priorities, the less influence America will have' (Daalder and Lindsay 2003b: 375). Implicit in this judgement is the argument that America's best long-term interests, particularly in a world in which its power may be in relative decline, will be served by returning to a more multilateral approach to the conduct of its foreign policy, which commits the United States to an 'international order organised around rules and institutional cooperation' (Ikenberry 2003: 382). On the other hand, such a prospect has to overcome what Ikenberry describes as lurking imperial temptation, supported by powerful feelings of national insecurity, and rationalised through an ideological framework which emphasises America's distinctive destiny (ibid.: 382). President Obama's 2015 National Security Strategy talked about 'America's leadership role within a rules-based international order that works best through empowered citizens, responsible states, and effective regional and international organisations', but it remained uncertain in a rapidly changing environment how such a system could be fully implemented (National Security Strategy 2015).

REFERENCES AND FURTHER READING

ACLU (2005) *Civil Liberties After 9–11: The ACLU Defends Freedom*, at http://www. aclu.org/FilesPDFs/911_report.pdf (accessed 4/11/2005).
—— (2011) 'National Security', at http://www.aclu.org/national-security (accessed 13/3/2011).
Ambrose, S. (1998) *Rise to Globalism*, London: Penguin.
Appy, C. (1993) *Working-Class War: American Combat Soldiers in Vietnam*, Chapel Hill: University of North Carolina Press.
Bacevich, A. (2004) *American Empire: The Realities and Consequences of U.S. Diplomacy*, Cambridge: Harvard University Press.
—— (2009a) *The Limits of Power: The End of American Exceptionalism*, New York: Holt.
—— (2009b) *The Long War: A New History of U.S. National Security Policy since World War II*, New York: Columbia University Press.
—— (2010) *Washington Rules: America's Path to Permanent War*, New York: Metropolitan Press.
BBC (2004) 'Bush Sets Case as "War President"', at http://news.bbc.co.uk/2/ hi/americas/3470139.stm
—— (2011) 'Declinism', *Today Programme*, 16 February, at http://news.bbc.co.uk/ today/hi/today/newsid_9399000/9399134.stm
Bloom, A. (1987) *The Closing of the American Mind*, New York: Simon & Schuster.
Boot, M. (2003) 'Neither New nor Nefarious: The Liberal Empire Strikes Back', *Current History*, vol. 102, no. 667, November, pp. 361–7.
Bourne, R. (1992) 'The State' in O. Hansen (ed.) *Randolph Bourne, Selected Writings, 1911–1918*, Berkeley: University of California Press.
Brinkley, A. (2007) *American History: A Survey*, New York: McGraw-Hill.
Burbach, R. and Tarbell, J. (2004) *Imperial Overstretch: George W. Bush and the Hubris of Empire*, London: Zed Books.

Bush G.W. (2001a) 'Inaugural Address', 20 January, at http://www.whitehouse.gov/news/inaugural-address.html
—— (2001b) 'Statement by the President in His Address to the Nation', 11 September, at http://www.whitehouse.gov/news/releases/2001/09/2001 0911–16.html
—— (2002) 'President Delivers Graduation Speech at West Point', 1 June, at http://www.whitehouse.gov/news/releases/2002/06
—— (2003) 'President Bush Discusses Iraq Policy at Whitehall Palace in London', 19 November, at http://www.whitehouse.gov/news/releases/2003/11/2003 1119–1.html
—— (2004a) 'State of the Union Address', 20 January, at http://www.whitehouse.gov/news/releases/2004/01/20040120–7.html
—— (2004b) 'President Addresses the Nation in Prime Time Press Conference', 13 April, at http://www.whitehouse.gov/news/releases/2004/04/20040413–20.html
Chomsky, N. (2004) Hegemony or Survival: America's Quest for Global Dominance, London: Penguin.
Cox, M. (2005) 'Empire by Denial: The Strange Case of the United States', International Affairs, vol. 81, no. 1, January, pp. 15–30.
—— (2012) 'Power Shifts, Economic Change and the Decline of the West?', at http://www.lse.ac.uk/IDEAS/pdf/Cox–Waltz.pdf (accessed 14/01/2015).
Cox, M. and Stokes, D. (2012) U.S. Foreign Policy, Oxford: Oxford University Press.
Cox, M., Lynch, T. and Bouchet, N. (eds) (2013) U.S. Foreign Policy and Democracy Promotion, Abingdon: Routledge.
Crockatt, R. (1995) The Fifty Years War, London: Routledge.
—— (2003) America Embattled: Sept. 11th, Anti-Americanism and the Global Order, London: Routledge.
Daalder, I. and Lindsay, J. (2003a) America Unbound: The Bush Revolution in Foreign Policy, Washington, DC: Brookings Institution.
—— (2003b) 'Bush's Revolution', Current History, vol. 102, no. 667, November, pp. 367–77.
De Tocqueville, A. (1965) Democracy in America, London: Oxford University Press.
Donoghue, D. (1988) 'The True Sentiments of America' in L. Berlowitz et al. (eds) America in Theory, New York: Oxford University Press.
Easley, J. (2010) 'Sarah Palin Attacks President Obama's Patriotism', Politicus USA, 1 July, at http://www.politicususa.com/en/palin-obama-america
Eisenberg, C. (2005) 'The New Cold War', Diplomatic History, vol. 29, no. 3, June, pp. 423–7.
Ferguson, N. (2004) Colossus: The Rise and Fall of the American Empire, London: Allen Lane.
Foner, E. (2000) 'American Freedom in a Global Age', American Historical Review, vol. 106, no. 1, February, pp. 1–16.
Gaddis, J.L. (1997) We Now Know: Rethinking Cold War History, Oxford: Clarendon.
—— (2004) Surprise, Security, and the American Experience, Cambridge, MA: Harvard University Press.
—— (2005) 'Grand Strategy in the Second Term', Foreign Affairs, vol. 84, no.1, pp. 1–8.
Gardner, L. (1984) A Covenant with Power: America and World Order from Wilson to Reagan, London: Macmillan.

Gienow-Hecht, J. (2006) 'AHR Forum: Always Blame the Americans: Anti-Americanism in Europe in the Twentieth Century', *The American Historical Review*, vol. 111, no. 4 at http://www.historycooperative.org/journals/ahr/111.4/gienowhecht.html (accessed 15/03/2011).

Greene, G. (1955) *The Quiet American*, London: Heinemann.

Halliday, F. (2005) 'It's Time to Bin the Past', *The Observer*, 30 January.

Hastedt, G.P. (2014) *American Foreign Policy: Past, Present, and Future*, 10th edn, Lanham, MD: Rowman & Littlefield.

Hayden, P. *et al.* (2003) *America's War on Terror*, Aldershot: Ashgate.

Hellman, J. (1986) *American Myth and the Legacy of Vietnam*, New York: Columbia University Press.

Herring, G. (2008) *From Colony to Superpower, U.S. Foreign Relations since 1776*, Oxford: Oxford University Press.

Hogan, M. (ed.) (1999) *The Ambiguous Legacy: U.S. Foreign Policy in the American Century*, Cambridge: Cambridge University Press.

Hollander, P (1995) *Anti-Americanism: Critiques at Home and Abroad 1965–1990*, Oxford: Oxford University Press.

Holloway, D. (2008) *9/11 and the War on Terror*, Edinburgh: Edinburgh University Press.

Hunt, M. (1988) *Ideology and US Foreign Policy*, New Haven: Yale University Press.

Huntington, S. (1998) *The Clash of Civilizations and the Remaking of World Order*, London: Touchstone.

Ikenberry, G. (2002) 'America's Imperial Ambition', *Foreign Affairs*, vol. 81, no. 5, Sept.–Oct., pp. 44–60.

—— (2003) 'America and the Ambivalence of Power', *Current History*, vol. 102, no. 667, November, pp. 377–83.

—— (ed.) (2002) *America Unrivaled: The Future of the Balance of Power*, Ithaca: Cornell University Press.

Ions, E. (ed.) (1970) *Political and Social Thought in America, 1870–1970*, London: Weidenfeld & Nicolson.

Johnson, C. (2002) *Blowback*, London: Time-Warner.

—— (2004) *The Sorrows of Empire: Militarism, Secrecy, and the End of the Republic*, London: Verso.

Johnson, L.B. (1965) 'Peace Without Conquest' at http://www.lbjlib.utexas.edu/Johnson/archives.hom/speeches.hom/650407.asp

Kaplan, A. (2004) 'Violent Belongings and the Question of Empire Today', *American Quarterly*, vol. 56, no. 1, pp. 1–18.

Katzenstein, P. and Keohane, R. (2006) 'Anti-Americanisms', *Policy Review*, no. 139, at http://www.hoover.org/publications/policy-review/article/7815 (accessed 3/01/2011).

Kellner, D. (2003) *From 9/11 to Terror War: The Dangers of the Bush Legacy*, Lanham, MD: Rowman & Littlefield.

King, M.L. (1967) 'Beyond Vietnam: A Time to Break Silence' at http://www.stanford.edu/group/King/publications/speeches/Beyond_Vietnam.pdf

Kissinger, H. (2002) 'Preemption and The End of Westphalia', vol. 19, no. 4, at http://www.digitalnpq.org/archive/2002_fall/kissinger.html (accessed 23/01/2011).

Kristol, I. and Brooks, D. (1997) 'What Ails Conservatism', *Wall Street Journal*, 15 September.

LaFeber, W. (2002) 'The Bush Doctrine', *Diplomatic History*, vol. 26, no. 4, pp. 543–58.

Layne, C. (2012) 'U.S. Decline or Primacy' in M. Cox and D. Stokes (eds) *U.S. Foreign Policy*, Oxford: Oxford University Press.

Leffler, M. (2005) '9/11 and American Foreign Policy', *Diplomatic History*, vol. 29, no. 3, pp. 395–413.

Lynch T. (2010) 'American Foreign Policy in the 2010s' in G. Peele *et al.* (eds) *Developments in American Politics, 6*, Basingstoke: Palgrave Macmillan.

Mann, J. (2004) *The Rise of the Vulcans: The History of Bush's War Cabinet*, New York: Viking.

McAlister, M. (2001) *Epic Encounters: Culture, Media, and U.S. Interests in the Middle East, 1945–2000*, Berkeley, CA, London: University of California Press.

McCormick, T. (1995) *America's Half-Century: United States Foreign Policy in the Cold War and After*, Baltimore: Johns Hopkins University Press.

McNamara, R. (1999) *Argument Without End: In Search of Answers to the Vietnam Tragedy*, New York: Public Affairs.

National Security Strategy (2002) *The National Security Strategy of the United States of America: September 2002*, at www.state.gov/documents/organization/63562.pdf

—— (2010) *The National Security Strategy of the United States of America: May 2010*, at http://www.whitehouse.gov/sites/default/files/rss_viewer/national_security_strategy.pdf

—— (2015) *The National Security Strategy of the United States of America: February 2015*, at https://www.whitehouse.gov/sites/default/files/docs/2015_national_security_strategy.pdf

Niblett, R. (ed.) (2010) *America and a Changed World: A Question of Leadership*, Oxford: Wiley Blackwell.

Nobel Foundation (2009) 'Nobel Peace Prize 2009', at http://www.nobelprize.org/nobel_prizes/peace/laureates/2009/press.html

Nye, J. (2003) *The Paradox of American Power: Why the World's Only Superpower Can't Go It Alone*, Oxford: Oxford University Press.

Obama, B. (2008a) 'Address to the People of Berlin', 24 July, at http://www.american rhetoric.com/speeches/barackobamaberlinspeech.htm

—— (2008b) *The Audacity of Hope: Thoughts on Reclaiming the American Dream*, Edinburgh: Canongate.

—— (2009) 'April 4 News Conference, Strasbourg, France' at http://www.white house.gov/the-press-office/news-conference-president-obama-4042009 (accessed 5/1/2011).

—— (2011) 'State of the Union Address', at http://www.whitehouse.gov/the-press-office/2011/01/25/remarks-president-state-union-address (accessed 10/2/2011).

—— (2014a) 'Remarks by the President on Review of Signals Intelligence', 17 January at https://www.whitehouse.gov/the-press-office/2014/01/17/remarks-president-review-signals-intelligence (accessed 14/01/2015).

—— (2014b) 'Remarks by the President at the United States Military Academy Commencement Ceremony', 28 May, at https://www.whitehouse.gov/the-press-office/2014/05/28/remarks-president-united-states-military-academy-commencement-ceremony (accessed 14/01/2015).

O'Sullivan, J. (1839) 'The Great Nation of Futurity', *The United States Democratic Review*, vol. 6, no. 23, pp. 426–30.

Pence, M. (2010) 'Statement on the New Republican Majority' at http://www.mikepence.com/news/110210.html

Pew (2005) 'U.S. Image up Slightly, but Still Negative' at *Global Attitudes Project* http://pewglobal.org/reports/display.php?ReportID=247 (accessed 6/11/2005).

—— (2010) 'Obama More Popular Abroad than at Home, Global Image of U.S. Continues to Benefit', at http://pewglobal.org/2010/06/17/obama-more-popular-abroad-than-at-home/

—— (2015) at http://www.pewglobal.org/ (accessed 23/6/2015).

Pieterse, J. (2003) 'Hyperpower Exceptionalism: Globalization the American Way' in U. Beck, N. Sznaider and R. Winter (eds) *Global America? The Cultural Consequences of Globalization*, Liverpool: Liverpool University Press, pp. 76–91.

Roper, J. (2005) 'The Contemporary Presidency: George W. Bush and the Myth of Heroic Presidential Leadership', *Presidential Studies Quarterly*, vol. 34, pp. 132–40.

Rosenberg, E. (1982) *Spreading the American Dream*, New York: Hill & Wang.

—— (2002) 'Rescuing Women and Children', *Journal of American History*, vol. 89, no. 2, September, pp. 456–65.

Singh, R. (2006) 'Are We All Americans Now? Explaining Anti-Americanisms' in B. O'Connor and M. Griffiths (eds) *The Rise of Anti-Americanism*, London: Routledge.

Slotkin, R. (1998) *Gunfighter Nation*, New York: Atheneum.

Steinmetz, G. (2003) 'The State of Emergency and the Revival of American Imperialism: Toward an Authoritarian Post-Fordism', *Public Culture*, vol. 15, no. 2.

Stephanson, A. (1995) *Manifest Destiny: American Expansion and the Empire of Right*, New York: Hill & Wang.

Thorne, C. (1979) *Allies of a Kind*, Oxford: Oxford University Press.

Tyrrell, I. (2015) *Transnational Nation*, Basingstoke: Palgrave Macmillan.

Weinkopf, C. (2003) 'Anti-Patriot Feminists', *FrontPage Magazine*, 10 July, at http://archive. frontpagemag.com/readArticle.aspx?ARTID=17316.

Younge, G. (2004) '*New York Times* Admits Failures in Run-up to War', *Guardian*, 27 May.

—— (2005) 'America's Top Paper Rethinks its Journalism', *Guardian*, 10 May.

FOLLOW-UP WORK

There are a number of additional resources, assignments and other materials to be found on the website that accompanies this new edition: http://www.routledge.com/cw/campbell/

1 The concept of 'exceptionalism' has long guided how many Americans have thought about their own history, but comparisons of the American experience with those of other nations may suggest common themes. How does the expansionist ideology of nineteenth-century America fit with the imperialist rhetoric of European powers during the same period? Has empire meant the same thing in America as in Europe, and, if not, how has American empire differed?

2 To what extent did American foreign policy change as a result of the attacks of September 11th? How did the policies of President George W. Bush compare with those of his predecessors? It may be instructive

here to compare specific examples, e.g. the Clinton administration's policies in the former Yugoslavia with that of the Bush administration in Iraq.

3 Examine the extent to which contemporary American power depends on military strength. Influential works by Chalmers Johnson (2004) and Bacevich (2004) portray a country whose civic and political culture is threatened by militarism. To what extent do you share these views? What prospects do you see for a greater degree of accountability in terms of the conduct of American military policies?

4 Examine the debate about the relative strengths of the American economy in the early twenty-first century, and assess its implications for the future of American political and military power. What responsibilities do you think the United States has to promote a stable international economic order?

5 Explore a case study in American nation-building (e.g. South Vietnam, Afghanistan, Iraq). What kind of problems arise when attempts are made to create stable democratic societies in the aftermath of military intervention? What do you make of the American commitment to the 'single model' of development?

6 Explore the ways in which the American military are depicted in popular culture, particularly by Hollywood. To what extent are the experiences of the American military overseas regularly represented in terms of earlier American mythology? Although this chapter hasn't looked at Vietnam, there is now a sizeable body of films dealing with American intervention in Southeast Asia which repay careful study.

7 Assess the tension between unilateralism and multilateralism in contemporary American policy.

8 Assess Randolph Bourne's judgement that war tends to encourage an oppressive state, in the light of the measures taken to promote domestic security after 9/11.

9 How do you assess the open American commitment to the promotion of democracy in the world?

10 Discuss the arguments for and against theories of American decline.

Chapter 10

The transmission of American culture

AMERICANISATION

In 1901 the English journalist W.T. Stead published a short tract entitled *The Americanisation of the World* in which he welcomed the growing power of the United States not only in military and economic terms but also in the area of ideas, values and culture. American energy and vitality, through their relentless involvement in other countries, would restore the strength of the British Empire and ensure the continued triumph of the Anglo-Saxon race. Forty years later, writing on the eve of America's entry into the Second World War, Henry Luce, the publisher of *Life*, coined the phrase 'The American Century' as part of a determined attack on American isolationism. The twentieth century was 'baffling, difficult, paradoxical, revolutionary'. If it was to come to life 'in any nobility of health and vigor, [it] must be to a significant degree an American century'. Like Stead, Luce stressed the importance of both American culture and values. 'American jazz, Hollywood movies, American slang, American machines and patented products' were already the 'only things that every community in the world, from Zanzibar to Hamburg, recognise[d] in common'. They must now be joined to a commitment to an internationalism 'of the people, by the people, and for the people'. The United States had a responsibility to spread 'great American ideals' and become 'the powerhouse of the ideals of Freedom and Justice'. Luce hoped that this kind of optimistic identification of American interests with those of the world would enhance 'the triumphal purpose of freedom' and that American internationalism would lift the life of mankind to 'a level a little lower than the angels'. It became clear, however, as the twentieth century developed, that the debates swirling round the process and impact of Americanisation suggested something much more ambiguous and complex than either he or Stead had anticipated (Luce 1999).

Clearly, American products and American culture were often eagerly consumed in many different places, but their spread also aroused considerable distrust and suspicion, as well as accusations of imposition. Americanisation, in Stead's formulation, above all raised questions to do with the nature of modernity linked to systems of mass production, relentless innovations in communications and the arrival of full–scale democracy. Debates over what form modernisation should take in places outside of America kept reverting to what David Ellwood has described as 'the cultural dimensions of American power, and the power dimensions of American culture' (Ellwood 2012: 1). As this suggests, there were elements of both change and continuity in the debates that took place about America's impact on the wider world and its symbolic role as the flag-leader for modernity. Context mattered since debates about cultural transfer have always taken place in the shifting patterns of history, politics and economics. At the same time, there were persistent themes in the way in which American culture and power were assessed, welcomed, contested and condemned.

In this chapter we will examine different aspects of these issues as American popular culture has spread beyond the country's borders. Their analysis is important because it has implications both for understanding American culture, as well as for the practice of American Studies. Exploring Americanisation is revealing because it can tell us something about the impact of American culture on the lives of those beyond the territorial boundaries of the United States. How peoples have responded to the presence of 'America' reminds us that the assumptions that lie behind much American rhetoric and many American cultural products may be interpreted and understood in different ways. At the same time, analysing Americanisation can also help us interrogate America itself. One key theme in the country's experience has been a temptation to see itself as exceptional. (See also the introduction and Chapters 1 and 9.) Determining what was American and what was un-American was a process carried out within America's borders. 'America' was defined as part of a national process of self-assertion. However, through analysing Americanisation, alternative definitions of America may emerge, which challenge the power of 'domestic' versions of the country's experience. America's identity in the world becomes something constructed not only by Americans, but also by the interactions other peoples and cultures have had with the country (Tyrrell 2015). In this respect debates over Americanisation can have revealing consequences for the practice of American Studies itself, by contributing to the way in which it increasingly takes into account a range of relationships between 'America', however that term is defined, and the rest of the world. Examining Americanisation invites us as students of America to reflect critically on the role it plays in our lives.[1]

COMING TO TERMS WITH AMERICA

As this suggests, the presence of the United States has been felt, over time, in the lives of peoples beyond its borders both through military might, economic power and cultural influence, as well as through reflection on the very idea of America. As non-Americans examined the development of their own societies, 'America often served as a model for rejection or emulation, providing views of a future seen in either a negative or positive light' (Kroes 1999: 464). Marcus Cunliffe, among many others, has pointed out the vast literature of responses to the country, which have often fallen into a series of broad classifications despite variations according to time and place (Cunliffe 1964: 492–514). He grouped these responses into two main historical categories: the heroic, which included such images as 'the land of liberty', 'the earthly paradise', and the villainous, which emphasised America as a place of excess or libertinism. Both went back to the age of exploration. America in this sense was imagined as much as discovered. It was, however, the developing capacity of America to spread her culture beyond her own borders that gave these images an added potency. As a range of American cultural products became increasingly widely dispersed throughout the world, partly through the energies of capitalist production and partly through the active encouragement of the United States government, particularly but not only during the Cold War, so the debate intensified about their impact on other cultures and peoples.

When people in other countries worried, however, about the effects American culture was having on their own lives, they were not thinking of America's novels, sculpture or ballet. 'Americanisation', as Richard Pells has argued, 'generally meant the world-wide invasion of American movies, jazz, rock 'n' roll, mass circulation magazines, best-selling books, advertising, comic strips, theme parks, shopping malls, fast food, and television programs' (Pells 2000: 495). In this respect concern about 'America' was frequently linked to the ongoing debate about the effects of popular culture in a way which often chimed with views expressed in America itself about its standardising tendencies. These issues were raised, for instance, during the 1940s by American cultural critics such as Dwight Macdonald, who argued that mass culture was 'imposed from above' on audiences who were 'passive consumers' of material that 'mixes and scrambles everything together, producing what might be called homo-genized culture' (Storey 1994: 30, 32). The effects of such a culture, for Macdonald, were 'narcotized acceptance . . . as a substitute for the un-settling and unpredictable . . . joy, tragedy, wit, change, originality and beauty of real life' previously captured in works of high culture. In place came 'standardization' and the 'spreading ooze of Mass Culture' (ibid.: 42) which was particularly associated with all things American. As the mass production techniques of industrial capitalism could reproduce endless copies of the same, standardised objects, for example sitcoms, records or paperbacks, fears grew that a similar process would occur in all cultural practices. The poet Allen Ginsberg asked in 1956, 'Are you going to let your emotional life be run by *Time* Magazine?' (Charters 1994: 75) and used the name 'Moloch' to characterise the interlinked technologies of consumerism, capitalism, weapons and the media that represented for him, and many during the 1950s and 1960s, a fearful imperial force threatening not only the health of the republic but also the rest of the world.

In Europe, American popular culture provoked similar denunciations across the political spectrum. In Britain, for instance, the spread of American cultural products in the years after the First World War encouraged a widespread reaction on the right to what was seen as a threat to established standards. Often, fear of cultural decline was explicitly conflated with anxiety about the full implications of democratisation. The literary critics F.R. and Q.D. Leavis quoted the words of the Victorian writer Edmund Gosse as part of their worries over the impact of American values on British life: 'The revolution against taste, once begun, will land us in irreparable chaos' (Webster 1988: 180). America, from this perspective, became a symbol of both cultural and political levelling, in a manner that endangered educated values. Similar concerns were expressed in Germany and France (Fluck 2004; Kuisel 1996). These alarms found an alternative form of expression after 1945 among a number of cultural critics on the left across Western Europe, who worried that the intervention of America into working-class culture, in particular, would result in the promotion of a superficial consumerism, dominated by the market, at the expense of political solidarity and the cohesiveness of traditional patterns of community which nourished it.

In Britain, Richard Hoggart, in *The Uses of Literacy* (1957), described what he saw as the success of a 'shiny barbarism' associated with the import of American goods and values, which rendered its consumers less capable of responding openly and responsibly to life. This was reflected above all in the lifestyle of jukebox boys, who spent their time 'listening in harshly lighted milk-bars to the nickelodeons . . . living to a large extent in a myth world compounded of a few simple elements which they take to be those of American life'. For Hoggart, this was all a thin and pallid form of dissipation, 'a sort of spiritual dry-rot' which affected the 'quality of ordinary working-class life' (Hoggart 1958: 247–50). America was seen as 'the homogenising agent' in the modern world, serving as 'the image of industrial barbarism; a country with no past, and therefore no real culture, a country ruled by competition, profit and the drive to acquire' (Hebdige 1988: 47–54). Though Hoggart in 1957 retained some optimism that British workers still retained sufficient moral resources to resist the worst effects of mass consumerism, his position reflected a wider set of assumptions about the one-way process of cultural transmission across the Atlantic, which was shared in other European countries as well as Britain. In France plans to market Coca-Cola more widely during the late 1940s provoked opposition from across the political spectrum. For *Le Monde* Coca-Cola threatened the moral landscape of France. A Catholic newspaper warned that Coca-Cola was the avant-garde of an offensive aimed at economic colonisation. In 1951 the communist poet Louis Aragon condemned the United States as 'a civilisation of bathtubs and frigidaires', accusing it of being more arrogant than the Nazis through its substitution of the machine for the poet, Coca-Cola for poetry (Kuisel 1996: 24). As these comments suggest, across Europe from the 1930s to the 1950s, 'wherever elites stood politically, one thing united most of them; their cultural anti-Americanism' (Wagnleitner 1999: 511).

In other parts of the world the dangers of Americanisation called for stronger responses. In Egypt, the Islamic fundamentalist, Sayyid Qutb, who was executed in 1966 for plotting against President Nasser, used the example of America to argue for the creation of fundamentalist societies in the Middle East, where a purified Islam would regulate life totally, in an effort to resist the social consequences of unrestrained individualism. After a two-year stay in America during the late 1940s he concluded that the churches were 'entertainment centres and sexual playgrounds'. The people 'had no faith in themselves or in life around them'. They were, on the one hand, as 'machines that move with madness, speed, and convulsion that does not cease', but they were also taken with 'indulgent pleasure'. Both trends had to be resisted if God's sovereignty was to prevail (Rippin 1993: 92). His writings would later have a strong influence on the Taliban in Afghanistan, as well as on al-Qaida as it aimed for an international jihad that would implement Shari'a, or religious law. For Osama bin Laden, America had to be forced to leave the Arabian Peninsula, and the wider Islamic world, because its way of life was 'defiling the Islamic home' (Friedman 2000: 395).

If we turn to later periods, it is striking that many of these attitudes have persisted. Although the international reaction to September 11th focused on American foreign policy, a powerful strain of cultural antagonism was also apparent in a range of critiques of what America stood for in the world. *Why Do People Hate America?* Sardar and Davies asked in 2002. Among their answers was the assertion that 'America was taking over the lives of ordinary people in the rest of the world and shrinking their cultural space – their space to be themselves, to be different, to be other than America'. America projected itself on the rest of the world 'as though it were a hamburger: a commodity, a brand, out to capture all cultural space for itself' (Sardar and Davies 2002: 104–5). Harold Pinter, the 2005 Nobel Prize winner for literature, bitterly linked what he saw as the brutalism of the 'Nazi' American military with the way in which the culture industry exercised control through propaganda (Chrisafis and Tilden 2003). In France, a range of responses to September 11th linked it to the aggressive ambitions not only of the American state but also the country's popular culture (Roger 2005: 1).

Concern among politicians and cultural critics about Americanisation has also been accompanied by more sustained theoretical assessments of mass culture. In the vanguard, and influential in both Europe and America, was the Frankfurt School, exemplified by the work of Theodor Adorno and Max Horkheimer, who saw mass culture as a product of state monopoly capitalism, which worked to deny genuine individualism. The media in this context ensured passivity by stifling oppositional thinking. In particular, they sought to mould the minds of ordinary citizens by encouraging false needs while diminishing alternative ways of thinking. The result was a 'culture industry' that ensured conformity in contemporary society by merchandising banality, and weakening high culture's ability to challenge reality. Combining standardisation with predictability, 'Its products encourage conformity and consensus which ensure obedience to authority, and the stability of the capitalist system' (Strinati 1992: 64). Mass culture was a way of maintaining the status quo through channelling any desire for utopian or even alternative modes of expression into passive consumption. Herbert Marcuse called this idea 'one dimensionality', arguing that in advanced industrial societies, of which America was the prime example, the individual was reduced to acquiescence, alienated from the possibilities of his own liberation.

> The products [of mass culture] indoctrinate and manipulate; they promote a false consciousness which is immune against its falsehood ... it becomes a way of life ... and as a good way of life, it militates against qualitative change.
>
> (Marcuse 1967: 27)

The American critic Theodore Roszak wrote of 'technocracy' and its intention to 'charm conformity from us by exploiting our deep-seated commitment to the scientific world-view' (Roszak 1970: 9).

Another term frequently assigned to this process was 'cultural imperialism', which has been developed as a key analytical concept in the assessment of Americanisation, and has stimulated considerable debate about the workings of popular culture. It is, however, a broad concept which has a range of different emphases, including media imperialism, the domination of one national culture by another, the global domination of capitalism and the critique of modernity (Gienow-Hecht 2000: 472–9). As it expanded into Europe and then other parts of the world, it is argued, American mass culture imposed its values on other societies and cultures, incorporating them into the values of the American state, to the detriment of local or national needs (see, for example, Schiller 1969, 1989). Hollywood, in particular, was singled out for the way in which it bedazzled whole cultures, leaving them susceptible to American manipulation: 'The Yanks have colonized our subconscious', one of the German characters says in Wim Wenders's 1976 movie *Kings of the Road*. Whether it was Walt Disney in Chile (Mattelart and Dorfman 1975) or American movies more generally in Western Europe (De Grazia 1989, 2005), the result was the same – the integration of local, regional or national societies into a wider international economic system. Such a process might not take the form of 'older, cruder and obsolete methods of colonisation', but the incursion of the American model of commercial media amounted to a form of 'neo-imperialism' that brought the countries concerned into the orbit of the dominant power (Herman and McChesney 1997: 137, 153).

Another influential theoretical perspective on mass culture as a system of control has been the work of George Ritzer, who coined the phrase 'the McDonaldisation of society' to describe the rationalisation of contemporary life. For Ritzer, writing from a Weberian rather than a Marxist perspective, McDonald's provides the paradigm of 'the process by which the principles of the fast-food restaurant are coming to dominate more and more sectors of American society as well as of the rest of the world' (Ritzer 2000: 1). It is a model for understanding a number of different aspects of modern societies beyond the fast-food industry itself, including credit cards, the sex industry, marketing, leisure, education and the media. In particular, he argues that McDonaldisation encompasses four key concepts: increased efficiency, calculability, predictability and control. Efficiency is revealed in both consumer satisfaction and in the organisational rules and regulations of McDonald's itself. Calculability emphasises the quantitative aspects of products at the expense of quality. Predictability ensures that products and services will be the same over time and in different places. Surprise is avoided in favour of reliability. All of this leads to control over both those who enter McDonald's and those who work there. Control is especially reflected in the way in which people's actions in this kind of setting are increasingly shaped by non-human technology. While conceding that McDonaldisation has 'led to positive changes', he emphasises what amounts to a fifth aspect of rationalisation, 'the irrationality of rationality', and in particular the way in which it has encouraged a range of problems which overwhelm any advantages. These include 'inefficiency ... relatively high costs, illusory fun and reality, false friendliness, disenchantment, threats to health and environment, homogenisation and dehumanisation' (ibid.: 145). While the processes of McDonaldisation were strongly linked to the more general phenomenon of modernity, it nevertheless remained the case, Ritzer argued, that they were originated and received their most thoroughgoing application in America.

In subsequent work he has gone on to explore what he describes as 'the new means of consumption', which he defines as 'the proliferation of settings that allow, encourage, and even compel us to consume innumerable goods and services'. Under this heading Ritzer includes franchises, shopping malls, superstores, theme parks, cybermalls and home shopping television. Taken together such developments have 'dramatically transformed the nature of consumption'. Moreover, 'what is critical about [them] is that they are powerful representations of American culture and they all bring that culture to any nation to which they are exported' (ibid.: 97–118).

GLOBALISATION

The analysis of 'Americanisation', or American cultural influence, has been complicated by the processes associated with the related concept of globalisation. The latter is notoriously difficult to pin down but may be defined here as the process of increasing connectivity, through which ideas, capital, goods, services and people are transferred across national borders. The concept has a long history, but it is revealing that in its new formulation, from the 1980s on, it is often used interchangeably with Americanisation. As Richard Crockatt has noted, 'America stands for many as a symbol of globalisation', perhaps because 'the expansion of American power happened at the same time as the growth of international capitalism' (Crockatt 2003: 57, 122).

This is certainly how it has often been seen by peoples outside of the United States. Globalisation, Thomas Friedman suggested in 2000, was viewed as wearing

> Mickey Mouse ears; it eats Big Macs, drinks Coke or Pepsi and does its computing on an IBM PC, using Windows 98, with an Intel Pentium II processor, and a network link from Cisco Systems. . . . In most societies, people cannot distinguish anymore among American power, American exports, American cultural assaults, American cultural exports and plain vanilla globalisation.
>
> (Friedman 2000: 382)

For former president Bill Clinton this easy identification of globalisation with America was misleading. It had more general benefits for international society. The global economy, the information technology revolution, scientific advance and 'the explosion of democracy and diversity within democracy' together would help 'to make the twenty first century the most peaceful, prosperous, interesting time in all human history'. He admitted there were problems – global poverty, the global environment, the rise of global epidemics and hi-tech terrorism – but he declared a more general confidence in the progressive benefits that globalisation would bring (Clinton 2001).

Others put it less diplomatically. Andrew Rothkop argued in 1997 that

> It is in the general interest of the United States to encourage the development of a world in which the fault lines separating nations are bridged by shared interests. And it is in the economic and political interests of the United States to ensure that if the world is moving toward common telecommunications, safety and quality standards, they be American; that if the world is becoming linked by television, radio and music, the programming be American; and that if common values are being developed, they be values with which Americans are comfortable.
>
> (Rothkop 1997: 5)

Another American assessment argued that 'a fair appraisal of [the] economic landscape suggests that struggling countries in general do not suffer from too much market liberalisation and exposure to international competition – they suffer from too little'. Nations fared better if they merged into the expanding global marketplace (Sorensen 2004: 405). In a survey published just after the attacks on the World Trade Center, *The Economist* insisted that globalisation was the only cure for international poverty (*Economist* 2001: 3).

Arguments, however, about the benefits of globalisation are a notorious battlefield. What had already become clear both from protests at World Trade Organization meetings around the turn of the century, the fallout from September 11th was that there was no general consensus about globalisation's potential benefits either on an international or a local scale, or about the way in which it might be used to promote the American example of development. Naomi Klein, the author of the influential *No Logo*, had already argued that 'the brutal economic model advanced by the World Trade Organization [was] itself a form of war' (Klein 2003). It encouraged global inequality by promoting privatisation and deregulation in a way that enhanced the fortunes of the richest fifth of the world at the expense of the poorest fifth. Globalisation, from this perspective, was anti-democratic because it denied popular choice in much of the world and favoured the interests of corporate elites. Fredric Jameson had made a similar point more trenchantly twelve years earlier:

> American, postmodern culture is the internal and superstructural expression of a whole new wave of American military and economic domination throughout the world: in this sense, as throughout class history, the underside of culture is blood, torture, death, and terror.
>
> (Jameson 1991: 5)

This was felt all the more clearly after the economic recession which hit much of the world in 2007–8. Klein argued in October 2008 that the crisis reflected the abandonment of the idea of 'the government as regulator, of protecting citizens and consumers from the detrimental impact of greed' (Klein 2008). A corollary of the economic and political indictments of globalisation has been its supposed encouragement of cultural homogenisation. Even an (American) supporter of the phenomenon admits that it has 'tended to involve the spread [for better and for worse] of Americanisation' (Friedman 2000: 9). Others put it more strongly. Globalisation involved 'a declaration of war upon all other cultures. And in cultural wars, there is no exemption for civilians; there are no innocent bystanders' (Seabrook 2004b). It relentlessly works to impose cultural control over peoples and nations in a manner that stifles opposition and promotes sameness (Seabrook 2004a). The world becomes 'more Americanised, rationalised, codified, and restricted' (Ritzer and Ryan 2004: 42).

A ONE-WAY PROCESS?

However, the processes of globalisation themselves raise questions about the assumptions of a one-way model of cultural expansion. Ritzer argues that while it is undeniable that there are global processes, which operate free of any nation-state, one nation-state remains disproportionately important in globalisation. Globalisation is persistently tied to the United States and American culture. Nonetheless, it is also the case that although the United States is often seen as the key agent in the process of globalisation, it is itself also susceptible to its impact. This has been true for much of its history. Luce in the 1940s saw America as the decisive actor in the world, and American values and cultural products as distinctively home-grown, whereas a wider perspective suggests something more complex. American political and social values originated in the transmission of European ideas across the Atlantic in the seventeenth and eighteenth centuries and America continued to be influenced in the nineteenth and twentieth centuries through the impact of transnational cultural forces, particularly from Europe. The mass migrations of the eighteenth and nineteenth centuries created a 'globally sourced, multicultural and multiracial population for the United States' (Hodson 2001: 81). The same process can also clearly be seen in the recent upsurge in immigration. In 2010 13 per cent of American residents were foreign-born as the country re-emerged as a nation of immigrants. The increasing variety of the sources of immigration, particularly from the developing world, also has profound consequences for the future of American culture and society. The US Census Bureau projects that the non-Hispanic, white population will comprise just 50.1 per cent of the total population in 2050, compared with 69.4 per cent in 2000. The Hispanic population is expected to grow from 35.6 million to 102.6 million, an increase of 188 per cent, meaning that their share of the nation's population would nearly double, from 12.6 per cent to 24.4 per cent, with potentially far-reaching consequences for national cultural identity (see Chapter 2). As Richard Pells has argued, the cultural connections between the United States and the rest of the world have often been reciprocal, and the United States has been affected by transnational cultural flows as much as Europe and elsewhere (Pells 2012: 2). Globalisation, from this perspective, has a long history, which has shaped America itself in significant ways since the early days of the republic, and which will continue to breach American borders, despite what is sometimes described as 'American self-absorption and lack of awareness of the bigger world' (Friedman 2000: 276).

There are a range of different areas of American cultural life which have been marked by this process. Hollywood has throughout its history regularly used actors, writers, musicians and directors from across the world and Pells has closely illustrated the impact of European culture on the American film industry (Pells 2012). Another recent example is its 'borrowings of Asian film aesthetics, movie stars, concepts and screenplays' (Goss and Yue 2005: 254). A musical form like jazz, often described as quintessentially American, has its roots in a mix of sources from Africa and Europe. Although it may have first become identifiable in the American South, as it developed it consistently drew on contributions from musicians and performance styles from across the world (Shipton 2001). The United States in this light may be seen as 'a participant in a global flow of people, ideas, texts, and products – albeit a participant who often tries to impede those flows' (Fishkin 2005: 24). In such a world accepted notions of a clearly defined American national culture imposing itself on other cultures become increasingly contested by the ways in which the construction of the idea of America itself is constantly under challenge from both internal and external forces which are difficult to resist. This is not to deny that struggles will take place for the power to articulate American identity, but it is to suggest that those struggles themselves, in a globalised world, will inform how America is seen and understood by others. As Amy Kaplan argues 'the Americanisation of global culture is not a one way street, but a process of trans-national exchange, conflict and transformation' that may create new cultural forms which express their own dreams and desires (Kaplan 2004: 7).

At the same time, the pace of globalisation by the early twenty-first century suggested it was becoming an increasingly free-floating process, less attached to specific national roots. Popular culture, for instance, has become increasingly deracinated as the forces of transnational communication have gathered pace. As the world has become a more interconnected and interdependent place, promoted by transformations in electronic technology, so the notion of American cultural dominance finds itself increasingly challenged from a range of alternative sources. The decisive force of globalisation in the contemporary world has raised questions about continuing American power as much as it has promoted its extension. The widespread temptation to describe American culture in terms of the values of the imperialist adventures of President George W. Bush needs to qualified by an appraisal of some of the ways in which the United States itself has been unable to escape the implications of 'global connectivity' (Tomlinson 1999: 12). America, from this perspective, is becoming increasingly decentred, and this is a process which is likely to continue into the future.

ASSESSING AMERICANISATION

If globalisation complicates narratives of Americanisation, so too do a range of assessments which focus on how 'America' has been received and interpreted in specific places and specific periods. From this perspective it may be too simplistic to read cultural trends as simply reflecting both economic and political developments and the meanings invested by producers in their creations. In *Cultural Imperialism* (1991), John Tomlinson argued against the idea that there are straightforward connections between a cultural product, the ideas it represents and the manner of its consumption in places outside of its place of production. The mediated nature of global communication systems and their highly charged, complexly coded forms and representational practices and the variegated contexts in which a slew of images and ideas about America circulate across the world and are consumed non-passively by people who were not quite the 'target consumers' should warn us not to assume that American hegemony, and cultural imperialism, work in predictable, totalising ways. Audiences are generally more reflective and critical about what they consume, and more aware about the threats of manipulation. Fluck emphasises the importance of 'models of negotiation, hybridisation and creolization' in helping us to come to terms with processes of cultural transfer (Fluck 2004).

Shelley Fishkin makes a similar point: 'Cultural imperialism has turned out to be too simple a model to understand how culture works.' It may be more appropriate instead to place an emphasis on the way in which American popular culture abroad is in a constant state of negotiation with other cultures, and how societies outside the United States use it to negotiate with aspects of their own cultures (Fishkin 2005: 33). The move away from a cultural imperialist model also helps to emphasise the significance of human agency. Both the Frankfurt School and cultural imperialism arguments, as well as Ritzer's iron cage of McDonaldisation, tend to portray those on the receiving end of American popular culture as objects, 'passive bod[ies] appropriated by hegemonic discourse' (Ang

1996: 152). At the same time, cultural imperialism, by assuming that self-contained and authentic national or local cultures are threatened by an 'equally self-contained "dominant culture" . . . often tends to collude with a defence of conservative positions of cultural Puritanism and protectionism' (ibid.: 152). Moving to a different kind of explanatory framework helps to 'understand contact, translation, exchange, negotiation, conflict and other dynamics that attend the constitution of social relationships across cultural and national borders' (Ngai 2004: 60–1).

Cultural artefacts, it is argued, 'change their meanings, transform their messages, acquire local meanings and become new signifiers as soon as they cross borders' (Wagnleitner 1999: 500). This not to deny the comparative advantage of the United States in terms of the transfer of culture, but it is to link it to the processes of selection and adaptation. As Rob Kroes has suggested, conventional notions of Americanisation may not be the most appropriate way of describing this process. Analysis of the 'motifs and organising views' of the producers of American cultural products remains important, but it needs to be accompanied by awareness of 'a freedom of reception, a freedom to re-semanticize and recontextualize meaningful messages reaching audiences across national and cultural borders' (Kroes 1999: 463). Aspects of American culture could provide an encouragement to liberation in one context, while acting as a threat in another.

Put another way, America provided itself as a text which contained its own ambiguities and contradictions, which allowed its readers to adopt and adapt meanings and pleasures for their own purposes. America, for the British critic and novelist Malcolm Bradbury, looking back on his own education in the 1950s, provided a direction 'in which the mind might go to look for images of alternative and otherness' (Bradbury 1979: 120). This is not to deny the context within which American cultural products were produced or the resources which supported their availability, but it is to suggest audiences have often exercised discretion in using America in ways that suited them. As Richard Pells has argued in assessing the worldwide impact of American culture, 'foreigners have regularly demonstrated "the ability" to adapt America's cultural exports to their own needs and traditions' (Pells 2012: x).

The case of broadcast media is illuminating here. If the cultural imperialism model were accurate, Jeremy Tunstall has argued, 'false consciousness would be plugged into every human home' with the growth of media technology ensuring that American mass culture would 'rule the global village' (Tunstall 1994: 39, 18). However, he suggested, it contains misleading assumptions about the ways in which popular culture operates at the point of consumption. The spread of American media in the world may not produce homogeneity at all, but respond to and facilitate 'the world . . . splitting up into smaller units and ethnic identities'.

New technical developments in the media would enable 'localism, separatism, talking back to, and switching off from, authority, the centre, the national and foreign media' (ibid.: 273–4). Under these conditions, he argued in 2008, local and regional media were becoming as significant as the American media, which once effectively dominated the international arena. Rather than moving towards some form of monolithic control, American media were in fact in relative decline, particularly in the areas of broadcasting and cinema, in the face of challenges at a regional level from countries like India, Japan and Mexico (Tunstall 2008: 253). This argument was earlier developed by Morley and Robins (1995), who explore the tension between globalism and localism, stressing that the two can and do coexist, and perhaps offer the 'possibility of reinventing and rearticulating international and local cultures and identities' (ibid.: 2). Rather than the threat of an imperialist media culture, with America at the centre, in which everything becomes the same, they suggested an alternative through which the local and the global could coexist, namely, that the media offered the possibilities of empowerment as much as the downside of suppression. Although large multinational media corporations exercise enormous influence and control, 'what is doubted is the cultural implications of this presence' (Tomlinson 1991: 57). This is partly to do with how audiences receive these messages, as we shall see later, and also connected to the explosion of media technologies which have provided new avenues for communication and expression to a wider base of people. This 'new regionalism' values 'diversity and difference of identities . . . and seeks to sustain and conserve the variety of cultural heritages, regional and national' (Morley and Robins 1995: 17), especially through television. Newer media such as the Internet and digital technology have only increased the channels of communication that may work to resist and counter the potentially hegemonic, corporate power of the multinationals.

In terms of transnational television programming, for instance, it used to be asserted both by corporate executives and academic critics that technological innovation, particularly the development of satellites, would lead to the rapid expansion of American provision around the world. Both advocates and critics shared what has been described as 'a strong technological and economic determinism. . . . [which] would automatically reinforce the reach and power of the major existing communications powers and corporations' (Straubhaar and Duarte 2005: 220). Audiences would be forced into a kind of cultural dependency as they passively consumed American products. The global would swamp the local. In fact, a range of empirical studies on television programming in Latin America and Asia have suggested that these predictions remain unrealised. Audiences have retained an active and powerful role in making choices about what they want to watch. In particular, they have often preferred programmes reflecting their own culture or that of their neighbour. In Asia, News Corporation first developed Star TV as a transnational broadcasting system with a limited menu of five channels, but was forced by audience demand to diversify into dozens of localised channels in order to succeed (ibid.: 221). In Latin America one recent study concludes, 'if the major systems want to grow their audiences, they will have to increase the number of locally produced channels they carry'. As this suggests, 'the American media industry has consistently had problems in determining what will sell, prospering, instead, by remaining competitive and eclectic, offering a multiplicity of icons and viewpoints that have different meanings for different audiences at different times in different countries' (ibid.: 248). Eric Hobsbawm has argued that 'tailoring the product to specific markets is the logic of the consumer global economy' and that 'at the consumer end globalisation needs diversification' (Hobsbawm 1998b: 7). What some of this evidence suggests, however, is that the choices of consumers themselves as much as the hard-nosed business sense of those doing the selling have often formed a part of the resistance to standardisation.

As far as programmes themselves are concerned, their meanings are often as much about how they are received and used by their audiences and consumers as they are about the 'intentions' of the corporate 'sender' or provider. That is, we can read them in different ways so that their meanings are plural and provisional rather than single, monologic and fixed. In the 1980s the top-rated US soap opera *Dallas* was watched throughout the world as it took the realm of the family, with its struggles for power and influence, into new territory. However, it became a focus for those like Jack Lang, French Culture Minister, who saw it as 'the symbol of American cultural imperialism' eating its way into French national life. Like McDonald's restaurants, *Dallas* was assumed to represent the worst facets of a homogenising American culture, with all the fears of the Frankfurt School realised. However, Ien Ang's analysis of audience responses to the programme suggested significant differences in the way the series was received and interpreted. Viewers demonstrated an awareness of what she calls 'the ideology of mass culture', and in particular the negative image of the American mass media and its tailored ideological messages. They appeared to be fully aware of the 'norms and prescriptions [that] exert pressure on them' (During 1993: 415). This argument suggests that audiences come up with a range of 'strategies' to resist, to some extent, the hegemony of the media. It is therefore misleading 'to pretend that the ideology of mass culture exercises dictatorial powers' since 'alternative discourses do exist which offer alternative points of identification' for *Dallas* watchers (ibid.: 416). Ang goes on to make an important point about the media, which is that it is 'talked about' in one way and yet in 'practice' may have a very different role. In consuming popular culture, people might mix, combine and 'pluralise' their use of the media in a manner that cuts across many of the theoretical groupings that appear to be significant and thus injecting pleasure into the process. The satisfaction gained from watching *Dallas* or similar media products does not replace real life but exists alongside it, and 'need not imply that we are bound to take up . . . positions and solutions in our relations to our loved ones and friends, our work, our political ideals, and so on' (Ang 1985: 135). Ang's findings suggest that arguments about the manipulative abilities of the mass media position may be misleading, particularly when scrutinised as part of the process of reception. Plural and diverse audiences use the media in a range of ways which resist the expectations of mass culture theorists (ibid.: 136).

'Cultural material', Fluck argues, is never simply absorbed as a model of behaviour but is reappropriated in different contexts for different needs and purposes (Fluck 2004). Audiences, moreover, have often acted in this way in the face of opposition or hostility from their own governments. In Fascist Italy, for example, efforts to impose nationalised codes of dress for women were ineffective as consumers chose to follow the American-influenced fashion industry instead (De Grazia 2005). In China, the American sitcom *The Big Bang Theory* recently achieved tremendous popularity, gaining more than 1.3 billion viewings through the streaming service SOTU by 2014. Its following eventually alarmed the Chinese State Administration of Radio, Film and Television (SARFT), which took it off the service in April 2014. It cited 'content that violates China's constitution, endangers the country's sovereignty and territorial integrity, provokes troubles in society, promotes illegal religion and triggers ethnic hatred' (Sheehan 2014). However, the difficulties the Internet has created for state control were soon displayed. Opponents to the ban used Sina Weibo, the country's most popular micro-blogging platform to register their concerns. One participant declared, 'You really have to feel bad for Chinese people. Everything is constricted, there's no freedom of speech, our thinking has been kidnapped, and now we can't even relax and watch a little American TV' (ibid. 2014).

As this example suggests, through use of blogs, Twitter, Facebook and other social media, individuals and groups can praise, denounce and criticise, what they see and hear. In more regulated societies this may allow individuals or groups to stake out their own position on controversial topics, programmes and texts. More generally the Internet can provide an accessible and immediate forum for discussion and review, which only reinforces the arguments above about the significance of audience engagement. The spread of long–form television, discussed in the introduction, is relevant here. In Britain, the significance of a series like *Breaking Bad* has only been enhanced by dedicated blogs, postings, discussion groups and other online contributions (*Guardian* 2015a).

As Arjun Appadurai argues, this kind of evidence suggests that 'the consumption of the media often provokes resistance, irony, selectivity, and in general, *agency*' (Appadurai 1996: 7).

HOLLYWOOD

The case of Hollywood illustrates the four themes we have been following. First it emphasises the scale of American cultural exports and their dominance at particular times and in particular places. Second, it shows how 'America' itself has been constructed out of a range of transnational forces. Third, it shows the importance of the issue of reception in terms of America's cultural impact. Fourth, it raises questions about the continuing significance of America, and the way it is being challenged by new processes of production and transmission.

Hollywood's international dominance since the 1920s is well documented, but it is worth emphasising here the continuing scale of its impact. American exports in the 2010s continued to dominate the international film industry with around 63 per cent of worldwide box office receipts in 2013 (*Guardian* 2013). Hollywood's share of the world market had effectively doubled between 1990 and 2000 to around 60 per cent and remained at that level for much of the next decade (Motion Picture Association of America 2010). About 70 per cent of Hollywood's annual revenue in 2013 came from international markets. Eighteen of the top twenty films at the box office in 2014 were American and the remaining two were joint productions, largely financed with US dollars (*Guardian* 2015a). In many European countries in the early twenty-first century the percentage of box-office takings on domestic products was in rapid decline to as low as 10 per cent in Germany and 12 per cent in Britain and Spain (Miller *et al.* 2005: 4). In Britain's case, this rose to 22 per cent by 2013, but the US still took 72.7 per cent of overall receipts (British Film Institute 2014). The success of James Cameron's *Avatar* in 2010 symbolised Hollywood's continuing dominance, as it was screened in 122 countries across the world to become the most successful production in terms of earnings in movie history (Ellwood 2012: 515). Jack Valenti, head of the MPAA at the turn of the century, offered a celebratory justification of the scale of American dominance:

> it is a fact, blessedly confirmed, that the American movie is affectionately received by audiences of all races, cultures and creeds on all continents amid turmoil and stress as well as hope and promise. This isn't happenstance. It's the confluence of creative reach, storytelling skill, decision making by top studio executives and the interlocking exertions of distribution and marketing artisans.
>
> (Ibid.: 1)

One argument here, however, is that Hollywood's development after the Second World War not only involved 'affectionate reception' but also the expansion of global capitalism, supported by Washington's trade policies, and the evolution of international agreements under GATT (General Agreement on Tariffs and Trade) and the WTO (World Trade Organization), which encouraged American access to foreign markets. The emphasis on media systems based on a market-led approach favoured American cultural industries because of their inherent advantages in terms of size and flexibility. Hollywood, from this perspective, maintained its international dominance not just through the appeal of its products but as much through its control of methods of production. Economic muscle was also regularly supported by state institutions. In occupied countries such as Germany and Austria both the presence and the educational policies of the US army actively encouraged consumption of American goods and practices (Wagnleitner 1994, 1999), and as a result rapidly spread into much of the rest of Western Europe. The special case of military occupation drew on a range of earlier precedents like the Creel Committee during the First World War, the Motion Picture Section of the Department of Commerce in the 1920s, and the close links between Hollywood and Washington during the Second World War. The development of the Cold War also included attempts to propagate the American way on the other side of the Iron Curtain. The Marshall Plan further integrated Western Europe into the American system by promoting the virtues of transnational communication as well as the promise of erasing social conflict through economic growth. At some point in the post-1945 era, Richard Kuisel argues, 'Americanisation became an essential aspect of American power' (Kuisel 2000: 513). Moreover, a continuing military presence in Europe, the Middle East and East Asia outlived the Cold War, as discussed in Chapter 9. At one level the subsequent proliferation of bases served as outposts of the American cultural economy. At another they provided a symbolic presence which local peoples often felt they were unable to contain. As part of the response to September 11th, moreover, cultural diplomacy was given renewed attention as an important aspect of the War on Terror. American beliefs and values needed to be promoted to support American interests in an increasingly antagonistic world (Kennedy 2003).

The appeal of American popular culture, and Hollywood in particular, was also helped by the ways in which it developed from its earliest days. As noted above, transnational currents ensured that production systems had to cater for the country's multi-ethnic population. This gave it an advantage over the less diverse societies of Western Europe, and prepared it to meet the needs of global audiences. The heterogeneity of the American audience 'anticipated (the) global market in its diversity and multi-linguistic nature' (Fluck 2004). At the same time, Hollywood itself drew on a range of foreign expertise in terms of film production as it grew in the early twentieth century. Hollywood's emergence as a cultural capital, Richard Pells argues, was based on it becoming a home 'to an international community of artists and their merchandisers', and therefore 'reliant on the skills and imagination of foreigners' (Pells 2012: 202). This was reinforced by what Fluck has described as 'dehierarchisation', the openness of access to cultural products and the relatively weak control by elites of cultural expression in the United States. Hollywood from the outset benefitted from its ability to bridge the gap between high and low culture in a manner which allowed it to bring sophisticated production techniques to popular film. In such a context, Hollywood managed to create, first for the domestic market, but also for foreign export, a democratic vision of the possibilities of modern life (Fluck 2004). Critics may have charged that American films were superficial products made for rapid consumption, but their immediate popularity in Western Europe by the mid-1920s, where they accounted in many countries for over 80 per cent of domestic viewing figures, testified to their transnational appeal.

At the same time, studies of the reception of Hollywood in specific settings, as in the case of broadcast media discussed above, often worked to complicate the relationship between production and consumption. Studio products might be carefully designed to appeal to mass markets, both at home and abroad, but they were often appropriated by audiences in different places and at different times, in ways which connected with local needs. In Britain, for instance, in the 1930s and 1940s, the success of American cinema was based on its 'idealism, its depictions of glamour and abundance, and its democratic story lines, which featured ordinary men and women in a sympathetic light'. Its approach contrasted with 'the flatness and rigidity' of many British films in which class-bound expectations governed how feelings were expressed (Nava 1999: 86). Hollywood's appeal was particularly attractive to working-class female audiences. Contemporary critics, like the socialist novelist John Summerfield, might declare that they were simply 'silly girls', with 'synthetic Hollywood dreams, pathetic silk stockings and lipsticks, [and] foolish stirrings', but as Mica Nava has persuasively argued, films provided an opportunity to resist 'the constraints of femininity as well as Englishness' (Nava 1999: 88–9). The readiness of American films to tackle such issues as 'crime, corruption, passions and violence' made them 'more adequate vehicles for contemporary emotions and expression than the insular universe of the British cinema' (Chambers 1988: 42). These kinds of findings are echoed in a range of other studies which suggest that, while audiences for Hollywood films were certainly targeted as part of a global market, the narrative of their reception was more one of adoption and adaptation than of domination (Jancovich and Faire 2003; Stokes and Maltby 2005).

On the other hand, evidence suggested that by the beginning of the 2010s Hollywood itself was no longer quite the monolithic presence it had been even twenty years before. A UNESCO (United Nations Educational, Scientific and Cultural Organization) survey in 2007 found that both India and Nigeria produced more films annually than the United States. While most of these were for local consumption, they nevertheless reflected a production model others might follow in the future, and suggested that rapidly expanding markets like China would increasingly restrict foreign film distribution in favour of domestic products. Hollywood movies too have increasingly used cross-national production processes in which the place of Los Angeles at the centre of the industry has been giving way to a wider network of other key cities like London, Buenos Aires, Paris and Shanghai in terms of studio space and post-production work. As a result, Hollywood is 'no longer rooted in clearly defined local and national contexts' and has become increasingly deterritorialised as it has been 'stretched and scattered across the globe' (McDonald and Wasco 2008: 6–7). Hollywood, McDonald argues, may in this sense be turning into something that in the future will be less straightforwardly thought of as 'American'.

THE INTERNET

The inaugural European edition of the magazine *Wired*, published in April 1995, had on its cover a startling fluorescent image of Tom Paine, the radical eighteenth-century writer, with the famous line from his pamphlet, 'Common Sense': 'We have it in our power to begin the world over again.' The magazine sought to reclaim Paine for the age of the Internet as a 'patron saint' of the new worlds of cyberspace and computer technology. The magazine developed connections between Paine's vision and the potential of the Internet as a new means of democratic global communications. His words were used as a clarion call for a new age born out of technological revolution, one in which the free flow of information could 'spread ideas . . . allow fearless argument . . . challenge and question authority, [and] set a common social agenda' (Katz 1995: 64). Just as Paine had employed the rotary press of the 1770s to disseminate radical opinions, so too could the Internet be used to challenge corporate and governmental authority. This anti-authoritarian stance was also reflected in the 'mission statement' of the Electronic Frontier Foundation, founded in 1990, which spoke of 'a new world arising in the vast web of digital, electronic media which connects us. . . . These communities without a single, fixed geographical location comprise the first settlements on an electronic frontier' (Rucker 1993: 88). The Foundation's aim was to make the Internet 'truly useful and beneficial not just to a technical elite, but to everyone' so that it 'threaten[ed] the hegemony of the government/corporate paradigm by empowering millions of individuals' (ibid.: 88). As this suggests, there was in its early days almost a counter-cultural fervour surrounding the Internet, or 'cyberspace' in its more mystical form, one that harked back to the 1960s when new technologies could operate as a form of 'radical politics that could bypass institutions and nations and go directly to the people' (Mellencamp 1992: 56). This has been reflected in a range of critical and political debates as use of the Internet has dramatically expanded over the last twenty years. It could offer, for instance, the possibility of side-stepping hierarchical modes of communication through the creation of a decentred system of information flow, 'potentially making for an equivalence of senders and receivers' (Kroes 2003: 237). Google's chief executive declared in 2006 that 'the internet is helping to satisfy our most fundamental needs – our desire for knowledge, communication and a sense of belonging' (Ellwood 2012: 500). Hillary Clinton, the American Secretary of State, in 2010 characteristically sought to link the liberating power of the Internet to American values. The more freely information flowed, the stronger societies would become. America stood for a world 'where all of humanity has equal access to knowledge' and 'a responsibility to help ensure the free exchange of ideas' (Clinton 2010).

On the other hand, it is argued, the growth of the Internet clearly became entwined in the processes of Americanisation. In terms of infrastructure, servers, users and content it had been dominated by the United States from its very inception. While it was based on the 'supposedly genuine American values of open access to information, liberalization, and privatization', this access was 'provided, guided, and controlled by multinational media and telecommunications companies'. From this perspective communication was 'more akin to a one way street rather than to a dialogue of equals' (Wagnleitner 2005). America was effectively at the centre of the map of the Internet with other nations at the periphery. Domain names in nations other than the USA always have a two-letter suffix and although an American suffix exists, it is rarely used. The Internet, argues Rob Kroes, may be 'only the latest medium for the global transmission of a culture crucially cast in an American mould. Rather than being a vehicle for a multiplication of people's affiliations, it may narrow their options, subjecting them to an Americanization by stealth' (Kroes 2003: 236). American domination of the Internet was also reflected in the way both English was its primary language and increasing commercialisation might negatively affect the free flow of information. Some critics have also charged, for instance, that the dramatic growth of a popular search engine like Google, which has well over half the world's Internet users, has significant implications for access to knowledge. Through its role as a gatekeeper it has intensified the so-called digital divide between producers and users by 'organising the world's information with a clear, if not always intentional bias towards commercial and popular trends, which in many cases take the form of U.S.-centric or mainstream views' (Segev 2010: xx). Individual users may feel that they are being empowered in terms of their ability to discover new information, but Google, in its role as the leading information agent, works to influence and shape the outcome of their searches (ibid.: xviii). Moreover, the concept of the search itself has implications for what is deemed to be valuable. To Google and its advertisers, it is not so much the answer to a search that matters, but the information it provides about the searcher, which can then be used to provide what might be appropriate supplementary material on the web page. One commentator has noted that despite the opportunities searching has provided, 'the line from commerce to surveillance turned out to be short and straight' (Halpern 2014).

However, whereas in 1995 users in North America constituted more than two-thirds of all Internet users worldwide, that figure had dropped to c. 50 per cent in January 2000, and was down to 10.7 per cent by December 2010. Every prognostication suggested that percentage was likely to fall further. By 2014, 87 per cent of the American population were Internet users, compared to 34.8 per cent of Asians, and yet Asians made up 45.6 per cent of world users. If the early growth of the Internet has been identified as a renewed means of spreading American cultural products across the globe, then it may be that this period is soon likely to come to an end (Internet World Stats 2015). What in its origins may have been developed in an American context, with an American imprint, is increasingly being used by a range of groups across the world, marked by significant differences in language and culture (Lull 2001). The Internet never quite had a 'centre' as it developed, but its revolutionary expansion around the globe has raised a fresh set of questions about its 'American-ised' characteristics.

This is what gave debates within the United Nations (UN) and else-where about the governance of the Internet such resonance. Since its inception, the United States had regulated the Internet's basic infra-structure through its control of the Internet's domain name systems, which were maintained by organisations contracted to the US Department of Commerce. Allocation and coordination of the names and numbers from a central authority is crucial to linking the multiple, scattered networks that constitute the Internet. A number of countries, in an effort to try to gain more control over how the Internet operates, argued that such regulation would be more appropriately managed by an international body under the auspices of the UN. Michael D. Gallagher, US Assistant Secretary of Commerce for Communications and Information, articulated the American position in 2005: 'We embrace [the] concepts of the private sector, the marketplace and freedom of expression' rather than inter-national bureaucratic management. Maintenance of the Internet was safer in the hands of the United States (Sparshott 2005). There were clear echoes here of the American battle with UNESCO in the 1970s and 1980s over the creation of a New World Information Order that would circumscribe the power of the Western media in order to ensure the right of individual nations, particularly in the developing world, to protect their cultural and social identity from what they saw as the propagation of false, distorted and potentially harmful information (Calabrese 2005). At the World Summit on the Information Society (WSIS), held in Montreal, Canada, in October 2012, aimed at exploring the governance of the Internet, among those arguing for a greater degree of state control in Internet governance were the leaders of Russia, Iran, China, Saudi Arabia and Zimbabwe, where state censorship already existed in other areas of the media. Indeed, since 2005 China had been able to use filtering technology in an increasingly successful way to control access to Internet information by its citizens. The Montreal Summit maintained the status quo, but it raised the revealing picture of an Americanised (commercialised) Internet committed to the market and free expression, in contrast to a more Balkanised version where national authorities sought to retain a degree of supervision over its use. An example of this had been the protracted struggle between China and Google over freedom of access. Google first compromised with the Chinese desire that the Internet within its borders should be under the jurisdiction of Chinese sovereignty, but then pulled its operations out of the country in protest against state interference within its operations, before reaching a compromise in 2010. The Chinese took the position that the American campaign for the uncensored and free flow of information on an unrestricted Internet was a disguised attempt to impose its values on other cultures in the name of democracy. Imbalances in the 'global information order' favoured the West and so countries like China, which were disadvantaged in this order, needed to take steps 'to protect their national interest' (BBC 2010). But nothing is straightforward here. It was the 'Americanised' Internet that anti-globalisation protestors used so successfully to coordinate protests against what they saw as the rampant aggression of the market. On the other hand, the American commitment to the free exchange of ideas on the Internet did not go so far as to accept the right of WikiLeaks in 2010 to publish the secret cables of US embassy staff working in foreign countries. Faced with widespread condemnation by governments for his actions, Julian Assange, WikiLeaks' founder, asserted in 2011 that the Internet had as much potential to implement totalitarian spying regimes, as it did to promote freedom of speech (*Guardian* 2011). American inconsistencies in this regard were underlined in 2013 by evidence of abuse of mass surveillance programmes by the National Security Agency (see discussion in Chapter 9). This provided support for the charge from a number of countries which wanted more national control of the Internet, that the American commitment to freedom was a mask for its own efforts to use cyberspace to its own advantage, both in terms of politics and commerce. All of this gave added force to Manuel Castells's argument that 'perhaps the most decisive social movements of our age are precisely those aimed at preserving a free internet . . . carving a space of communication autonomy that constitutes the foundation of the new public space of the Information Age' (Castells 2009: 415).

CASE STUDY 3: MUSIC

Another revealing case study is the spread of American popular music through the twentieth century. At one level, by the end of the century, the popular music industry was marked by a relentless process of mergers on a global scale, resulting in a market dominated by a small number of giant corporations that captured 76 per cent of the five main national markets (the United States, Germany, the United Kingdom, France and Japan), which themselves made up 70 per cent of world record sales (Leyshon *et al.* 1998: 10). One consequence, some critics have argued, was the creation of a homogeneous popular music culture dominated by American products, which stifled national or local alternatives. At the 2010 World Music Awards, presented to the world's best-selling acts, a clear majority of the winners were American. However, an alternative perspective suggests that it is misleading to treat both America as undifferentiated threat and the consumers of its products as uncritical and unquestioning. European audiences, for instance, frequently proved adept at selecting and adapting those elements in American culture that had meaning and value for them in their own lives, while rejecting other aspects that they distrusted, and the same has been true of other non-European societies. It is mistaken, as Roy Shuker has argued, to see the popular music audience as a mass of passive recipients. Such a view 'is totally at variance with contemporary audience studies which suggest that the consumption of music is an active rather than a passive process', one which contains oppositional possibilities (Shuker 2008: 23). Moreover, the rise of new forms of music production and distribution on the Internet also worked to challenge both American-centred dominance, and the opportunities for music producers to develop a greater degree of autonomy.

American popular music as it spread to Europe clearly offered alternatives to existing forms of provision, which was a great part of its appeal. Jazz, for Eric Hobsbawm, was democratic and classless, the sound of modernity and urban culture, and thus offered a challenge to accepted tradition (Hobsbawm 1998a: 267). Paul Oliver has noted how in the aftermath of the Second World War in Britain 'jazz had become a symbol of the irrepressible creative spirit of Blacks in the face of racial and economic oppression . . . a symbol of revolt against their parents, against war, against commercialism'. This had paradoxical political implications, as what was, after all, an American cultural form was taken up by the left as the Cold War got under way (Oliver 1990: 80–1). In Paris in the early 1940s, French youth, or Zazous, also used jazz as a form of cultural resistance to the German military occupation. Mica Nava talks about the way in which American popular music and dance provided opportunities for young women in England during the 1930s and 1940s to confront assumptions about acceptable behaviour: 'America operated psychically . . . as an imaginary somewhere else; as a refuge and a fantasy of a better future, as a means of breaking away from the constraints of class and parental conventions of deference, denial and despair' (Nava 1999: 76). Across Europe, in successive generations after the Second World War, the young, in particular, while on the receiving end of American popular music, regularly adapted it to their own ends (Kroes 1999: 466). In Britain, for instance, Peter Wicke has argued that

> Rock and Roll promoted the utopia of a distant America, a utopia which could encourage the everyday experiences of British working-class teenagers with all their longings, desires, hopes, frustrations and leisure needs. . . . [It] achieved a significance in Britain which it never possessed in America.
>
> (Wicke 1993: 61–2)

The foreignness of the music itself provided an opportunity to challenge conventional assumptions about place, class and parental authority within the narrow confines of British society.

Though Elvis Presley never performed outside of north America, his appeal through records, and later films, provided a set of challenges to existing patterns of society and culture and a model for Fluck's concept of individualisation, discussed above. 'Elvis' from this perspective offered 'more effective ways for imaginary self-empowerment, and self-fashioning' to new audiences, ready for the liberation of taste from hierarchical controls (Fluck 2004). Something similar happened in Italy where the young used new musical styles to differentiate themselves from tradition (Ellwood 2012: 412). In the late 1950s and early 1960s in Britain the popularity of the blues as a musical form had a profound influence upon a generation of musicians, reinvigorating local popular music by providing it with a sense of liberation and energy. Its downside was a tendency to 'minstrelsy', and often what amounted to a parody of black performance styles, but at its best, for a good number of performers, playing the blues was a first step, in the context of British life, to finding their own voice. The Beatles, for their part,

> started off by imitating Elvis, Buddy Holly, Chuck Berry, Carl Perkins, Gene Vincent, the Coasters, the Drifters – we just copied what they

Plate 10.1 Elvis performs on *The Ed Sullivan Show*, October 1956.
© CBS Photo Archive / Getty Images

did. . . . The people we copied were all American of course, because there was no one good British.

(Wicke 1993: 64)

Both British blues bands and the Beatles, however, adapted and re-exported what they had learned back to America, transforming it along the way into distinctive fresh forms which in their turn would have a dramatic impact on American popular culture (Philo 2014).

In France in the 1980s, the rapid growth of hip hop was initially inspired by American performance styles, but it quickly adapted them to local circumstances. French rappers performed in their own language, developed their own forms of dance and graffiti/tagging and incorporated a range of African influences into their music. In particular hip hop provided the opportunity for the children of immigrants from Algeria, Morocco or Tunisia to negotiate their own identities within the context of wider French culture. By 2000 France had become the second biggest market for rap after the United States. Moreover, just as American rap had crossed borders, French rap influenced artists in the rest of the Francophone world, especially western Africa and Quebec (Durand 2002). A study of hip hop in Germany has emphasised how it is used 'to define . . . personal identity and, hence, for individualization' (Winter 2003: 212). Similarly, Paul Gilroy has shown how aspects of American culture provided 'powerful sources of solidarity and pleasure as well as a means to organise themselves' for black minority groups in Britain. African America, in particular, was 'a source of cultural and political raw material for UK blacks in the post-war period' (Gilroy 1992: 171). It was not only the narrative of black political protest that acted as an inspiration here, but also the cultural expressiveness which developed alongside it, through a range of musical forms like soul, jazz and rap, 'which exported to Europe the idea that black communities in the inner city, particularly the young, could define themselves politically and philosophically as an oppressed "nation", bound together in the framework of the diaspora by language and history' (ibid.: 184). In a very different vein, while country music is often identified with a strong sense of American patriotism, one aspect of its appeal in Britain was to working-class and regional groups who did not fit easily into conventional notions of mainstream British culture, and who used the music to assert a sense of identity. Difference, in these varied cases, is expressed 'by using, and at the same time enjoying, mainstream music' (Winter 2003: 214).

As these examples suggest, audiences were often ready to adopt and adapt American popular music for their own ends. Of course, these were not always in conditions entirely of their own choosing, and the power of American record companies to promote particular artists or styles abroad always remained significant. However, the argument that a narrowing of musical expression resulted from the consolidated power of the music industry was also challenged by the powerful impact of the Internet. Alex Seago, for instance, argues that 'we can no longer sensibly define the music market in nationalistic terms with some countries such as the United States imposing their culture upon others', suggesting that there is a 'contradiction between the rapid centralisation and rationalisation of the music industry and the development of a global culture in which the relationships between identity, locality, and nationality are becoming disembedded' (Seago 2000: 134). New technologies and forms of communication have both weakened distinctive national identities and encouraged cooperative, localised patterns of resistance to mainstream culture. The music industry may well wish to create global cultural products, but it has frequently found itself confronted with musical trends, developed in a diverse range of locales that create new kinds of fusions by drawing on an eclectic mix of sources and styles. Increasingly, too, these fusions are distributed and consumed through new media such as social networks which challenge older concepts of production and distribution. This in practice has worked not only to undermine the power of the major record companies, but to encourage very different patterns of production, promotion and marketing which are far less tied to a sense of national, particularly American, identity. As in the case of Hollywood, models of national ownership and methods of production may be becoming less appropriate for the analysis of the continuing spread of popular music. George Lipsitz warned that new kinds of inter-cultural communication do not 'automatically lead to inter-cultural cooperation especially when participants in the dialogue speak from positions of highly unequal access to power, opportunity, and life chances', but he nevertheless concedes that they could link with 'currents of culture and politics emerging from fundamentally new geopolitical realities' (Lipsitz 1994: 5).

CONCLUSION

Many of these examples and approaches indicate that ambiguity and variety often characterise responses to the spread of American culture. Different groups have often accepted, altered or rejected it according to the specific circumstances in which they have found themselves. This process has of course to be seen in the context of the scale and potency of American cultural production, but it must also take into account its attractiveness and flexibility. This perspective makes it clear that 'a process such as Americanization does not run uniformly and is not imposed from above. It leads to heterogeneous answers and different accentuation' (Sznaider and Winter 2003: 5). Both positions need to be explored alongside each other. This involves examining how people incorporate American culture into their fantasies and values, as well as the 'multifarious and contradictory meanings' they attach to it. The official definition of 'Americanisation' as an unambiguous threat should be relativised by looking at the 'contradictory losses and opportunities allowed by it' (Ang 1996: 148). Moreover, as some of the examples cited above suggest, the forces of globalisation have thrown up new departures and connections that complicate explanations of cultural transfer and problematise, in particular, the scenario of prolonged American cultural hegemony. However hard it might try to resist it, America from this perspective may be becoming increasingly de-centred, and its influence and impact qualified and changed by the pace of cultural transformation across the world.

NOTE

1. George McKay has provocatively asked whether American Studies outside of America exists 'solely or primarily in order to maintain American cultural, economic – even, let's go for it, imperial – hegemony?' One response here may be to emphasise the importance of arguments over Americanisation as a counter to uncritical acceptance of what he describes as an exported 'cultural chauvinism' (McKay 1998: 29–30).

REFERENCES AND FURTHER READING

Ang, I. (1985) *Watching Dallas: Soap Opera and the Melodramatic Imagination*, London: Methuen.

—— (1996) *Living Room Wars*, London: Routledge.

—— (2005) 'De-Americanising the Global: Overcoming Fundamentalism in a Volatile World', *Comparative American Studies*, vol. 3, no. 3, September, pp. 267–82.

Appadurai, A. (1996) *Modernity at Large: Cultural Dimensions of Globalization*, Minneapolis: University of Minnesota Press.

Basu D. and Lemelle, S. (eds) (2006) *The Vinyl Ain't Final: Hip Hop and the Globalization of Black Popular Culture*, London: Pluto.

BBC (2005) 'Microsoft Censors Chinese blogs' at http://news.bbc.co.uk/1/hi/technology/4088702.stm (accessed 18/11/05).

—— (2010) 'China Defends Internet Censorship', at http://news.bbc.co.uk/1/hi/8727647.stm (accessed 23/10/2014).

Beck, U., Sznaider N. and Winter, R. (eds) (2003) *Global America? The Cultural Consequences of Globalization*, Liverpool: Liverpool University Press.

Bradbury, M. (1979) 'How I Invented America', *Journal of American Studies*, vol. 14, no. 1, pp. 115–46.

British Film Institute (2014) *Statistical Yearbook 2014*, at http://www.bfi.org.uk/sites/bfi.org.uk/files/downloads/bfi-statistical-yearbook-2014.pdf (accessed 14/02/2015).

Calabrese, M. (2005) 'The McBride Report', at https://www.globalpolicy.org/component/content/article/157/27023.html (accessed 10/9/2015).

Campbell, N., Davies J., and McKay, G. (eds) (2004) *Issues in Americanisation and Culture*, Edinburgh: Edinburgh University Press.

Castells, M. (2009) *Communication Power*, New York: Oxford University Press.

Chambers, I. (1988) *Popular Culture: The Metropolitan Experience*, London: Methuen.

Charters, A. (1994) *The Penguin Book of the Beats*, Harmondsworth: Penguin.

Chrisafis A. and Tilden, I. (2003) 'Pinter Blasts "Nazi America" and "Deluded Idiot" Blair' *Guardian*, 11 June.

Clinton, H. (2010) 'Remarks on Internet Freedom' at http://www.state.gov/secretary/rm/2010/01/135519.htm (accessed 7/11/2010).

Clinton, W. (2001) 'The Struggle for the Soul of the 21st Century', *BBC Richard Dimbleby Lecture*, at http://www.clintonfoundation.org/121401-nr-sp-cf-spespe-wjc-at-bbc-richard-dimbleby-lecture.htm (accessed 5/10/2005).

Crockatt, R. (2003) *America Embattled: Sept. 11th, Anti-Americanism and the Global Order*, London: Routledge.

Cunliffe, M. (1964) 'European Images of America' in A. Schlesinger and M. White (eds) *Paths of American Thought*, London: Chatto & Windus.

De Grazia, V. (1989) 'Mass Culture and Sovereignty: The American Challenge to European Cinema, 1920–1960', *Journal of Modern History*, vol. 61, no. 1 March, pp. 52–87.
—— (2005) *Irresistible Empires: America's Advance Through Twentieth-Century Europe*, Cambridge: Harvard University Press.
Deibert, R. (2015) 'The Geopolitics of Cyberspace after Snowden', *Current History*, vol. 114, no. 68.
Durand, A.-P. (2002) *Black, Blanc, Beur: Rap Music and Hip-Hop Culture in the Francophone World*, Lanham, MD.: Scarecrow.
During, S. (ed.) (1993) *The Cultural Studies Reader*, London: Routledge.
Economist (2001) 'Globalisation and its Critics', *The Economist*, 27 September.
Ellwood, D. (2012) *The Shock of America*, Oxford, Oxford University Press.
Ellwood, D. *et al.* (1994) 'Questions of Cultural Exchange: The NIAS Statement on the European Reception of American Mass Culture', *American Studies International*, vol. 22, no. 2, pp. 33–47.
Fishkin, S.F. (2005) 'Crossroads of Culture: The Transnational Turn in American Studies', *American Quarterly*, vol. 57, no. 1, March, pp. 17–58.
Fluck, W. (2004) 'The Americanisation of German Culture? The Strange Paradoxical Ways of Modernity' in A. Mueller (ed.) *German Pop Culture. How 'American' Is It?*, Ann Arbor: University of Michigan Press, available at https://www.press.umich.edu/pdf/0472113844-ch1.pdf (accessed 3/05/2014).
Focus (2009) 'World Film Market Trends', at http://www.obs.coe.int/online_publication/reports/focus2009.pdf
Friedman, T. (2000) *The Lexus and the Olive Tree*, New York: Anchor.
Gienow-Hecht, J. (2000) 'Academics, Cultural Transfer and the Cold War – A Critical Review', *Diplomatic History*, vol. 23, no. 3, Summer, pp. 465–515.
Gilroy, P. (1992) *There Ain't No Black in the Union Jack: The Cultural Politics of Race and Nation*, London: Routledge.
Goss, J. and Yue, M. (2005) 'De-Americanising the Global: Cultural Studies Interventions from Asia and the Pacific', *Comparative American Studies*, vol. 3, no. 3, September, pp. 251–66.
Guardian (2011) 'Julian Assange Tells Students That the Web is the Greatest Spying Machine Ever' at http://www.guardian.co.uk/media/2011/mar/15/web-spyingmachine-julian-assange (accessed 21/3/2011).
—— (2013) 'Hollywood's Hold Over Global Box office – 63% and Falling', 2 April, at http://www.theguardian.com/film/filmblog/2013/apr/02/hollywood-hold-global-box-office (accessed 10/09/2014).
—— (2015a) 'Breaking Bad', at http://www.theguardian.com/tv-and-radio/breaking-bad (accessed 15/02/2015).
—— (2015b) '2014 Global Box Office in Review', at http://www.theguardian.com/film/2014/dec/31/transformers-4–2014-global-box-office-in-review (accessed 04/03/2015).
Halpern , S. (2014) 'Are We Puppets in a Wired World?' *New York Review of Books*, 7 Nov.
Hebdige, D. (1988) *Hiding in the Light*, London: Methuen.
Herman, E. and McChesney, R. (1997) *The Global Media: the New Missionaries of Corporate Capitalism*, London: Cassell.
Hobsbawm, E. (1998a) *Uncommon People*, London: Weidenfeld & Nicholson.
—— (1998b) 'The Nation and Globalisation', *Constellations*, vol. 5, pt. 1, pp. 1–9.

Hodson, J. (2001) '"Intercourse in Every Direction": America as Global Phenomenon', *Global Networks*, vol. 1, no. 1, pp. 79–87.

Hogan, M. (ed.) (2000) *The Ambiguous Legacy, U.S. Foreign Relations in the American Century*, Cambridge: Cambridge University Press.

Hoggart, R. (1958) (first 1957) *The Uses of Literacy*, Harmondsworth: Penguin.

Horn, A. (2009) *Juke Box Britain: Americanisation and Youth Culture, 1945–60*, Manchester: Manchester University Press.

Ignatieff, M. (2003) 'The American Empire: The Burden', *New York Times Magazine*, 5 January, p. 22.

Internet World Stats (2015) 'Internet Usage Statistics', at http://www.Internet worldstats.com/stats.htm (accessed 21/03/15).

Jameson, F. (1991) *Postmodernism, or, The Cultural Logic of Late Capitalism*, London: Verso.

Jancovich, M. and Faire, L. (2003) *The Place of the Audience*, London: British Film Institute.

Kaplan, A. (2004) 'Violent Belongings and the Question of Empire Today', *American Quarterly*, vol. 56, no. 1, March, pp. 1–18.

Kaplan, A. and Pease, D. (eds) (1994) *Cultures of United States Imperialism*, Durham: Duke University Press.

Katz, J. (1995) 'The Age of Paine', *Wired*, vol. 1, no. 1, April, pp. 64–9.

Kennedy, L. (2003) 'Remembering 9/11: Photographic Diplomacy', *International Affairs*, vol. 79, no. 2, March, pp. 315–26.

Klein, N. (1999) *No Logo*, London: Flamingo.

—— (2003) 'Free Trade is War' at http://www.nologo.org/

—— (2008) 'Wall St. Crisis Should be for Neoliberalism What Fall of Berlin Wall Was for Communism' *Democracy Now!*, 8 October, at http://www.democracy now.org/2008/10/6/naomi_klein (accessed 23/01/2015).

Kroes, R. (1996) *If You've Seen One, You've Seen the Mall: Europeans and American Mass Culture*, Chicago: University of Illinois Press.

—— (1999) 'American Empire and Cultural Imperialism: A View from the Receiving End', *Diplomatic History*, vol. 23, no. 3, pp. 463–77.

—— (2003) 'The Internet: An Instrument of Americanization?' in U. Beck, N. Sznaider and R. Winter (eds) *Global America? The Cultural Consequences of Globalization*, Liverpool: Liverpool University Press.

Kuisel, R. (1996) *Seducing the French: The Dilemma of Americanization*, Berkeley: University of California Press.

—— (2000) 'Americanisation for Historians', *Diplomatic History*, vol. 24, no. 3, Summer, pp. 509–15.

Lauter, P. (2001) *From Walden Pond to Jurassic Park: Activism, Culture and American Studies*, Durham: Duke University Press.

Leyshon, A., Matless, D., and Revill, G. (eds) (1998) *The Place of Music*, London: Guilford Press.

Lipsitz, G. (1994) *Dangerous Crossroads*, London: Verso.

Luce, H. (1999) 'The American Century', *Diplomatic History*, vol. 23. no. 3.

Lull, J. (2001) 'Superculture for the Communication Age' in J. Lull (ed.) *Culture in the Communication Age*, London and New York: Routledge, pp. 132–63.

Marcuse, H. (1967) *One Dimensional Man*, London: Paladin.

Mathe, S. (ed.) (2000) *Anti-Americanism at Home and Abroad*, Aix-en-Provence: University of Provence Press.

Mattelart, A. and Dorfman, A. (1975) *How to Read Donald Duck: Imperialist Ideology in Disney Comic*, New York: International General.

McDonald, P. and Wasco, J. (eds) (2008) *The Contemporary Hollywood Film Industry*, Oxford: Blackwell.

McKay, G. (1998) *Yankee Go Home (And Take Me With U): Americanization and Popular Culture*, Sheffield: Sheffield Academic Press.

Mellencamp, P. (1992) *High Anxiety: Catastrophe, Scandal, Age and Comedy*, Bloomington: Indiana University Press.

Miller, T., Govil, N., McMurria, J., Maxwell, R., and Wang, T. (2005) *Global Hollywood*, London: British Film Institute.

Morley, D. and Robins, K. (1995) *Spaces of Identity: Global Media, Electronic Landscapes and Cultural Boundaries*, London: Routledge.

Motion Picture Association of America (2010) *Theatrical Market Statistics*, at http://www.mpaa.org/Resources/93bbeb16–0e4d-4b7e-b085–3f41c459f9ac. pdf

Murphy, R. (ed.) (2000) *British Cinema of the 90s*, London: British Film Institute.

Nava, M. (1999) 'Wider Horizons and Modern Desire: The Contradictions of America and Racial Difference in London 1935–45', *New Formations*, no. 37, Spring, pp. 71–91.

Ngai, M. (2004) 'Transnational and the Transformation of the "Other"', *American Quarterly*, vol. 57, no. 1, March, pp. 59–66.

Oliver, P. (ed.) (1990) *Black Music in Britain*, Milton Keynes: Open University Press.

Pells, R. (1997) *Not Like Us: How Europeans Have Loved, Hated, and Transformed American Culture*, New York: Basic Books.

—— (2000) 'Who's Afraid of Steven Spielberg', *Diplomatic History*, vol. 24, no. 3, Summer, pp. 495–502.

—— (2012) *Modernist America*, New Haven: Yale University Press.

Philo, S. (2014) *British Invasion: The Crosscurrents of Musical Influence*, Lanham: Scarecrow.

Rippin, A. (1993) *Muslims: Their Religious Beliefs and Practices*, London: Routledge.

Ritzer, G. (2000) *The McDonaldisation of Society*, Boston: Pine Forge Press.

Ritzer, G. and Malone, E. (2000) 'Globalisation Theory: Lessons from the Exportation of McDonaldisation and the New Means of Consumption', *American Studies*, vol. 41, nos. 2/3, pp. 97–118.

Ritzer, G. and Ryan, M. (2004) 'Americanisation, McDonaldisation and Globalisation' in N. Campbell, J. Davies and G. McKay (eds) *Issues in Americanisation and Culture*, Edinburgh: Edinburgh University Press.

Roger, P. (2005) *The American Enemy: The History of French Anti-Americanism*, Chicago: Chicago University Press.

Rosenberg, E. (1982) *Spreading the American Dream*, New York: Hill & Wang.

Roszak, T. (1970) *The Making of the Counter Culture*, London: Faber and Faber.

Rothkop, D. (1997) 'In Praise of Cultural Imperialism? Effects of Globalisation on Culture', *Foreign Policy*, 22 June, pp. 1–9.

Rucker, R. (ed.) (1993) *Mondo 2000: A User's Guide to the New Edge*, London: Thames & Hudson.

Sardar, Z. and Davies, M. Wyn (2002) *Why Do People Hate America?*, Cambridge: Icon Books.

Schiller, H. (1969) *Mass Communications and American Empire*, New York: A.M. Kelly.

—— (1989) *Culture Inc.: The Corporate Takeover of Public Expression*, Oxford: Oxford University Press.

Seabrook, J. (2004a) *Consuming Cultures: Globalization and Local Lives*, Oxford: New Internationalist.

—— (2004b) 'Localizing Cultures', *Korean Herald*, 13 January, at http://www.global policy.org/globaliz/cultural/2004/0113jeremyseabrook.htm (accessed 8/11/ 2005).

Seago, A. (2000) '"Where Hamburgers Sizzle on an Open Grill Night and Day": Global Pop Music and Americanisation in the Year 2000', *American Studies*, vol. 41, nos. 2/3, pp. 119–36.

Segev, E. (2010) *Google and the Digital Divide: The Bias of Online Knowledge*, Oxford: Chandos.

Sheehan, M. (2014) 'Chinese Say They're Living In "West North Korea" After Popular U.S. Shows Banned', *Huffington Post*, at http://www.huffington post.com/2014/04/28/china-tv-bans_n_5227340.html (accessed 3/04/2015).

Shipton, A. *(2001) A New History of Jazz*, London: Continuum.

Shuker, R. (2008) *Understanding Popular Music*, London: Routledge.

Slater, D. and Taylor, P. (eds) (1999) *The American Century: Coercion and Consensus in the Projection of American Power*, Oxford: Blackwell.

Sorensen, T. (2004) 'The Global Liberal Order: A Progress Report', *Current History*, vol. 103, no. 677, pp. 403–7.

Sparshott, J. (2005) 'U.S. Domination in Internet Regulations Under Fire', *Washington Times*, 25 October.

Stead, W.T. (1901) *The Americanisation of the World: The Trend of the Twentieth Century*, London: Horace Markey.

Stokes, M. and Maltby, R. (eds) (2005) *Hollywood Abroad: Audiences and Cultural Exchange*, London: British Film Institute.

Storey, J. (1993) *An Introductory Guide to Cultural Theory and Popular Culture*, Edinburgh: Edinburgh University Press.

—— (ed.) (1994) *Cultural Theory and Popular Culture*, Hemel Hempstead: Harvester Wheatsheaf.

—— (ed.) (1998) *Cultural Theory and Popular Culture: A Reader*, London: Prentice Hall.

Straubhaar, J. and Duarte, L. (2005) 'Adapting U.S. Television Channels to a Complex World: From Cultural Imperialism to Localisation to Hybridisation' in J. Chalaby (ed.) *Transnational Television Worldwide: Towards a New Media Order*, London: I.B. Tauris.

Strinati, D. (1992) 'The Taste of America: Americanisation and Popular Culture in Britain' in D. Strinati and S. Wagg (eds) *Come on Down? Popular Media Culture in Post-war Britain*, London: Routledge.

Sznaider, N. and Winter, R. (2003) 'Introduction' in U. Beck, N. Sznaider and R. Winter (eds) *Global America? The Cultural Consequences of Globalization*, Liverpool: Liverpool University Press.

Tomlinson, J. (1991) *Cultural Imperialism: A Critical Introduction*, Baltimore, MD: Johns Hopkins University Press.

—— (1999) *Globalisation and Culture*, Oxford: Polity.

Tunstall, J. (1994) *The Media Are American: Anglo-American Media in the World*, London: Constable.

—— (2008) *The Media Were American, U.S. Mass Media in Decline*, Oxford: Oxford University Press.

Tyler May, E. and Wagnleitner, R. (eds) (2000) 'Here, There and Everywhere': The Foreign Politics of American Popular Culture, Hanover, NH: University Press of New England.

Tyrrell, I. (2015) Transnational Nation, London: Palgrave.

UNESCO (2007) Analysis of the UIS International Survey on Feature Film at http://www.uis.unesco.org/ev.php?ID=7651_201&ID2=DO_TOPIC (accessed 21/03/2011).

Wagnleitner, R. (1994) Coca-Colonisation and the Cold War: The Cultural Mission of the United States in Austria After the Second World War, Chapel Hill: University of North Carolina Press.

—— (1999) 'The Empire of the Fun, or Talkin' Soviet Union Blues: The Sound of Freedom and American Cultural Hegemony in Europe', Diplomatic History, vol. 2, no. 3, Summer, pp. 499–524.

—— (2005) 'United States Culture and Communications Policy and the Internet at the End/the Beginning of the "American Century"', at http://www.sbg.ac.at/ges/research/projekte/wagnleitner.htm (accessed 21/11/05).

Webster, D. (1988) Looka Yonder! The Imaginary America of Populist Culture, London: Routledge.

Wicke, P. (1993) Rock Music: Culture, Aesthetics and Sociology, Cambridge: Cambridge University Press.

Willett, R. (1989) The Americanisation of Germany, 1945–1950, London: Routledge.

Winter, R. (2003) 'Global Media, Cultural Change and the Transformation of the Local: The Contribution of Cultural Studies to a Sociology of Hybrid Formations' in U. Beck, N. Sznaider and R. Winter (eds) Global America? The Cultural Consequences of Globalization, Liverpool: Liverpool University Press.

World Music Awards (2010) at http://www.worldmusicawards.com/index.html

FOLLOW-UP WORK

There are a number of additional resources, assignments and other materials to be found on the website that accompanies this new edition: http://www.routledge.com/cw/campbell/

1 Paul Lauter has argued that 'the globalization of American culture requires the localization of its study' (Lauter 2001: 35). Explore the implications of this statement with regard to the workings of an aspect of American popular culture in the world in which you live. In particular, pay attention both to the production process as well as to the act of consumption. To what extent is consumption constrained by the way in which a specific cultural product is structured and distributed? How do specific historical, political or social contexts affect the reception of American culture?

2 Examine Arjun Appadurai's suggestion that 'images of the media are quickly moved into local repertoires of irony, anger, humour, and resistance' (Appadurai 1996: 7). How might this relate to the consumption of cultural products such as music, television and film?

3   To what extent do you think the reassertion of American military power in the world after the September 11th attacks has affected arguments about how American culture is consumed? Try to make connections between the issues discussed in Chapter 9 about the exercise of American political and military power, and the processes of Americanisation.

4   Using your local environment as a resource, go out with a digital camera and record how the cultural landscape has been Americanised. Examine leisure, retail, fast-food outlets, supermarkets, billboards and fashion. All these are sources of imagery and ideas that can then be analysed in the light of readings and debates suggested in this chapter. Produce a photographic essay with analysis on the themes of local Americanisation.

5   Assess the impact of the Internet on patterns of cultural flow. Does it enhance or undermine American dominance?

Index